W9-BAF-569

PESTS OF LANDSCAPE TREES AND SHRUBS:
AN INTEGRATED PEST MANAGEMENT GUIDE

Pests

of Landscape

Trees

and Shrubs

An Integrated Pest Management Guide

Steve H. Dreistadt

Jack Kelly Clark
Principal Photographer

Mary Louise Flint
Technical Editor and Director

IPM EDUCATION AND PUBLICATIONS, UC DAVIS
STATEWIDE INTEGRATED PEST MANAGEMENT PROJECT

COLLABORATORS, UC BERKELEY
Carlton S. Koehler, *Extension Entomologist Emeritus*
Arthur H. McCain, *Extension Plant Pathologist Emeritus*
Robert D. Raabe, *Professor of Plant Pathology*

UNIVERSITY OF CALIFORNIA
DIVISION OF AGRICULTURE AND NATURAL RESOURCES
PUBLICATION 3359

PRECAUTIONS FOR USING PESTICIDES

Pesticides are poisonous and must be used with caution. READ THE LABEL BEFORE OPENING A PESTICIDE CONTAINER. Follow all label precautions and directions, including requirements for protective equipment. Use a pesticide only against pests specified on the label or in published University of California recommendations. Apply pesticides at the rates specified on the label or at lower rates if suggested in this publication. In California, all agricultural uses of pesticides must be reported, including use in parks, golf courses, roadsides, cemeteries, and schoolyards. Contact your county agricultural commissioner for further details. Laws, regulations, and information concerning pesticides change frequently, so be sure the publication you are using is up to date.

Legal Responsibility. The user is legally responsible for any damage due to misuse of pesticides. Responsibility extends to effects caused by drift, runoff, or residues.

Transportation. Do not ship or carry pesticides together with food or feed in a way that allows contamination of the edible items. Never transport pesticides in a closed passenger vehicle or in a closed cab.

Storage. Keep pesticides in original containers until used. Store them in a locked cabinet, building, or fenced area where they are not accessible to children, unauthorized persons, pets, or livestock. DO NOT store pesticides with foods, feed, fertilizers, or other materials that may become contaminated by the pesticides.

Container Disposal. Dispose of empty containers carefully. Never reuse them. Make sure empty containers are not accessible to children or animals. Never dispose of containers where they may contaminate water supplies or natural waterways. Consult your county agricultural commissioner for correct procedures for handling and disposal of large quantities of empty containers.

Protection of Non-Pest Animals and Plants. Many pesticides are toxic to useful or desirable animals, including honey bees, natural enemies, fish, domestic animals, and birds. Certain rodenticides may pose a special hazard to animals that eat poisoned rodents. Plants may also be damaged by misapplied pesticides. Take precautions to protect non-pest species from direct exposure to pesticides and from contamination due to drift, runoff, or residues.

Permit Requirements. Many pesticides require a permit from the county agricultural commissioner before possession or use.

Plant Injury. Certain chemicals may cause injury to plants (phytotoxicity) under certain conditions. Always consult the label for limitations. Before applying any pesticide, take into account the stage of plant development, the soil type and condition, the temperature, moisture, and wind. Injury may also result from the use of incompatible materials.

Personal Safety. Follow label directions carefully. Avoid splashing, spilling, leaks, spray drift, and contamination of clothing. NEVER eat, smoke, drink, chew while using pesticides. Provide for emergency medical care IN ADVANCE as required by regulation.

ISBN 1-879906-18-X

Library of Congress Catalog Card No. 94-60514

© 1994 by the Regents of the University of California

Division of Agriculture and Natural Resources

All rights reserved.

No part of this publication may be reproduced, stored in a retrieval system, or transmitted, in any form or by any means, electronic, mechanical, photocopying, recording, or otherwise, without the written permission of the publisher and the author.

Printed in the United States of America.

The University of California, in accordance with applicable Federal and State law and University policy, does not discriminate on the basis of race, color, national origin, religion, sex, disability, age, medical condition (cancer-related), ancestry, marital status, citizenship, sexual orientation, or status as a Vietnam-era veteran or special disabled veteran. The University also prohibits sexual harassment. This nondiscrimination policy covers admission, access, and treatment in University programs and activities.

Inquiries regarding the University's nondiscrimination policies may be directed to:
The Affirmative Action Director,
University of California,
Agriculture and Natural Resources,
300 Lakeside Drive, 6th Floor,
Oakland, CA 94612-3560. (510) 987-0096.

ORDERING

For information about ordering this publication, write to:
ANR Publications
University of California
6701 San Pablo Avenue
Oakland, California 94608-1239

or telephone (510) 642-2431
or FAX (510) 643-5470

Publication #3359

Other books in this series include:

Integrated Pest Management for Walnuts, Publication #3270

Integrated Pest Management for Tomatoes, Publication #3274

Integrated Pest Management for Rice, Publication #3280

Integrated Pest Management for Citrus, Publication #3303

Integrated Pest Management for Cotton, Publication #3305

Integrated Pest Management for Cole Crops and Lettuce, Publication #3307

Integrated Pest Management for Almonds, Publication #3308

Integrated Pest Management for Alfalfa Hay, Publication #3312

Integrated Pest Management for Potatoes, Publication #3316

Pests of the Garden and Small Farm, Publication #3332

Integrated Pest Management for Small Grains, Publication #3333

Integrated Pest Management for Apples and Pears, Publication #3340

Integrated Pest Management for Strawberries, Publication #3351

 Printed on Recycled Stock.

Contributors and Acknowledgments

THIS BOOK WAS PREPARED under the auspices of the University of California Statewide Integrated Pest Management Project, Frank G. Zalom, Director.

TECHNICAL ADVISORS

Pamela S. Bone, *Urban Horticulture Advisor, Cooperative Extension, Sacramento County*
Richard Cowles, *Extension Entomologist, U.C. Riverside*
Clyde L. Elmore, *Extension Weed Scientist, U.C. Davis*
John N. Kabashima, *Ornamental Horticulture Advisor, Cooperative Extension, Orange County*
Carlton S. Koehler, *Extension Entomologist Emeritus, U.C. Berkeley*
Arthur H. McCain, *Extension Plant Pathologist Emeritus, U.C. Berkeley*
Robert D. Raabe, *Professor of Plant Pathology, U.C. Berkeley*
Pavel Svihra, *Environmental Horticulture Advisor, Cooperative Extension, Marin County*

CONTRIBUTORS AND PRINCIPAL REVIEWERS

Entomology:
Walter J. Bentley, Richard Cowles, Donald L. Dahlsten, James A. Downer, Lester E. Ehler, Thomas D. Eichlin, Raymond J. Gill, John N. Kabashima, Carlton S. Koehler, Vernard R. Lewis, Timothy D. Paine, Michael P. Parrella, Pavel Svihra

Horticulture:
Dave Adams, Michael Baefsky, Pamela S. Bone, Laurence R. Costello, Richard Cowles, Debbie Flower, Richard W. Harris, Donald R. Hodel, John N. Kabashima, John F. Karlik, John M. Lichter, Richard A. Molinar, Edward J. Perry, Dennis R. Pittenger, Dan Pratt, Pavel Svihra, Ellen M. Zagory

Nematology:
Armand R. Maggenti, Michael V. McKenry, Philip A. Roberts, Becky B. Westerdahl

Plant Pathology:
Dave Adams, Michael Baefsky, Laurence R. Costello, Donald M. Ferrin, Janine Hasey, John R. Karlik, James D. MacDonald, Arthur H. McCain, Edward J. Perry, Robert D. Raabe, Timothy E. Tidwell

Weed Science:
Dean R. Donaldson, James A. Downer, Clyde L. Elmore, John N. Kabashima, Thomas W. Lanini, Richard A. Molinar, Robert F. Norris, Dennis R. Pittenger

SPECIAL THANKS

The following persons generously provided information, offered suggestions, reviewed draft manuscripts, helped obtain photographs, or otherwise helped in manuscript preparation:

M. S. Barzman, A. M. Berry, R. L. Bugg, G. Chun, P. da Silva, K. M. Daane, J. A. De Benedictis, T. Eager, H. Elting-Ballard, D. K. Fitch, R. C. Gay, P. Gouveia, J. E. Gray, K. Grimes, M. Grimes, K. S. Hagen, L. M. Hanks, J. Hing, M. P. Hoffman, C. Joshel, H. K. Kaya, S. T. Koike, W. H. Krueger, V. F. Lazaneo, D. Lesser, T. Lindsey, P. Lindsey, D. Lofgren, P. A. Luft, P. J. Marer, P. M. McCool, J. E. Milstead, J. M. Nelson, K. Numes, T. M. ODell, J. D. Radewald, J. Rentner, K.L. Robb, A. S. Robertson, R. Rosetta, D. Sanders, G. Sandoval, M. Schmit, J. N. Sorensen, L. L. Strand, R. L. Tassan, S. A. Tjosvold, L. Tolmach, D. L. Wagner, D. Walker, D. Weddle, R. Zerillo, R. Zuparko

PRODUCTION

Design and Production Coordination:
 Seventeenth Street Studios
Drawings: David Kidd
Editing: Andrew L. Alden

Contents

CHAPTER ONE

What's in this Book

THIS BOOK is for landscape professionals, pest managers, and homeowners interested in woody ornamental plants. Its purpose is to encourage maintenance of healthy landscapes through integrated pest management (IPM). IPM is a strategy to prevent and suppress pest problems with minimum adverse impacts on human health, the environment, and nontarget organisms. IPM requires identification of plants and pests and knowledge of their biology. Selecting an appropriate plant for a location and providing for its basic growth requirements are other critical aspects of landscape IPM. Plants must be inspected regularly to detect any problems. Appropriate actions must be taken to promote beneficial organisms and minimize pest damage.

Landscape managers have numerous tools available; the key to their successful use is knowing when and how to apply them. The best approach is an integrated program that includes regular monitoring and relies on a combination of techniques to prevent and control problems.

Methods include selecting plants that are well adapted to the environment and resistant to pests, as well as adopting appropriate cultural practices, biological controls, and physical controls. Pesticides are also essential in many integrated pest management programs, but this book generally does not make specific recommendations because availability and appropriate and legal uses of pesticides frequently change. Where pesticides are mentioned, less toxic materials, such as insecticidal soap, narrow-range or horticultural oil, microbials, and botanicals are emphasized because they generally are more compatible with IPM programs. Your local Cooperative Extension office, other experts, or University publications can provide more specific and current information on pesticides.

Chapter 2 describes how to develop an IPM program. Landscape design, planting, and cultural care activities that prevent and minimize damage to woody landscape plants are detailed in Chapter 3. Subsequent chapters cover pest identification, biology, monitoring, and management. Pests include insects, mites, and snails and slugs (Chapter 4), plant pathogens (Chapter 5), weeds (Chapter 7), and nematodes (Chapter 8). Abiotic or environment-caused disorders are also discussed in Chapter 6. Vertebrate pests are covered in *Wildlife Pest Control Around Gardens and Homes*, University of California (UC) Publication 21385.

If you are uncertain of the cause of a problem and don't know which chapter to go to for solutions, two tables are provided at the back of the book (Chapter 9) to help with diagnosis. The Problem-Solving Guide briefly summarizes damage symptoms that can occur on many woody landscape plants and directs readers to sections of the book that discuss common causes of these problems.

The Tree and Shrub Pest Tables are more extensive and are organized according to host plants. They list the common problems of many woody plants occurring in California landscapes.

A list of references, a glossary, and an index are provided at the back of the book.

Designing an IPM Program

Landscape managers have many opportunities to make decisions that minimize serious pest problems over the long run. The choices of the species and varieties planted and the planting method and location are flexible. With careful planning, managers or homeowners should be able to establish a well-balanced system for maintaining long-term plant health. This ecological approach to preventing unacceptable pest presence or damage is called integrated pest management (IPM).

Which Organisms are Pests?

Many types of organisms can damage trees and shrubs or otherwise be undesirable inhabitants of landscapes. Common pests include insects, mites, snails, vertebrates, weeds, nematodes, and pathogens. However, in each of these groups there are many related species that do not harm cultivated plants or are beneficial; in fact, the great majority of organisms in the landscape are desirable components of the ecosystem.

Even the presence of organisms with the potential to become pests may not be cause for alarm. For example, many fungi and other microorganisms that can cause disease are continually present in the environment; they usually become damaging only when conditions are favorable for disease development or unfavorable for plant growth, such as when poor cultural practices weaken the plant. Insects, mites, and nematodes that can cause damage when they are abundant can be harmless or even beneficial when their numbers are low; the presence of a few of these plant-feeding pests provides food to maintain natural enemies that help prevent outbreaks.

The extent to which insects, fungi, weeds, and other organisms are pests depends on how much they interfere with the specific purposes for which plants are grown. Location, plant vigor, the species of plant-feeding organisms present, and the attitude and knowledge of people using the landscape also influence whether certain organisms are a pest problem.

Components of an IPM Program

Effective, environmentally sound pest management requires considerable forethought, knowledge, and observation. Most landscape pest problems can be avoided by taking several steps: choose pest-resistant varieties and species that are well adapted to local conditions, correctly prepare sites before planting, use proper planting techniques, and provide optimum conditions for plant growth.

Take action to prevent problems in established landscapes. If you wait until a tree or shrub is nearly dead or heavily damaged by pests, the only recourse might be to spray it with a fast-acting pesticide, which normally does not permanently correct the problem, or to remove the plant. Plan for possible problems before they occur. Learn the potential pest problems and damage symptoms of plants in your landscape areas by reviewing the Tree and Shrub Pest Tables at the back of this book and by consulting other resources and experts. Talk to other homeowners and landscape professionals in your area to learn of their experience with these plant species.

Examine valued plants regularly for pests, damage, and inappropriate cultural practices; keep records of any problems you encounter. Learn to recognize when a plant appears abnormal or if pest abundance or damage is approaching levels that require control. Select control methods that are effective under your growing conditions and least likely to cause adverse effects on the environment. Often more than one method can be employed to give the most reliable control. Five components are key to successful integrated pest management:

- prevention
- pest and symptom identification
- regular surveying for pests
- action thresholds and guidelines
- sound management methods

PREVENTION

Prevention is the most important component of landscape IPM. Weed problems in landscapes can be largely avoided by careful landscape design, preparing soil before planting, and proper planting, irrigating, and mulching. Poor choice of plant species or variety, improper site design and preparation before planting, or incorrect planting and maintenance aggravate or cause most

Landscape planners can choose from among many plant species and varieties, choices that will minimize or promote pest problems.

common problems. For example, many insect and disease problems are caused by overwatering or underwatering, overfertilizing, or other improper plant care activities. Furthermore, if the symptoms caused by these poor cultural practices are incorrectly blamed on disease or insect pests, then pesticide applications that are unwarranted might be made. Chapter 3 details cultural practices essential for maintaining healthy plants and preventing pest problems.

PEST AND SYMPTOM IDENTIFICATION

Many pests look similar, especially to the untrained eye; some pests can be easily confused with beneficial or innocuous organisms. Frequently, people blame damage symptoms on insects or other organisms that happen to be on the plant at the time symptoms are observed when, in fact, those organisms are not causing the problem. The pest causing the damage may have left the site or may be hard to detect, such as pathogens within the roots or the plant's water-conducting vessels. Symptoms caused by factors other than pests, things like overwatering, nutrient deficien-

Proper identification is essential. Some people may mistake this large hover fly, *Scaeva pyrastri*, larva for a caterpillar; it eats aphids, not plants.

cies, pesticide toxicity, air pollution, or choosing the wrong plant for that location, can be incorrectly blamed on insects, mites, or pathogens. Similar looking symptoms may have very different causes; spotted leaves, for example, may result from disease-causing microorganisms as well as certain insects. Plants also are frequently subject to more than one stress or problem at a time. Diagnosing the specific causes behind a set of symptoms can be a challenge.

Proper identification is essential for choosing the right control actions. Even closely related species often require different management strategies, and some species require no action at all. Accurate identification of plant problems depends on a combination of knowledge, observation, and available resources. The first step is to learn the cultural and environmental conditions required by each plant and check that these are being adequately provided. Look for sometimes subtle differences between the appearance of unhealthy plants or their environment and healthy plants of the same species. Patterns in the symptoms may provide clues to the cause. Obtain information about the recent history of affected plants, weather, the site, and cultural practices. Use appropriate tools, including a soil sampling tube, pocket knife, hand lens or binoculars, sample collecting containers (plastic bags or vials), and reference material like this book.

The descriptions and photographs in this book will help you recognize many common pests of woody ornamental plants in California, other western states, and the United States. However, because of the broad scope of this book and because new plant and pest species are often introduced from elsewhere, some of the pests you may encounter are not pictured

or described here. Check other references at the back of this book for additional information sources. *Insects That Feed on Trees and Shrubs* and *Diseases of Trees and Shrubs* are especially useful publications. Some pest problems can only be diagnosed reliably by experienced professionals; do not hesitate to seek their help. Your Cooperative Extension advisor, qualified horticultural consultant, certified arborist, or certified nursery-person may be able to make an identification or direct you to professional diagnostic services.

REGULAR SURVEYING FOR PESTS

Go out to the landscape on a regular basis and systematically check for pests and damage symptoms. Develop a routine that is adequate and efficient for the areas under your management. Although sophisticated sampling programs and monitoring techniques have been developed for use in agricultural crops and a few major landscape pests, monitoring in most landscape situations is a less formalized process.

Learn the problems that commonly occur in your area on each species of plant that you manage so that you know what to monitor for and where to look on and around the plant. Learn to recognize the stages of common pests and to distinguish them from beneficial organisms. Check regularly for adequate cultural care and damage. Frequency of inspection varies with the season, potential problems, plant value, and resources. Weekly inspections may be needed for certain plants during times of the year when problems can develop quickly. Time invested in monitoring can avoid plant damage and reduce the extent of any necessary management actions. If problems are not detected until they become more

Examine valued plants regularly for pests, damage, and inappropriate cultural practices. Keep records of any problems that you encounter.

People's aesthetic tolerance for pest damage varies. The yellow blotches on these Chinese lantern leaves are caused by abutilon mosaic virus, some people like these variegated plants.

obvious, your management options may be limited to pesticide use or removing the plant.

Examine plants systematically. Use a predetermined pattern of inspection to collect information in the same manner each time, allowing you to compare results among inspection dates. Thoroughly inspect all plant parts that may be infested or show symptoms that you are looking for. Examine plants in locations with different environmental conditions, such as both sunny and shady sites.

Check soil compaction and moisture conditions, for example by using a soil probe or tube.

Keep written monitoring records. Suggested monitoring forms are provided in this book for insects and weeds. Some professional landscape managers enter these records into a computer and summarize and analyze them using a data base or statistical software program. Compare monitoring results from different dates to determine if problems are increasing or decreasing, whether control action is needed, and how effective management activities are. Record the date, specific location, host plant, pests, natural enemies, who sampled, description of procedures, and counts or results. Note pest management activities, such as any pesticide applications. Record other actions and weather that may influence pests. For example, the reproductive and feeding rates of most insects and mites increase with increasing temperature; monitoring temperature and time in units called degree-days helps when managing certain pests. Specific monitoring methods are discussed in each section on particular pests.

ACTION THRESHOLDS AND GUIDELINES

A certain number of pest individuals and some amount of damage usually can be tolerated; this concept is fundamental to integrated pest management. The difficulty is in determining the action threshold—the point at which some action must be taken to prevent unacceptable damage.

Researchers have developed control action thresholds or guidelines for some pests in agriculture, especially insects and mites. Crops are grown for profit, so control action thresholds in agriculture are based largely on economic criteria; action is warranted when it will improve crop quality or yield and provide increased

BOTH COMMON AND SCIENTIFIC NAMES are used to identify organisms. Because different humans (*Homo sapiens*) may use different names for the same organism, names are often a source of confusion.

SCIENTISTS USE A UNIQUE, two-word combination for each animal, plant, pathogen, and other organism. This scientific name provides the surest identification because scientific names are used according to agreed-upon rules and each organism has only one valid scientific name, which is used throughout the world. The first word, the genus or generic name, is capitalized. The second word, the species or specific name, is not. Both words are italicized or underlined and are Latinized so scientists can understand what plant or animal others are referring to, regardless of nationality and native language. After its first use in the text, the genus name is often abbreviated; for example *Eucalyptus globulus* is shortened to *E. globulus*. When several species within the same genus are discussed together, species may be abbreviated as "spp." When referring to only one species, "sp." is used.

SCIENTIFIC NAMES ARE USED IN A HIERARCHICAL organization or ranked order that includes the family and order names sometimes used in this book. These hierarchical names show relationships among organisms, as illustrated here for the common convergent lady beetle:

> Kingdom: Animalia (animals)
>   Class: Insecta (insects)
>   Order: Coleoptera (beetles)
>   Family: Coccinellidae (lady beetles)
>   Genus: *Hippodamia*
>   Species: *convergens*

MANY PLANTS, INSECTS, AND DISEASES also have common names as well as the two-part scientific name. Common names are familiar to more people than scientific names and they're often easier to pronounce and remember. However, there are serious problems with common names. Unlike scientific names, there are no clear rules for deciding what is the correct common name of most organisms. Some common names, such as lilac and laurel, are used to refer to several distinctly different plants. The same organism can have several common names, some of which may be known and used only by people in certain locations. For example, what is commonly known in California as avocado is in some parts of the southern United States called alligator-pear! Common names may also be ridiculous or inaccurate; pineapple refers to a plant that is very unlike pines or apples. Ladybug refers to certain beetles, which are very different from the insects that scientists classify as true bugs. Many important organisms, such as beneficial predators or parasites, have no common name, often because they are tiny and known only to scientists.

BOTH COMMON AND SCIENTIFIC NAMES are used in this book. The scientific name and one or more common names of each pest can be found in the index at the back of the book, and both names are used together in the major section discussing that pest (that section listed in the table of contents). Scientific names (as well as common names) are also used for plants in the Tree and Shrub Pest Tables and for pests not detailed elsewhere in the text.

PLANT SCIENTIFIC NAMES are generally avoided in this book, except in the index and in tables. Common names are more widely known for most plants in comparison with insects and diseases. Common plants such as oaks (*Quercus* spp.) are mentioned so often here that using their scientific names would consume much space and be awkward. For many plants such as camellia, citrus, and rhododendron, the genus name and common name are the same, except that the common name is not capitalized or italicized.

PRIMARY SOURCES for names used in this book are *Common Names of Insects & Related Organisms 1989*, *Fungi on Plants and Plant Products in the United States*, and *An Annotated Checklist of Woody Ornamental Plants of California, Oregon, & Washington* (UC Publication 4091).

revenue that exceeds the extra cost of management.

Almost no formalized control action guidelines have been developed for pests on landscape trees and shrubs. There are several reasons for this, including a lack of research. However, the most important factor is the difficulty in defining what level of pests or damage is intolerable.

Although the death of an attractive plant can be an economic loss to the property owner, the most common landscape pests are those that are annoying to some people or that make plants unsightly; many of these pests do not kill the plant. The pest population or damage level when action must be taken to deter undesirable damage to ornamental plants often depends on people's attitudes and is commonly referred to as the "aesthetic threshold."

Aesthetic tolerance varies with the attitude and knowledge of people using the landscape. For example, certain annual plants growing wild as ground covers are tolerated or enjoyed by one segment of the public, while another group considers them weeds and insists on bare soil beneath shrubs. Defining an aesthetic threshold that people can agree on is difficult and subjective. Damage that is acceptable on out-of-the-way plants may not be tolerable on prominent plants. Organisms such as gall-forming insects and mites or a few leaf-chewing caterpillars may cause no real harm to plants but can be annoying or even frightening to some people.

Despite the lack of numerical action guidelines for landscape trees and shrubs, you will find recommendations throughout this book to help you determine whether actions may be needed and the best time to take action to avoid or reduce specific pest problems. Many plants are more vulnerable to pest damage at certain times in their development—especially during the first year or two after establishment or during certain seasons. These differences in susceptibility mean that the control action guidelines also differ over the growing season and as the plant develops. Other conditions affect a plant's ability to tolerate pest damage; for example, plants weakened by water stress, weed competition, root disease, nematodes, or injury must be more carefully protected because they are less tolerant of additional stresses or more pests.

Timing of actions is often critical for effective management. For example, once symptoms become apparent, it is often too late to effectively control many plant diseases. Many times the appropriate action is not to apply pesticide but to use cultural practices such as pruning, fertilizing, or irrigating. If you are limited to methods that take several days or months to provide control or that kill a smaller fraction of the pests, you have to allow for more lead time than you would with faster-acting measures.

Modify monitoring techniques, action thresholds, and management methods as appropriate. Control action guidelines are helpful only when used with accurate pest identification and careful monitoring. Keep records of pests, how you determined when to treat, and the results of management activities. These records will help you to develop action guidelines that work best for your situation in the future.

SOUND MANAGEMENT METHODS

Integrated pest managers must consider the interrelation of cultural practices, environmental conditions, and the biology of plants, pests, and beneficial organisms in order to provide healthy plants. Primary methods used specifically for pest management are cultural, mechanical, physical, biological, and chemical control.

Before applying these methods, determine whether action is needed

Prevent weeds and improve plant growth by applying an attractive and effective mulch to bare soil.

and likely to be effective. If it is too late for control to be effective or if the problem is minor or doesn't threaten plant health, consider taking no action or applying other methods. When action is needed, use more than one method in combination to provide more effective control. Methods are summarized below and detailed in later chapters.

Cultural Control. Cultural controls are modifications of normal plant care activities that reduce or avoid pest problems as detailed in Chapter 3. Some landscape designs, and selecting resistant species and varieties, can minimize pest problems. Plant properly and irrigate, fertilize, and prune plants appropriately. Providing plants with proper care is the most important component of pest management. Good care can prevent many pests from adversely affecting plants; for certain problems, such as root diseases and most wood-boring insects, cultural control is the only effective method.

Mechanical Control. Mechanical controls use labor, materials not usually considered as pesticides, and machinery to reduce pest abundance directly. For example, control weeds with mulch, mowing, weed eaters, flamers, and hand-pulling where appropriate (see Chapter 7). Install copper bands around trunks and planting areas to exclude snails and slugs. Apply sticky material around trunks to prevent canopies from being infested by ants, flightless weevils, and snails. Clip and dispose of foliage infested with insects that feed in groups, such as tentmaking caterpillars. Hand-pick snails or leaves infested with insects or disease. Prune out or rake up foliage and twigs infected with disease, such as leaf spots and anthracnose.

Physical Control. Physical controls are environmental manipulations that indirectly control or prevent pests by altering temperature, light, and humidity. Control black scale and possibly similar species by thinning canopies in hot areas of California, thereby increasing scale mortality due to heat exposure. Control certain foliar diseases by thinning the plant canopy to improve air circulation and reduce humidity. Apply white interior (not exterior) latex paint, diluted 50% with water, to trunks of young or heavily pruned woody plants to reduce light exposure and prevent sunscald. Avoid cold damage to small trees and shrubs by covering them to retain warmth or by hanging outdoor lights to generate heat.

Biological Control. Biological control is the use of beneficial organisms to control unwanted organisms. Biological control has been used most

Apply sticky material around trunks to prevent canopies from being invested by ants, flightless weevils, and snails.

Biological control has been used most successfully to control pest insects and mites. This bigeyed bug nymph, *Geocoris* sp., is feeding on a bollworm or corn earworm caterpillar egg.

successfully to control pest insects and mites, as detailed in Chapter 4. Under certain circumstances biological control is also effective against weeds, snails, nematodes, and plant diseases. For example, control honeydew-seeking ants, reduce dust, and avoid persistent pesticides to enhance the effectiveness of certain natural enemies of insect and mite pests. Plant a diversity of flowering and nonflowering species to provide habitat and food for beneficial predators and parasites. Periodically releasing commercially available natural enemies may control pests under certain circumstances. Avoid cultivating soil deeply to prevent burying weed seeds where they are protected from decay microorganisms or cannot be reached by seed-eating insects and small vertebrates.

Chemical Control. Pesticides are chemicals that control, prevent, or repel pests or mitigate the problems they cause. You can quickly obtain temporary control of certain pests if you choose the correct pesticide and apply it at the right time in an appropriate manner. *Follow all label directions*—if you use an incorrect pesticide, the wrong rate, or improper application methods, you can do more harm than good.

Broad-spectrum pesticides can sometimes be used selectively. Spot spraying an area encircling the trunk (bark banding) kills elm leaf beetle larvae as they crawl down to pupate around the tree base. Wear a washable hat when spraying overhead.

Consider alternatives as discussed above before using a pesticide; cultural practices and other alternatives often provide more long-lasting control. If you use a pesticide, combine its use with nonchemical control methods. Respect pesticides for their hazards; many pesticides are poisonous to other living things besides the pest you wish to control. Use the least hazardous pesticide where possible. Avoid broad-spectrum, persistent pesticides when possible or apply them in a selective manner as dis-

cussed below. Read the label carefully before you buy the pesticide so you will understand its hazard, and be certain it is registered and appropriate for use on the plants or site where it will be applied. Read the label again before using it and follow all the precautions and application directions.

Types of Pesticides. Pesticides are categorized several ways, most commonly according to the type of organism controlled. Insecticides control insects. Miticides or acaricides control mites. Herbicides control weeds. Fungicides control disease-causing fungi. Molluscicides control snails and slugs. Rodenticides control mice and other rodents.

Mode of action (for example, contact or systemic) and chemical class (for example, carbamate or organophosphate) are other classification systems. Pesticides are also categorized by the source of the material: naturally occurring pesticides are derived from organisms, such as botanicals that are extracted from plants. Inorganic pesticides like sulfur and copper are refined from minerals. Synthetic pesticides such as organophosphates and chlorinated hydrocarbons are manufactured from petroleum.

Some specific pesticides are discussed in each chapter, but read the following sections before choosing a pesticide. See *The Safe and Effective Use of Pesticides* (UC Publication 3324) and *Pesticides: Theory and Action*, listed in References, for more details on pesticides.

Pesticides Are Toxic. All pesticides are toxic (poisonous) in some way. The degree of toxicity ranges from slight to extreme. The distinction between toxicity and hazard is important. Toxicity is the capability of a substance to cause injury or death. Hazard is a function of two factors—toxicity and potential exposure to the toxic substance. Toxic substances pose a relatively low hazard if their use can minimize or avoid exposure to people and other nontarget organisms. For example, some toxic compounds are used in low concentrations and enclosed in containers with a bait. Pests are attracted to feed by entering the container openings, which are small enough to exclude children and pets. These enclosed baits, such as "ant stakes,"

TABLE 2-1

Pesticide Toxicity Categories.[a]

HAZARD INDICATORS	I DANGER	II WARNING	III CAUTION
Oral LD$_{50}$	Up to 50 mg/kg	50-500 mg/kg	>500 mg/kg
Inhalation LC$_{50}$	Up to 0.2 mg/L	0.2-2 mg/L	>2 mg/L
Dermal LD$_{50}$	Up to 200 mg/kg	200-2,000 mg/kg	>2,000 mg/kg
Eye effects	Corrosive	Persistent irritation	Reversible irritation
Skin effects	Corrosive	Severe irritation	Moderate irritation

a. See text for explanation.

minimize nontarget exposure, thereby greatly reducing hazard.

Pesticides sold in the United States must have a signal word on their label indicating potential hazard of immediate or acute injury. Signal words are CAUTION (the least hazardous), WARNING, and DANGER (the latter the most hazardous, often including a skull and crossbones and also labeled POISON). Hazard is estimated primarily by assessing potential exposure and performing toxicity studies on laboratory mammals that are affected similarly to people. Toxicity is assessed through several means of exposure, such as oral (ingestion), inhalation (breathing), and dermal (through skin). Toxicity is reported as the amount in milligrams (mg) of toxic material per kilogram (kg) of animal body weight or liter (L) of air that is lethal to 50% of the test animals. The lethal dose (LD$_{50}$) or lethal concentration (LC$_{50}$) and corresponding signal words are listed in Table 2-1. Some pesticides are suspected of causing long-term health effects, but this information is not provided on the label. A Material Safety Data Sheet (MSDS) detailing potential hazards is available for each pesticide; request and read the MSDS for more information.

The most hazardous pesticides (DANGER or POISON) generally are available only to certified applicators. These pesticides require special training and equipment and generally should not be used in ways or places where people or pets may be exposed.

Pesticide Selectivity. Selective pesticides are toxic only to the target organism and related species, in contrast with broad-spectrum pesticides, which kill many different species. For example, certain strains of *Bacillus thuringiensis*, or Bt, kill only moth and butterfly larvae, while most synthetic insecticides kill both caterpillars and their natural enemies. Use selective pesticides where possible because they are generally less damaging to nontarget organisms and are safer for use around people.

In addition to describing the inherent toxicity of a pesticide, selectivity also refers to the manner of use. Broad-spectrum pesticides sometimes can be used selectively by modifying application timing, equipment, and method. For example, dormant season application of narrow-range oil to kill scale insects may reduce the impact on natural enemies in comparison with a foliar season spraying, because the beneficials tend to be inactive during the winter or are not present in the treatment area. Insecticides for ant control and rodenticides can be mixed with bait and enclosed in a container that prevents most nontarget organisms from being exposed to pesticides. Spot treatments, such as insecticide bark banding instead of spraying the whole plant canopy, help control elm leaf beetle without killing predators and parasites that live on leaves. Selective application methods and pesticides are discussed in the chapters on invertebrates, weeds, and diseases.

Pesticide Persistence. Persistence, the length of time after application during which a pesticide remains active, is important in determining how long a pesticide controls the target pest. Persistence may also influence the extent to which a pesticide can harm beneficial organisms. Longer persistence sometimes may be desirable. For example, a more persistent pre-emergent herbicide (as listed in Table 7-8) suppresses weed seedlings longer, providing desirable plants with more time to grow larger and become established without having to compete for moisture and nutrients. Conversely, a more persistent insecticide can be undesirable to suppress pests when effective natural enemies are present.

Pests often become temporarily abundant before natural enemies become common enough to provide control. Most predators and parasites also are more sensitive to pesticides than are pests. If a persistent insecticide is applied to control a pest that has temporarily escaped biological control, its residues can continue to kill natural enemies that migrate in after spraying, long after the insecticide has ceased to kill the pests. Therefore, persistent residues can prevent natural enemies from providing biological control, leading to another outbreak or resurgence of the pest population. Insecticides with little or no persistence or residual toxicity as listed in Table 4-6 are

frequently preferable when controlling landscape pests.

Pesticides Can Damage Plants. Herbicides are designed to kill plants, so they can injure or kill desirable species if they are applied improperly or drift onto nontarget plants. Some nonherbicide pesticides, such as insecticides and fungicides, also can damage plants; this damage is called phytotoxicity. Damage usually occurs because pesticides have been used carelessly or in a manner contrary to the label. Common mistakes are applying excess amounts, allowing spray to drift, failing to obey label precautions, or using a sprayer contaminated with herbicides to apply other materials. Environmental stress, such as drought, heat, or wind, or sensitivity of particular plant varieties can also lead to phytotoxicity from exposure to pesticides.

Because herbicides are made specifically to kill plants, they probably pose the greatest risk of unintended damage to desirable plant species. Each kind of herbicide causes characteristic damage symptoms as discussed in Chapter 6.

Narrow-range oil, insecticidal soap, and other pesticides also can damage certain plants under specific conditions. Pesticide labels often list sensitive plants to avoid spraying. When in doubt as to whether the plant species is sensitive to a pesticide, spray a small out-of-the-way area of the plant and observe it for several days for any signs of damage before spraying it further.

Choose the Correct Pesticide. Make sure you have correctly identified the pest and have considered nonchemical alternatives before you purchase or apply a pesticide. Read the label carefully before deciding which pesticide to purchase and apply. Do not use a pesticide unless the host plant

or location to be sprayed is listed on the label and the pest is listed on the label or on a written University guideline. The oral LD_{50} values for some common pesticides are listed in Table 2-2. Although pesticides with a high LD_{50} are less acutely toxic than those with a low LD_{50}, a high LD_{50} doesn't necessarily mean that a pesticide is "safe." Some pesticides with a relatively high LD_{50}, like sulfur and glyphosate, can be very irritating to the eyes, skin, or lungs. Others may cause long-term or chronic diseases, even if doses are relatively low. Pesticides that have a low toxicity to people can be very toxic to beneficial organisms.

Read the precautionary statement on the label. Consider hazards to humans, pets, desirable plants, beneficial organisms, wildlife, and the rest of the environment. Note the signal word and choose the least toxic pesticide available for the job. Purchase only the amount of pesticide you expect to use up within a few months; proper disposal of unused pesticide may be difficult.

Transport Pesticides Safely. Do not carry pesticides in the passenger compartment of any vehicle. Do not carry pesticides in the same compartment as food or drink. Make sure that containers are tied down or are in an attached compartment so they cannot fall or be knocked over. Protect bottles by wrapping them in paper to reduce the chance of breakage if they fall over or crash together. Protect bags from damage by sharp objects. Protect containers from moisture. Do not leave pesticides unattended unless they are in a locked container.

Store Pesticides Safely. Store pesticides only in the original labeled container. Never store pesticides in soft-drink bottles or other food or drink containers. Store pesticides in a

TABLE 2-2

Approximate Oral LD$_{50}$ Values for Some Pesticides.[a]

CHEMICAL	LD$_{50}$	TYPE OF PESTICIDE
Nicotine	50	insecticide
Paraquat	150	herbicide
Chlorpyrifos	160	insecticide
Carbaryl	260	insecticide
Fluvalinate	270	insecticide
Diazinon	300	insecticide
Dimethoate	300	miticide
2,4-D	400	herbicide
Copper sulfate	500	fungicide
Acephate	900	insecticide
Bensulide	900	herbicide
Dicofol	900	miticide
Copper hydroxide	1,000	fungicide
Ryania	1,200	insecticide
Malathion	1,400	insecticide
Pyrethrum	1,500	insecticide
EPTC	1,600	herbicide
Pendimethalin	2,500	herbicide
DCPA	>3,000	herbicide
Trifluralin	3,700	herbicide
Sabadilla	4,000	insecticide
Glyphosate	4,300	herbicide
Oil, narrow-range	>4,300	insecticide, miticide
Napropamide	>4,600	herbicide
Simazine	5,000	herbicide
Benefin	>5,000	herbicide
Sulfur	>5,000	fungicide, miticide
Oxadiazon	>5,000	herbicide
Oxyfluorfen	>5,000	herbicide
Captan	9,000	fungicide
Benomyl	>10,000	fungicide
Chlorothalonil	>10,000	fungicide
Oryzalin	>10,000	herbicide
B. thuringiensis	15,000	insecticide
Insecticidal soap	>16,900	insecticide

a. LD$_{50}$ values are in milligrams of pesticide per kilogram of body weight. Lower LD$_{50}$ values indicate higher toxicity; for example, acephate (900) is more acutely toxic than narrow-range oil (>4,300). Actual values vary depending on the pesticide formulation. LD$_{50}$ values are only one of several considerations when selecting a pesticide (see text). > indicates that the LD$_{50}$ value is higher than the number listed.

locked and labeled area or cabinet that is out of reach of children and pets. Do not store pesticides near food, feed, beverages, clothing, or rags. Protect stored pesticides from moisture and extreme heat or cold. Be sure the storage area is well ventilated to prevent the accumulation of toxic fumes. Check pesticide containers periodically for leakage or corrosion.

Use Appropriate Application Equipment. Pesticide application equipment ranges from simple devices attached to a garden hose to power-driven machines. Consult Tables 2-3 to 2-5 for help in choosing the proper equipment. For more details see *The Safe and Effective Use of Pesticides* (UC Publication 3324).

Check Equipment Before Use. Fill the sprayer with clean water and operate it before use. Look for leaking hoses, connections and tanks, and worn or plugged nozzles. Repair or replace faulty equipment before use.

Mix Pesticides Properly. Pesticides are in their most hazardous form when you mix and handle the concentrated material. Choose an outdoor or open location with good light and ventilation. Read the label carefully and make sure that you are upwind before you open the container. Wear any safety equipment listed on the label, such as plastic or rubber gloves and tightly woven clothing with long sleeves and pant legs worn outside of (not tucked into) gloves and boots. Wear eye protection, even if it's not listed on the label. It is also a good idea to wear a rubber apron while mixing pesticides. Do not wear leather gloves or boots; wear rubber or neoprene unless otherwise designated on the label. Keep the container below eye level when pouring

TABLE 2-3

Selection Guide for Nonpowered and Hand-Operated Application Equipment for Liquid Pesticides.[a]

	TYPE	USES	SUITABLE FORMULATIONS	COMMENTS
	AEROSOL CAN	Insect control on house or patio plants, small areas.	Liquids must dissolve in solvent; some dusts are available.	Very convenient. High cost per unit of active ingredient. Good for spot applications.
	HOSE–END SPRAYER	Home garden and small landscaped areas. Used for insect, weed, and pathogen control, where water pressure is sufficient.	All formulations. Wettable powders and emulsifiable concentrates require frequent shaking.	Convenient and low-cost way of applying pesticides to small outdoor areas. Cannot spray straight up. Install an anti-siphon device on the hose-end connector to prevent pesticide from being sucked into the water line if water pressure drops.
	TRIGGER PUMP SPRAYER	Indoor plants and small home yard areas. Used for insect and pathogen control.	Liquid-soluble formulations best.	Low cost and easy to use. Good for spot applications.
	COMPRESSED AIR SPRAYERS	Many commercial and homeowner applications. Can develop fairly high pressures. Used for insect, weed, and pathogen control.	All formulations. Wettable powders and emulsifiable concentrates require frequent shaking.	Good overall sprayer for many types of applications. Needs thorough cleaning and regular servicing to keep sprayer in good working condition and prevent corrosion of parts.
	BACKPACK SPRAYERS	Same uses as compressed air sprayers.	All formulations. Wettable powders and emulsifiable concentrates require frequent shaking.	Durable and easy to use. Requires periodic maintenance.
	WICK APPLICATORS	Used for applying contact herbicides to emerged weeks. Landscape and agricultural uses.	Only water-soluble herbicides.	Simple and easy to use. Clean frequently. Avoids drift onto desirable plants.

a. Once used with herbicides, do not use the sprayer for other pesticides.

TABLE 2-4

Selection Guide for Powered Liquid Pesticide Application Equipment.[a]

	TYPE	USES	SUITABLE FORMULATIONS	COMMENTS
	POWERED BACKPACK SPRAYER	Landscape, right-of-way, aquatic, forest, and agricultural applications.	All. Some may require agitation.	May be heavy for long periods of use. Requires frequent maintenance.
	CONTROLLED DROPLET APPLICATOR	Used for application of contact herbicides and some insecticides. Some are hand-held while others are mounted on spray boom. May also be used with air blast sprayers. Produces uniform droplet sizes.	Usually water-soluble formulations.	Plastic parts may break if handled carelessly.
	LOW-PRESSURE SPRAYER	Very common type of sprayer used in commercial applications for weed, insect, and pathogen control. Used with spray booms of hand-held equipment.	All. Equipment may include agitator.	Frequent cleaning and servicing is required. Powered by own motor or external power source.
	HIGH-PRESSURE HYDRAULIC SPRAYER	Landscape, right-of-way, and agricultural applications. Use on dense foliage and large trees and shrubs.	All. Equipment may include agitator.	Important to clean and service equipment frequently. Requires own motor or external power source. Abrasive pesticides may cause rapid wear of pumps and nozzles.

a. Once used with herbicides, do not use the sprayer for other pesticides.

pesticide. Mix only the amount needed to complete the immediate job. Use measuring tools specifically reserved for this purpose.

Clean Any Spills Immediately. Wear protective equipment when cleaning any spills. Sweep or shovel any spilled pesticide dust or powder into a container, such as a plastic bag. Absorb liquid spills with sand, sawdust, or cat litter, then shovel it into a container. Dispose of any spilled pesticide and contaminated substances at a hazardous materials disposal site. Do not allow any wash water to enter bodies of water or sewer systems. Special absorptive materials are available that allow pesticide spilled on an otherwise clean surface to be collected and put back into the spray tank where it dissolves and can be sprayed; this avoids the expense of disposing of spilled pesticide and cleaning material as a hazardous waste. Report all spills to the County Department of Agriculture, which can provide information and assistance.

Dispose of Containers Properly. Consult the pesticide label or the County Department of Agriculture for instructions on disposing of pesticide containers. Some communities have special collections or drop-off points where small amounts of household hazardous waste, such as pesticides, can be disposed of occasionally. The best method is to pur-

TABLE 2-5

Selection Guide for Dust and Granule Application Equipment.[a]

	TYPE	USES	SUITABLE FORMULATIONS	COMMENTS
	MECHANICAL DUST APPLICATOR	For landscape and small agricultural areas.	Dusts.	Avoid drift. Do not breathe dust. May have bellows to disperse dust.
	HAND-OPERATED GRANULE APPLICATOR	Landscape, aquatic and some agricultural areas.	Granules or pellets.	Suitable for small areas. Easy to use.
	MECHANICALLY DRIVEN GRANULE APPLICATOR	Turf and other landscape areas. Also commonly used in agricultural areas.	Granules or pellets.	Requires accurate calibration.
	POWERED GRANULE APPLICATOR	Large landscape applications (e.g., golf courses).	Granules or pellets.	Frequent servicing and cleaning is required. Some units may have blowers to disperse granules. Others may distribute granules along a boom.

a. Once used with herbicides, do not use the sprayer for other pesticides.

chase only the amount of pesticide that will soon be used; use up all the material as directed on the label so that no pesticides in need of disposal are left over.

Some pesticide vendors and manufacturers accept empty pesticide containers for recycling. Many containers can be disposed of in a sanitary landfill if containers have been properly rinsed (triple rinsed) and, where required, inspected by the County Department of Agriculture.

Rinse empty containers three times (triple rinse them) immediately after emptying them and before you finish filling the spray tank. First drain the empty container into the spray tank for at least 30 seconds. Next fill the container about one-quarter full with clean water, close the container, and gently shake or roll it to rinse all interior surfaces. Drain the rinse material into the spray tank and continue to let the material drain for at least 30 seconds after the container is mostly empty and has begun to drip. Repeat this rinse procedure two more times, then fill the spray tank to the proper level.

Use Effective Methods. Proper methods and timing are critical for effective pesticide application. Spraying is the most common application method, and spot spraying (spraying only small areas) is preferable when effective. Baits for rodents or ants and wick or wiper applicators for herbicides are examples of other methods that are more effective or preferred in certain situations. Systemic insecticides can be injected or implanted into tree trunks or roots to control many insects that chew foliage or suck plant juices. This method minimizes environmental contamination but can seriously damage trees, especially through repeated or improper use. Injections and implants are not effective against wood-boring pests such as bark beetles, flatheaded and roundheaded borers, and clearwing moths. Nonchemical methods (such as proper plant care) are the only effective control for most of these pests.

Correct timing of control is vital. For example, *Bacillus thuringiensis* (Bt) must be applied to cover foliage thoroughly when young caterpillars are actively feeding or it will not be effective. Application of oil during the dormant season (after leaves have dropped) to kill scale insects and overwintering stages of some mites and aphids may provide better control than foliar season spraying. Less spray volume is needed because leaves are not present and timing is less critical than during the foliar season, when applications must coincide with the activity of young crawlers, which must be monitored closely.

Many fungicides must be applied before infection takes place, especially when using inorganic or organically acceptable materials. Most of these protect undamaged tissue, but they do not cure tissue once it becomes infected. Some herbicides must be

applied before weeds emerge; others are effective only when weeds are actively growing.

Apply pesticides at the correct time and in the proper manner (according to label directions or University guidelines) or else your effort is wasted, the environment is needlessly contaminated, and target pests are not controlled.

Apply Pesticides Safely. Read the label instructions again and follow them exactly before applying pesticides. It is illegal and may be dangerous to disregard label instructions. Clear any people or pets from the area to be treated. Wear protective clothing, including eye protection, gloves, and any protective equipment listed on the label. Never apply pesticides when it is windy or raining. Avoid drift over water and do not fill, drain, or rinse equipment near water. Provide buffer zones when spraying near water. Do not apply more pesticide than is indicated on the label.

All people who mix, apply, or otherwise handle pesticides at work must be trained each year by their employer. Employers must maintain written evidence of this training. Many people using pesticides as part of their job must also be licensed or certified by passing an examination administered by the state and then attending continuing education courses, or they must work under the supervision of a licensed or certified applicator. Contact the County Department of Agriculture to determine the legal requirements before handling any pesticides in connection with your employment.

Wear Protective Clothing. Always wear at least as much protective clothing as specified on the pesticide

Figure 2-1. Minimize your exposure to pesticides. Unless otherwise stated on the label, wear rubber or neoprene gloves and boots, eye protection that covers the brows and temples, and long pants, long-sleeved shirt, and a hat that can be washed after each use. It is also a good idea to wear a rubber or neoprene apron.

label (Figure 2-1). Always wear protective eyewear that covers the brow and temple when applying or handling pesticides, even if no eyewear is specified on the label. Minimize your exposure to pesticides, even if the material has a high LD_{50}. Unless otherwise specified on the label, rubber or neoprene gloves and boots, eye protection, and a washable hat, long pants, and a long-sleeved shirt that are laundered after each use are the minimum protective clothing that should be worn, even when applying "safe" materials such as oil or soap. A rubber or neoprene apron provides additional protection.

Consult *The Safe and Effective Use of Pesticides,* and *Residential, Industrial, and Institutional Pest Control,* listed in References, for more information.

CHAPTER THREE

Growing Healthy Trees and Shrubs

Selecting an appropriate plant for each location and providing for its basic growth requirements are the most important aspects of pest management. If plants are well adapted to local conditions, receive proper care, and are relatively free of other stresses, they typically are more tolerant of pests. Plants stressed from adverse environmental conditions or a lack of proper care may be damaged by even a small number of pests. The purpose of an integrated pest management program is not to kill pests, but to cultivate healthy plants that can tolerate some pests while serving your needs. This chapter summarizes basic woody-plant care to minimize pests and provide healthy plants. For more detailed information, consult *Arboriculture: Integrated Management of Landscape Trees, Shrubs, and Vines* and other publications listed in References.

Growth Requirements

Plants are living organisms that require energy, water, and oxygen. Energy is provided by oxidation of food (primarily sugars and starches) in the process known as respiration. Unlike animals, most plants produce their own food using solar energy. This food-producing process, called photosynthesis, occurs in green tissue, primarily leaves. Plants need essential nutrients, carbon dioxide, and appropriate light, water, and temperatures to carry out photosynthesis.

People modify the landscape environment and control the availability of resources that plants need. Water and oxygen availability to roots are affected by irrigation, drainage, aeration, and changes in the grade, composition, and texture of soil.

Plants are living organisms that require energy, water, oxygen, and adequate space for growth.

appropriate environment and adequate care increases the likelihood that pests will damage or kill plants. Most plants are particularly vulnerable to damage during certain stages of their growth or under specific environmental conditions; under other circumstances or at other times, plants are relatively resistant or can tolerate more pests or damage.

Plant Development and Seasonal Growth

Trees and woody shrubs are perennial plants; they live for many years. Deciduous perennials typically drop leaves in the fall before entering winter dormancy and regrow foliage in the spring. However, some species like the California buckeye adapt to drought by dropping leaves during hot, dry weather and regrowing foliage after the winter rainfall begins. Evergreen perennials retain some foliage year around. They still exhibit seasonal changes in growth, flowering, and foliage production. Conifers, for example, typically drop their oldest needles in the fall while retaining their youngest needles, those produced during the last several years.

Perennial plants are alive the year around. Although deciduous perennials may be without leaves for several months each year, tissue beneath bark and in roots is still living. Improper watering, excessive light, extreme temperatures, drying winds, and other adverse conditions can cause damage even when plants are dormant.

Changes in temperature, moisture, and especially in the amount and length of daylight induce seasonal changes in plant growth and appearance, such as flowering or leaf flush and growth. Each species or variety responds differently to these condi-

Fertilizing, applying amendments and mulches that add organic matter or change soil acidity or alkalinity (measured in pH units), and allowing fallen leaves to remain and decompose, alter nutrient availability. Temperature and light vary according to weather, but can be manipulated locally by pruning, adding or removing plants, modifying structures or pavement, and by planting in a suitable location at the proper time of year. Depending on their type and location, mulches or ground covers can increase or decrease heat or light around plants.

All the basic requirements for growth must be properly maintained for plants to have maximum resistance to diseases and be less susceptible to damage by insects, weeds, and other pests. Failing to provide an

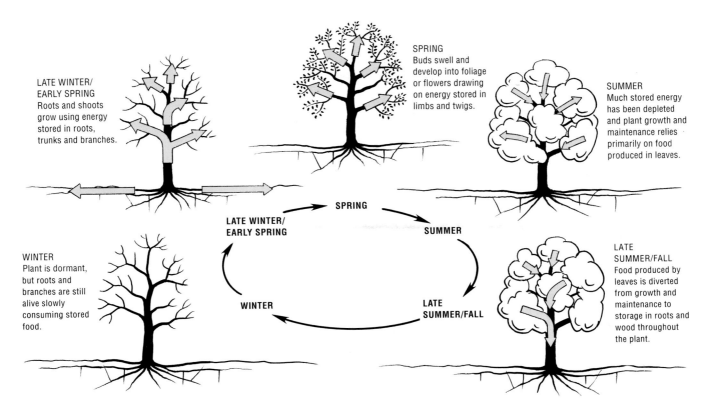

LATE WINTER/ EARLY SPRING
Roots and shoots grow using energy stored in roots, trunks and branches.

SPRING
Buds swell and develop into foliage or flowers drawing on energy stored in limbs and twigs.

SUMMER
Much stored energy has been depleted and plant growth and maintenance relies primarily on food produced in leaves.

WINTER
Plant is dormant, but roots and branches are still alive slowly consuming stored food.

LATE SUMMER/FALL
Food produced by leaves is diverted from growth and maintenance to storage in roots and wood throughout the plant.

LATE WINTER/ EARLY SPRING → SPRING → SUMMER → LATE SUMMER/FALL → WINTER → (cycle)

Figure 3-1. The seasonal growth cycle of a typical deciduous, perennial plant. Wide arrows indicate the direction of major energy flow in the form of carbohydrates.

tions. Seasonal growth usually begins with root and shoot elongation in the spring. In deciduous plants, this early growth starts before foliage is present. Early growth relies on energy produced from food stored in roots or aboveground wood as starch and carbohydrates, which are converted to sugars and transported and used throughout the plant. After root and shoot growth begin, buds swell and expand into foliage or flowers. Some species produce one flush of growth during a short period in the season (determinate growth); other species produce continuous flushes of foliage or flowers until dormancy (indeterminate growth), as long as conditions are favorable.

Once their foliage has developed, deciduous plants have depleted much of their stored energy; continued growth and maintenance rely on food produced by leaves. In most woody deciduous plants, buds for the next season's growth develop on stems during the summer and fall. As the dormant season approaches, food produced by leaves is increasingly diverted from growth and maintenance to storage in roots, trunks, and limbs. During dormancy, the plant slowly consumes the stored food by converting it to energy until conditions again become favorable and the seasonal growth cycle is repeated (Figure 3-1).

Planting, fertilizing, and irrigating must be done during the appropriate growth period or plants do not benefit or perform well. Pest abundance and damage are also linked to this seasonal cycle of plant growth. Actions to prevent and manage pests must be properly timed to be effective.

Good design minimizes pest problems; for example, this close planting shades out weeds.

Designing a Pest-Tolerant Landscape

Effective pest management begins before the landscape is planted. Design landscapes to provide an optimal living environment for plants. Minimize pest problems by selecting relatively pest-resistant species and varieties that are well adapted to local conditions and group the plants that have similar cultural requirements.

CHOOSE A GOOD LOCATION

Consider soil quality, water quality and availability, drainage, and other conditions before selecting a planting location and the species to grow there. Determine proximity to structures, pavement, overhead lines, and underground utilities that may be damaged by growing roots.

Determine how much light and heat occur at that location based on

Choose plants by looking to see what species or varieties are doing well in that neighborhood or in nearby parks or botanical gardens. This blue-flowering ceanothus and yellow-flowered flannel bush in the University of California Davis Arboretum are well adapted to dry areas of central and southern California.

climate and nearby structures, pavement, and plants; choose species suited to those conditions. Examine the space available for growth and learn about the mature size of candidate plants. Give limbs and roots plenty of room to grow and use only plants that will fit at maturity. Most small

trees should be placed at least 5 feet from structures and at least 3 feet from any paved area; larger trees should be placed even farther away. Look for overhead obstacles. Do not plant tall-growing species beneath utility lines. Utility companies prune trees that grow into overhead lines,

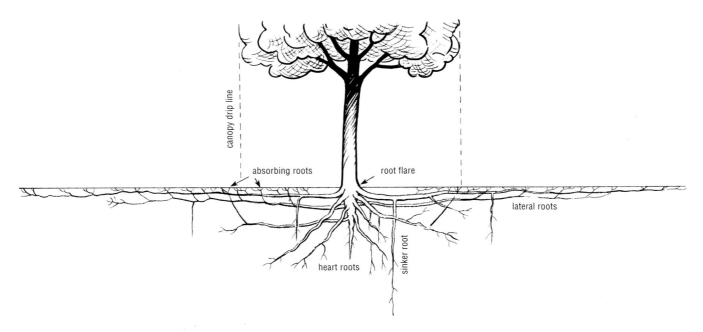

Figure 3-2. Healthy roots are vital to plant survival. Woody plants have several different types of roots and about 90% of roots grow in the upper 3 feet of soil. Up to about 70% of roots are in the top 1 foot, and because roots need air, even more of a tree's roots are near the surface if soils are compacted or water-logged. Conversely, drought-adapted species and trees in deep or well-drained soil have more of their roots growing deeper below ground than shown here. Roots typically extend beyond the tree canopy drip line.

which can severely disfigure trees and promote decay, structural failure, insect attacks, and increase utility costs. Consult *Trees Under Power Lines: A Homeowner's Guide* (UC Leaflet 21470) for more details.

PROVIDE FOR ROOTS

Healthy roots are vital to plant survival. Water, nutrients, and oxygen are absorbed by root tips and mycorrhizae (see below). Roots eliminate waste carbon dioxide, store food, reduce erosion, produce compounds essential to the plant, and support the aboveground plant structure.

Damage appearing on aboveground parts may occur because roots have been smothered, cut, crushed, poisoned, overwatered, underwatered, or otherwise improperly cared for; excessively wet conditions and soil compaction are probably the most common problems. Insects and diseases that attack trunks, limbs, or foliage also can cause more serious damage if roots are unhealthy.

Roots are often neglected because they grow underground and are not seen. Provide them with proper soil conditions and adequate space. Examine the surrounding soil for barriers to root growth before planting. After the first few years of growth, roots of healthy plants extend well beyond the canopy or drip line of the plant; these horizontally growing or lateral roots often extend for a distance equivalent to two to three times the diameter of the drip line. Woody plants also have heart roots, which grow downward and help anchor the tree, and absorbing roots, which have concentrations of root hairs that absorb water from the soil. Commonly, about 90% of woody plant roots grow in the top 3 feet of soil, most in the top 1 foot (Figure 3-2). However, breaking up hardpans or compacted soils deeper than 3 feet before plant-ing can improve plant growth by increasing drainage and facilitating development in some species of sinker roots, which grow near the trunk and deep into the soil. Breaking up hardpan is especially important in arid areas, where hard crusts often form near the soil surface.

CONSIDER MYCORRHIZAE

Most healthy trees have beneficial fungi growing in or on their roots; these are called mycorrhizae or mycorrhizal root tips. Hundreds of different species of soil-dwelling fungi are involved in these symbiotic associations; each plant species tends to be associated with certain species of fungi. Mycorrhizal root tips are the location where plants absorb water and nutrients. Mycorrhizae may also help protect plants from harmful nematodes and pathogenic microorganisms in the soil. Many trees grow poorly and die in the absence of

Avoid plants like this with major roots that are kinked or circling the container.

Reject container-grown plants with poor structure, like this kink in the crown area.

mycorrhizae, especially if plants are stressed from other environmental conditions.

Endomycorrhizae occur mostly within roots; colonized roots appear normal. *Ectomycorrhizae* form a sheath or mantle around short lateral roots. Roots colonized by ectomycorrhizal fungi are often devoid of root hairs and may appear swollen. Beneficial nitrogen-producing bacteria, damaging nematodes, and pathogens also change the outward appearance of roots. With either type of mycorrhizae, fragile hyphae extend from the root into the soil and provide a conduit for water and mineral flow into the plant. Mushrooms growing out of the ground near conifers may be the reproductive structures of mycorrhizal fungi.

Mycorrhizae are common in soils where the plant species they are associated with have grown previously. They disperse in soil, with roots of host plants that are moved, or by spores, which can be windblown or occur in litter on the soil. It may be beneficial to introduce mycorrhizae when planting new species that have not previously grown at that site. One way to do this is to collect soil or litter—if it is known to be free of pathogens—from around established older plants of that species and rake it into the soil around the young plants to be inoculated.

Mycorrhizal fungi are already present in most soils. Promote mycorrhizal growth and development by providing plants with appropriate growing conditions. Avoid soil compaction, overwatering, or underwatering. Prevent changes in soil grade or drainage. Apply mulch as detailed in Chapter 7 to moderate soil temperatures around plants. Avoid contaminating soils with toxic materials. Fumigating soils kills beneficial fungi. Avoid overfertilization, particularly with phosphorus or quick-release, synthetic formulations.

CHOOSE THE RIGHT TREE OR SHRUB

Pest problems commonly occur because people have chosen plants that are poorly suited to local conditions. Each plant species or variety thrives or survives only if conditions are within a certain range, which may be different from the conditions needed by other plants. Plants poorly adapted to conditions at their sites are problem-prone, require frequent pest management action, and do not perform well. Soils, temperature, and seasonal rainfall vary throughout California and are different from most other parts of the United States, so many of the plants that thrive in the eastern states or other areas of the world do not do well in most of California. Likewise, a plant that does well along California's coast may grow poorly in the warmer, drier interior valleys. Determine what plant species or varieties are adapted to local conditions and look to see what plants are doing well in that neighborhood or in nearby parks or botanical gardens; choose from among those. Consult local Cooperative Extension personnel, other experts, and publications listed in References.

Soil. Determine the physical properties of the soil where you plan to plant. Many California soils are alkaline, compacted, and poorly drained, especially in urban areas. Consider having soils tested by a laboratory for texture, salinity, and pH. Learn which plants tolerate local soil conditions and choose from among those species and varieties. If necessary, aerate, amend, change grade, provide a sump for excess water drainage (Figure 3-4), or install drain pipe or drain tile before planting.

Water. Choose plants that thrive within the water limitations at that site. If summer rainfall-adapted species are planted, they may need irrigation throughout their life or they will perform poorly and be problem-plagued. If drought-adapted species are planted in areas provided with irrigation, watering may need to be modified as frequent summer irrigation can damage or kill such plants. Consider water quality in addition to quantity. For example, certain plants grow poorly if water mineral content is high as it is in some irrigation well water.

Climate. Most landscape plants are adapted to either summer drought or summer rainfall. Summer rainfall-adapted species are generally those native to the eastern United States, northern Europe, or eastern Asia where summer rainfall occurs. Most of California has a Mediterranean climate. Winters are cool and wet, summers are hot, and much of the state

Shrubs and trees have different irrigation requirements than turf; separate them by using sidewalks, driveways, or headers.

receives little or no precipitation from late spring through early fall. Californians should consider planting native California species or exotics from other parts of the world that also have a Mediterranean climate (Figure 3-3); these species should require significant irrigation only during establishment.

California encompasses many different climate zones, so even native plants must be matched to local conditions and provided the cultural care to which they are adapted. For example, Monterey pine and Monterey cypress from the coast and giant sequoia from the Sierra do poorly in hot, dry, interior areas of the state regardless of how much water they are given. For more information on selecting drought-adapted and native California plants, see publications in References.

Light and Heat. Consider local climate and choose plants that can tolerate the coldest and hottest conditions expected in that area. Determine the direct and reflected light conditions at that site and choose plants that tolerate those conditions. In urban areas, light and heat can vary dramatically between locations only a few feet apart due to the influence of buildings and pavement. Too much or too little sunlight causes foliage of susceptible species to discolor, die, and drop. Excess heat, or light that converts to heat when it contacts surfaces, causes cracked and sunken bark. These wounds promote wood-boring insects, bark cankers, and decay fungi. Plant only species that are well adapted to the amount of light and heat at that location. See Abiotic Disorders (Chapter 6) for more discussion of light and heat damage.

Select Healthy Plants. Choose good-quality nursery stock (Table 3-1). Investment in better quality plants can pay great dividends in lower maintenance costs and better performance. Avoid improperly pruned trees. Nurseries sometimes clip the main terminal to produce more compact lateral growth that appears attractive when plants are young; improper pruning of young trees can lead to serious structural problems once the plants mature.

Check roots in container-grown plants. Feel below the soil surface or use a hose to wash away some topsoil, which can be replaced; examine smaller plants by temporarily removing them from the container. Avoid plants with major roots kinked or circling the container; these will eventually become girdled by their own root system and grow poorly, break off, or die. Smaller roots circling the con-

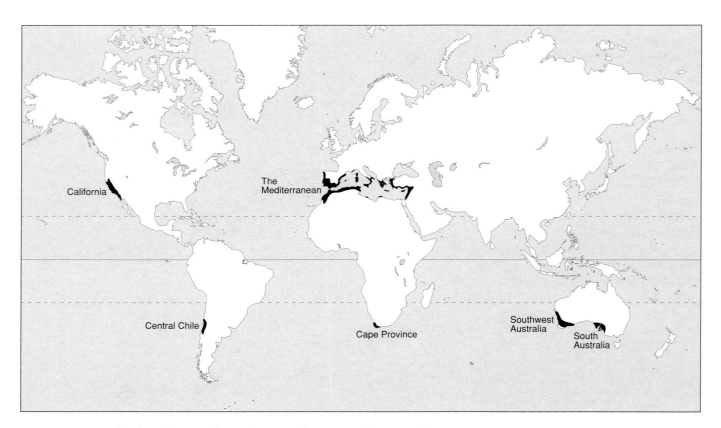

Figure 3-3. Central and southern California have a Mediterranean climate: cool, moist winters and hot, dry summers. Native plants and species from other Mediterranean regions labeled on the map are generally better adapted to California climates.

tainer periphery can be spread or cut before planting, but if larger roots or roots near the trunk are kinked, reject the plant. If possible, select trees that are not staked; they will have sturdier trunks.

Root and crown rots, such as *Phytophthora*, may develop in certain susceptible nursery plants and lead to poor growth and death after transplanting. Avoid plants infested with insects or diseases that may cause problems in landscapes. See Table 3-1 for a nursery plant selection checklist. Consult *Arboriculture: Integrated Management of Landscape Trees, Shrubs, and Vines* for more detailed suggestions.

Pest Resistance. In some cases, pest-resistant varieties or species can be selected that otherwise perform and look similar to susceptible plants. Avoid planting species or varieties known to be prone to serious problems in your area. Do not replant in locations where plants have been killed or severely damaged by disease unless you select a highly disease-resistant species or variety. Do not plant species highly susceptible to root and crown diseases in poorly drained, compacted soils.

Consult Table 3-2 and the appropriate text for resistant species or varieties before selecting plants. For example, tables on species resistant or susceptible to *Verticillium*, *Phytophthora*, and *Armillaria* serve as a guide for selecting plants to avoid these diseases. However, choosing resistant or less susceptible species or varieties does not guarantee that problems will be avoided. Resistant plants may become affected if they are stressed because of poor cultural care or other factors. Insect pests and disease can also evolve to overcome resistant plants, and new pests are often introduced from foreign places.

TABLE 3-1

Nursery Tree and Shrub Selection Checklist.

LOOK FOR:
Species or varieties well adapted to soil, water, light, heat, wind, and other environmental conditions prevailing where they will be planted.
A plant that at maturity will fit into the space provided for roots and branches.
Pest-resistant species or varieties.
Roots and crown area free of rot, galls, wounds, and insects.
Roots that are not kinked or circling the trunk or main roots.
Roots that aren't a solid mass or too small in comparison with aboveground parts.
Good overall plant appearance, color, leaf size, and vigor.
A smaller plant, one more likely to survive transplanting.
A tree trunk that has not been headed back or topped.
A trunk without wounds that can stand without being staked.

AVOID:
Species or varieties poorly adapted to local environmental conditions.
Plants that at maturity will be too large for the available space.
Species or varieties prone to pest problems.
Injured, distorted, diseased, or girdled trunks, roots, or crown area.
Encircling or kinked roots or a root mass too small in comparison with above ground plant parts.
Discolored, undersized, or distorted foliage.
Tree trunks that have been topped or lack a single dominant leader.
Tree trunks that can't stand without being staked.

New plant varieties and better information are constantly being developed; consult knowledgeable Cooperative Extension personnel, horticultural consultants, or a certified nurseryperson for assistance in selecting pest-resistant plants.

Plant Compatibility. Group together plants having compatible growth characteristics and similar needs for irrigation and other cultural care. For example, some ground cover and turf species can spread rapidly and overgrow nearby shrubs and young trees. Turf and trees have different soil moisture and irrigation requirements.

Separate incompatible species with structures, pavement, or headers (wood, metal, or concrete barriers extending 8 inches or more below ground).

TABLE 3-2

Pest-Resistant Alternative Species or Varieties for Common Problems on Woody Landscape Plants.

HOST PLANT	PEST	RESISTANT OR LESS SUSCEPTIBLE ALTERNATIVES
Many species	Verticillium wilt	Table 5-2, page 192
Many species	Armillaria root rot	Table 5-4, page 208
Many species	Phytophthora root rot	Table 5-5, page 211
Many species	crown gall	page 203
Many species	large-leaf mistletoes	page 252
Acacia	acacia psyllid	Table 4-9, page 105
Alder	flatheaded alder borer	Italian alder, page 158
Ash	anthracnose	'Moraine,' 'Raywood,' page 185
Box elder	boxelder bug	male box elder, page 136
Ceanothus	ceanothus stem gall moth	Table 4-10, page 145
Crape myrtle	powdery mildew	'Catawba,' 'Cherokee,' 'Seminole,' page 193
Cypress	cypress canker	page 202
Cypress	cypress tip miner	Table 4-11, page 147
Elm, Chinese	anthracnose	'Drake' cultivar, page 202
Elm	Dutch elm disease	hackberry, zelkova, Chinese elm, page 192
Elm	elm leaf beetle	hackberry, zelkova, Chinese elm, page 81
Elm	European elm scale	hackberry, zelkova, page 131
Eucalyptus	eucalyptus longhorned borer	page 161
Euonymus	euonymus scale	page 125
Fuchsia	fuchsia gall mite	Table 4-13, page 175
Juniper	cypress tip miner	Table 4-11, page 147
Juniper	juniper twig girdler	page 169
Pear, ornamental	fireblight	'Bradford,' 'Capital,' 'Red Spire,' page 190
Pepper tree	peppertree psyllid	page 108
Pine	Nantucket pine tip moth	Table 4-12, page 151
Pine	pine pitch canker	brutia pine, page 201
Poplar	Cytospora canker	'Easter,' 'Nor,' 'Mighty Mo,' 'Platte' poplar hybrids, page 201
Rhododendron	root weevils	Table 4-8, page 89
Rose	powdery mildew	'Simplicity,' 'Meidiland' series, page 193
Sycamore	anthracnose	'Bloodgood,' page 185
Sycamore	powdery mildew	'Yarwood,' page 193

Site Preparation and Planting

Properly prepare the soil and control weeds before planting as discussed in Chapter 7. Do not wait until weeds appear after planting. It is easier and more effective to control weeds if you take action and properly design landscapes before planting.

PREPARE THE SITE

Many urban soils are compacted and drain poorly. Drainage must be improved and soil must be loosened if young trees and shrubs are to grow well. It may be necessary to break up or penetrate hardpan, for example with a jackhammer, auger, or backhoe, to provide greater soil depth. Install drain pipe, drain tile, or a sump (Figure 3-4) if needed to ensure adequate drainage and good plant growth.

Before planting, mark out a planting area that is at least two to three times the diameter of the rootball. Rototill, shovel, bore, or use an auger to mix the soil within this area to the depth of the plant's rootball. Deep ripping or plowing may be necessary. Mix the soil well.

Adding organic matter to the planting hole of trees and large shrubs has not shown consistent benefits. Amending the entire potential root zone of trees is generally not practical, and amending soils around established plants will damage roots. Amendments can help before planting certain shrubs. Species like camellias and azaleas are adapted to well-drained, acidic soils. Without amendment, they will do poorly in alkaline, poorly drained soils.

If organic matter is added to soil, it should be at least partially decomposed or well-composted and constitute no more than about 25% of the soil volume in the upper 12 inches of soil. Thoroughly mix the organic matter into the topsoil. Appropriate amounts of sulfur can also be mixed in to increase soil acidity.

Provide for necessary irrigation. Low-volume emitter systems conserve water and reduce weed and some disease problems, as discussed later in this chapter.

PLANT PROPERLY

Early spring and late fall are generally the best times to plant; avoid planting during hot summer weather. Depending on conditions and preparations needed at that site, weed control and other work may need to begin well before planting.

Dig a shallow hole in the center of the prepared soil area and set the plant on firm or settled ground in the center of the hole. Make sure the top of the plant's root crown is level with or slightly above surrounding soil. Plant the crown about 1 to 2 inches higher than soil level if the soil is compacted, will drain poorly, has been loosened deeper than the rootball, or if soil is highly amended so the plant is likely to settle as organic matter decays. Avoid planting in a hole or low-lying area (Figure 5-3), except that planting 1 to 2 inches below the surrounding surface may be acceptable in sandy soils.

Planting too deep or too shallow are common problems. Deep planting favors root and crown diseases to which young plants are especially susceptible. Planting too shallow leads to root damage from exposure and excessive drying.

Place the plant in the hole and position the main stem perpendicular to the ground. Cut any wires or rope around the rootball and pull them away. If the plant has a container, remove it before planting. Check for roots that circle the container and gently spread them before planting. Cut any broken or encircling roots that are too large to spread. Do not use the plant if it is extensively root-bound with major roots kinked or encircling the trunk or rootball; the plant will perform poorly and die sooner than normal. Backfill the hole after properly positioning the plant and preparing the roots.

Do not cover container soil with field soil, as the difference in texture can prevent water penetration into container soil around the roots. Settle the soil after planting by watering; don't stamp soil down or you may overpack it. Keep a 4 foot diameter or larger area around the trunk free of turf or other vegetation. Apply 3 to 4 inches of organic mulch over the entire prepared area. Keep mulch 4 to 6 inches away from the stem or trunk or apply it thinly there to avoid moist trunks, which may promote disease.

Remove any trunk wrapping or protective tape that came with the

Figure 3-4. Provide adequate drainage before planting. One method is to create a sump by augering one or more holes, each 1 to 4 inches in diameter, through impermeable soil or hardpan. Auger down at least 3 feet or deeper if necessary to penetrate to more permeable soil. Fill the holes with pea gravel or sandy loam soil before planting.

Planting too shallow leads to root damage from exposure and excessive drying.

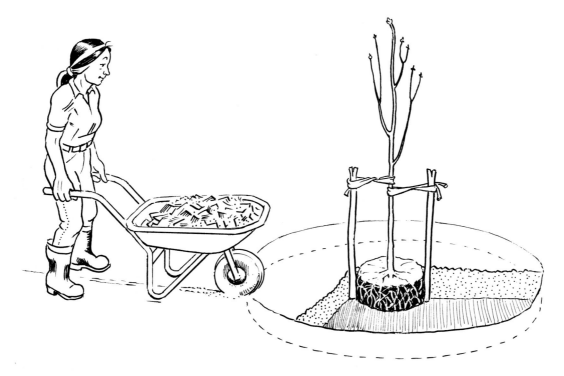

Figure 3-5. Plant new trees properly. Prepare an area several times wider than the rootball. Place the rootball on solid ground in a hole so that the root crown is level with, or slightly higher than, the surrounding soil. Use two stakes, each with one tie near the top, such as rubber tubing in a figure eight that allows the trunk to flex but prevents the trunk from rubbing the stake. Apply mulch over the entire prepared area, but keep organic mulch and waterproof synthetics 4-6 inches away from the trunk or apply mulch thinly there.

new plant. Trunk wrapping or staking material that restricts trunk growth can seriously injure young plants. Prevent sunscald by applying white interior latex paint, diluted 50% with water, to the trunk. Nursery plants are commonly grown close together so their trunks are shaded; planting in the landscape exposes tender bark to sun damage.

STAKING

Stake trees only if needed to protect or support the trunk or anchor the rootball during the first year or so after planting. If the tree was rigidly staked in the nursery container, remove this and restake the plant. Do not fasten trunks firmly; they must be allowed to flex some with the wind in order to develop stem strength. Use two stakes and tie the trunk at just one level near the top of the stakes.

After tying the trunk, cut the stakes off several inches above the ties.

To determine the proper staking height of trunks that cannot stand upright without support, hold the lower part of the trunk in one hand, bend the top of the trunk to one side, then release the top. Locate the ties about 6 inches above the lowest level at which the trunk can be held and still return upright after the top is deflected.

Ties should have a broad surface that contacts the trunk without cutting into bark. Ties should be flexible or elastic and form a loose loop around the trunk. One way is to use two sections of rubber tubing, each about 18 inches long, attached to opposite posts. Circle each tie around the trunk, cross the ends to form a figure-eight, then attach the free ends of the rubber to the stake (Figure 3-5). Another method is to use two ties, each attached to both posts. Overlap the ties twice, once on each side of the trunk between the trunk and each post (Figure 3-6). Remove any staking after a year or so; if the trunk is then unable to stand alone, determine the cause before restaking. Consult *Staking Landscape Trees* (UC Leaflet 2576) or *Arboriculture: Integrated Management of Landscape Trees, Shrubs, and Vines* for more details.

CARE FOR YOUNG TREES AND SHRUBS

Learn the cultural requirements of plants under local conditions. Water, fertilize, and prune young plants correctly. Proper cultural care is critical to minimize pest damage. If pests or damage do appear, reevaluate cultural practices to determine if inadequate or improper care have contributed to the problem. Proper cultural care alone may provide the solution. Other activities, such as pesticide applications, may be of little benefit to plants if cultural care is inadequate.

Keep soil moist but not soggy around newly planted trees and shrubs. Proper irrigation frequency depends on the plant, soil, and weather. New plantings for about the first 2 months may need to be irrigated almost daily during hot, dry weather because their roots are confined to the small volume of soil that was the old soil ball in the container. Because of the difference in texture between potting mix used in the nursery and natural soil, water often does not move easily from surrounding soil into the rootball. Therefore, be sure to wet the rootball directly; however, avoid wetting the trunk and do not allow water to puddle around the crown.

Allow the soil surface to dry between waterings. Dig a shallow hole or use a soil tube or moisture indicator probe to check that soil several inches deep is remaining moist. Increase the interval between irrigations as plants become established and encourage good root growth through infrequent, thorough soakings. Avoid frequent sprinkling that only wets the surface; this encourages undesirable shallow root growth.

Fertilize woody plants sparingly or not at all during their first growing season in the landscape. Nitrogen is usually the only nutrient to which woody plants respond. Slow-release fertilizers are better because quick-release fertilizers can injure and kill young roots and retard early plant growth if applied heavily or incorporated into the planting hole.

During the first four or five years of growth, prune young woody plants to encourage good structure and remove damaged or diseased stems; establish-

Ties were left on this young tree too long, causing wood to grow around the top tie. The branch at the right has a canker from rubbing a stake that is too tall and too close.

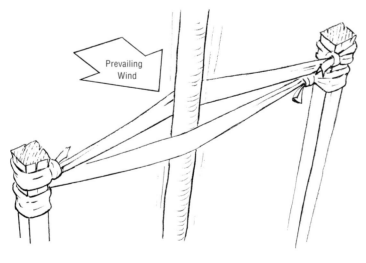

Figure 3-6. Overhead view of one method of staking tree trunks. Each of two ties is attached to both stakes. Ties cross over between the stake and trunk, providing support but allowing the trunk to flex, which is necessary for developing strength. The imaginary line between the stakes should be at a right angle to the prevailing wind.

Prevent sunscald by applying white interior latex paint diluted 50% with water to young trunks. If you must plant trees in lawn, keep a 4-foot-diameter or larger area around the trunk free of turf or other vegetation.

Water Management

Poor water management is probably the biggest problem suffered by landscape trees and shrubs. Each species has a different range of maximum and minimum water necessary for survival. Learn the water requirements of plants at each location. Monitor soil moisture around the plant's root zone and adjust irrigation according to seasonal need. Maintain adequate but not excessive water in the soil to ensure plant survival and good growth. Dig up and examine small roots to become familiar with their appearance. Healthy root tips are generally cream colored and firm; unhealthy roots are often dark, water-soaked, and soft. Excess water can cause fine roots to decay and slough off when dug from the soil.

WATER AND PEST PROBLEMS

Too much or too little water damages or kills plants (Tables 3-3 and 3-4). Insufficient water causes leaves to wilt, droop, and drop. Drought stress promotes sunburn and sunscald, shoot and branch dieback, bark cracking, cankers, and some fungi, such as *Cytospora* canker fungus. *Botryosphaeria* fungus commonly causes cankers and branch dieback on drought-stressed giant sequoia planted outside its native range; other species can also become infected. Monterey and Leyland cypress planted in hot, dry locations are highly susceptible to cypress canker disease and insect attack; few Monterey cypress survive to maturity when they aren't planted in the cool, moist coastal areas they prefer.

Mites and some leaf-chewing and leaf-sucking insects are more damaging to plants receiving insufficient moisture. Most wood-boring insects such as bark beetles, flatheaded and

ing a central leader or dominant main terminal is especially important. Avoid excessive pruning, which may ruin tree structure and retards overall growth by removing food-producing foliage. Leave some temporary, short branches along the trunk or main stem during the first few years; these protect tender bark from injuries and sunscald, improve trunk growth and strength, and nourish the tree.

Prevent weeds, turf, and ground covers from growing near the trunk of young trees and shrubs. Nearby plants can seriously retard young woody plant growth. Apply 3 to 4 inches of mulch over a 4-foot-diameter or larger area beneath new plants. Mulch reduces weed competition, retains soil moisture, moderates root-zone temperatures, and reduces compaction.

longhorned beetles, and clearwing moths primarily attack plants stressed from drought or other unfavorable conditions. Prevent damage through proper plant care; once trees and shrubs become severely infested by borers, plants do poorly and usually die. When these pests appear on plants, prune out and destroy infested limbs and identify and apply cultural practices that improve plant vigor.

Overwatering is probably a more common problem in landscapes than underwatering. Excess water excludes oxygen from soil that plant roots need to survive. Excessive water in the root zone, especially near the root collar, is a primary cause of root and crown diseases such as *Armillaria*, *Phytophthora*, and *Dematophora*. The fungi causing these diseases are present in many soils, but usually become damaging only when conditions favor them.

Poor water placement also promotes some diseases. Splashing water spreads fungal spores and wet foliage promotes some foliar and fruit diseases, such as leaf spots, rusts, anthracnose, and brown rot. Minimize or prevent many foliar diseases by using low-volume drip irrigation or minisprinklers instead of standard overhead sprinkling.

The seasonal timing of irrigation also is important in disease development. For example, *Armillaria mellea*, the oak root fungus, becomes active when soils are warm and moist. Because California's rainfall naturally occurs during the winter when soils are cool, oaks growing in dry summer soils usually escape damage. However, when people frequently water native oaks during the summer, or alter soils through compaction or changes in grade, moist roots and warm soils may coincide, predisposing oaks and many other species to infection and death by the *Armillaria* fungus.

TABLE 3-3

Common Problems Associated With Underwatering Woody Landscape Plants.

DAMAGE SYMPTOMS	CAUSE	MANAGEMENT
Leaves drop prematurely	abiotic disorder	pages 32, 215
Leaves spotted	abiotic disorder	pages 32, 185
Leaves bleached/stippled	mites insects that suck plant juices	page 170 page 135
Shoot or branch dieback	abiotic disorder *Botryosphaeria* canker wood-boring insects	pages 32, 215 page 203 page 151
Bark cracking	abiotic disorder	pages 32, 215
Bark or branch cankers	abiotic disorder *Botryosphaeria* canker cypress canker *Cytospora* canker	page 32 page 203 page 202 page 201
Bark weeping	abiotic disorder wood-boring insects *Botryosphaeria* canker bacteria	pages 32, 200 page 151 page 203 pages 197, 204
Bark with holes	wood-boring insects	page 151
Bark with sawdust	wood-boring insects	page 151

TABLE 3-4

Common Problems Associated With Overwatering or Poor Water Placement.[a]

DAMAGE SYMPTOMS	CAUSE	MANAGEMENT
Leaves drop prematurely	anthracnose diseases	page 185
Leaves spotted/discolored	fungal and bacterial diseases	page 185
Foliage yellows/wilts	root and crown diseases vascular wilt diseases abiotic disorder	page 206 pages 190–193 pages 32, 215
Fruit spotted/discolored	fungal diseases	pages 185–189
Branch cankers	anthracnose diseases	page 185
Branches die back	root and crown diseases abiotic disorder	page 206 pages 32, 215

a. Poor water placement includes overhead watering, wetting trunks, and allowing water to pond around trunks.

Basin irrigation with a water tank truck is useful in dry locations that do not have an installed water system.

Drought-adapted plants such as oaks and eucalyptus may benefit from deep, supplemental water at 1 or 2 month intervals during the summer, especially during years of abnormally low rainfall. Irrigation should be provided to simulate natural patterns and applied mostly during the normal rainy season, tapering off during the dry season. Water around and beyond the drip line, not near the trunk (see Figure 5-2).

IRRIGATION

Irrigation is required to maintain most urban landscapes in California, where rainless weather prevails throughout much of the growing season. Early morning or just before dawn is the best time to irrigate; irrigating at this time reduces water loss from evaporation. Predawn irrigation also improves sprinkler efficiency and the uniformity of water distribution because there is generally less wind and more water pressure. Predawn irrigation minimizes the length of time when foliage is wet, thereby discouraging the development of certain foliar diseases.

Irrigation frequency and the volume of water to apply at any one time varies greatly according to many factors, such as past irrigation practices, moisture demand by plants, microclimate, root depth, drainage patterns, irrigation system efficiency, and soil texture, structure, and depth. Several terms are used to describe the water-holding capacity of soil. *Pore spaces* are the openings between soil particles, which fill with air or water or both. *Field capacity* is the amount of water that can be held in pore space by capillary action, after excess water has moved down through the soil by the force of gravity. *Capillary action* is the term used to describe the attraction of water to the surface of soil particles. Because of this attraction between particles and water, only a portion of the water in soil—the *available water*—can actually be extracted by plants. The *wilting point* occurs when plants have extracted all the available water. Loam soils (clay, sand, and silt combined) that are not compacted generally provide the best combination of available water (Table 3-5) and adequate oxygen for roots

(Figure 3-7); they provide a range of pore sizes with the smaller pores holding moisture while the larger pores drain and allow air to enter the soil.

Rooting depth varies according to plant age, type, species, soil, and moisture conditions. Plants generally have more shallow roots when they are young, receive relatively frequent and light irrigations, or are growing in compacted or poorly drained soils. Roots are usually deeper in older plants, as well as plants growing in well-aerated soils with good drainage and less frequent but deep irrigation. However, about 90% of tree and shrub roots are in the top 3 feet of soil (Figure 3-2).

Water demand or loss varies greatly depending on the environment and plant species. Water lost through a combination of evaporation from soil and transpiration by plants is called evapotranspiration (ET). A plant's demand for water increases when weather is sunny, hot, and windy and when humidity is low. A solitary, exposed plant growing near pavement or other heat-absorbing and light-reflecting surfaces requires more water than that same plant growing where it's sheltered or grouped with other plants.

TABLE 3-5

Approximate Amounts of Available Water When Soils Are at Field Capacity.

SOIL TEXTURE	INCHES OF AVAILABLE WATER PER FOOT OF SOIL
Sand	0.5-1.0
Sandy loam	1.0-1.5
Clay loam	1.5-2.0
Clay	1.5-2.0

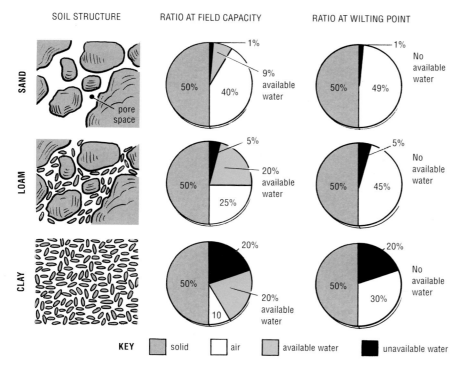

SOIL STRUCTURE RATIO AT FIELD CAPACITY RATIO AT WILTING POINT

SAND

LOAM

CLAY

KEY solid air available water unavailable water

Figure 3-7. Pore spaces are the openings between soil particles that contain water and air. Sandy soils have big pore spaces that contain large amounts of air, but allow water to drain quickly. Clay soils have more small pore spaces and retain more water, resulting in poor drainage and often insufficient oxygen for roots. Loam soils are a mixture of sand, silt, and clay that are not compacted; loam provides the best balance between water-holding ability and adequate air.

Estimating Irrigation Needs.

Schedule irrigation by observing plants or monitoring soil or evapotranspiration. Combine more than one method for the best results. These estimates assume the plant is correctly planted and rooted and has been growing well.

Observe Plants. Examine plants regularly for symptoms of water stress. Early drought-stress symptoms exhibited by broadleaf plants include wilting of leaves and normally shiny green foliage that becomes faded, dull, or grayish. Growing tips may wilt in the afternoon and recover as evening approaches. As drought stress becomes more severe, plants may not recover from wilt, leaf margins or interiors turn yellow or brown, foliage dies and drops, and

twigs, branches, and eventually the entire plant may die. Certain plants may exhibit symptoms first because they are more isolated and exposed, are planted on higher ground, or are less drought-tolerant species. Inspect these plants more frequently and use them as indicators of drought stress and irrigation need.

Monitor the Soil. Schedule irrigation by monitoring soil moisture. Frequency of monitoring varies greatly depending on the factors discussed above. Soil around young plants during hot weather may need to be monitored daily; every few weeks may be adequate when monitoring around mature trees during more favorable weather.

Dig a shallow hole or use a soil sampling tube and examine soil in the

rooting zone to a depth of about 1 foot; soil lightens in color when it is dry. Feel the soil; medium- and fine-textured soils such as loam and clay can be molded, or rolled or squeezed into a ball when wet. If soil does not mold, it is too dry. If soil molds into a ball but does not crumble when rubbed, it is too wet. If the soil can be molded and crumbles when rubbed, the moisture content is probably suitable, except that sandy soil crumbles even when wet. Sample soil from the root zone in several different areas of the landscape to assess overall irrigation needs and determine whether water is being applied deeply and uniformly enough.

Another way to monitor soil moisture is to install a tensiometer or other reliable soil moisture sensor. A tensiometer is a closed tube containing a porous, water-filled cup at the bottom. The tube is buried so that its bottom is in contact with the water film surrounding soil particles in the root zone, usually about 1 to 2 feet deep. As the soil dries, water is sucked out of the cup, creating a vacuum, which is measured by a gauge. The entire unit can be secured below ground, and some tensiometers can be wired into irrigation system controls to trigger watering automatically when needed. For more details on using a tensiometer see *Questions and Answers About Tensiometers* (UC Leaflet 2264).

Irrigation may also be scheduled by monitoring evapotranspiration, using an electrical-resistance block (gypsum block), or with a capacitance sensor as discussed in *Arboriculture: Integrated Management of Landscape Trees, Shrubs, and Vines.*

IRRIGATION METHODS

Basin, sprinkler, and low-volume soaker or drip irrigation systems are common in landscapes. Form a basin by creating a berm of soil several

This drip system, which will be covered with organic mulch, wastes comparatively little water. Low-volume irrigation also reduces compaction, salinity, and weed growth problems associated with sprinklers.

inches high that encompasses the drip line of the tree or shrub bed. Provide water within the berm by installing an irrigation head, using a hose or tank truck, or by relying on runoff or precipitation. Slope soil within the berm away from the plant's base and break down berms during prolonged rainy weather to prevent water from ponding around the trunk (see Figure 5-2).

Sprinklers are a common irrigation method. They wash dust from plants and increase humidity in landscapes, as well as irrigate the soil. However, sprinklers may distribute water unevenly and waste water, especially in windy conditions. They can compact the surface of bare soil and promote certain foliar diseases by splashing fungal spores and increasing humidity. In comparison with low-volume irrigation systems, sprinkler irrigation of trees and shrubs is less efficient because water is dispersed widely, making it suitable only for relatively large plantings with uniform water needs.

Low-volume systems emit water directly on or below the soil surface using porous hoses, drippers, or emitter nozzles. Low-volume systems can be more expensive than sprinklers and require more skill to use, especially in developing appropriate irrigation schedules. When using a low-volume system, shrubs in dry areas may need to be occasionally washed of dust to keep them healthy. However, low-volume systems waste comparatively little water and reduce or avoid compaction, salinity, and weed growth problems associated with sprinkler irrigation.

CONSERVE WATER IN LANDSCAPES

Conserve water by installing an efficient irrigation system. Maintain and operate irrigation equipment properly. Irrigate only when needed; monitor plants or soil as discussed above to determine when to irrigate.

Choose species that are tolerant of the heat, exposure, soil, and moisture conditions at that specific site. Group together plants with similar water requirements. Use plant species adapted to the local climate. Many California natives and plants from

other areas of the world with a Mediterranean climate require little or no irrigation once they become established.

Fertilizing Woody Plants

Sixteen elements are required for plant growth; they usually occur naturally in sufficient quantities. Carbon, hydrogen, and oxygen are the most common and are provided to plants by air and water. Depending on the soil, environment, and host plant, providing nutrients or fertilizer in small amounts may improve the growth and appearance of landscape plants and reduce plant susceptibility to pests.

Nitrogen, and to a lesser extent iron, are the only nutrients in which woody plants are commonly deficient. Most plants respond to the addition of nitrogen, which is available in various organic and inorganic forms. Iron is usually present in soils in adequate amounts; however, many plants cannot absorb iron if soils are either too alkaline or poorly drained. Fertilization with other nutrients is not needed unless a specific deficiency exists. Improper or excessive fertilization damages plants, can cause pest problems, and may pollute water. Fertilization does not overcome harmful effects from improper watering or other cultural practices.

FERTILIZATION AND PESTS

Fertilize only as needed and only if other problems have been eliminated as the cause of poor growth. Some abiotic disorders, such as mineral deficiencies that cause undersized, discolored, or distorted foliage, can be remedied by adding nutrients.

Avoid overfertilization, especially with high nitrogen fertilizers. Overfertilization promotes excessive foliage that undesirably shades the inner canopy and understory plants. Fertilization results in the need for more frequent pruning and can shorten the life of plants by causing them to outgrow available space. Rapid growth from excess fertilizer can cause bark to crack, allowing entry of fungi. Excessive fertilizer kills roots and "burns" or kills foliage. Application of nitrogen late in the growing season may delay dormancy in deciduous plants; if cold weather occurs early, plants can be damaged.

Too much fertilizer promotes excessive succulent foliage, which can increase populations of pests, such as mites, aphids, and psyllids, that prefer new growth. Cypress bark moth larvae in natural situations feed primarily on Monterey cypress cones. In landscapes, they often infest trunks and limbs because landscape cypresses are fertilized and watered to promote rapid growth, resulting in thin bark susceptible to bark moth attack. Fertilizing oaks may promote distorted terminals. These "witches' brooms" are caused by powdery mildew, which readily infects and damages succulent new growth caused during the dry season by fertilization. Do not fertilize pines that exhibit cankers or rosaceous plants infected with fireblight as fertilization increases plant susceptibility to these diseases.

WHEN TO FERTILIZE

With the possible exception of young plants and fruit and nut trees grown for their yield, woody species in landscapes should not be routinely fertilized. Nutrients should be provided only selectively in response to identified needs. As long as woody plants exhibit normal leaf size and color and desired growth, nutrients are probably adequate.

Young trees and shrubs, especially those growing in infertile soil, may grow more quickly after fertilization;

which people usually desire. Species poorly adapted to local soils may also benefit from fertilization; however, avoid planting these and consider replacing them with plants better adapted to local conditions.

NUTRIENT DEFICIENCIES

Learn to recognize symptoms of nutrient deficiency in established plants; nitrogen and iron are the common deficiencies. Deficiencies cause foliage to discolor, fade, distort, or become spotted, sometimes in a characteristic pattern that can be used to identify the cause. Fewer leaves, flowers, and fruit may be produced and these can develop later than normal and remain undersized if plants are deficient. More severely deficient plants become stunted and exhibit dieback.

Common nutrient deficiencies and their symptoms are summarized in Table 6-2, and proper fertilization is discussed in Chapter 6. More detailed discussions on fertilization and nutrient problems are available in *Fertilizing Woody Plants* (UC Leaflet 2958), *Arboriculture: Integrated Management of Landscape Trees, Shrubs, and Vines*, and *Western Fertilizer Handbook: Horticultural Edition* listed in References.

Pruning

Removing or pruning off parts is common practice to direct plant growth and performance. Improper pruning damages plants and can cause pest problems.

REASONS FOR PRUNING

Prune landscape plants to remove diseased wood, to induce strong structure in young plants, and to maintain mature plant health and structure. Stands of naturally growing plants may be "self-pruning" because lower and inner branches become

shaded, weaken, and die. Many landscape trees need to be pruned to obtain the desired spacing of main branches vertically and radially around the trunk. Remove branches to provide more light to the plants below and to reduce wind resistance, which can lead to deformities or breakage. Prevent obstruction of views or interference with utility lines by pruning plants that grow too large for the space provided. Only qualified arborists should prune large trees or those near power lines.

Minimize pruning requirements by selecting species that mature to a size appropriate for that location. Select plants that have been well cared for and correctly pruned in the nursery. Properly prune young plants during their first few years of growth so that structural problems are minimized as plants mature.

Leave temporary branches along the trunk of young trees to nourish and strengthen the trunk and to shade and protect the lower trunk from injury; keep these temporary branches less than 12 inches long. Remove the largest temporary branches during dormant season pruning each year during the first four or five years of a tree's growth. The remaining branches should then provide the maturing tree's structure.

PRUNING AND PEST MANAGEMENT

Proper pruning can control or prevent certain pests. Prune plants properly when young to minimize the need to remove large limbs later, resulting in large wounds. Remove damaged or diseased limbs and consider pruning out pests confined to a small portion of the plant. Pruning can increase air circulation within the canopy, which reduces humidity and the incidence of certain diseases. Avoid unnecessary pruning; pruning causes wounds, which are entry sites for decay and disease organisms.

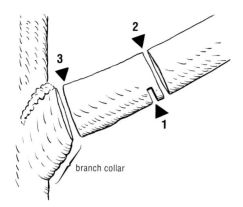

Figure 3-8. Remove a branch by making the pruning cut just outside the branch collar, as indicated by number 3. When removing a limb larger than about 2 inches in diameter, make three cuts in the order indicated. Make the first cut from below, about one-fourth of the way through the limb and 1 or 2 feet from the trunk. Make the second cut about 2 inches beyond the first cut, cutting from above until the limb drops. Make the final cut at number 3.

Make pruning cuts correctly, just outside the branch collar as illustrated in Figure 3-8.

Do not prune too much too soon. Plants store energy in their trunk and limbs (in addition to roots) and sufficient photosynthetic surface (primarily foliage) is required to manufacture enough food. Topping trees or otherwise removing excess wood in one season results in vigorous, dense growth, which is susceptible to breakage and shades interior branches. Large wounds close slowly, increasing the likelihood of decay, disease, and infestation by termites. Removing too much foliage exposes previously shaded bark, causing sunscald. Sunscald leads to cankers or attack by wood-boring insects and disease-causing fungi.

Check the host tables at the back of this book to learn what problems each plant species is prone to; prune at the proper time to avoid these problems. For example, prune eucalyptus during December through

This black walnut was topped, encouraging growth of branches weakly attached below the cut on both limbs. A major limb was also removed below the first main branch crotch, leaving a large wound, which closes slowly and has developed decay.

March to avoid attracting eucalyptus longhorned borers. Prune elms only during the late fall and winter, when the bark beetles that spread Dutch elm disease are not active. Beetles are attracted to fresh wounds and introduce disease spores when they feed or lay eggs. Prune off and dispose of declining limbs that are infested with wood-boring insects. Such practices eliminate beetle breeding sites and remove developing insects before

they can emerge and attack other parts of the plant or nearby plants. Avoid pruning plants susceptible to powdery mildew during the dry season. Pruning stimulates new growth, which is susceptible to powdery mildew fungi during dry weather.

Keep pruning tools clean. Contaminated tools may spread bacterial gall of oleander and olive and fireblight of fruit trees and other rosaceous plants. Sterilize tools before each cut with a

The center pine was topped to prevent damage to power lines. Terminals are dying back and bark beetles are attacking the tree, which died 3 months after this photograph was taken. Do not plant tall growing species beneath overhead utility lines.

commercial disinfectant as directed on the label when pruning these hosts if infections are a problem.

WHEN TO PRUNE

The correct time to prune depends on plant species and condition and the purpose of pruning. Remove damaged or hazardous branches whenever they appear. Prune to improve structure and shape, especially when plants are young. Remove one or both branches that cross, are attached to the trunk at a sharp angle with included bark, or have a branch diameter that is about one-half or more that of the trunk and compete with the main leader. If many branches should be removed, reduce excessive shoot growth and dwarfing by spreading pruning over several years. Prune deciduous plants during the dormant season if possible. Avoid pruning deciduous plants once they have begun to grow through midsummer. Minimize dwarfing of evergreen species by pruning just before their normal growth season, usually in the spring. Check the Tree and Shrub Pest Tables and discussion above to see how pruning time affects certain pest problems.

HOW TO PRUNE

Heading and thinning are the two primary types of pruning cuts; each promotes a different plant response. Heading removes a branch to a stub, a bud, or a small branch. Pinching, tip pruning, shearing, stubbing, and topping are all types of heading cuts. Heading stimulates new growth from buds just below the cut. The resulting foliage and shoots are often dense, may be weakly attached to the old branches, and may break off easily. In some cases, branch stubs die or produce only weak sprouts.

A thinning cut removes a branch at its point of attachment (Figure 3-8) or shortens it to a lateral large enough to assume the terminal role. Compared with a heading cut, growth near the pruning site is less vigorous after a thinning cut; thinning cuts promote more evenly distributed growth throughout the plant. Thinning cuts are more selective and time consuming, but result in stronger structure and retain more of the plant's natural shape.

The location of the pruning cut in relation to the branch attachment influences the size of the wound, extent of callusing, and potential decay. Make most pruning cuts just outside the branch collar or bark ridge. Do not cut flush with the main limb or trunk and don't leave stubs. Cutting just outside the branch collar reduces the wound size, reduces the exposure of trunk tissue to infection, and preserves the attachment zone, which is most resistant to decay and contains tissue best able to close after a cut.

Shears can be used for small diameter cuts. Use a saw when cutting branches greater than about 1 inch in diameter. On branches larger than about 2 inches in diameter, avoid tearing bark or splitting the wood by making three cuts as illustrated in Figure 3-8. Consult *Arboriculture: Integrated Management of Landscape Trees, Shrubs, and Vines* for more details.

AVOID TOPPING TREES

Topping, also called stubbing or dehorning, is the drastic heading of large branches in mature trees. Main limbs are often sheared as with a hedge, leaving stubs. Topping is a poor pruning practice sometimes used to shorten tall trees, remove hazardous or diseased limbs, or to prevent interference with overhead utility lines.

Drastic pruning is rarely justified simply because trees are believed to be too tall. Removing extensive canopy may not leave enough foliage to manufacture sufficient food and may cause roots to die and the tree to decline. The large wounds left by topping often fail to close and are susceptible to internal decay and attack by wood-boring insects. Topping encourages growth of branches weakly attached below the cut, which become susceptible to wind breakage.

Prune trees properly when they are young to minimize the need for severe pruning when trees mature. Instead of topping, selectively remove upper limbs back to lower lateral branches. This proper method is more time consuming and expensive, but avoids future expense from improper pruning and provides a more attractive, healthier, and safer tree.

Injuries, Hazards, and Protecting Landscapes

Bark, wood, and roots can be wounded or injured by people, animals, or adverse environmental conditions. Wounds can attract boring insects, serve as entry sites for disease-causing organisms, and lead to limb, root, or trunk failure or death. Injuries are caused by pruning, injections or implants, and by vehicles or equipment striking bark or compacting soil over roots. Deer, gophers, rabbits, mice, and other animals damage plants by gnawing bark and wood. Drought, frost, hail, ice, snow, and lightning also can cause injuries.

Prevent injuries by fencing off landscape plants beyond their drip line during construction. Make pruning cuts properly, just outside the branch collar (Figure 3-8). Keep weed trimmers and lawn mowers away from trunks. Choose plants that are well adapted to local environmental conditions so they are less likely to be injured by sunlight, temperature, or moisture extremes. Provide proper cultural care so plants are less likely to be injured and better able to tolerate damage.

Wounds, such as these made to implant insecticide in a tulip tree trunk, provide entry sites for bacterial wetwood and other disease-causing organisms.

Protect trees from likely injury by installing barriers to keep vehicle bumpers away from trunks.

PROTECT TREES DURING CONSTRUCTION

Forests, oak woodlands, and urban lots are often developed because mature trees make these sites desirable to people. However, in constructing homes and roads, and in installing amenities, trees are often killed outright or their lives are greatly shortened. Stress imposed by construction can increase tree susceptibility to many pests. Negligent or thoughtless construction activities wound trunks, limbs, and roots. Changes in soil grade or drainage adversely alter the root environment and deprive roots of water or oxygen, promote decay and root and crown diseases, and make trees susceptible to attack by bark beetles and other wood-boring insects. Adverse effects may not become apparent until several years after the injury or stress. Protect trees during construction or they may decline, become hazardous, or die.

Check county or city ordinances before working around mature trees. Fence off individual trees or groups of trees around the drip line or beyond to prevent equipment and activities from damaging roots or trunks. Most roots are near the soil surface and many extend much farther than the tree crown spread (Figure 3-2). Minimize changes in soil grade and drainage; compaction and changes in soil contour alter surface and subsurface water flow on which established vegetation may depend.

Do not place fill around trunks. If the grade must be elevated, construct a stone or concrete well around each trunk. Before placing the fill, install a drainage system on top of the existing soil to provide oxygen and appropriate water to established roots once the original soil level is covered. If grade must be lowered, construct walls to retain as much of the original grade, soil, and roots as possible, at least within the drip line of established plants. If soil is undisturbed on one side, removing soil on the other side halfway between the trunk and drip line may allow the tree to survive if adequate cultural care is provided. If grade must be lowered near trunks, consider removing these plants as they are likely to become diseased, hazardous, and die.

Be realistic in assessing which trees are worth saving and are likely to survive construction. Remove trees that are likely to die rather than leaving them to become a hazardous and expensive problem after sites are occupied; trees can be left to protect

At construction sites, fence off trees around the drip line or beyond to prevent equipment and activities from damaging roots or trunks.

Minimize trenching near trees; digging damages roots.

other trees during construction, then removed soon afterward. Remove declining or severely injured trees. Consider removing trees if the root zone, soil grade, or drainage will be seriously disturbed or if species with incompatible cultural needs will be planted nearby.

Remove and dispose of all recently dead wood and dying trees. Bark beetles may emerge from recently dead wood and attack nearby healthy trees. Seal fresh firewood beneath clear plastic tarps in a sunny location for at least six months through the warm season; after this time, the wood is no longer suitable for bark beetles. Remove bark from cut wood to hasten its drying and reduce the likelihood of beetles emerging and reinfesting nearby trees. Apply borax (sodium tetraborate decahydrate) to freshly cut pine stumps in areas where pines grow naturally. This helps prevent infection by airborne spores of annosus root disease that can spread from stumps through roots to nearby living trees.

Trench for utilities away from roots, combine utilities in a single trench, and consider tunneling beneath roots to minimize cutting of roots. Locate septic systems away from trees; chemicals used in these systems may leach and damage roots or roots may infiltrate the systems and cause damage.

Use partially permeable materials near trunks (like bricks instead of concrete) if extensive areas must be paved. Use caution when applying wood preservatives; they may kill nearby vegetation through direct contact or by leaching. Use good judgment by planting around an existing landscape with species with compatible water requirements. Irrigation of turf and other new landscape plants can kill nearby established plants that are adapted to summer drought. Consult Table 7-2 and *Compatible Plants*

Under and Around Oaks before planting and see *Protecting Trees When Building on Forested Land* (UC Leaflet 21348) for more information. Be aware of fire hazards from natural or planted vegetation around buildings.

MINIMIZE FIRE HAZARDS

Fire is a serious hazard throughout much of California, where hot, dry weather prevails. All plants will burn if conditions are suitable, but appropriate plant selection and maintenance dramatically reduce the likelihood that vegetation fires will burn structures. Structure type, building materials, topography, and other factors are also important, but only landscape plants are discussed here.

Large plants provide more fuel than small plants and present a greater fire hazard the closer they are to structures. Nearby trees may provide a barrier that can prevent airborne, burning debris from reaching buildings. However, prevent large plants from contacting structures or overhanging roofs. Laws in some

areas require a vegetation-free area around structures; consult local fire officials.

Provide plants with proper cultural care, especially appropriate irrigation, to improve plant resistance to fire. Even drought-adapted species may benefit from watering every 1 or 2 months during the dry season and the increased moisture may decrease their flammability. Prune lower limbs to provide a fuel break between the ground and tree canopies. Prune out dead branches and remove dead or dying plants. Thin crowns by pruning limbs that form bridges between tall plants. Avoid grouping together a progression of shorter to taller plants near structures; these provide a fuel "ladder" allowing fire to spread readily from one canopy level to the next. Minimize the buildup of litter.

Unwatered landscapes generally increase the risk of fire, except for succulent ground covers (such as ice plant) and groves of cleanly maintained trees. Yuccas, cacti, and similar succulents retain water during dry

A 1991 fire in Oakland and Berkeley, California, killed 25 people and destroyed over 3,000 houses. Appropriate plant selection and maintenance dramatically reduce the likelihood that vegetation fires will burn structures.

TABLE 3-6

Shrubs and Trees that Are Drought-Adapted and More Fire Resistant.[a]

COMMON NAME	SCIENTIFIC NAME
SHRUBS	
Manzanita	*Arctostaphylos* spp.
Caucasian artemisia, silver	*Artemisia caucasica*
Carmel creeper	*Ceanothus griseus* var. *horizontalis*
Rock rose[b]	*Cistus crispus, C. salviifolius*
Hopseed bush	*Dodonaea viscosa*
Toyon	*Heteromeles arbutifolia*
Oleander[b]	*Nerium oleander*
Carolina cherry laurel	*Prunus caroliniana*
Italian buckthorn	*Rhamnus alaternus*
Lemonade berry	*Rhus integrifolia, R. ovata*
TREES	
Carob	*Ceratonia siliqua*
Coast live oak	*Quercus agrifolia*
California pepper tree	*Schinus molle*
Brazilian pepper tree	*Schinus terebinthifolius*
California bay laurel	*Umbellularia californica*

a. All plants will burn if conditions are suitable, but these species resist fire if properly maintained (see text).

b. Keep these plants pruned low.

Any one of these signs—mushrooms around the trunk, brackets on bark, or damaged bark—can indicate a hazardous tree.

periods and are more fire resistant. Other drought-adapted plants can be more fire-resistant if properly maintained (Table 3-6). Consult *Landscape for Fire Protection* (UC Leaflet 2401) for more information.

RECOGNIZE HAZARDOUS TREES

Damaged or unhealthy trees that may fall over or drop limbs are hazardous. In more natural settings, dead or declining trees provide benefits such as wildlife habitat and recycled nutrients. In urban or recreational areas, hazardous trees can injure people or damage property.

Prevent injuries to roots and aboveground parts. Examine trees regularly to see that they are receiving proper cultural care and are not hazardous. Look for dead or dying limbs, wounds, cankers, and mushrooms or other decay fruiting bodies around the tree base or on bark. Some hazards are difficult to detect, such as internal decay or unhealthy roots. Have a certified arborist or other competent professional inspect regularly for potential hazards if trees are located where their failure could cause injury or damage property. Correct any hazardous conditions; replace the plant where necessary. See *Evaluation of Hazard Trees in Urban Areas* listed in References.

CHAPTER FOUR

Insects, Mites, and Snails and Slugs

INSECTS, MITES, and other invertebrates commonly live on and around landscape trees and shrubs. Some are pests because they annoy us or injure ornamentals, but most are innocuous or beneficial and should not be destroyed. Many invertebrates are necessary food for birds and other wildlife that live in urban areas. Some invertebrates are valuable parasites or predators that destroy pests. Others are scavengers that break down organic matter so that nutrients are available for plant growth. Insects, including honey bees, are essential for pollinating plants so that seeds and fruit are produced. Many invertebrates are neither damaging nor clearly beneficial, but removing them disrupts the natural relationships among organisms and may lead to problems.

This chapter discusses common species that sometimes become pests. Some level of invertebrate pests can usually be tolerated without harm to landscape plants. When control is appropriate, selective methods are often available and preferable.

Actions you take to control pests may also damage the beneficial species on which people and other organisms depend.

Damage

Invertebrate pests are a very diverse group. Most of them damage plants through their feeding, but few other generalizations can be made. The damage is determined by many factors, including plant age, plant part affected, species, location, the size and stage of the pest, and the extent of any other stresses on the plant.

The type of damage depends on the pest's mouthparts. Invertebrates generally have chewing or sucking mouthparts. Beetles, caterpillars, and other insects with chewing mouthparts cause identifiable holes in leaves, twigs, stems, or fruit. They sometimes cut parts completely from plants. Snails and slugs also chew and clip succulent plant parts and occasionally chew young bark and fruit.

Bark beetles, flatheaded and round-headed borers, clearwing moth larvae, and some other insects with chewing mouthparts feed inside trunks and limbs. Weevil larvae and some other insects chew on roots. These insects that feed inside plant tissue or chew on roots can cause discolored or wilted leaves and other symptoms of plant decline that may be confused with diseases or cultural problems.

Pests with tubular sucking mouthparts feed on plant fluids and never cut away pieces of tissue. These insects and mites cause buds, leaves, or fruit to discolor, distort, or drop. Sucking pests include aphids, scales, true bugs, leafhoppers, thrips, and mites.

Life Cycles

Most invertebrates begin life as an egg, which hatches into an immature form called a nymph or a larva. Aphids can lay eggs or give birth to live, active young (Figure 4-1). Immature insects and mites grow by periodically forming a new outer skin or exoskeleton (molting) and shedding their old skin. In addition to the change in size, many insects modify their shape with each successive molt, a process known as metamorphosis.

Insects, the most common invertebrate pests, can be divided into two major groups depending on their type of metamorphosis. Some species undergo major changes in form between the immature stages and adult. This transformation occurs within the nonfeeding pupal stage, and these insects are said to have

Insects with chewing mouthparts, like this California oakworm, make distinct holes in leaves, fruit, or stems.

Sucking pests, like this adult southern green stink bug, *Nezara viridula*, insert their tubular mouthparts into plants, causing plant parts to discolor, distort, or drop.

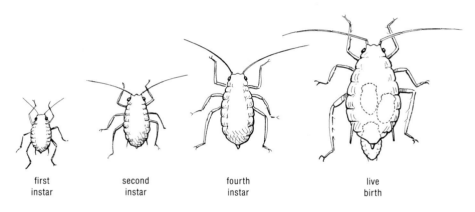

first instar   second instar   fourth instar   live birth

Figure 4-1. Development of aphids—gradual or incomplete metamorphosis. Many species of aphids give birth to live aphid nymphs rather than laying eggs.

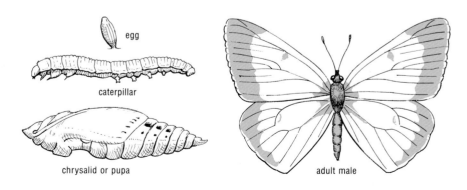

egg

caterpillar

chrysalid or pupa

adult male

Figure 4-2. Stages of development of a typical moth or butterfly showing complete metamorphosis. Most moths and butterflies go through 4 or 5 molts during the caterpillar stage.

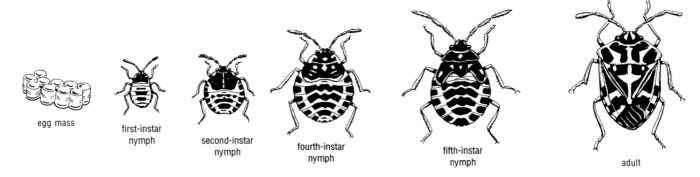

egg mass   first-instar nymph   second-instar nymph   fourth-instar nymph   fifth-instar nymph   adult

Figure 4-3. Development of a stink bug species, the harlequin bug, showing incomplete metamorphosis with wing development.

complete metamorphosis (Figure 4-2). Species that undergo complete metamorphosis, such as beetles and butterflies, commonly have different feeding habits during their immature and adult stages. Their immatures are called larvae and in many cases, such as among butterflies, moths, and flies, only the larval stage causes damage; the adults take in only nectar and water. Many beetle species chew plant parts as both larvae and adults. One stage typically is more damaging than the other, in part because the immatures and adults often feed on different parts of the plant.

Insects in the other major group, such as aphids and true bugs, go through gradual or incomplete metamorphosis. They have no pupal stage. Their immatures are called nymphs and differ from adults primarily in their smaller size, lack of wings, and often different color (Figure 4-3).

The development of mites is similar to the gradual metamorphosis of insects; however, the stage that hatches out of the egg usually has six legs and is normally called a larva. Later stage immatures (nymphs) and adults usually have eight legs, but otherwise look similar to mite larvae (Figure 4-4).

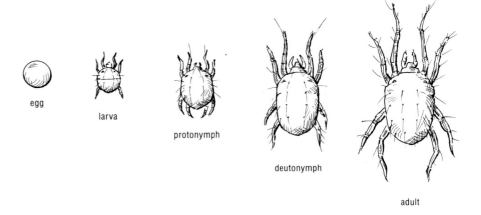

egg   larva   protonymph   deutonymph   adult

Figure 4-4. Development of a typical plant-feeding spider mite. The stage that hatches out of the egg is called a larva. Remaining immatures are nymphs.

Monitoring and Diagnosing Problems

Regularly inspect valued plants to determine what invertebrate species are present and to get a general idea of their relative abundance. Insect and mite populations can increase rapidly; regular monitoring or sampling allows you to recognize developing problems and take action at the proper time. Once pest populations are high and damage becomes extensive, your management options become more limited because you did not act early; pesticide applications or replacing the plant may be the only options.

Proper identification of pest and natural enemy species is essential for successful pest management. One approach to pest identification is to identify the host plant, then use the Tree and Shrub Pest Tables at the end of this book to help diagnose the problem. Alternatively, if you know what kind of pest you have (say, caterpillars or scale insects), you can go to that section of the book and use the photographs and descriptions to help identify common species. Because of the broad scope of this book and because new species are frequently introduced from other places, not all possible landscape pests are included in this book. Take pests or

Monitor certain species like adult acacia psyllids by branch beating or dislodging them onto a collecting surface.

to implement controls, and to evaluate the effectiveness of management actions.

Keep good written records. Record the number of plant parts (samples) that you inspect. Write down the date, specific location, host plant and pests sampled, and the results or counts from your samples. Record what management action you took and when you took it. Use a 10-power hand lens to help identify small insects and mites.

An alternative to counting each individual insect in samples is to determine the percent of samples with pests or damage. This presence-absence sampling is quicker, but less precise than counting each individual. Inspect each sample and record whether it is damaged or infested with one or more pests. Calculate and record the percent of infested or damaged samples:

$$\frac{\text{Number of samples infested or damaged}}{\text{Total samples inspected}} \times 100 = \text{Percent of samples infested or damaged}$$

Specialized techniques and equipment are often useful for monitoring. Sticky traps, branch beating, and degree-day (temperature) monitoring are discussed here; other methods are detailed in the sections on individual pests.

Sticky Traps. Adult whiteflies, thrips, and some other pests and beneficial parasitoids can be monitored with sticky traps (Table 4-1). Hang several bright yellow cards (each 3 by 5 inches or larger) covered with clear sticky material near plants to detect the adults and get a rough estimate of changes in their numbers. To catch the most insects when monitoring around small plants, hang the traps so that the bottom of the trap is even

damaged plant parts you can't identify to a local Cooperative Extension or Agriculture Department office.

After identifying the invertebrates on your plants, learn about their biology and potential damage. You may find that some species, while present near the damage or symptoms, are actually innocuous or beneficial. Even those species that cause damage can usually be tolerated at moderate levels without apparent harm to the plants.

Monitor for pests or damage by regularly inspecting a number of leaves, shoots, branches, or terminals or by using other techniques (Table 4-1) instead of or in addition to

inspecting plant parts. Select an appropriate monitoring method based on knowledge about pest biology, the goals of your monitoring, and available resources. Keep a written description of your sampling and inspection methods and follow those directions every time you monitor. In addition to detecting the presence of pests or damage, another purpose of sampling is to determine whether pest populations or damage are increasing or decreasing; so you must sample the same way every time to make the results comparable. Compare the results of samples taken on several different dates to help decide if action is needed, when and where

TABLE 4-1

Insect and Mite Monitoring Methods.

METHOD	INVERTEBRATE SPECIES
Visual inspection of plant parts	Most exposed-feeding species, including evidence of parasitism and predation. Monitoring tiny pests requires a hand lens
Branch beating	Most exposed, readily dislodged species, especially the adults, including leaf beetles, mites, thrips, psyllids, true bugs, leafhoppers, weevils, non-webbing caterpillars, lady beetles, green and brown lacewings
Sticky traps	Adult whiteflies, thrips, leafhoppers, psyllids, fungus gnats, *Liriomyza* spp. leafminers, winged aphids, parasitoids
Double-sided sticky tape	Scale crawlers
Burlap trunk bands	Adult weevils, gypsy moth larvae
Trap boards	Snails, adult weevils, predaceous beetles
Pheromone traps	Adults of certain moths and scales, including clearwing moths, fruittree leafroller, omnivorous looper, Nantucket pine tip moth, gypsy moth, San Jose scale, California red scale
Pitfall traps	Adult weevils, predaceous ground beetles
Timed counts	Pest individuals that are relatively large and obvious, such as caterpillars, and occur at relatively low density so they are not observed faster than they can be counted
Honeydew monitoring	Aphids
Frass dropping	Non-webbing caterpillars
Degree-day monitoring	Species for which researchers have determined development thresholds and rates, including elm leaf beetle, Nantucket pine tip moth, California red scale, San Jose scale

with the top of the plant canopy. Orient the longest part of the trap vertically (up and down).

If you are counting large numbers of trapped insects, research shows that for some pests, including greenhouse whitefly, western flower thrips, certain aphids, and the *Liriomyza trifolii* leafminer, it is not necessary to examine the entire trap; counting the insects in a vertical, one-inch-wide stripe on both sides of the card gives results that are representative of the entire trap. For example, when using 3 by 5 inch cards, count only the insects in a 1 by 5 inch vertical column on both sides of each card, then multiply your results by 3 to get a good estimate of the overall number of insects in each trap. When using traps to detect pest presence or when monitoring less abundant species, it is best to examine the entire trap.

Inspect trap cards about weekly whenever adults may be present. Replace disposable traps (available from most garden supply centers) or clean other types of traps when they become fouled. Yellow wood, metal, or plastic traps can be periodically cleaned and the sticky material reapplied. An organic solvent must be used to remove commercial Tanglefoot or Stickem. However, traps can be wrapped with a clear plastic wrapping, sealed with transparent tape, then covered with sticky material. The wrapping can then be replaced when it becomes dirty and the trap can be reused. Alternatively, an adhesive of one part petroleum jelly or mineral oil and one part household detergent can be used and washed off with soap and water. While easy to clean, this mixture is less sticky and does not last as long as commercial sticky materials, especially during warm weather.

Carefully identify insects in traps before taking action, since many of them may be harmless or beneficial. Even large numbers of pest species in traps do not necessarily indicate that control action is needed. There are no specific guidelines for when treatment is warranted in landscapes based on the number of insects caught in traps.

Branch Beating. Branch beating is used for monitoring invertebrates that are readily dislodged from foliage as listed in Table 4-1. Sample by holding a special beating tray, sheet, or a clipboard with a white sheet of paper beneath the branch as a collecting surface. Shake the branch or hit it two or three times with a stick. Use the same size collecting surface and the same number of beats or shakes per branch each time you sample so that results are comparable between locations or over time. Monitor about the same time of day on each date, preferably in the morning when temperatures are cool and invertebrates are less active.

Beat two to four branches from different parts of each of several plants on each sample date. Count and record separately the number of individuals of each pest species and beneficial species that are dislodged in

TABLE 4-2

Approximating Degree-Days (DD) Manually.[a]

Add the daily minimum and maximum temperature and divide by 2 to get the average daily temperature.	$\dfrac{74°F + 54°F}{2} = 64°F$
Subtract the lower threshold temperature (for example 52°F for elm leaf beetle) from the average daily temperature. The result is the approximate number of degree-days accumulated that day.	$64°F - 52°F = 12\ DD$
Add up the degree-days accumulated for each day until you reach the sum when specific actions are recommended.	

a. This "manual" method of DD estimation becomes significantly inaccurate when temperatures are near the threshold; computerized sine wave estimations are more accurate and recommended.

each sample. Total the insects counted and divide this sum by the number of branches beaten to determine the average insect density. If insect densities are relatively high, consider dividing your collecting surface into equal-sized subunits. Count only the insects on one or several representative subunits. Estimate the number of insects on the entire collecting surface by dividing your count by the number of subunits examined and then multiplying by the total number of subunits on the collecting surface.

Degree-Day Monitoring. The growth rate of plants and invertebrates is closely related to temperature; generally, the higher the temperature, the more rapid the development. Because of variation in weather, calendar dates are not a good guide for carrying out management actions. Measuring the amount of heat accumulated over time provides a physiological time scale that is biologically more useful than calendar days. The unit used to measure physiological time is the "degree-day." One degree-day is defined as one degree above the threshold temperature maintained for a full day.

The lower threshold temperature is the temperature below which no development or activity occurs. Pests do not feed, grow, or reproduce unless temperatures are above this threshold. Development also slows and eventually stops if temperatures are too warm, so an upper threshold is sometimes used in calculating degree-days. Each plant and invertebrate species has a specific lower and upper development threshold. The lower development threshold and the number of degree-days required to complete each life stage must be known in order to use degree-days for pest management. Researchers have determined the threshold temperature and developmental times for some important pests.

Degree-days for each day are estimated by subtracting the threshold temperature from the average daily temperature for that date as in Table 4-2. Computerized "sine wave" calculation methods are also available and recommended because they provide more accurate estimates. Degree-day monitoring does not tell you whether control action is warranted; you must still monitor plants to decide whether thresholds are exceeded. Degree-day

monitoring tells you when pests will reach susceptible life stages. If pests are abundant, monitoring degree-days helps eliminate the guesswork otherwise required to determine when to time a control action.

For example, elm leaf beetles do not develop below 52°F. First- and second-instar larvae of first-generation elm leaf beetle are most abundant in California at about 700 degree-days above 52°F accumulated from 1 March. If populations are high and damage is anticipated, a foliar insecticide applied at about 700 degree-days will catch susceptible larvae at their greatest abundance.

Current temperatures for calculating degree-days and timing control actions in your area can be obtained from the University of California Statewide IPM Project computer system (IMPACT), or you can use temperatures you record or obtain from the local newspaper. IMPACT provides an easy-to-use menu selection program for calculating degree-days using virtually any microcomputer equipped with a telephone modem. Free computer access accounts and instructions for using IMPACT can be obtained from the IPM Implementation Group at UC Davis, which also distributes degree-day software for use on microcomputers without connecting to the University's computer system. Electronic temperature recorders are also available that can directly calculate degree-days.

Management

Integrated pest management (IPM) is a strategy for preventing and minimizing pest damage. IPM employs various techniques or controls, including biological, cultural, and chemical controls. As detailed in the previous chapters, effective pest management begins when you select plants that are well adapted to that location and properly plant and care for them. By providing proper cultural care, such as appropriate watering, pruning, and fertilizing, you keep landscape plants vigorous so they are less likely to be attacked by certain pests and are better able to tolerate any damage. An overview of biological and selective chemical controls is provided below. Consult the individual pest sections for more detailed information.

BIOLOGICAL CONTROL

Biological control—the use of predators, parasites, and pathogens to control pests and reduce damage—is very important in the management of invertebrate pests. Classical biological control, conservation, and augmentation are three tactics for using natural enemies. Classical biological control is the importation, release, and establishment of natural enemies of pests. Conservation is the use of management practices that preserve beneficial organisms that are already present. Augmentation is the manipulation of pests or natural enemies to make biological control more effective.

Classical Biological Control. Classical biological control is used primarily against pests that have been introduced from elsewhere. Many organisms that are not pests in their native habitat become unusually abundant when they arrive in a new area without their natural controls. Researchers go to the pest's native habitat and collect and study the natural enemies that kill the pest. Natural enemies found to be beneficial are introduced into the new environment. If they become established, these introduced natural enemies may reduce their host to a low

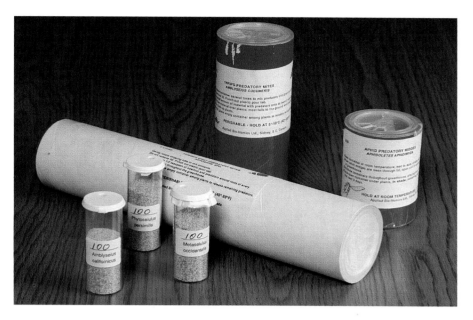

Many natural enemies are available for purchase and release, but there has been relatively little research on their use in landscapes.

enough level so that it is no longer a pest. Many insects that were formerly widespread pests in California landscapes are now partially or completely controlled by introduced natural enemies (see Table 4-3), except where these natural enemies are disrupted, such as by pesticide applications or honeydew-seeking ants. Introduction of exotic natural enemies from foreign countries by law must be done only by qualified scientists, but it is important for landscape managers to be aware of these natural enemies and to conserve them.

Conservation. Preserve resident natural enemies whenever you can by choosing cultural, mechanical, or selective chemical controls that do not interfere with or kill natural enemies. Avoid applying broad-spectrum or persistent pesticides (Table 4-6) or apply them in a selective manner. Natural enemies are often more susceptible to pesticides than are pests. In addition to immediately killing natural enemies that are present at the time of spraying (contact toxicity), many pesticides leave residues on foliage that kill predators or parasites that migrate in after spraying (residual toxicity). Even if beneficial organisms survive an application, low levels of pesticide residues can interfere with natural enemies' abilities to reproduce and to locate and kill pests.

Some ants are important predators of pests, but the common Argentine ant and certain other species in landscapes are pests because they attack predators and parasites of honeydew-producing Homoptera insects and disrupt biological control. Control ants that feed on honeydew produced by sucking insects such as aphids, soft scales, whiteflies, and mealybugs. Reduce dust, for example, by planting ground covers. Dust can interfere with natural enemies and cause outbreaks of pests such as spider mites.

Plant a variety of species including flowering plants to improve certain biological controls (Table 4-4). Flow-

TABLE 4-3

Woody Landscape Pests Reported as Substantially Controlled by Natural Enemies Introduced for Classical Biological Control in California.

PEST COMMON NAME	PEST SCIENTIFIC NAME	INTRODUCED NATURAL ENEMIES	SEE PAGE NO.
Acacia psyllid	*Acizzia uncatoides*	*Diomus pumilio* lady beetle *Anthocoris nemoralis* minute pirate bug	105
Ash whitefly	*Siphoninus phillyreae*	*Encarsia partenopea* parasitic wasp *Clitostethus arcuatus* lady beetle	110
Black scale	*Saissetia oleae*	*Metaphycus helvolus, Metaphycus* spp. parasitic wasps	126
Brown soft scale	*Coccus hesperidum*	*Metaphycus luteolus* parasitic wasp	126
California red scale	*Aonidiella aurantii*	*Aphytis melinus, Aphytis lingnanensis, Comperiella bifasciata, Encarsia perniciosi* parasitic wasps	121
Citrophilus mealybug	*Pseudococcus calceolariae*	*Coccophagus gurneyi, Arhopoideus pretiosus* parasitic wasps	
Citrus whitefly	*Dialeurodes citri*	*Encarsia* spp. parasitic wasps	111
Comstock mealybug	*Pseudococcus comstocki*	*Allotropa convexifrons, Allotropa burrelli, Pseudaphycus malinus* parasitic wasps	
Cottony cushion scale	*Icerya purchasi*	*Rodolia cardinalis* lady beetle *Cryptochaetum iceryae* parasitic fly	130
Elm aphid	*Tinocallis platani*	*Trioxys tenuicaudus* parasitic wasp	
Linden aphid	*Eucallipterus tiliae*	*Trioxys curvicaudus* parasitic wasp	
Longtailed mealybug	*Pseudococcus longispinus*	*Anarhopus sydneyensis, Arhopoideus peregrinus* parasitic wasps	116
Nantucket pine tip moth	*Rhyacionia frustrana*	*Campoplex frustranae* parasitic wasp	150
Nigra scale	*Parasaissetia nigra*	*Metaphycus helvolus* parasitic wasp	
Olive scale	*Parlatoria oleae*	*Aphytis maculicornis, Coccophagoides utilis* parasitic wasps	122
Purple scale	*Lepidosaphes beckii*	*Aphytis lepidosaphes* parasitic wasp	
San Jose scale	*Quadraspidiotus perniciosus*	*Prospaltella perniciosi* parasitic wasp	124
Walnut aphid	*Chromaphis juglandicola*	*Trioxys pallidus* parasitic wasp	122
Woolly whitefly	*Aleurothrixus floccosus*	*Amitus spiniferus, Cales noacki* parasitic wasps	114

ers provide nectar and pollen for parasitic wasps and adult insects with predaceous larvae, such as syrphid flies and green lacewings. A diverse landscape generally harbors low populations of different plant-feeding arthropods, which may serve as alternate hosts for the more general natural enemies. Obtain a colorful *Natural Enemies Are Your Allies* poster (UC Publication 21496) and display it so you and others that see it can become familiar with common beneficial species.

Augmentation. When resident natural enemies are insufficient, their populations can be increased (augmented) in certain situations through the purchase and release of commercially available beneficial species. Natural enemy releases are most likely to be effective in situations similar to those where researchers or pest managers have previously demonstrated success. This includes situations where certain levels of pests and damage can be tolerated. Augmentation may be more effective for perennial plants of relatively high value. Avoid using pesticides that may harm beneficials in systems where natural enemies are released. Desperate situations where pests or damage are already abundant are not a good opportunity for augmentation.

Inoculation and inundation are two tactics for augmenting natural enemies. In inoculative releases, pest populations are low and relatively few natural enemies are released. The progeny of these predators or parasites, not the same individuals released, are expected to eventually provide biological control. Releasing the mealybug destroyer lady beetle, *Cryptolaemus montrouzieri,* in the spring to control mealybugs is an example of inoculative release. The mealybug destroyer is effective in killing mealybug species that feed openly on foliage or bark, but it overwinters poorly in California and often needs to be reintroduced to target areas in the spring.

Inundative releases involve large numbers of natural enemies, often released several times over a growing season. The natural enemies released, and possibly their progeny, are expected to provide biological control. Periodically releasing *Trichogramma* species (parasitic wasps) to kill caterpillar eggs is an example of inundative biological control.

Releasing Natural Enemies Effectively. There has been relatively little research on how to effectively release commercially available natural enemies in landscapes. Most research and use is in agricultural crops or greenhouses, and much of the information in this book has been extrapolated from those situations.

Take steps to increase the likelihood that any natural enemy releases will be effective. Accurately identify the pest and its life stages. Learn about the biology of the pest and its natural enemies. Release the appropriate natural enemy species when the pest is in its vulnerable life stage; most parasitic insects attack only certain stages of their host. Many parasites lay their eggs in one host life stage, but the parasite doesn't kill its host and emerge until the host has developed to another stage. For example, the holes in mature female scales are often caused by parasites that attacked and laid their eggs in the host when it was immature. The

pest life stage that can be effectively controlled with natural enemies may also be different from the pest stage that damages plants. For example, *Trichogramma* species only kill moth and butterfly eggs; they are not effective against caterpillars. *Trichogramma* must be released when moths or butterflies are laying eggs, before plant-damaging caterpillars become abundant.

Anticipate pest problems and plan releases ahead of time; begin making releases before pests are too abundant or intolerable damage is imminent. Avoid applying broad-spectrum or persistent pesticides, or use them as spot sprays. Be prepared to tolerate some pests and possible damage since pests must be present to provide food for natural enemies. Remember that natural enemies are living organisms that require water, food, and shelter. Natural enemies may be adversely affected by extreme conditions such as hot temperatures. Keep them in a cool place and release them early or late in the day if temperatures are hot.

Effectively releasing natural enemies requires knowledge, practice, and imagination. Releases often fail because information or experience was inadequate, the wrong species was released, timing was incorrect, or pesticides were applied. Obtain

beneficials from a quality supplier; the quality of commercially available natural enemies is not regulated and sometimes may be poor. Some of the natural enemy species that are sold evidently are available because they are the easiest and most economical to produce and sell, not because they are the most effective species. Available natural enemies may not always be able to keep pest populations below acceptable damage thresholds. In some cases, the value of the plants and availability of alternatives may not justify the cost and effort of releasing natural enemies. Common pests for which natural enemies can be purchased and released are listed in Table 4-5, which also includes beneficial nematodes and bacteria that are discussed in sections on biological pesticides. Specific strategies for augmentative releases are discussed in the sections on that particular pest.

The convergent lady beetle, *Hippodamia convergens,* is probably the most widely sold natural enemy. Natural populations of these lady beetles, sometimes incorrectly called "ladybugs," are important aphid predators. *Hippodamia* that are sold have been collected from overwintering aggregations and they have a tendency to fly. Releasing a significant number of bee-

TABLE 4-4

Sequentially Flowering California Native Plants That Can Provide Nectar and Pollen for Beneficial Insects Throughout Much of the Year.

COMMON NAME	SCIENTIFIC NAME	FLOWERING PERIOD
Sumacs	*Rhus* spp.	late winter to early summer
Wild lilacs	*Ceanothus* spp.	late winter to spring
Coffeeberry	*Rhamnus* spp.	spring
Toyon	*Heteromeles arbutifolia*	late spring
Wild buckwheat	*Eriogonum* spp.	summer to fall
Coyote brush	*Baccharis pilularis*	late summer to fall

TABLE 4-5

Some Woody Landscape Invertebrate Pests With Commercially Available Natural Enemies.[a]

PEST	NATURAL ENEMIES COMMON NAME	SCIENTIFIC NAME	SEE PAGE NO.
Aphids	lacewings lady beetle	*Chrysopa* and *Chrysoperla* spp. *Hippodamia convergens*	57, 100 60, 99
Carpenterworm	parasitic nematodes	*Steinernema carpocapsae*	168
Caterpillars	egg parasites microbial insecticide	*Trichogramma* spp. *Bacillus thuringiensis* variety *kurstaki*	66 61, 68
Clearwing moth larvae	parasitic nematodes	*Steinernema carpocapsae*	162
Elm leaf beetle	microbial insecticide	*Bacillus thuringiensis* var. *tenebrionis* or *san diego*	61, 81
Japanese beetle	microbial insecticide parasitic nematodes	*Bacillus popilliae* *Heterorhabditis bacteriophora,* *Steinernema glaseri*	90
Mealybugs	lacewings mealybug destroyer citrus mealybug parasite	*Chrysopa* and *Chrysoperla* spp. *Cryptolaemus montrouzieri* *Leptomastix dactylopii*	57 116
Spider mites	lacewings predatory mites	*Chrysopa* and *Chrysoperla* spp. *Amblyseius, Metaseiulus,* and *Phytoseiulus* spp.	57, 170 170
Scale insects	red scale parasite black scale parasite predaceous lady beetle	*Aphytis melinus* *Metaphycus helvolus* *Rhyzobius* or *Lindorus lophanthae*	121 126 120
Snail, brown garden	predatory snail	*Rumina decollata*	176
Thrips	predatory mites minute pirate bug greenhouse thrips parasite lacewings	*Amblyseius* and *Euseius* spp. *Orius tristicolor* *Thripobius semiluteus* *Chrysopa* and *Chrysoperla* spp.	57, 174 58, 140 141 57, 139
Weevils	parasitic nematodes	*Steinernema carpocapsae,* *Heterorhabditis bacteriophora*	86
Whiteflies	predaceous lady beetle parasitic wasps	*Delphastus pusillus* *Encarsia* species	109 112

a. See Suppliers for sources of natural enemies.

tles may temporarily reduce aphids on small plants. However, most lady beetles will soon leave the site where they are released, even if food is plentiful.

Releases of preying mantids are not recommended. Preying mantids feed indiscriminately on pest and beneficial species, including other mantids and honey bees. Their release is unlikely to provide effective pest control.

Types of Natural Enemies. Three primary groups of natural enemies are used in biological pest control: pathogens, parasites, and predators.

Many natural enemies, including most parasites, pathogens, and some predators, attack only one or several closely related pest species. For example, syrphid fly larvae and the convergent lady beetle feed primarily on aphids. More specialized natural enemies are discussed in the individual pest sections.

Pathogens. Pathogens are microorganisms including bacteria, fungi, nematodes, and viruses that infect and kill the host. *Bacillus thuringiensis* or Bt is a naturally occurring bacterial disease of insects that is commercially available and is discussed in the sections on biological and microbial pesticides. Bt is the microorganism most widely used for pest control; different varieties are available for controlling foliage-feeding caterpillars, certain leaf beetle larvae, and immature mosquito, black fly, and fungus gnat lar-

TABLE 4-6

Some Insecticides and Miticides Used in Landscapes and Their Toxicity to Natural Enemies.

MATERIAL	NATURAL ENEMIES AFFECTED	TOXICITY TO NATURAL ENEMIES CONTACT[a]	RESIDUAL[b]
Acephate	most predators and parasites	high	high to moderate
Bacillus thuringiensis	most predators and parasites	no or very low	no or very low
Carbaryl	parasites	high	moderate to high
	lady beetles	moderate to high	moderate to high
	predaceous mites	moderate to high	moderate to low
Chlorpyrifos	parasites	high	moderate to low
	lady beetles	low	low
	predaceous mites	moderate	moderate to low
Diazinon	most predators and parasites	moderate to high	moderate
Dicofol	parasites	moderate to low	no to low
	most predaceous insects	no to low	no to low
	predaceous mites	high	moderate to high
Dimethoate	parasites	high	moderate to high
	lady beetles	moderate to low	moderate to low
	predaceous mites	high	moderate to high
Fluvalinate	most predators and parasites	moderate to low	low
Insecticidal soap	most predators and parasites	moderate to high	no or very low
Malathion	most predators and parasites	high to moderate	moderate
Oil, narrow-range	most predators and parasites	moderate to high	no or low
Permethrin	most predators and parasites	high to moderate	moderate to high
Pyrethrum	most predators and parasites	moderate to high	no to low
Rotenone	parasites	moderate to high	low to moderate
	predaceous insects	low to high	low to moderate
Ryania	most predators and parasites	no to low	no to moderate[c]
Sabadilla	most predators and parasites	no to low	no or very low
Sulfur	parasites	low to high	low to high[c]
	predaceous insects	no to low	no to low
	predaceous mites	moderate to high	moderate

a. Contact toxicity is the immediate killing of natural enemies at the time of spraying.

b. Residual toxicity results from persistant residues that affect natural enemies migrating in after an application.

c. Effect of persistent residue may be similar to dusts: acts as an irritant and/or interferes with natural enemy searching ability.

vae. As with most bacteria, Bt must be eaten by the insect before it can infect and kill its host. Some fungi can infect their host on contact, though most require humid conditions to be effective.

Parasites. Insect parasites (more precisely called parasitoids) are smaller than their host and develop inside, or attached to the outside, of the host's body. Often only the immature stage of the parasite feeds on the host, and it kills only one host individual during its development (see Figure 4-5).

Most parasitic insects are either flies (Diptera) or wasps (Hymenoptera). The most common parasitic flies are in the family Tachinidae. Adult tachinids often resemble house flies and their larvae are maggots that feed inside the host they parasitize.

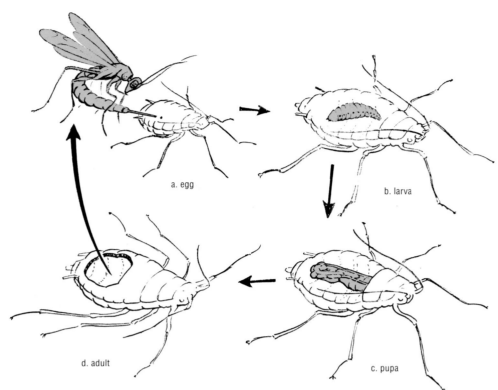

a. egg

b. larva

d. adult

c. pupa

Figure 4-5. Life cycle of a typical parasite or parasitoid, illustrated with a species that attacks aphids: (a) an adult parasite lays an egg inside a live aphid, (b) the egg hatches into a parasite larva that grows as it feeds on the aphid's insides, (c) after killing the aphid the parasite pupates into an adult wasp, (d) the wasp chews a hole and emerges from the dead aphid, then (a) flies off to find and parasitize other aphids.

some food is always available for predators. Avoid using pesticides, and treat only heavily infested spots instead of entire plants. Encourage general predators so that if pest outbreaks do develop, the predators will already be present to help provide control. Because they depend on specific prey, more specialized predators (and many parasites and pathogens) may not provide much control until pest populations become abundant. Once outbreaks develop, these more specialized natural enemies may rapidly increase in abundance and are more often responsible for reducing high pest populations than are more general predators.

Birds and Other Vertebrates

Insects are important food for many birds, mammals, reptiles, and amphibians. Some birds feed almost exclusively on insects, and many species that normally feed on seeds rely on insects to feed their nestlings. Caterpillars are apparently the pests most commonly fed upon by many birds. Populations of desirable birds can be increased by growing a mixture of trees, shrubs, and ground covers of different size, species, and density and by providing water and supplemental food. Many species of insect-eating birds nest in cavities in dead trees. Dead and dying trees can rarely be left in the landscape because they are hazardous and may fall; a practical alternative is to provide nesting boxes or bird houses. The value of dead and dying trees as wildlife habitat should be assessed along with hazard when considering tree removal.

Parasitic Hymenoptera occur in over three dozen families. Aphelinidae is one of the most important, with about 1,000 known species of tiny wasps that attack aphids, caterpillars, mealybugs, psyllids, scales, true bugs, and whiteflies. The Encyrtidae family includes over 1,500 species that attack primarily scales and mealybugs, but also beetles, bugs, flies, and moths. Braconidae and Ichneumonidae are often large wasps, with about 5,000 species in North America that commonly parasitize beetle, caterpillar, and sawfly larvae and pupae. Most Aphidiidae attack aphids and most Trichogrammatidae parasitize insect eggs. Wasps in the family Eulophidae attack beetles, caterpillars, flies, scales, and thrips.

Predators. Predators feed on more than one individual host during their lifetime and are commonly about the same size or larger than the animals they eat. Many predators feed on a variety of insects and mites. These "general predators" feed opportunistically on any currently abundant prey and can be important in suppressing pests. Some also feed on pollen, nectar, and honeydew in addition to prey species. Encourage general predators by maintaining landscapes with diverse plant species. Tolerate low populations of plant-feeding insects and mites so that

Spiders

Spiders are very common invertebrates. Unlike insects, which have six legs and three main body parts, spiders have eight legs, two main body parts, and are classified in the arachnid group along with mites. Most spiders feed entirely on insects, commonly capturing prey in webs or stalking them across the ground or vegetation and pouncing on them. Spiders seek to avoid people, and most are harmless to humans.

An adult funnel weaver spider, *Hololena nedra*, Agelenidae family.

Mites

Although some mites feed on plants and can become pests, many species of mites are predators of pest mites and insects (Table 4-14). Mites often go unnoticed because they are tiny and natural controls frequently keep their populations low. Mites, unlike insects, do not have antennae, segmented bodies, or wings. Most mites pass through an egg stage, a six-legged larval stage, and two eight-legged immature stages before becoming adults (Figure 4-4).

Most predaceous mites are long-legged, pear-shaped, and shiny. Many are translucent, although after feeding they often take on the color of their host, and may be bright red, yellow, or green. Predaceous mite eggs are colorless and oblong, compared with the eggs of plant-feeding mites, which are commonly spherical and colored to opaque. One way to distinguish plant-feeding mites from the predaceous species on your plants is to closely observe them with a good hand lens. Predaceous species appear more active than plant-feeding species; they stop only to feed. See the section on mites for details.

This adult green lacewing, *Chrysoperla* sp., is named for its green body and wings with netlike veins. Adult brown lacewings look similar, but are usually about one half as large and are brownish.

GREEN LACEWING

adult

0   1/2   1 in.
       mm
   10   20

BROWN LACEWING

adult

0   1/2   1 in.
       mm
   10   20

Green and Brown Lacewings

Lacewing larvae are flattened, tapered at the tail, and have distinct legs. Their long, curved mandibles are used for grasping their prey. Lacewing larvae look like tiny alligators and are sometimes called aphidlions because they often feed on aphids. However, they also feed on a wide variety of other small insects, including leafhoppers, mealybugs, whiteflies, caterpillars, psyllids, and insect eggs. Adults have large, lacy-veined wings. Depending on the species, adults may feed on insects or only on honeydew, nectar, and pollen. The green lacewings, *Chrysopa* and *Chrysoperla* spp. (family Chrysopidae), have green slender bodies and green wings with netlike veins. Adult brown lacewings (such as the *Hemerobius* species, family Hemerobiidae) look like green lacewings, except that brown lacewings are typically about half as large and brown. Green lacewings lay their spherical green to gray eggs on slender stalks, either

This alligatorlike green lacewing larva, *Chrysoperla rufilabris*, is grasping a rose aphid with its mandibles.

A green lacewing, *Chrysoperla carnea*, pupating or changing from larva to adult within a loosely-woven silken cocoon.

singly or in groups. Brown lacewings' oblong eggs are laid singly on plants and look like syrphid eggs.

Minute Pirate Bugs

Minute pirate bugs, family Anthocoridae, are small, oval insects. The adults of many species are black or purplish with white markings and have a triangular head. As with most true bugs, adults have a triangle or X-pattern on the back caused by the folding of their half-dark and half-clear wings. The small nymphs are commonly yellowish or reddish brown and may be overlooked in monitoring. *Orius* and *Anthocoris* are two common genera. Adults and nymphs commonly feed on aphids, mites, thrips, psyllids, and insect eggs.

Green lacewings lay their spherical eggs on slender stalks. Depending on the species, eggs are laid singly or, as shown here for *Chrysopa nigricornis*, in groups.

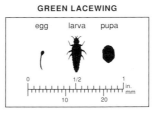

GREEN LACEWING

egg   larva   pupa

0   1/2   1 in.
                           mm
     10   20

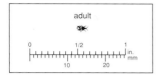

MINUTE PIRATE BUG

adult

0   1/2   1 in.
mm
10   20

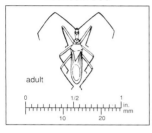

ASSASSIN BUG

adult

0   1/2   1 in.
mm
10   20

An adult flower bug or minute pirate bug, *Anthocoris nemoralis*, feeding on an acacia psyllid nymph.

Assassin Bugs

Assassin bugs, family Reduviidae, are oval or elongate. Most are black and reddish or brown. Assassin bugs have a long narrow head with an extended, needlelike beak and are larger and have longer legs than most other predaceous bugs. They feed on most insect species.

Predaceous Flies

Larvae of many flies in the families Syrphidae, Cecidomyiidae (gall midges), and Chamaemyiidae (aphid flies) prey on soft-bodied insects, such as aphids, mealybugs, and some scales. Larvae are maggotlike and can be green, yellow, brown, orangish, or whitish. Adult syrphids, also known as hover flies or flower flies, look like honey bees but do not sting. They are often seen feeding on flower nectar. Adult aphid flies are small and chunky; gall midges are slender and delicate.

An adult assassin bug adult, *Zelus renardii*, eating a lygus bug.

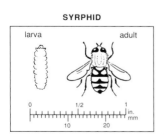

SYRPHID

larva   adult

0   1/2   1 in.
mm
10   20

An adult syrphid, commonly called a flower fly or hover fly, requires pollen to reproduce. It is sometimes mistaken for a honey bee; syrphid flies cannot sting.

Syrphid fly eggs are elongate-oval and are laid singly near aphid colonies.

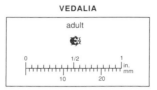

Lady Beetles

Adults and larvae of lady beetles, family Coccinellidae, are predators of pest mites and most soft-bodied or sessile (immobile) insects, including aphids, whiteflies, scales, and mealybugs. About 500 different species occur in the United States. The common convergent lady beetle, *Hippodamia convergens*, feeds primarily on whatever species of aphids are abundant. The vedalia beetle, *Rodolia cardinalis*, feeds on only one pest species, the cottony cushion scale, *Icerya purchasi*. Other species of lady beetles specialize on mites or certain insects and are discussed elsewhere with their hosts.

This adult predaceous ground beetle, *Calosoma* sp., stalks its prey on soil or in litter.

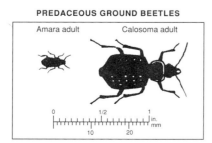

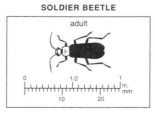

Predaceous Ground Beetles

Adult predaceous ground beetles, family Carabidae, are commonly black or dark reddish, although some species are brilliantly colored or iridescent. They dwell on the ground, have long legs, and are fast runners. Larvae dwell in litter or the soil and are elongate and have a large head with distinct mandibles. Carabids feed on snails, slugs, root feeding insects, and insect larvae and pupae.

Soldier Beetles

Adult soldier beetles, family Cantharidae, are long, narrow beetles, usually red or orange with black, gray, or brown wing covers. Adults are often observed on flowers. The dark, flattened larvae are predaceous, as are the adults of many species.

They feed on aphids and the eggs and larvae of beetles, moths, and butterflies.

PESTICIDES

Pesticides, substances applied to kill or repel pests or control damage, can provide a quick but temporary reduction in pest populations. Many pesticides of low toxicity to humans and pets are available, including microbials, insecticidal soap, narrow-range oil, and botanical insecticides. These selective, less toxic, or less persistent pesticides can reduce, delay, or prevent future outbreaks (pest resurgence) or outbreaks of other potential pests (secondary pest outbreaks), in part because they are not as harmful as other pesticides to natural enemies. If an application needs to be made, whenever possible choose a pesticide with little or no contact or residual toxicity to natural enemies (Table 4-6).

Some pests develop resistance to pesticides so that spraying becomes less effective. Resistance develops because the genetic makeup of some individuals in a pest population happens to make them less susceptible to pesticides. These tolerant individuals are more likely to survive an application and produce descendents. Repeated applications over several generations eventually result in a pest population composed primarily of tolerant or resistant individuals.

Pesticides sometimes damage plants (cause phytotoxicity), especially if plants lack proper cultural care, environmental conditions are extreme, or pesticides are used carelessly (see Pesticides and Phytotoxicity, Chapter 6). Check the label for plant species that should not be sprayed with that material. Before spraying a plant with a new pesticide, consider spraying a small portion of it and examining it for damage during

This adult soldier beetle, *Cantharis* sp., eats aphids and the eggs and larvae of beetles, moths, and butterflies.

the following week before spraying the rest of the plant.

Understand the relative toxicity, mode of action, persistence, and safe and legal use of pesticides. You can then more favorably manage natural enemies in the landscape and avoid other potential problems. For more discussion on pesticides see Chapter 2 and *The Safe and Effective Use of Pesticides* (UC Publication 3324).

Microbial or Biological Insecticides. Microbial insecticides are diseases of insects that are produced commercially, often in a process similar to brewing beer. Each kind affects only a certain insect group, and does not affect humans or most beneficial species. *Bacillus thuringiensis* (Bt) variety *kurstaki* is the most commonly used microbial insecticide; it kills only moth and butterfly larvae. Bt variety *tenebrionis* or *san diego* kills only some beetles. Bt variety *israelensis* is applied to water to kill mosquito and black fly larvae and to soil to kill fungus gnat larvae. *Nosema locustae*, a disease-causing protozoan, is com-

mercially available for controlling crickets and grasshoppers.

Microbial insecticides may also be called biological insecticides, but biologicals is a broader term that also includes commercially available beneficial nematodes (tiny roundworms) that are effective against certain insects that contact soil or bore into wood. Abamectin is the natural product of a fungus, *Streptomyces avermitilis,* and is commercially available (for example under the name Avid) for killing mites and certain insects.

Insecticidal Soap. Insecticidal soap is effective against mites, whiteflies, and other soft-bodied pests including aphids, thrips, immature scales, and leafhoppers. Insecticidal soap has low toxicity to humans and wildlife, but can damage some plants, especially species with dull leaf surfaces or many hairs. Before treating a plant, consider making a test application to a portion of the foliage and observing it for damage over several days before spraying it any more. Do not treat water-stressed plants or spray when it is expected to be hot, windy, or humid. Early morning or late afternoon may be the best application times.

Narrow-Range Oil. Narrow-range or horticultural oil, also called supreme or superior oil, is a highly refined petroleum product manufactured specifically to control pests on plants. Plant-derived oils, such as those made from cottonseed, may also be available. In comparison with motor oils or many other petroleum products, narrow-range oils have low toxicity to humans and most wildlife. Some products may irritate skin and, as with all pesticides, should be kept away from eyes.

Oil smothers insects by clogging spiracles, the tiny openings in insect bodies through which they breathe. Narrow-range oil apparently also disrupts cell membranes, interfering with normal metabolic activities. Oils are effective against exposed eggs and soft-bodied immature and adult pests, including scales, aphids, mealybugs, and whiteflies.

Oils have traditionally been applied to deciduous trees during the winter as "dormant oil" sprays. Delayed dormant season sprays, commonly applied before leaves flush but after buds have begun to swell in the spring, control scales, mites, aphid eggs, and other pests overwintering on bark. A dormant season or delayed dormant application may require less gallons than foliar sprays and may have less impact on some natural enemies.

Narrow-range oils can control most soft-bodied insects when applied as a foliar spray during the spring or summer. Check the label and avoid spraying plants identified as susceptible to foliar damage, such as some arborvitae, juniper, maple, and blue spruce. Do not apply oil when plants are

drought-stressed, when it is windy, or when temperatures are over 90°F or below freezing. Do not spray when the relative humidity is expected to be above 90% for 48 hours, and avoid spraying oil when it is very foggy. High humidity reduces the evaporation of oil, increasing its effectiveness against pests but also increasing the likelihood of phytotoxicity. For summer or dormant season applications, use only oils that say "supreme" or "superior" or "narrow-range" on the label. These have a minimum unsulfonated residue (UR) of 92 and a minimum percent paraffin (% Cp) of 60%, characteristics that make an oil relatively safe for plants. For more details on effectively using oils see *Managing Insects & Mites with Spray Oils* (UC Publication 3347).

Botanicals. Botanical pesticides are derived from plants. Most botanicals are of low toxicity to humans (nicotine sulfate is a notable exception) and are effective against many exposed feeding insects. Botanicals break down rapidly after application, which makes them relatively safe for the environment, but they must be applied precisely when and where pests are present to be effective.

Pyrethrum, rotenone, ryania, sabadilla, and azadirachtin are available botanicals. Pyrethrum is derived from chrysanthemum flowers grown in Africa and South America. Rotenone is obtained from the roots of certain tropical plants. Ryania is made from the ground roots of a shrub grown in Trinidad. Sabadilla is extracted from the seeds of a lily. Azadirachtin is extracted from the seeds of the neem tree. Neem extracts are apparently very toxic to a wide range of invertebrate pests, yet quite nontoxic to humans.

Read the labels carefully before use and observe all recommended pre-

cautions; for example, rotenone is extremely toxic to fish and must be used with great care near water. Insects and fish metabolize rotenone into breakdown products that are highly toxic to them. Most mammals produce almost exclusively nontoxic metabolites, accounting for rotenone's selective toxicity to certain organisms.

Pyrethroids. Pyrethroids are synthesized from petroleum and have chemical structures similar to naturally occurring pyrethrum insecticides. Pyrethroids, such as fluvalinate and permethrin, are more persistent and more toxic to pests than natural botanicals. Pyrethroids have a relatively low toxicity to humans and other mammals. However, like many other pesticides, pyrethroids can be very toxic to natural enemies (see Table 4-6) and pests may readily develop resistance to them, so try to avoid their use in landscapes.

Inorganics. Inorganic insecticides are elements or salts usually refined from minerals. Sulfur, probably the first effective pesticide discovered, is commonly used as a dust to control plant fungal diseases and mites. Do not treat plants labeled as susceptible to damage by sulfur and do not apply it during very hot or humid weather. Sulfur can irritate the skin and is harmful if inhaled, so wear a dust mask and other protective clothing during application.

Synthetics. Acephate, chlorpyrifos, diazinon, and malathion (all organophosphates) and carbaryl (a carbamate) are commonly used insecticides synthesized from petroleum. Organophosphates and carbamates inhibit cholinesterase, an important enzyme in the nervous system. Because all insects and mammals use cholinesterase to regulate nerve activity, these pesticides can adversely affect nontarget organisms. Pets and people may be harmed if they are exposed to a large enough dose, such as from careless use or accidents.

Most organophosphates and carbamates kill a wide variety of pests that are directly sprayed or that touch or eat treated foliage. They also kill many natural enemies and promote the development of resistance. Carbaryl is especially toxic to honey bees and can cause mite outbreaks, in part because it kills spider mite natural enemies. Avoid using these materials if less toxic materials or nonchemical alternatives are available.

FOLIAGE-FEEDING CATERPILLARS

Caterpillars are the larval stage of moths or butterflies and are in the insect order Lepidoptera. Don't confuse them with the immature stages of other caterpillarlike insects covered elsewhere in this book, including beetles and sawflies that also feed on foliage. Hundreds of different leaf-chewing caterpillars feed on landscape plants, but most are so uncommon that they are not pests. Many species are important food for birds or mature into attractive butterflies.

DAMAGE

Some caterpillars fold or roll leaves together with silk to form shelters. Others feed on leaves beneath a canopy of silk, sometimes creating dense "nests" in foliage. Many species chew irregular holes in leaves, some tunnel within foliage, and others devour entire leaves along with stems, and in some cases, flowers or fruit as well. This damage can be

unsightly, but it often looks more serious than it is. The importance of the injury depends on the age, species, and health of the plant and the level of aesthetic quality desired for that location. A relatively small number of caterpillars can retard the growth of plants that are young or already stressed from other causes, such as a lack of proper cultural care. Severe defoliation, especially during consecutive years, may cause branch dieback or kill entire plants. However, most mature trees and shrubs tolerate extensive feeding by caterpillars, especially later in the growing season, with little or no loss in plant growth or vigor.

IDENTIFICATION AND BIOLOGY

After mating, the female moth or butterfly lays her eggs singly or in a mass on the host plant. These eggs hatch after several days, except in the case of species that spend the winter in the egg stage. The emerging larvae move singly or in groups to feeding sites on the plant. In addition to three pairs of legs on the thorax (the area immediately behind the head), caterpillars have leglike appendages (called prolegs) on at least some segments of the abdomen, but there are no prolegs on at least the first two abdominal segments. These features distinguish

caterpillar larvae from similar-appearing larvae of certain beetles and sawflies. Beetle larvae have no legs on the abdomen, while sawfly larvae have six or more pairs of legs on the abdomen in addition to their three pairs of thoracic legs (Figure 4-6).

Most caterpillars eat voraciously and grow rapidly, shedding old skins three to five times before entering a nonactive pupal stage; some species pupate within silken cocoons (Figure 4-2). Most species pupate in a characteristic location, such as in litter beneath the tree, on leaves, or the trunk. The adult moth or butterfly emerges from the pupal case after several days to several months, depending on the species and season. Some common caterpillar pests, such as the fruittree leafroller and most tussock moths, have one generation a year. Other species have several generations annually and can cause damage throughout the growing season.

CONTROL ACTION THRESHOLDS

Plants tolerate feeding by moderate populations of caterpillars, and control is not needed merely because caterpillars are present. No thresholds have been established for caterpillar numbers or damage on most landscape plants, although action guidelines have been suggested for

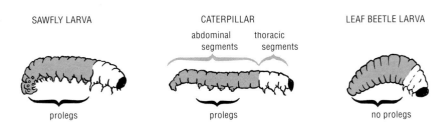

Figure 4-6. Caterpillars can be distinguished from larvae of beetles and sawflies by the number and arrangement of their appendages. All of these insect larvae have three pairs of true legs, one pair on each thoracic segment. Sawfly larvae also have appendages (called prolegs) on all of their abdominal segments. Caterpillars have prolegs on some abdominal segments, but never on their first two abdominal segments. Beetle larvae have no prolegs.

the California oakworm. Suggested control action thresholds for healthy, mature deciduous plants in landscapes are approximately 20% defoliation in the spring and 30–40% in the summer. In the fall, it is generally inappropriate to control leaf-feeding insects regardless of damage levels, since the leaves will be shed soon. A 30% defoliation level may warrant control on conifers. Tolerance for injury varies among locations and host plants. Some people are bothered by observing insects or damage that does not actually threaten plant health. Monitor plants as discussed below and use that information to develop and modify action thresholds that are appropriate for your situation.

Identify the species present and learn about their biology before taking action. Some caterpillars have only one generation a year, and it may be too late for control to be effective once mature caterpillars or their damage are observed. Keep thorough records of your insect or damage monitoring. Record the location, date, and specific reason why pests were considered a problem. Adjust your thresholds based on experience or special circumstances, such as weakened plants that are less tolerant of defoliation. Some pesticides may also adversely affect weakened plants.

MONITORING

The first step toward preventing unacceptable damage is to learn how to recognize infestations early. Plants with a history of damage, or that are prone to certain pests, may need to be monitored every week for certain pest life stages during critical parts of the year. Monitoring is necessary to determine whether populations warrant control and to time management efforts so that they are effective. Plants should also be monitored at least once after taking control action

to assess the effectiveness of your management. Monitoring provides only a relative measure of insect abundance; for example, it alerts you to whether insect numbers are going up or down. Several sampling methods are available. The most important considerations in monitoring are to choose a sampling method appropriate to your host plant and pest situation and to be consistent in your method so that results are comparable among sample data.

Sweep Net Shake or Branch Beating. Sweep net or branch beat samples are appropriate for caterpillars that are easily dislodged from foliage. Neither technique is effective for caterpillar species that web themselves in leaves. Insert new growth flushes into a standard sweep net and shake vigorously. Alternatively, hold a light-colored tray, framed cloth, or clipboard beneath foliage and shake or beat the branch to dislodge insects. One shake or beat from each of about four locations per plant on each of about four plants may be adequate for sampling at each location. Empty the samples onto a clean surface and record the number of larvae collected per beat or shake (total larvae divided by total beats or shakes).

Timed Counts. Timed counts can be used to monitor any type of caterpillar that can easily be observed in foliage. Inspect foliage and record the number of caterpillars, rolled leaves, or webbing "nests" seen in 1 or 2 minutes. Pull apart rolled leaves or webbing and count them only if they contain live caterpillars. Make several timed searches on different plants or on different parts of the same large plant. To keep track of time while counting insects, time your counts with an alarm watch or work with a second person who can time and record. Timed counts are not useful if

populations are so high that the number of insects recorded is limited by how quickly each can be seen and counted.

Visual Inspection. A common method for sampling foliage-chewing insects is to visually inspect a set number of randomly selected leaves or growth terminals for caterpillars or their eggs. Record the number of insects found on each leaf or terminal. Determine the average number of insects per sample by adding up the total number of insects found and dividing by the number of samples inspected.

Foliage may also be inspected for damage instead of, or in addition to, counting insects. Record the number of chewed or skeletonized leaves or terminals and the total number of leaves or terminals sampled. To obtain a more exact estimate of damage, assign each sample a damage rating from 0 to 10, where zero equals no damage, 1 equals about 10% damage, 2 is about 20% damage, and so on. About 30 samples at each site may be adequate. Take the average of all samples to estimate overall damage at that location. For insects that occur in groups, such as fall webworms or tent caterpillars, a timed count or whole plant count is more useful because of the clumped distribution.

Damage sampling indicates past insect activity. Insect populations may change rapidly because of factors such as weather or natural enemies, so make sure that the damaging life stages susceptible to treatment are still abundant before using damage as the basis for your control actions.

Pheromone-Baited Traps. Traps are commonly used for monitoring the gypsy moth and are commercially available for other lepidopterans, including the fruittree leafroller, Nantucket pine tip moth, omnivorous looper, and some clearwing moths. Traps typically consist of a sticky surface and a dispenser containing a pheromone (sex attractant) to lure adults of one sex (usually the male). Because both sexes are active around the same time, traps can be used to determine when females are laying eggs and to time control actions. For example, *Bacillus thuringiensis* (Bt) is effective against young lepidopteran larvae that feed openly on foliage. If you know how long it takes for larvae to hatch from eggs after adults are caught, you can use traps to time applications for insects like the omnivorous looper. Because rate of development is related to heat, monitoring temperatures in degree-days is the most reliable method for determining time to hatching. Although traps can help time your controls for some pests, traps do not reliably indicate numbers of an insect in landscapes. Therefore traps should not be used for deciding whether insects are abundant enough to warrant control action.

No specific trapping recommendations have been developed for landscape plants. However, to determine when specific moths are active in an area, hang one trap at chest height in each of two host trees spaced at least several hundred feet apart. Deploy traps during the season when adults are expected, and check them about once a week. Reapply sticky material or replace the traps when they are no longer sticky. Pheromone dispensers may need to be replaced about once monthly, especially if the weather has been hot. Check with trap distributors for specific recommendations.

Frass Collection. Several methods of monitoring fecal pellets (frass) have been used by researchers to estimate density and damage by caterpillars, including the California oakworm and gypsy moth. Each type of caterpillar excretes characteristic droppings, which fall to the ground beneath the plant. These fecal pellets increase in size as the larvae grow and pellets are generally produced in greater amounts with an increase in the number of larvae or an increase in temperature, which causes caterpillars to feed faster. Because California oakworms are generally more abundant in the west part of the tree canopy, concentrating monitoring in the west side of trees provides an earlier and more sensitive measure of their feeding.

Place three to five light-colored sticky cards, shallow trays, or cups beneath the canopy at regular intervals, such as for 24 hours each week. Place these frass traps when no rain or sprinkler irrigation is expected. After monitoring with sticky cards, allow the frass to dry somewhat then cover the cards with clear plastic and save them for comparison with cards from other sample dates. If cups or trays are used, combine in one container all the frass collected from one tree or from all trees. Use the same number of sticky cards or the same size and number of cups on each sample date. Save the frass or record its volume for comparison with the amount collected on other sampling dates or at other locations.

Initially you may want to conduct both frass monitoring and foliage inspection. This provides a record of the proportion of leaves eaten or the

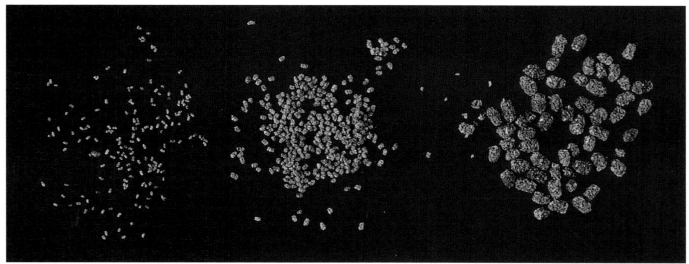

Frass collection can be used to monitor the California oakworm, which has five different larval instars. These three piles of frass (from left to right) were produced by the smallest larvae (first instars), third instars, and fifth-instar larvae. Pellets average 0.3, 0.6, and 1.4 mm long, respectively.

number of larvae present and the corresponding density or volume of frass produced. With experience, frass monitoring alone may be used to estimate caterpillar density and damage and to help in deciding if control is warranted. Fecal trap monitoring is not useful for sampling tent-making and leaf-rolling caterpillars, because little of their frass falls to the ground.

MANAGEMENT

Cultural Controls. Proper cultural care allows landscapes to tolerate moderate levels of defoliation without harm to the plants. Provide proper fertilizer and water, depending on soil type, location, and plant species. Protect roots and trunks from damage, and prune trees properly when needed.

Biological Controls. Predators, parasites, and natural outbreaks of disease sometimes kill enough caterpillars to control populations. Predators include spiders, bigeyed bugs, pirate bugs, lacewing larvae, ground beetles, damsel bugs, assassin bugs, and birds. Many caterpillar eggs are destroyed by tiny parasitic wasps, such as *Trichogramma* species. Most larvae are attacked by one or more larger

species of wasp. For example, red-humped caterpillars are often controlled by two species of parasitic wasps.

Caterpillars are often killed by diseases caused by naturally occurring bacteria, fungi, or viruses. Caterpillars killed by viruses and bacteria may turn dark and their bodies become soft and limp. These carcasses hanging limply from foliage or twigs, eventually degenerate into a sack of liquefied contents. When broken, they release more viral particles or bacterial spores that infect other caterpillars that eat contaminated foliage. Such disease outbreaks can rapidly reduce populations under favorable conditions, although outbreaks are difficult to predict and may not occur until caterpillar populations have become high.

You get the greatest benefit from natural enemies if you avoid the use of insecticides that destroy them. For instance, among materials used for control of caterpillars, the biological insecticide *Bacillus thuringiensis* leaves most natural enemies unharmed.

When monitoring for pests, also look closely for the presence of predators, parasites, and other evi-

dence of biological control; record this information. Evidence of natural enemy activity includes disease-killed caterpillars, pupae or eggs with holes from which parasites emerged, unhatched eggs that are darker than normal indicating they may contain parasites, or hatched caterpillar eggs with no evidence of caterpillars or damage. If you have an increasing number of pests but also many natural enemies, wait a few days before using insecticides. Monitor again to determine whether pest populations have declined, or natural enemies are increasing to levels that may soon cause pest numbers to decline. Although selective insecticides such as *Bacillus thuringiensis* may not provide such rapid insect control as broad-spectrum sprays, where natural enemies are active, better long-term control is provided by using methods that conserve natural enemies.

Mass Releases of Trichogramma *Wasps. Trichogramma* are tiny wasps that attack the eggs of many moths and butterflies, adults are the size of a period. Although they often occur naturally on plants infested with caterpillar eggs, several species are available by mail from commercial insectaries (see Suppliers for publications listing current vendors). University researchers have successfully used *Trichogramma* releases to control a few agricultural pests that lay exposed eggs, including omnivorous leafroller, tomato fruitworm, and loopers. Although some of these same pest species occur on ornamentals, no research has demonstrated the effectiveness of *Trichogramma* releases against pests in landscapes. *Trichogramma* released for controlling pest caterpillars may also kill nearby eggs of innocuous or desirable species of moths and butterflies.

The parasitic wasp, *Hyposoter* sp., is laying an egg in a caterpillar.

The two silverspotted tiger moth caterpillars, *Lophocampa argentata*, hanging beneath this Monterey pine twig have been killed by a naturally occurring disease. A healthy larva is at top.

Most insectaries claim to sell one or more of three species: *T. pretiosum*, *T. platneri*, and *T. minutum*. *Trichogramma platneri* has been effectively used against caterpillars on fruit trees in southern California. *T. pretiosum* controls caterpillars in tomatoes. Only certain *Trichogramma* species may be adapted for your situation.

Commercial suppliers of *Trichogramma* normally ship the parasite in the form of parasitized caterpillar eggs glued to a piece of cardboard. The wasps, which complete their immature stage within the caterpillar eggs, should emerge as adults soon after the shipment arrives. *Trichogramma* are more likely to be effective if they are allowed to emerge in containers *lightly* streaked with honey diluted with water and permitted to feed for 24 hours before

release. Using clear containers covered with tightly woven cloth allows you to observe the tiny wasps and permits some air flow while preventing their escape.

Trichogramma must be released in large numbers just before or at peak pest-egg laying for any likelihood of effectiveness. Monitor plants regularly to determine when adults or eggs first appear, then order your *Trichogramma*. Pheromone-baited traps are available for some pest species, including the omnivorous looper and fruittree leafroller, to indicate when egg-laying moths become active. If necessary, *Trichogramma* may be refrigerated (not frozen) for a while then released at intervals around when pest egg-laying peaks. They will probably survive best if they are refrigerated as parasite pupae, before the adult wasps emerge. If they are

refrigerated as adults, allow them to warm to room temperature and feed on honey water for several hours each day. Parasite mortality increases and the survivors' egg-laying ability decreases dramatically if they are refrigerated longer than about 2 weeks.

Based on research against *Amorbia cunea* and omnivorous looper in avocado and citrus orchards, weekly releases each of 10,000 or more *Trichogramma* per 20-foot tree over a period of 3 weeks or longer may be effective if releases coincide with peak butterfly or moth egg-laying.

Physical Controls. Many species, such as the spiny elm caterpillar, red-humped caterpillar, mimosa webworm, fall webworm, and tent caterpillars, feed in groups, which in some species are evidenced by silken webbing on foliage. Clip and dispose of infested foliage; a pole pruner or ladder may be needed for this. Effective physical control may require monitoring to identify infestations while the caterpillars are still young, because some group-feeding species disperse as the larvae mature. Clipping is best done on cool, rainy, or overcast days when young caterpillars remain in tents or inactive groups. Heavily infested plants can be sprayed if necessary, preferably with a selective insecticide, then monitored during subsequent seasons when populations are lower and physical control is more practical.

Some caterpillars, such as the tussock moths and gypsy moth, overwinter in obvious egg masses on bark or other objects. After leaves have dropped, inspect the bark and area around susceptible plants. Scrape any egg masses into a bucket of soapy water and dispose of them.

Microbial Insecticides. Microbial insecticides are commercially available formulations of naturally occurring diseases of insects. They are almost ideal insecticides from an environmental and safety point of view. They are generally very selective, killing only a particular life stage of certain insects. The bacterium *Bacillus thuringiensis* variety *kurstaki* (Bt) is effective against many leaf-eating caterpillars when larvae are young. The disease destroys the caterpillars' digestive system and causes larvae to stop feeding within about a day. Most infected caterpillars die within a few days.

Unlike broad-spectrum insecticides that kill on contact, caterpillars must eat sprayed foliage in order to be killed. Proper timing and thorough spray coverage is therefore very important for effective application, so monitor caterpillar populations before treatment. For example, to control tussock moths, monitor several overwintering egg masses on bark and spray foliage when most of the eggs are observed to have hatched. A high-pressure sprayer should be used to provide adequate spray penetration when treating leafrolling and tentmaking species. *Bacillus thuringiensis* should be applied during warm, dry weather when caterpillars are feeding actively. Because sunlight quickly decomposes Bt on foliage, most caterpillars hatching after the application are not affected. A second application about 7 to 10 days after the first may be required. Follow label directions for mixing and applying. *Bacillus thuringiensis* is available in formulations that are diluted with water and sprayed on and in ready-to-apply dust formulations in hand shaker type packages.

Narrow-Range Oil. Spraying trees during the dormant season with specially refined narrow-range or horticultural oils, also labeled "superior" or "supreme," kills overwintering eggs of fruittree leafroller, tussock moths, gypsy moths, and other caterpillars on bark, thereby substantially lowering summer populations of these pests. The primary reason for applying oil during the dormant season is to control scales or overwintering eggs of aphids and mites; high caterpillar populations the previous spring or summer may also warrant a dormant season oil spray. See the section on scale insects for more information on dormant season oil treatments.

Other Pesticides. If more toxic pesticides than the ones discussed above are needed, confine treatments to those plants or portions of plants that are infested. Time treatments to coincide with the pest's most vulnerable life stage—usually the newly hatched larvae. Some synthetic pesticides such as organophosphates, carbamates, or pyrethroids rapidly reduce populations of most caterpillar species. However, these broad-spectrum insecticides also kill beneficial organisms and may cause outbreaks of other pests such as mites. Avoid using these pesticides if less toxic materials (see Table 4-6) or nonchemical alternatives are available. Do not apply broad-spectrum insecticides to flowering plants if honey bees are present. For specific insecticide recommendations see *Insect Pest Management Guidelines for California Landscape Ornamentals* (UC Publication 3317).

A number of broad-spectrum but "organically acceptable" insecticides are effective against some caterpillars, including certain botanicals (pesticides extracted from plants) such as pyrethrum, rotenone, and ryania. Check labels to determine whether these materials are registered for ornamentals and what pests are likely to be controlled.

Insecticide injections or implants can control caterpillars and other leaf-feeding insects while avoiding spray drift and contamination problems associated with foliar applications. However, injections or implants damage trees and should be avoided; do not inject or implant trees more than once a year.

California Oakworm
Phryganidia californica

The California oakworm, family Dioptidae, is one of many species of caterpillars that feed on oaks in California; it is especially numerous in some years in the San Francisco Bay area and Monterey Bay region. The adult is a uniform tan to gray moth, distinguished by its prominent wing veins. The tiny round eggs are laid in groups of about two or three dozen on twigs or leaves. The eggs are white when laid, but develop red centers that become pinkish to brownish gray before hatching. The young larvae are yellowish green with dark stripes on their side and have overly large brown heads. Mature larvae are variable in color, commonly dark with prominent lengthwise yellow or olive stripes. Pupae are white or yellow with black markings and are found on bark or suspended from limbs, leaves, or objects near trees.

Two generations a year typically occur in northern California; a third generation sometimes occurs in southern California and in northern California in years of uncommonly warm, dry winters. The oakworm overwinters as young larvae on the lower leaf surface. Young larvae skeletonize the lower leaf surface, while mature larvae chew all the way through the leaf. Overwintering larvae in northern California mature about May or early June, when defoliation on live oaks may become extensive. Large populations of the spring generation generally do not occur on deciduous oaks because these trees drop their leaves in the fall, causing the overwintering generation larvae and eggs to die. The spring generation larvae produce moths often seen fluttering around oaks in the late afternoon in June and July. These adults lay eggs that hatch into larvae that may cause noticeable defoliation in July through September. Second-generation moths are present in October and November when they lay eggs that hatch into the overwintering larvae. Development in southern California is more variable, and moths may appear almost any time from March through November.

Thresholds and Management.
Healthy oaks tolerate extensive defoliation without serious harm. Well-cared for oaks not otherwise subject to serious stress survive being totally defoliated. If trees need protection from defoliation because they are stressed or of especially high aesthetic value, regularly inspect foliage for larvae and spray only when caterpillars are abundant. No thresholds have been established, but some guidelines have been suggested: If more than 8 to 10 larvae greater than 1/4 inch long are observed after inspecting 25 young (lighter green) shoots, defoliation may become apparent on untreated oaks. A density of 25 California oakmoth larvae per 100 twigs has also been suggested as the population density that may warrant control action to prevent annoying levels of defoliation. Frass collection is useful for oakworm monitoring.

Young larvae are most susceptible to *Bacillus thuringiensis*, but because

The adult male (left) and female (right) of the California oakworm are tan to grayish moths with prominent wing veins, as seen here on coast live oak.

CALIFORNIA OAKWORM

egg mass   larva   pupa   adult

they only scrape the lower leaf surface, spraying is less effective at that stage unless you thoroughly treat the underside of leaves. It can be more effective to thoroughly treat foliage when larvae are first observed to be chewing completely through the leaf or chewing at the leaf edge.

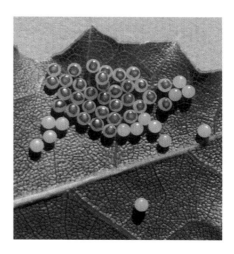

California oakworm eggs are whitish when laid, but develop red centers that become pinkish to brownish gray before hatching. See chapter introduction for a larval photograph.

Tussock Moths

Many tussock moths, family Lymantriidae, especially *Orgyia* species, occur in the United States. One or more kinds of tussock moths can feed at least occasionally on most species of deciduous and evergreen trees.

Adults are hairy, brownish to white moths. Females of some species are flightless because they are heavily laden with eggs or their wings are reduced to small pads (vestigial wings). Females produce a sex pheromone, which attracts the night-flying males. After mating, females lay their tiny whitish eggs in a mass of several hundred covered with hairs from the female's body. In species that overwinter as eggs, eggs hatch in the spring into tiny, dark caterpillars, which may travel on the wind. Full-grown caterpillars have prominent hairs that protrude, sometimes in tufts, from colored tubercles along their body. These hairs readily detach from the larvae and are often irritating to human skin. Pupation occurs on or near the host plant.

The western tussock moth, *Orgyia vetusta,* occurs from southern California to British Columbia. Its hosts include fruit and nut trees, hawthorn, manzanita, oak, pyracantha, toyon, walnut, and willow. Mature caterpillars are gray and have numerous bright red, blue, and yellow spots from which gray to white hairs radiate. They have four dense white tufts of hair on the back, two black tufts on the head, and a black and a white tuft at the rear. After emerging from the overwintering eggs and feeding during the spring, the larvae pupate on the bark of the trunk or main limbs. Cocoons are a tan brown. Adults emerge from late spring through early summer. Males are brown with gray markings. The western tussock moth usually has one generation a year, although in southern California two generations may occur. Second-generation larvae are present about late August to October, and adults lay the overwintering eggs in September and October.

Rusty tussock moth, *Orgyia antiqua,* occurs throughout the United States on many different deciduous and evergreen plants. Its hairy, blackish larvae have three projecting tufts of black hair, two in front and one at the rear, and four orangish tufts along the back.

The Douglas-fir tussock moth, *Orgyia pseudotsugata,* occurs only in

The western tussock moth larva has bright colored spots and dense tufts of hairs.

Tussock moth cocoons occur near or on host plants, such as this coast live oak.

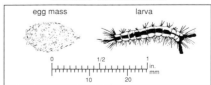

WESTERN TUSSOCK MOTH

egg mass   larva

0   1/2   1 in.
              mm
      10   20

the western states, primarily on Douglas fir and true firs. It also has two tufts of black hair in front and one at the rear, but lighter colored tufts of hair along the back, red spots on top, and an orange stripe along each side distinguish its mature larvae from those of the rusty tussock moth.

Whitemarked tussock moth, *Orgyia leucostigma,* occurs mostly in the eastern states. Its larvae are yellowish along the sides with a bright orangish red head.

Naturally occurring diseases and parasites often keep tussock moth populations at low levels. For example, a tiny purplish black parasitic wasp, *Telenomus californicus,* kills many western tussock moth eggs. *Bacillus thuringiensis* controls tussock moth larvae, especially if applied when young larvae are the predominant stage present.

ROGER ZERILLO, USDA-FOREST SERVICE

Mature gypsy moth larvae are hairy, with a row of five pairs of blues spots and 6 pairs of red spots on their back. In the western United States, report suspected gypsy moths to your County Department of Agriculture.

Gypsy Moth
Lymantria dispar

The gypsy moth, family Lymantriidae, was introduced from Europe and is the most serious caterpillar pest of deciduous trees in the northeastern states. Scattered infestations have been discovered in the West and are the target of eradication programs. Larvae prefer alder, basswood, some poplars and flowering fruit trees, willows, and especially oaks, but high populations will feed on many other plants.

Mature larvae are dark, and rows of blue dots near the front and red dots toward the rear may be visible along the back at the base of tufts of dark hairs. Mature larvae feed at night, then crawl down the trunk to hide during the day in bark crevices or litter on the ground. This behavior allows populations to be monitored

by wrapping a folded burlap band around host tree trunks and checking beneath it during spring days for hiding larvae. Larvae can be scraped into a bucket of soapy water or otherwise destroyed, which may provide some control. Larvae feed for about one and a half months during the spring, then form large, dark, oblong pupae. Pupation occurs on or near the host plant, commonly in leaf litter, bark crevices, or on manmade objects.

Adults emerge from the pupae in about 10 days. Female moths are whitish with inverted dark V-patterns on their wings. Gypsy moth females in the East do not fly, but females of the Asian gypsy moth strain do fly and are sometimes introduced, especially in the West. Male gypsy moths are brownish and tan with wavy black

bands on their wings. Gypsy moths overwinter as immatures in masses of eggs laid on bark or objects near host plants. If laid on manmade items, egg masses may be inadvertently transported on vehicles or outdoor equipment, thereby introducing this pest into new locations.

The sex pheromone females emit to attract males is commercially available. Sticky traps baited with pheromone are used to monitor populations. *Bacillus thuringiensis* provides control if applied to thoroughly cover foliage when young caterpillars are predominant. In the western United States, report suspected gypsy moths to the County Department of Agriculture, which will take action to prevent this pest from becoming permanently established.

Redhumped Caterpillar
Schizura concinna

The redhumped caterpillar, family Notodontidae, feeds on a variety of hosts throughout the U.S., including aspen, birch, cottonwood, fruit and nut trees, liquidambar, poplar, redbud, walnut, and willow. In California, high populations are usually only found in the inland valleys. Adult moths are reddish brown or gray and first appear about early May. After mating, the females lay pearly white, spherical eggs in masses of 25 to 100 on the underside of leaves. The larvae are yellow or reddish and have dark lines and projections along their bodies. The fourth segment behind the head is red and distinctly humped with two black projections. Larvae feed in groups, particularly when young. They consume the entire leaf, except for the major vein, and often feed only on a single branch. The insect overwinters as reddish brown pupae in the soil or in organic debris on the ground and has one to three generations a year.

Redhumped caterpillar populations are often controlled by two species of wasps, *Hyposoter fugitivus* and *Apanteles schizurae*. The female wasps lay their eggs in caterpillars and the wasp larvae hatch and feed inside. After killing the caterpillars, the *Apanteles* parasite larvae emerge and pupate in whitish, silken cocoons in groups that may be seen on leaves near dead caterpillars. *Hyposoter* pupae are oblong and mottled black or purplish. Parasite numbers can increase quickly, causing caterpillar populations to crash. Conserve these parasites by avoiding the use of broad-spectrum pesticides. Plant flowering species near host trees so that adult parasites have nectar to feed on (Table 4-4). Adult parasitoids live longer and can parasitize and kill more caterpillars when provided with nectar. Prune out and dispose of infestations that are on a limited portion of the plant. Apply *Bacillus thuringiensis* if spraying is necessary.

Older redhumped caterpillar larvae have two black projections on the distinctly reddish and enlarged fourth segment behind their head.

Hatched redhumped caterpillar eggs (upper right), unhatched eggs (below), and young larvae.

REDHUMPED CATERPILLAR

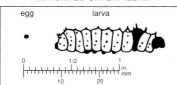

egg   larva

Omnivorous Looper
Sabulodes aegrotata or
S. caberata

The omnivorous looper, family Geometridae, occurs in the western states on several dozen plant species including acacia, box elder, California buckeye, chestnut, citrus, elm, eucalyptus, fruit trees, ginkgo, magnolia, maple, pepper tree, and willow. Young larvae are pale yellow and feed on the leaf surface, leaving a characteristic brown membrane. Older larvae are yellow to pale green or pink, with dark brown, black, or green lines along the sides and a gold colored head. In addition to the three pairs of legs behind the head, loopers have two additional prolegs near the rear (see Figure 4-6), allowing them to travel in the characteristic looping manner. They eat through the entire leaf, often leaving only the midrib and larger veins.

Larvae feed singly on the edge of leaves or twigs, or singly or in groups between two leaves tied with silk. After about 6 weeks, the larvae form pearly white to brown pupae, usually found in webbing between leaves. The adults that emerge are tan with a narrow black band across the middle of the wing and are active at night. The barrel-shaped eggs are laid in clusters of 3 to 80 on the underside of leaves. The eggs have a ring of tiny projections around one end and, after about 2 days, change from pale green to a shiny, reddish brown. The insect has up to five generations each year; all stages may be found whenever foliage is present. One or more applications of *Bacillus thuringiensis* can provide control when larvae are present.

These white cocoons were made by larvae of an *Apanteles* sp. wasp that emerged to pupate after feeding inside and killing these redhumped caterpillars.

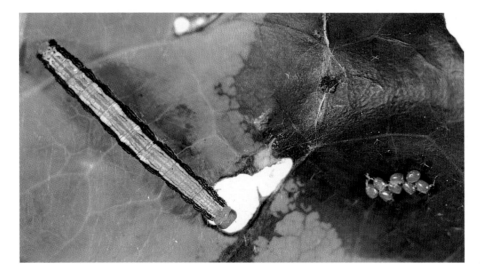

An older larva, eggs, and chewing damage of the omnivorous looper on ivy. The leaf blackening is probably caused by a foliar disease unrelated to the caterpillar.

OMNIVOROUS LOOPER

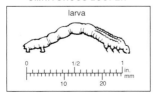

larva

Some species of caterpillars tie foliage together with silken threads and feed inside. This fruittree leafroller taken out of its leafroll is distinguished by its shiny black head.

The fruittree leafroller lays its irregular flat egg masses on twigs and small branches. The lower egg mass shows exit holes left by emerged larvae.

Fruittree Leafroller
Archips argyrospila

The fruittree leafroller, family Tortricidae, occurs throughout the U.S. on aspen, box elder, buckeye, citrus, cottonwood, elm, fruit and nut trees, hawthorn, locust, maple, oak, poplar, rose, and willow. The larvae feed only in the spring on new leaves, giving them a ragged or curled appearance. Unusually high populations can defoliate trees and understory plants and cover them with silken threads.

The fruittree leafroller overwinters in irregular, flat masses of eggs on twigs and small branches. Egg masses are coated with a dark gray or brown cement, which later turns white and becomes perforated as the larvae emerge. Larvae hatch in the spring, usually coincident with the flush of new leaves. Young caterpillars are green with a black, shiny head. They tie or roll leaves or blossoms together with silken threads and feed inside the nest. The caterpillars wriggle vigorously and often drop to the ground on a silken thread when disturbed. They frequently move to other leaves and construct a new nest, eventually pupating inside a nest or on bark in thin brown cocoons. The dark brown to yellowish tan, patterned moths emerge about 8 to 12 days after pupation. These adults soon mate and lay their overwintering eggs. The fruittree leafroller has one generation a year.

Pheromone-baited traps are commercially available for determining

FRUITTREE LEAFROLLER

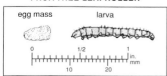

egg mass   larva

when moths are flying, usually in May or June. If fruittree leafroller damage has been a problem, apply oil in January or February to thoroughly cover limbs and small twigs infested with overwintering eggs. Alternatively, monitor several egg masses in spring when leaves begin to flush and apply *Bacillus thuringiensis* when about 25% to 50% of eggs have hatched. Repeat an application if necessary when most eggs have hatched. If larger larvae in rolled leaves are abundant, use high-pressure application equipment so that the insecticide penetrates into rolled foliage.

Spiny Elm Caterpillar
Nymphalis antiopa

The spiny elm caterpillar, family Nymphalidae, feeds on elm, poplar, and willow throughout the U.S. It causes ragged, chewed leaves, often on a single branch, which may be entirely defoliated. The group-feeding larvae produce dark fecal pellets. At maturity, larvae are mostly black with a row of orange-brown spots down the back and have minute rows of white dots on each segment. The most distinctive larval feature is the row of black spines around each segment, which may be mildly irritating to human skin.

Larvae form black, brown, or gray pupae from which strikingly beautiful butterflies emerge. The adult, known as the mourning cloak butterfly, is mostly brownish black to purple. Adult wing margins are ragged with yellow bands bordered inwardly by blue spots. The tiny eggs are orange or pink to brown, and almost cylindrical with eight longitudinal ribs. They are laid in masses of several dozen on leaves, limbs, or twigs. Spiny elm caterpillars have about two

generations a year, but in southern California, both adults and larvae may be observed during almost any month.

Spiny elm caterpillar larvae do not harm the tree and no control is needed. Clip and dispose of the infested branch if caterpillars cannot be tolerated.

Tent Caterpillars
Malacosoma spp.

Tent caterpillars, family Lasiocampidae, feed on deciduous trees and shrubs throughout the U.S. Depending on the species, their hosts include ash, birch, fruit and nut trees, madrone, oak, poplar, redbud, toyon, and willow. Adults are hairy, medium-size, day-flying moths, usually dull brown, yellow, or gray in color. Tent caterpillars overwinter in pale gray to dark brown eggs encircling small twigs or laid in a flat mass on bark. The larvae hatch and begin feeding in the spring, and some species form silken webs on foliage. After feeding, tent caterpillars spin silken cocoons in folded leaves, on bark, or in litter, and the adults emerge in mid-summer. Tent caterpillars have one generation a year.

Western tent caterpillar, *Malacosoma californicum*, larvae are reddish brown with some blue spots and are covered with tufts of orange to white hairs. They spin large silken webs in

SPINY ELM CATERPILLAR
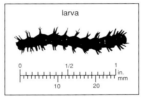

WESTERN TENT CATERPILLAR
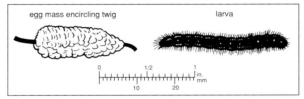

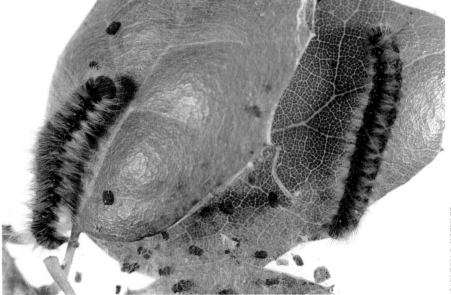

CARLTON S. KOEHLER

Western tent caterpillars are mostly reddish brown. Their dark frass or droppings are visible here caught in silken webbing they've make on coast live oak leaves.

which the larvae do most of their feeding.

The Pacific tent caterpillar, *M. constrictum*, looks very similar to *M. californicum*, except more blue is visible and the larvae usually feed only on oaks. Pacific tent caterpillars produce small tents a few inches wide. Larvae feed openly, in groups when they are young, and usually enter the tent only to molt.

The forest tent caterpillar, *M. disstria*, occurs throughout the U.S. Larvae are mostly dark blue, with wavy reddish brown lines and distinct white, keyhole-shaped markings down the back. Larvae feed in groups without making any webbing.

Inspect plants regularly and when larvae are young, prune out tents or clip and dispose of infested branches if this can be done without cutting major limbs. *Bacillus thuringiensis* provides control if high-pressure spray equipment is used so that insecticide penetrates any webbing.

Fall Webworm
Hyphantria cunea

The fall webworm, family Arctiidae, is one of several tentmaking species in the U.S. Its tents are formed over the foliage toward the outer portions of the tree, while the nests of the tent caterpillars (*Malacosoma* spp.) are usually formed around the juncture of branches. The hosts of fall webworm include aspen, birch, cottonwood, elm, fruit and nut trees, liquidambar, maple, mulberry, poplar, sycamore, and willow. Its feeding damage is rarely severe, and the presence of silken tents is its primary effect.

Adult moths emerge in the late spring or early summer and are mostly white, sometimes with black

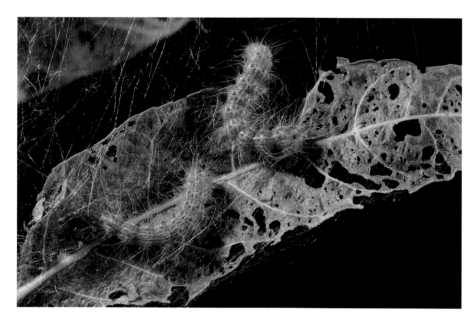

Fall webworms and their chewing damage within a silken tent on willow.

Fall webworm nests, as shown here on Lombardy poplar, are typically formed over outer foliage, which can be clipped and disposed of. This distinguishes them from tent caterpillars, which usually make nests around branch junctures.

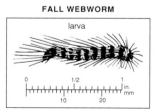

FALL WEBWORM
larva

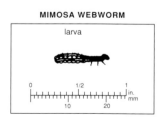

MIMOSA WEBWORM
larva

wing spots. In June or July, the females lay globular white or yellow eggs in large masses beneath leaves. These eggs hatch in about 10 days, and the larvae feed in silken tents until late summer or early fall. While feeding, the larvae enlarge their tents to include more leaves and shoots. Mature larvae are yellowish brown or gray with longitudinal stripes and have long white or black hairs arising from black and orange projections along the body. Fall webworms overwinter in dark brown cocoons, usually attached to the tree trunk or in organic debris on the ground. Fall webworm produces one or two generations a year.

Regularly inspect host plants for silken tents during late spring and summer. Prune out and dispose of caterpillar-infested tents as soon as they appear. If nests are abundant and cannot be pruned or tolerated, apply *Bacillus thuringiensis* with a high-pressure sprayer to penetrate webbed foliage. Inspect plants again the season after treating; populations should be lower and any remaining colonies can be pruned out.

Mimosa Webworm
Homadaula anisocentra

The mimosa webworm, family Plutellidae, was inadvertently introduced from China and occurs throughout the U.S. In California, it is a pest primarily in the Sacramento Valley. It feeds on *Albizia,* or mimosa, and especially on honey locust. Young larvae commonly feed in groups, covering foliage with silk and causing leaves to turn brown and die. Mature larvae vary from gray to blackish brown, have five longitudinal white stripes on the body, and commonly feed singly. They can move rapidly

when alarmed, and may drop from the foliage on a silken thread when disturbed. The adults are small, silvery gray moths with stippled black dots on their wings. They emerge in the late spring from whitish overwintering cocoons, which are found under bark scales on the trunk or in organic debris beneath host trees. After mating, females deposit pearly gray to pink eggs singly on foliage or on webbing formed by feeding larvae. The mimosa webworm usually has two generations a year.

Inspect plants for silken webbing and chewed or brown leaves and prune out and dispose of infested foliage while caterpillars are still young and feeding in groups. Apply *Bacillus thuringiensis* when young larvae are abundant if damage cannot be tolerated.

SAWFLIES

Sawflies are not true flies; they are in the order Hymenoptera, which includes ants, wasps, and bees. Sawflies are named for the adult female's sawlike abdominal appendage used for inserting eggs in foliage. Larvae of most conifer-feeding sawflies, family Diprionidae, feed externally on young conifer shoots or needles, and resemble butterfly caterpillars. Sawflies in the family Tenthredinidae, such as the willow leaf gall sawfly, pear sawfly, and bristly roseslug, feed mostly on or in broadleaf plants, including alder, birch, poplar, oak, and willow. A few species, such as the cypress sawfly, feed on evergreens. The tenthredinids are a diverse group of sawflies with different species that feed openly, in leaf mines, or in galls.

DAMAGE

Most conifer sawflies cause chewed needles or buds; a few mine in shoots and cause tip dieback. Broadleaf-feeding species cause more variable damage. Some skeletonize or chew holes in leaves; others mine tissue, causing winding, discolored tunnels. Different species roll leaves, web foliage, or cause plant galls. Sawflies in forests in the western states rarely cause serious damage, but high populations retard plant growth and occasionally kill trees in plantations and landscapes.

IDENTIFICATION AND BIOLOGY

Adult sawflies have two pairs of wings and are dark, wasplike, somewhat flattened insects, usually ½ inch long or shorter. They have a relatively wide abdomen, which is broadly attached to the thorax, in contrast to most other adult hymenopterans, which have a narrow "waist" between the thorax and abdomen. Most exposed-feeding larvae (the pearslug is an exception) have six or more prolegs on the abdomen (see Figure 4-6) and one large "eye" on each side of the head. This distinguishes them from butterfly caterpillars, which always lack legs on at least the first two segments of the abdomen and have a group of small eyespots but no large eyes.

Most sawflies in California overwinter as eggs in foliage or as pupae in litter. Sawflies that overwinter as eggs generally feed on older growth foliage, while those that overwinter as pupae feed on newer growth. Depending on the species, they have from one to several generations a year.

Young conifer sawflies, like these *Neodiprion fulviceps* larvae, often feed several to a needle with their heads pointed away from the twig. Unlike caterpillars and leaf beetle larvae, appendages can be seen on each sawfly larval segment.

Conifer Sawflies
Neodiprion spp.

Over two dozen *Neodiprion* species sawflies are native to the U.S. In the eastern states, several foreign species have also been introduced, including the European pine sawfly, *Neodiprion sertifer,* and the European spruce sawfly, *Gilpinia hercyniae.* Pines are the most common hosts; arborvitae, cypress, fir, hemlock, juniper, larch, and spruce are also fed upon, especially in the East. Most conifer sawfly adults are yellowish brown to black with yellowish legs. Females lay eggs in niches carved in needles. Larvae are commonly yellowish or greenish and develop dark stripes or spots as

CONIFER SAWFLY

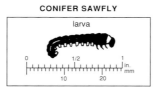

they mature. Young larvae often feed several to a needle with their heads pointed away from the twig. Older larvae may wrap their bodies around the needle on which they are feeding.

Several webspinning sawflies, *Acantholyda* spp. (family Pamphiliidae), occur on Monterey pine and other conifers in California. These sawflies spin nests or silken webs on foliage and feed inside in groups or singly. Unlike most free-feeding sawflies, these webspinning species have no prolegs and instead have a pair of three-segmented appendages on the last segment of the body. They pupate in an earthen cell in the ground.

Willow Leaf Gall Sawfly
Pontania pacifica

The willow leaf gall sawfly infests *Salix lasiolepis* and is one of several similar species that cause nearly identical damage on willow throughout the U.S. Adult males are shiny black; females are dull reddish. Females insert their eggs in young willow leaves and inject a fluid that causes the formation of reddish, berrylike galls. One larva develops in each of these galls, which are globular or elongate and about one-third inch long. Mature larvae emerge from the galls and pupate on the ground. This insect apparently has several generations a year.

Willow leaf gall sawflies apparently do not harm plants. No controls are recommended or known. The larvae of several wasps, and at least one weevil and moth, feed on the sawfly larvae or on the gall tissue, causing the sawflies to die. A wasp, *Eurytoma* sp., appears especially important in controlling willow leaf gall sawfly populations in California.

Willow leaf gall sawfly larvae feed within these reddish, berrylike galls.

Pear Sawfly
Caliroa cerasi

The pear sawfly, commonly called the pearslug, occurs throughout the U.S. Larvae skeletonize the leaf surface of most fruit trees, especially cherry and pear, and occasionally other plants such as ash and hawthorn. Larvae are dark olive green and covered with slime, so they look like slugs. Adults are shiny black with dark wings. There are generally two generations a year, and larvae are most abundant in the mid to late spring and again in mid to late summer.

Bristly Roseslug
Endelomyia aethiops

Bristly roseslug is one of several slug-like sawflies that feeds on roses. The larvae are shiny black to pale green and at maturity have many bristlelike hairs on their body. Unlike the pearslug, bristly roseslugs have apparent legs and prolegs. Young larvae skeletonize the lower leaf surface; mature larvae chew large holes in leaves. The bristly roseslug has several generations each year.

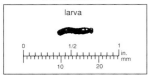

PEAR SAWFLY

larva

0   1/2   1
|||||||||||||||||||||| in.
        10   20   mm

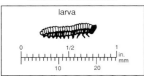

BRISTLY ROSESLUG

larva

0   1/2   1
|||||||||||||||||||||| in.
        10   20   mm

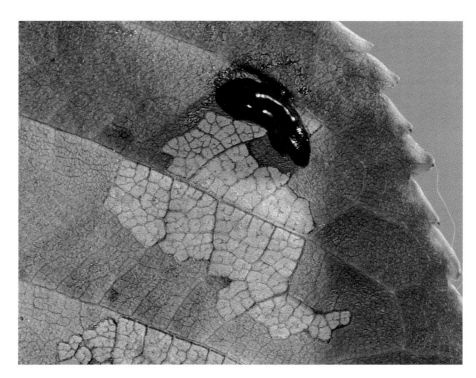

Pear sawfly larvae skeletonize leaves; their dark slimy coating gives them a sluglike appearance.

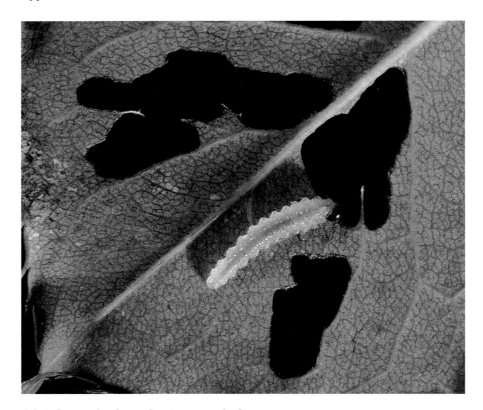

A bristly roseslug larva chewing a rose leaf.

Cypress Sawfly
Susana cupressi

The cypress sawfly in southern California damages cypress and reportedly also feeds on arborvitae, juniper, and larch. Adult wasps are black and yellow. Larvae are grayish green with rows of whitish dots. The cypress sawfly spends the winter in a cocoon in the soil and has one generation a year.

MANAGEMENT

Healthy trees and shrubs tolerate moderate defoliation without significant loss in growth, flowering, or fruit yield. Natural enemies are responsible for keeping most sawfly populations low and can cause outbreak populations to soon decline. Parasitic wasps, insectivorous birds and small mammals, predaceous beetles, or fungal and viral diseases commonly kill sawflies. Most broad-spectrum insecticides kill exposed-feeding sawfly larvae, but these should be avoided because of their adverse affect on natural enemies. Although some larvae look like caterpillars, sawflies are not controlled by *Bacillus thuringiensis*. In the eastern states some sawflies in forests have been managed by introducing and augmenting sawfly parasites and insect-specific viruses. Sawflies in the western states are mostly native species and rarely damage forest trees. There has not been sufficient research in landscapes or Christmas-tree plantations to allow recommendations on effectively using natural enemies.

Insecticidal soap or narrow-range oil kill exposed-feeding sawfly larvae, but sprays may damage blossoms. Pearslug larvae can be washed from plants with a forceful stream of water.

LEAF BEETLES AND FLEA BEETLES

Hundreds of species of leaf beetles and flea beetles, family Chrysomelidae, occur in the U.S., but only a few are common pests in landscapes. The elm leaf beetle is the major landscape pest in this group. Leaf beetles on alder, aspen, *Baccharis*, cottonwood, *Hypericum*, poplar, viburnum, and willow also are sometimes abundant enough to be pests.

DAMAGE

Leaf beetle adults and larvae scrape the surface or chew holes in leaves. Similar damage may be caused by larvae of some moths, butterflies, or sawflies, by adult weevils, or adult and immature grasshoppers, katydids, snails, and slugs. Damaged leaves may turn yellow or brown and drop prematurely. High leaf beetle populations cover leaves with their dark droppings and can skeletonize or defoliate entire plants. Repeated defoliation causes plants to decline, become susceptible to other problems, and in rare cases die. However, healthy deciduous plants tolerate extensive skeletonization or defoliation. Larvae of some species feed on roots, but these are not known to seriously damage established, woody plants.

IDENTIFICATION AND BIOLOGY

Most adult leaf beetles are less than ⅓ inch long, oval, blunt, and have threadlike antennae. The smallest species, called flea beetles, are metallic in color and often jump away when disturbed. Larger species may be colorful or blend with the colors of their host and usually drop when disturbed. Adults and larvae of many species feed on leaves, while other larvae, including cucumber beetles,

Diabrotica spp., feed on roots but cause no known damage to woody plants. Larvae of a few leaf beetles feed in stems or mine leaves. Exposed larvae are caterpillarlike, but unlike caterpillars and sawflies, they lack prolegs (see Figure 4-6). Many species feed in groups when young, then individually as they mature. Most leaf beetles pupate on the ground or attached to foliage or bark, and overwinter as adults in debris or protected places, such as bark crevices or inside buildings. Most species feed only on a few closely related plants.

MANAGEMENT

No thresholds have been established for leaf beetle numbers or damage on landscape plants; tolerance varies among individuals and location. Suggested control action thresholds for leaf beetle damage to healthy, mature deciduous landscape plants are approximately 20% defoliation in the spring, and 30% to 40% in the summer. In the fall, it is generally inappropriate to control leaf beetles on deciduous plants regardless of damage levels, since the leaves will be shed soon. Leaf beetle damage or larvae can be monitored by regularly inspecting leaves as discussed for foliage-feeding caterpillars. Degree-day monitoring is useful for timing control actions against elm leaf beetle.

Provide proper cultural care to keep plants vigorous and better able to tolerate defoliation. Many deciduous landscape plants, such as European and American elms, are adapted to frequent summer rainfall and require regular irrigation when grown in areas with summer drought. Consider replacing especially problem-prone trees with pest-resistant species or varieties.

A microbial insecticide, *Bacillus thuringiensis* variety *tenebrionis* or *san diego*, controls some leaf beetles including elm leaf beetle and cotton-wood leaf beetle. Broad-spectrum insecticides may also be applied, but treating foliage with these adversely affects natural enemies and may cause outbreaks of other pests such as mites.

Elm Leaf Beetle
Xanthogaleruca or *Pyrrhalta luteola*

Elm leaf beetle feeds on elms and zelkova throughout the United States. European elm species are most susceptible to damage, Siberian and American elm are somewhat resistant, and Chinese (evergreen) elm and zelkova are infrequently fed upon. Larvae skeletonize the leaf surface, while adults eat through the leaf, often in a shothole pattern. Adults are olive-green with black, longitudinal stripes along the margin and center of the back. Females lay their yellowish to gray eggs in double rows of about 5 to 25 on the underside of leaves. Newly hatched larvae are black. Mature larvae are a dull yellow or greenish with rows of tiny

dark tubercles that form two black stripes down the back. After feeding in the canopy for several weeks, larvae crawl down the tree trunk and form bright yellowish pupae around the tree base. After about 10 days, adult beetles emerge and fly to the canopy to feed and lay eggs. Elm leaf beetle has one to three generations a year in northern California; three or more annual generations can occur in central and southern California. Adults commonly overwinter in bark crevices or buildings.

Do not plant European elms such as English or Scotch elm and consider replacing these species because they are especially susceptible to elm leaf beetle. Provide elms with proper irrigation and avoid changes in grade and drainage around established trees. Check elms for dead or dying branches and properly prune these out during late fall and winter. Avoid pruning elms during the spring and summer; the European elm bark beetle, which vectors Dutch elm disease, is attracted then to feed around fresh pruning wounds. Control elm leaf beetle with an integrated program that includes good tree care, bark bands, and foliar sprays of selective

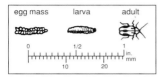

ELM LEAF BEETLE

egg mass   larva   adult

0   1/2   1 in.
    10   20   mm

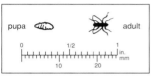

ELM LEAF BEETLE PARASITE

pupa   adult

0   1/2   1 in.
    10   20   mm

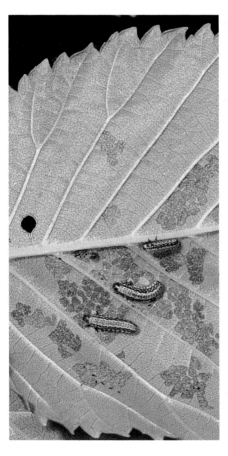

Several third-instar (mature) elm leaf beetle larvae on the lower surface of an English elm leaf they have skeletonized. Adult feeding, one hole chewed through the leaf, is visible at the left.

An elm leaf beetle adult, egg mass, and first-instar larva.

Curled elm leaf beetle prepupae and yellowish pupae around the base of an English elm. See the elm bark banding photograph on page 10.

A close-up of elm leaf beetle prepupae (left) and pupae (center) and pupae of the elm leaf beetle parasite *Erynniopsis antennata* (right).

or low residual toxicity insecticides that conserve natural enemies.

Biological Control. Several introduced and native natural enemies kill elm leaf beetles; however, at present they do not provide adequate control by themselves. *Erynniopsis antennata*, the most important in California, is a small, black tachinid fly that emerges from mature beetle larvae. Its black to reddish, cylinder- or teardrop-shaped pupae occur at the tree base among the bright yellow beetle pupae. *Tetrastichus brevistigma*, a tiny wasp, leaves one or more small, round holes in beetle pupae that it emerges from around the tree base; this species is uncommon in California but may be important in the eastern United States. An egg parasite, *Tetrastichus gallerucae*, occurs in California and Ohio. *T. gallerucae* leaves round holes when it emerges from beetle eggs, which remain golden. When beetle larvae have emerged, the egg shell is whitish with ragged holes. Conserve these natural enemies by avoiding foliar applications of broad-spectrum insecticides; use less toxic methods, such as narrow-range oil, *Bacillus thuringiensis*, and insecticide bark bands in an integrated program to obtain maximum benefits from biological control.

Thresholds and Treatment Timing. Defoliation to English elms (*Ulmus procera*) in northern California can be predicted by determining the percent of one-foot branch terminals infested with elm leaf beetle eggs. Egg presence-absence sampling must be done, and treatment decisions made separately, for each generation of beetles. Using a threshold of 40% defoliation, treatment is warranted when over 45% of branch terminals have beetle eggs during the week when egg density is at its maximum during the first generation. Treatment is warranted during the second generation if 30% or more of the terminals inspected have elm leaf beetle eggs on the leaves.

Monitor degree-days to determine when to sample. First-generation elm leaf beetle eggs in California are most abundant at about 510 degree-days above 52°F accumulated since March 1, as discussed in the section on degree-days. Second-generation egg density peaks at about 1,715 degree-days above 52°F accumulated since March 1. Begin weekly sampling about 150 degree-days before the predicted egg peak for each generation, at about 360 and 1,565 degree-days for the first and second generations, respectively. Continue sampling weekly until the percent of branches with eggs peaks then falls, until about 150 degree-days have accumulated after the predicted peak time, or until thresholds are exceeded on any one sample date, whichever comes first. This will usually mean sampling a maximum of four or five times per generation.

Use a pole pruner to clip one or more one-foot terminals from each of 8 segments of the lower canopy of each tree. Segments are north, east, south, and west, in both the inner canopy (from trunk halfway to the drip line) and the outer canopy. To reasonably predict defoliation, you must sample at least three trees, and a minimum of 25% of the trees, present at the site. Randomly select the trees to be sampled and sample those trees each week. Inspect a minimum of 120 total samples, 2 to 5 terminals in each segment of 3 or more trees. The number of samples needed per tree and the recommended number of elms to sample at each site are listed in Table 4-7.

TABLE 4-7

Suggested Sample Size for Elm Leaf Beetle Egg Presence-Absence Sampling on English Elm in Different Size Groups of Elms. Sample Eight Segments per Tree; North, East, South, and West in Both the Lower Inner, and Lower Outer Canopy.[a]

TOTAL TREES	SAMPLE TREES	SAMPLES PER TREE	SAMPLES PER SEGMENT	TOTAL SAMPLES	% OF TOTAL TREES SAMPLED
3	3	40	5	120	100%
4	4	32	4	128	100%
5	5	32	4	160	100%
6	6	24	3	144	100%
7	6	24	3	144	86%
8	7	24	3	168	88%
9	8	16	2	128	89%
10	8	16	2	128	80%
11	8	16	2	128	73%
12	8	16	2	128	67%
13	8	16	2	128	62%
14	8	16	2	128	57%
15	8	16	2	128	53%
16	9	16	2	144	56%
17	9	16	2	144	53%
18	9	16	2	144	50%
19	9	16	2	144	47%
20	9	16	2	144	45%
21	9	16	2	144	43%
22	10	16	2	160	45%
23	10	16	2	160	43%
24	10	16	2	160	42%
25	10	16	2	160	40%
26	10	16	2	160	38%
27	10	16	2	160	37%
28	10	16	2	160	36%
29	10	16	2	160	34%
30	10	16	2	160	33%
40	12	16	2	192	30%
50	15	16	2	240	30%
60	15	16	2	240	25%

a. Sample at least 25% of the trees at a site, examine a minimum of 16 samples (one-foot terminals) per tree, and inspect at least 120 total terminals.

From: D.L. Dahlsten, S.M. Tait, D.L. Rowney and B.J. Gingg. 1993. J. Arboriculture 19: 181-186.

An adult *Erynniopsis antennata* and two second instar elm leaf beetle larvae.

Two black second instar elm leaf beetle larvae killed by *Bacillus thuringiensis* and a healthy green larva.

Examine the leaves on each sample and record whether eggs are present or absent. Once you observe the first eggs on a sample, there is no need to examine it further; record it as infested and move on to inspect the next terminal. To determine the percent of samples (terminals) infested, divide the number of samples infested by the total number of samples inspected then multiply this by 100. Use this percent of terminals infested during the week of maximum percent infes-

tation to determine treatment need during the first or second elm leaf beetle generation as discussed above.

If a single foliar insecticide application is planned, spray at the peak density of early-instar larvae. In California, first-generation, early-instar larvae are most abundant at about the same time that mature larvae first appear, about 700 degree-days above 52°F accumulated from March 1. Second-generation early-instar larvae are most abundant at about about 2,000

degree-days. Because of field variation in development times and because beetles are not always abundant, inspect branch terminals weekly as this period approaches to confirm the need for, and exact timing of, treatment.

Bark Bands. Bark band elms by spraying a persistent insecticide with a hand pump sprayer or a hydraulic sprayer at low pressure. Spray an area of bark at least several feet wide encircling the trunk, around the first main branch crotch. Apply about one-half gallon of material at the rate labeled for elm bark beetle on each large tree. Larvae are killed when they contact the insecticide while crawling down to pupate around the tree base after feeding in the canopy. By reducing the number of larvae that pupate and emerge as adults, bark banding reduces damage by later beetle generations and their progeny.

Inspect foliage weekly from late April through June and band when mature larvae are first observed on leaves, before they begin to crawl down the trunk. Alternatively, monitor local temperatures and use a degree-day method to time the application in California. Spray at about 700 degree-days above 52°F accumulated since March 1, as discussed in the section on degree-days.

A single application of carbaryl to bark each spring can kill most beetle larvae that crawl over it all season long. If rain occurs after application, if trunks are wetted by sprinklers, or if a less persistent material like fluvalinate is used, regularly inspect around the base of trees throughout the season. If many beetles have changed from greenish prepupae (the stage killed by banding) to bright yellowish pupae (unaffected beetles), another application may be warranted.

Bark banding alone does not provide satisfactory control in many situ-

Adults, eggs, and larval chewing damage of the California willow leaf beetle, *Plagiodera californica*, which looks like the imported willow leaf beetle, *Plagiodera versicolora*. Black larval frass covers part of the chewed underside of the left willow leaf.

ations. Treatment of a single or few trees is unlikely to be as effective as banding all nearby trees in a neighborhood, because adult beetles can fly between treated and untreated trees. Not all beetles crawl down the trunk to pupate; some drop to the ground from branches or pupate in upper branch crotches or bark crevices. Because overwintering adults fly to the canopy and lay eggs, first-generation beetle populations or damage are not reduced by that season's banding. Study of Siberian elms (*Ulmus pumila*) in northern California found good control during the first season of banding, but beetles were not controlled during the first year on European elms, such as English elm and Scotch elm. This is because Siberian elms are less susceptible to elm leaf beetle and are not as seriously damaged by the first generation of beetles in comparison with European elms, which are often heavily damaged. Little or no control should be expected during the first year when banding the more susceptible species; banding all nearby elms over several consecutive years can provide control after the first year of treatment.

Narrow-Range Oil. Several low-toxicity insecticides are available to supplement banding during the first year or two of treatment or when early-season populations of elm leaf beetle are high. Narrow-range oil applied to foliage kills eggs and larvae; and oil may be applied in combination with Bt or another insecticide. Spray when early-instar larvae are most abundant. Consult *Managing Insects & Mites with Spray Oils* (UC Publication 3347) for details on effective oil use.

Bt. *Bacillus thuringiensis* (Bt) variety *tenebrionis* or *san diego* kills young beetle larvae. However, manufacturers' products vary in their effectiveness, and Bt products labeled for moth and butterfly caterpillars or mosquito larvae are not effective against elm leaf beetle. To obtain control, foliage must be thoroughly sprayed with an effective Bt during warm, dry weather when young larvae are actively feeding. Because only a portion of the beetle population is in the susceptible young larval stage at any one time, and Bt breaks down within a few days, several applications may be necessary beginning when young larvae are abundant. Bt can be applied in combination with oil.

Systemic Insecticides. Elm leaf beetle feeding can be controlled with injections or implants of systemic insecticides. Do not inject or implant trees more than once a year; injections and implants damage trees. For specific insecticide recommendations see *Insect Pest Management Guidelines for California Landscape Ornamentals* (UC Publication 3317).

Cottonwood Leaf Beetle *Chrysomela scripta*

The cottonwood leaf beetle feeds on cottonwood and willow. Several other similar *Altica, Calligrapha, Chrysomela,* or *Pyrrhalta* species throughout the U.S. also feed on alder, aspen, cottonwood, poplar, or willow. Adults are grayish or yellowish with variable black markings on the back. Females lay yellowish eggs in clusters of about 25 on the lower leaf surface. The young, black larvae feed in groups on the lower leaf surface. Mature larvae are yellowish, grayish, or reddish, often with rows of black tubercles. There are several generations a year.

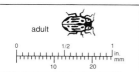

COTTONWOOD LEAF BEETLE

Provide regular, deep irrigation for hosts planted in areas with hot, dry summers. Vigorous host plants tolerate moderate leaf beetle feeding and control is generally not warranted. If populations are not tolerable, *Bacillus thuringiensis* variety *tenebrionis* or *san diego* and narrow-range oil provide control, as discussed above for elm leaf beetle. Make one or more applications if necessary when young larvae are abundant.

Klamathweed Beetle
Chrysolina quadrigemina

The Klamathweed beetle is one of several insects that was deliberately introduced into California during the 1940s to control *Hypericum perforatum,* a toxic rangeland weed. The beetle largely eliminated Klamathweed from several million acres and each year saves ranchers millions of dollars in otherwise lost grazing land and

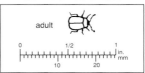

KLAMATHWEED BEETLE

adult

Klamathweed beetle adults are metallic dark brown to bluish green.

poisoned livestock. The ground cover *Hypericum calycinum,* which subsequently became a popular plant in landscapes, can be severely defoliated by this leaf beetle. The metallic bluish green to brown adults feed on foliage the year around, except during the hot, dry summer. Eggs are laid from fall through spring singly or in clusters on leaves where the grayish larvae feed. Larvae pupate just beneath the soil surface. Damage occurs during the spring when plants produce most of their growth flush.

Adult weevils characteristically chew irregular notches in leaf edges when they feed. Black vine weevil damaged this viburnum.

Insecticidal soap or another insecticide, applied when larvae or adults are feeding, can provide control. Removing litter accumulated beneath plants in hot areas may reduce the survival of adult beetles that rest there during the summer. Keeping soil beneath plants moist during the spring may increase disease and mortality of immature beetles that pupate near the soil surface. Applying parasitic nematodes to soil beneath plants, as discussed below for weevils, may provide control if applications are made when most beetles are pupating, before adults emerge. Pupation often occurs during April and May, but populations vary so monitor plants to determine when to treat; pupation occurs after mature larvae are observed on foliage.

WEEVILS

Many weevils, or snout beetles, family Curculionidae, feed on landscape plants. This is the most diverse group of beetles; over 1,000 species occur in California alone.

DAMAGE

Adult weevils generally feed on foliage. They cause leaves or flowers to appear notched or ragged, and leaves or needles may be clipped from twigs. This adult feeding is the primary damage caused by live oak weevils (*Deporaus glastinus*), pine needle weevils (*Scythropus* spp.), and Fuller rose beetle. Unless populations are high, this damage does not harm established woody plants and can be ignored. Larvae of *Otiorhynchus* species and whitefringed beetles, *Graphognathus* spp., can seriously damage roots and girdle plants near the soil surface, causing a general decline and death of young plants, such as rhododendron and yew. Larvae of the yucca weevil (*Scyphophorus yuccae*) tunnel in the base of green flowers and the heart of the plant and cause yuccas to decline.

IDENTIFICATION AND BIOLOGY

Adult weevils have the head elongated into a snout and have elbowed and clubbed antennae. Many weevils are flightless because their wing covers are fused. Females may feed for an extended period before laying eggs, and many species produce viable eggs without mating. Larvae of most species are whitish grubs that feed on roots and pupate in the soil. At least a dozen weevil species may damage woody ornamentals; black vine weevil, Fuller rose beetle, and conifer twig weevils are discussed here.

Black Vine Weevil
Otiorhynchus sulcatus

Adult black vine weevils feed on yew (*Taxus* spp.) and broadleaf evergreens such as azalea and rhododendron. Other hosts include euonymus, hemlock, liquidambar, and grape. Black vine weevil occurs throughout the U.S. and has one generation a year. In California, adults emerge from pupae in the soil and feed during the night from March through September. Larvae are the most damaging stage of this weevil, primarily in nurseries or on young landscape plants. Larvae feed on roots and bark near the soil surface. Most feeding and damage occurs in the spring. Even a few weevils or slight foliage damage may warrant control actions to prevent larvae from developing and causing damage to young plants; mature plants tolerate more extensive feeding.

An adult black vine weevil chewing a euonymus leaf edge.

A heathy black vine weevil pupa and larva (left) and two pupae and a larva infected with *Steinernema feltiae* nematodes (right).

Fuller Rose Beetle
Asynonychus godmani or *Pantomorus cervinus*

Fuller rose beetle is found in the southern and western states on many hosts including acacia, box elder, citrus, oak, photinia, *Rhaphiolepis*, rose, toyon, and *Prunus* and *Pyrus* species. These brown weevils lay their tiny eggs in organic matter on the soil or on branches, leaves, or fruit. The emerging larvae enter the soil and feed on roots for 6 to 10 months. Most adults emerge between June and November, but a few can emerge from pupae during each month of the year. The foliage- or blossom-feeding adults, not larvae on roots, are the damaging stage of this weevil, so low populations of adults can be ignored.

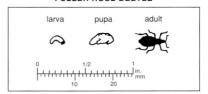

FULLER ROSE BEETLE

larva   pupa   adult

0   1/2   1 in.
                        mm
    10   20

Conifer Twig Weevils
Pissodes spp.

Conifer twig weevils feed on Douglas fir, fir, pine, and spruce throughout the U.S. Some species, such as the white pine weevil, *Pissodes strobi*, feed on shoots and needles both as larvae and adults and can severely distort terminals. Only the adults of other species, such as the Monterey pine weevil, *Pissodes radiatae*, feed on foliage; this foliage damage is minor. Monterey pine weevil larvae feed on roots and the trunk near the soil; this feeding can cause unsightly cankers on bark.

MONITORING

Regularly inspect the foliage, buds, and flowers of host plants for evidence of weevil feeding. Damage was likely caused by weevils if needles are clipped or notched or jagged-edged leaves are observed, but no slime trails from snails or slugs and no leaf-feeding caterpillars, katydids, or other insects are found on foliage. Monitor these plants as discussed below to determine whether adult weevils are present. Decide on the need for and timing of control actions based on the extent of observed damage and on the presence and abundance of adults. For species such as the Fuller rose beetle that are damaging only when adults are abundant, conduct control actions only if the apparent damage is intolerable or if it was high the previous season. For weevils such as *Otiorhynchus* species that cause damage primarily in the larval stage, even a few adults or low levels of foliage feeding warrant further investigation and possible control actions to prevent damage to young plants that tolerate relatively little damage to roots.

Several methods are available to determine if the night-feeding adult weevils are present. About 1 or 2 hours after dark, sweep foliage with a net or hold a tray, clipboard, or framed cloth beneath a branch and beat or shake it to dislodge any weevils. Sample several branches on each of several susceptible plants.

As an alternative to foliage sampling at night, adult *Otiorhynchus* weevils can be trapped by taking advantage of their need to seek shelter during the day. Burlap bands wrapped around trunks are an effective monitoring method in landscapes. Pitfall traps may be best in nurseries, but can also be useful in landscapes. Trap boards, though apparently a less effective method, can also be used.

Monitor weevils by banding trunks with a strip of burlap (approximately 3 by 4 feet) folded lengthwise several times, then wrapped snugly around the base of each plant. Once or twice a week, gently remove the trunk wrap, carefully unfold it, count and record the number of weevils, then dispose of them. Corrugated plastic tree wrap or corrugated cardboard with the smooth paper removed on one side may also be wrapped around trunks with the corrugated side placed against the bark.

Weevils may also be captured using a pitfall trap constructed from a several-inch-deep, wide-mouth plastic cup or dish and a funnel or smaller tapered cup. Cut off most of the funnel's spout or the bottom of the smaller cup and snugly insert it into the larger cup with the hole pointed down. A single plastic cup may be used if the sides are regularly lubricated with oil to prevent the beetles from climbing out. Bury your trap so its top is flush with, or slightly below, the soil surface (Figure 4-7). Drill

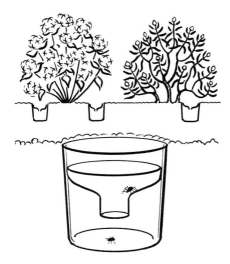

Figure 4-7. Pitfall traps can be used to monitor for adult weevils. These are constructed from a funnel or smaller cup fit inside a cup, then buried in the soil near plants so that beetles walking on the soil surface fall into them.

small holes in the bottom of the cup so that water can drain out. Alternatively, keep irrigation water out by covering each trap with an inverted gallon pot after first cutting legs into the rim. Bury one or more traps as close to the trunk as possible beneath the canopy of each of several host plants. Check each trap about weekly, and record the total number of weevils caught in all traps. Don't be surprised to find a variety of ground-dwelling creatures in your pitfall traps or trunk wraps, including beneficial predaceous carabid beetles. Release these predators as they help to control weevils.

Alternatively, small trap boards (about 10 by 10 inches) can be placed on the ground to attract adult black vine weevils and possibly other weevils in landscapes. Place one or more boards beneath each of several host plants. Inspect the underside of the trap boards and the ground beneath them during the day when beetles are resting.

MANAGEMENT

Plant less susceptible species to avoid weevil damage. Many rhododendron hybrids resist weevil damage (Table 4-8). Provide proper cultural care to keep plants vigorous and better able to tolerate damage. Many deciduous landscape plants are adapted to frequent summer rainfall and require regular irrigation when grown in dry-summer climates.

If plants have only one or a few trunks, flightless weevils such as the Fuller rose beetle and black vine weevil can be prevented from feeding on foliage by trimming branches that provide a bridge to other plants or the ground, then applying a 6-inch band of sticky material to trunks (see the Ants section). Persistent trapping year-round as discussed under monitoring may significantly reduce weevil populations in some situations.

Soil-dwelling immature weevils can be controlled with commercially available parasitic nematodes, *Heterorhabditis bacteriophora* (formerly *H. heliothidis*) or *Steinernema carpocapsae*, or by applying a broad-spectrum insecticide to soil as labeled. Apply nematodes (see References for suppliers) when weevil larvae or pupae are expected to be present. Apply nematodes in mid-summer to fall or before adults begin emerging in the spring; about mid-March for most weevil species in northern California. In hot areas, apply nematodes in the early morning or evening. Soil must be warm (at least 60°F) and moist (well irrigated) but not soggy before application and for 2 weeks afterwards. Irrigate it every 2 to 3 days for about 2 weeks after applying nematodes if needed.

A persistent insecticide may also be applied to foliage to control adults, but monitor weevil populations beginning early in the spring before spraying. If you can tolerate some foliage damage, do not spray until 4 or 5 weeks after first detecting feeding damage or weevils; few if any weevils will have laid eggs by then because snout beetles must feed for about a month before they start laying eggs. If adult feeding cannot be tolerated, spray about a week after first detecting adults or damage. The most effective time to make a single application to foliage is as soon as your regular sampling for adults indicates that weevil populations have peaked and begun to decline. If weevil emergence is prolonged, a second foliar spray may be warranted about 3 to 4 weeks after the first application. See *Insect Pest Management Guidelines for California Landscape Ornamentals* (UC Publication 3317) for specific insecticide recommendations.

TABLE 4-8

Hybrid Rhododendrons Resistant to Feeding Injury by Adult Root Weevils.[a]

RHODODENDRON HYBRID	RATING
P.J. Mezzitt	100
Jock	92
Sapphire	90
Rose Elf	89
Cilpimense	88
Lucky Strike	83
Exbury Naomi	81
Virginia Richards	81
Cowslip	80
Luscombei	80
Vanessa	80
Oceanlake	80
Dora Amateis	79
Crest	79
Rainbow	76
Point Defiance	76
Naomi	76
Pilgrim	76
Letty Edwards	76
Odee Wright	76
Moonstone	73
Lady Clementine Mitford	72
Candi	72
Graf Zeppelin	71
Snow Lady	71
Loderi Pink Diamond	71
Faggetter's Favourite	70

a. Ranked from highly (100 rating) to moderately resistant (70) to *Sciopithes obscures, Otiorhynchus sulcatus, O. singularis, Nemocestes incomptus,* and *Dyslobus* spp. From: A. L. Antonelli and R.L. Campbell. 1984. Root weevil control on rhododendrons. Wash. State Univ. Coop. Exten. Bull. 0970.

JAPANESE BEETLE
Popillia japonica

Japanese beetle, family Scarabaeidae, is established throughout the northeastern U.S. It has been found in California on several occasions, but was successfully eradicated in each case. Japanese beetle is primarily a pest of turf, but it attacks many different species including woody ornamentals such as American chestnut, apple, black walnut, crab apple, elm, grape, Japanese maple, linden, *Prunus* spp., and rose.

JAPANESE BEETLE

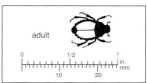

adult

DAMAGE

The most serious damage is caused by larvae feeding on roots of grasses and herbaceous species. Most damage to woody ornamentals is from adults feeding on foliage, flowers, and fruit. Adults chew out tissue between the veins, leaving a lacy skeleton of damaged leaves. Although this damage is unsightly, vigorous plants tolerate extensive defoliation. Beetles also congregate on individual fruit or blossoms, which they eat.

IDENTIFICATION AND BIOLOGY

Adult beetles are mostly a shiny, metallic green with coppery brown wing covers and tufts of short, whitish hairs along their sides. Larvae are plump, whitish grubs; it takes an expert to distinguish them from several other species of lawn-feeding beetle larvae.

In the northeastern United States, adults are present from about June through September; they lay eggs in moist soil or turf near where they feed on foliage, flowers, and fruit. Most of the life cycle is spent as larvae in soil. Larvae feed on small roots, mostly within about 2 inches of the soil surface; larvae can go several inches deeper, especially to overwinter as second or third instars. Larvae pupate underground, primarily during May and June, before emerging as adults. Females produce a sex pheromone, which attracts males. Adults tend to be active during warm, sunny weather, when they congregate on hosts to feed and mate.

MANAGEMENT

Established woody plants tolerate extensive defoliation and are unlikely to be seriously harmed by beetle feeding. Many varieties and species of woody ornamentals are rarely or not attacked. If you live in the eastern states where Japanese beetle is established, obtain information on nonhosts from a local Cooperative Extension office or a well-informed nursery person and consider planting these species. If you live in the western states, take suspected Japanese beetles to a Cooperative Extension or Department of Agriculture office; officials will take action to prevent this pest from becoming established.

The most effective control is against larvae in soil. A commercially available microbial insecticide, milky

Adult Japanese beetles are mostly shiny, metallic green with coppery brown wing covers and tufts of short, whitish hairs along the side. One beetle shown here has two white eggs of the tachinid parasite *Hyperecteina aldrichi* on its thorax. In the western United States, report suspected Japanese beetles to your County Department of Agriculture.

spore disease (*Bacillus popilliae*), can be applied to turf near trees and shrubs to infect and kill immature beetles before adults emerge. Some broad-spectrum insecticides are also effective, but unless a quicker kill of high populations is needed, it is better to use milky spore disease. It may take several years of annual treatment before milky disease provides good long-term control. However, this naturally occurring insect disease won't kill earthworms and other beneficial organisms in the soil and helps to conserve natural enemies, such as important *Tiphia* spp. parasitic wasps and other natural enemies that attack larval stages of Japanese beetle in the eastern states.

Parasitic nematodes are effective against immature Japanese beetles if applied to turf and to warm, moist soil around ornamentals, as discussed for weevil larvae. *Steinernema glaseri* and *Heterorhabditis bacteriophora* appear more effective against Japanese beetle than *Steinernema carpocapsae*. May or early June is probably the best time to apply nematodes; most Japanese beetles are then in the more susceptible late larval instar or pupal stages.

Commercially available traps designed for Japanese beetle can capture many adults, although the extent to which traps provide control is debatable. Suggested densities for reducing beetle populations range from one trap every 100 square feet to one trap per acre. If only one or a few traps are used, they should probably be located away from rather than near susceptible ornamentals. Traps do indicate when adult beetles are active so you know when to take action against them. Broad-spectrum, persistent foliar insecticides can be applied to protect foliage and flowers when adults are active, but this is generally not warranted on woody ornamentals unless they are of very

high aesthetic value, such as with rose blossoms. Broad-spectrum materials kill natural enemies, including a tachinid fly, *Hyperecteina aldrichi,* that attacks Japanese beetle adults. Spraying foliage may also cause outbreaks of other pests. Knocking or beating adults from branches onto a sheet or tray and disposing of them in a bucket of soapy water may provide control on shrubs or small trees if done daily during the cool morning from June through September. In infested areas, it is best to plan ahead and selectively control larvae in turf and soil around ornamentals before adults emerge.

ANTS

Ants, family Formicidae, are in the order Hymenoptera, along with bees and wasps. Many species of ants are important natural enemies of insect pests. A few species can tunnel in and damage woody plants. Ants are a pest in landscapes primarily when they feed on honeydew excreted by homopteran insects, including soft scales, mealybugs, whiteflies, and aphids. Ants protect these honeydew-producing insects from predators and parasites that might otherwise control them. Ants can also disrupt the biological control of some non-honeydew-producing pests, such as mites, armored scales, and certain gall-making cynipid wasp species, especially if these pests occur on the same plants as honeydew-producing species. Control honeydew-feeding ants and take other measures to enhance biological controls as discussed earlier in this chapter; populations of many pests, such as the homopteran species listed in Table 4-3, will gradually be reduced as natural enemies become more abundant.

IDENTIFICATION AND BIOLOGY

Ants are sometimes confused with termites. Ants have a narrow constriction between the thorax and abdomen, their antennae are distinctly elbowed, and winged ants have hindwings that are much shorter than the forewings. Termites have a broad waist, antennae that are not elbowed, and equal length wings (see Figure 4-8). Consult *A Key to Ants of California with Color Pictures* (UC Leaflet 21433) to identify common species.

Adult ants are divided into three social classes: winged males that occur only during the mating season, queens that spend most of their time in the nest laying eggs, and workers. Queens develop wings during the brief mating season, which is usually the only time they and the males are observed, often in large swarms outside of the nest. Most ants are wingless workers that spend their time foraging for food outside the nest or caring for the tiny, pale, grublike immatures in the nest. Most ants nest underground or beneath rocks, buildings, or other objects, where the tiny, elliptical eggs are laid.

MANAGEMENT

Inspect trees and shrubs for ants in spring, when honeydew-producing insects such as aphids appear. If ants descending from infested plants have swollen, almost translucent abdomens, this identifies them as honeydew-collecting species. Deny ants access to plant canopies by pruning branches that provide a bridge between buildings, other plants, or the ground, and by applying sticky material (for example, Tanglefoot or Stickem) to trunks. Applying a mixture of sticky material and copper sulfate (such as Stickem Green) prevents brown garden snails as well as ants and flightless weevils from climbing trunks.

Increase the persistence of sticky material by applying it higher above the ground, which reduces dust and dirt contamination and decreases sprinkler wash-off. Check the sticky material every one or two weeks and stir it with a stick to prevent the surface from becoming clogged with debris that allows ants to cross. Do not apply sticky material directly to the bark of young or thin-barked plants or plants that have recently

Argentine ants collecting poison bait from an ant stake.

been severely pruned; the material may have phytotoxic effects. Wrap the trunk with a strip of fabric tree wrap, duct tape, or another material and apply the sticky material to it to prevent damage to bark. Periodically remove and relocate any wrap to minimize injury to bark.

Enclosed pesticide baits, such as ant stakes, may be placed near nests or on ant trails beneath plants. Pesticide baits act slowly, but can be more effective than sprays because ants carry the pesticide back to their underground nests where reproductive queens are killed. For the most effective and economical ant control, treat in the late winter or early spring when ant populations are low. Periodic moistening and stirring of certain baits may improve their attractiveness to ants.

Argentine Ant
Iridomyrmex humilis

The Argentine ant is a common honeydew-feeding species in California and the southern states. The small workers are uniformly dark brown and travel in characteristic trails on bark or the ground. Argentine ants nest in soil and can quickly relocate nests in response to changes in food

and weather. Colony size varies, often numbering in the thousands. Unlike many social hymenopterans that have only one queen per nest, each Argentine ant colony may have many queens that contribute to this species' high reproductive capability. The winged reproductive males and females are about twice as long as workers and are rarely observed above ground, except sometimes in the spring. Argentine ant populations increase greatly in mid-summer and early fall. Apply sticky material or baits beginning in late winter or early spring, before ants and the pests they tend become abundant.

Carpenter Ants
Camponotus spp.

Carpenter ants nest underground or in wood, sometimes in structures or the interior of living trees. Carpenter ants do not eat wood, but their tunneling weakens limbs, which may drop. Carpenter ants feed on insects, honeydew, and plant sap. Columns of these relatively large, black or dark reddish ants may be observed foraging from nests. Wood borings may also accumulate beneath nest entrances.

Help prevent carpenter ants and termites from attacking trees by providing plants with proper cultural care. Prune plants properly when needed and prevent injuries to trunks and limbs as detailed in Chapter 3.

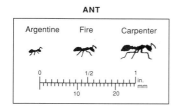

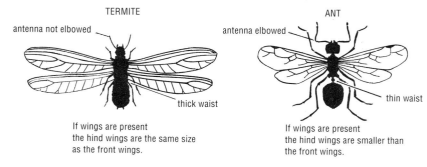

TERMITE

antenna not elbowed

thick waist

If wings are present the hind wings are the same size as the front wings.

ANT

antenna elbowed

thin waist

If wings are present the hind wings are smaller than the front wings.

Figure 4-8. Ants are distinguished from termites by their narrow waist, elbowed antennae, and if wings are present, by hindwings that are much shorter than the forewings.

Prenolepis imparis ants tending woolly aphids on shamel ash.

Fire Ants
Solenopsis spp.

Several *Solenopsis* species in the southern and western U.S. are important predators of insects; most species rarely injure plants. However, some ants, such as the southern or California fire ant, *Solenopsis xyloni*, nest in mounds around trees and shrubs and can inflict painful bites or stings on people and pets. The southern fire ant also girdles and kills young trees by feeding on bark. If fire ants nest in landscapes, consider thoroughly spraying an insecticide to run off around the lower trunk and trunk-soil interface or applying insecticide baits according to label directions.

APHIDS

Aphids, family Aphididae, are small, soft-bodied insects that suck plant juices. Over 200 species are occasional or frequent pests of landscape or agricultural plants.

DAMAGE

Feeding by high aphid populations can slow plant growth or cause leaves to yellow, curl, or drop early. Some species distort stems or fruit or cause galls on roots, leaves, or stems. Aphids are important pests of many annual crops because they transmit some viruses that cause plant diseases, but this is usually not a problem in landscape trees and shrubs.

Landscape plants commonly tolerate extensive feeding by aphids, and established woody plants are not killed by them. The whitish cast skins aphids produce may be unsightly, but the most bothersome aspect of aphids in landscapes is the honeydew they produce. Honeydew is sugary water excreted by many homopterans that ingest sap. It is harmless to plants, except if it becomes so abundant that black sooty mold grows on it, reducing light reaching foliage to the extent that it slows plant growth. Copious honeydew and sooty mold create a sticky and unsightly mess on trees, sidewalks, automobiles, and other surfaces beneath the plant.

IDENTIFICATION AND BIOLOGY

Aphids often feed in dense groups on leaves or stems and do not rapidly disperse when disturbed. Adults are usually 1/8 inch or less in length and are pear-shaped with long legs and antennae. They vary from green, yellow, white, brown, or red to black. Some species, such as the woolly aphids, are covered with a waxy, white to grayish coating. Adult aphids may be winged or wingless. A pair of tubelike projections (called cornicles) near the hind end of the body distinguishes most aphids from other insects.

During warm weather, aphids may go through a complete generation in less than 2 weeks. The outgrown and shed aphid skins from successive molts may dot foliage as small white

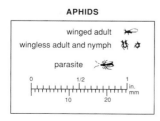

Shiny, sticky honeydew coats these flowering plum leaves infested with the waterlily aphid, *Rhopalosiphum nymphaeae*.

Blackish sooty mold on California bay infested with California laurel aphids.

flecks, often persisting long after aphids have left the plant. There are many generations per year and populations can increase rapidly, especially under conditions of moderate temperatures. Extreme temperatures may retard aphid growth and reproduction. Throughout most of the year, adult aphids (either winged or wingless) give birth to live young without mating (Figure 4-1). Aphids may produce overwintering eggs, especially in locations with cold winters.

Common Host-Specific Aphids. Although many aphids look similar, most species on woody landscape plants feed on only one or several closely related plant species and cannot spread to nearby plants of another species. These include the tuliptree aphid (*Illinoia liriodendri*), Norway maple aphid (*Periphyllus lyropictus*), linden aphid (*Eucallipterus tiliae*), and birch aphids, such as *Callipterinella calliptera*, *Betulaphis brevipilosa*, and *Euceraphis betulae*. The rose aphid, *Macrosiphum rosae*, may spend part of the summer on nearby herbaceous plants, but usually occurs on roses whenever succulent tissue is present.

Melon or Cotton Aphid
Aphis gossypii

The melon or cotton aphid feeds on many different plants, including apple, camellia, crape myrtle, euonymus, *Prunus*, and willow. It feeds and reproduces all year long in areas of California with mild winters where hosts are available. Melon aphids are commonly blackish or dark green, but pale yellow to whitish forms also occur.

Bean Aphid
Aphis fabae

Hosts of the bean aphid include elderberry, euonymus, jacaranda, pyracantha, and viburnum. Aphids are dark olive green to black with black appendages. As with melon aphid, they can occur in dense colonies, sometimes with both green and black individuals.

Green Peach Aphid
Myzus persicae

The green peach aphid is one of the most common species nationwide. It is green, yellow, or reddish, with black on the top of the head and thorax of winged adults. It feeds on a large variety of woody and herbaceous landscape plants, including *Prunus* species such as flowering plum. Because succulent foliage on some of its host plants is available the year around in mild winter areas, this insect can have up to two dozen generations a year, and overwintering eggs are produced only in cold-winter areas.

Giant Conifer Aphids
Cinara spp.

Giant conifer aphids commonly occur on fir, pine, and spruce. They are among the largest aphids, up to ⅕ inch long; at first glance they are sometimes mistaken for ticks. Giant conifer aphids have especially long legs and occur individually or in large colonies on foliage and bark. The purplish or black body may be covered with gray powder. Colonies on deodar cedar often infest only a single limb. These aphids may shift their

Melon or cotton aphids are smaller than many other aphid species. They are commonly green to blackish, but pale yellow to whitish forms also occur.

Giant conifer aphids are among the largest aphids and at first glance they are sometimes mistaken for ticks. This bow-legged fir aphid, *Cinara curvipes*, occurs on fir, spruce, and deodar cedar, often in large colonies.

bodies in unison when disturbed, apparently in response to an alarm pheromone they secrete. There are several dozen *Cinara* species and each species is specific to one or a few conifer species, but more than one aphid species may occur on the same plant. Giant conifer aphids give birth to live nymphs the year around in mild winter climates, but overwinter as eggs where winters are severe.

GIANT CONIFER APHID

adult

0   1/2   1
┝┷┷┷┷┷┷┷┷┷┷┷┷┷┷┷┷┷┥ in.
      10   20   mm

This gall on a poplar leaf petiole has been opened to reveal the waxy, grayish poplar gall aphids inside.

The manzanita leaf gall aphid, *Tamalia coweni*, caused these leaves to swell into harmless pod-shaped galls. This aphid feeds only on manzanita and is prevalent on new growth, such as that stimulated by frequent irrigation and shearing plants.

Crapemyrtle Aphid
Sarucallis or *Tinocallis* *kahawaluokalani*

The crapemyrtle aphid is occasionally so abundant on crape myrtle that plants may be defoliated. This aphid is mostly yellowish green, except for winged adults that have distinctive black marks on the abdomen, wings, and tips of the antennae.

Poplar Gall Aphids
Pemphigus spp.

Several aphids cause apparently harmless galls on cottonwood or poplar leaves. Their biology and damage are similar to the lettuce root gall aphid, *Pemphigus bursarius*, in California. Feeding by this aphid on poplar trees stimulates plant tissue to form a hollow gall around the aphid. The enclosed aphid gives birth to about 100 to 250 waxy, grayish nymphs, many of which develop wings and migrate up to several miles. Alternate hosts are mostly in the family Compositae, such as lettuce (*Lactuca* spp.), where it can be a serious pest, and related weeds. These aphids feed on the roots of their alternate hosts, then in the fall fly back to poplars where males are produced prior to mating and the laying of overwintering eggs.

Woolly Aphids

Woolly aphids cover themselves with white waxy material similar to that secreted by some adelgids and mealybugs. Some species feed in groups and cause gall-like swellings on bark or curled leaves. The woolly apple aphid, *Eriosoma lanigerum,* occurs on apple, cotoneaster, hawthorn, and pyracantha leaves and bark and sometimes causes gall-like swellings on bark. Woolly apple aphid and some other *Eriosoma* species also cause bark swellings on elm. The life cycles of most woolly aphids are poorly known. Some species move among plant species. For example, the ash leaf curl aphid or woolly ash aphid, *Prociphilus californicus,* apparently alternates between conifers and ash trees. The same species of aphid may look different depending on the host, season, and part of the plant it is feeding on. Some species feed on roots, especially during the winter, making them difficult to study.

Woolly apple aphids produced the white waxy material on this pyracantha stem. Bean aphids, both black and green forms, infest the plant tips.

THRESHOLDS

No thresholds have been established for aphid numbers in landscapes. Because of the large amounts of honeydew they can produce, aphids frequently become bothersome at levels too low to have any noticeable affect on the plant. Tolerance for honeydew varies among people and according to the species and location of plants. You can establish approximate action thresholds by monitoring aphids or honeydew, then comparing your results to when aphids or honeydew become a problem. Sample during subsequent seasons and take action if aphids or honeydew approach this previously bothersome level.

MONITORING

Monitor aphids by visually inspecting 5 to 10 or more leaves, new growth tips, or one-foot branch terminals on each of several plants. Aphids commonly occur on the lower leaf surface; clipping leaves may facilitate their inspection. Begin monitoring before aphids typically become a problem, usually in the spring. Record the number of aphids, parasitized aphids, and predators on each sample. Inspect foliage every 1 or 2 weeks in the spring and early summer. Estimate insect densities by separately totaling the number of aphids and natural enemies and dividing by the number of samples inspected.

Honeydew Monitoring. Honeydew production, not insects on leaves, is the primary problem with aphids. Monitoring honeydew provides a more direct measure of damage than counting insects and may require less time. Honeydew can be efficiently monitored using yellow water-sensitive paper or cards. These cards are often used for monitoring insecticide droplets and calibrating sprayers and produce distinct blue dots upon contact with honeydew (see Suppliers). Attach the cards to a stiff background and place the cards beneath plants. Cards can be suspended several inches beneath branches of trees using a bent wire coat hanger.

Begin monitoring before honeydew typically becomes a problem, usually in the spring. Use four cards per plant, one beneath the lower, outer canopy of each quadrant. Monitor several plants that have had honey-

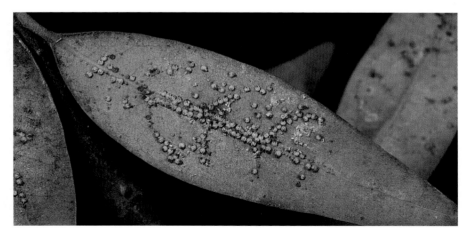

These round, gray California laurel aphids, *Euthoracaphis umbellulariae,* are sometimes mistaken for immature whiteflies or scale insects. They occur on the underside of California bay, often in rows along veins. Camphor tree and sassafras are occasionally infested. Even high populations apparently do not harm trees and can be ignored.

dew problems. Place the monitors beneath plants for the same period about once each week, such as from 11 a.m. to 3 p.m. on a day of typical weather when no rain or irrigation is anticipated. Handle the cards with forceps or gloves because they will change color from the moisture in your skin.

Determine the average honeydew density on each card by counting the total number of drops and dividing by the area of each card (Card area = Length in inches x Card width). For tuliptrees distinguish between aphid-produced honeydew and much larger droplets that may drip from the blossoms in the spring. Determine the overall average by adding up the average density from each card and dividing this sum by the total number of cards. Use a form such as Figure 4-9 to record your data and make your calculations. When honeydew becomes intolerable, note the average droplet density measured during that week and during previous weeks. Monitor honeydew next season and take control action if honeydew density approaches the level that you pre-

viously found to be intolerable.

Instead of counting each drop, you can estimate honeydew density by visually comparing each card to reference cards with a range of droplet densities previously determined. Record the average that appears closest to each of your monitoring cards. Add up all of these averages and divide the sum by the total number of cards to estimate the overall average honeydew density.

MANAGEMENT

Many natural enemies help to control aphids, but these predators and parasites may not always appear in sufficient numbers until after aphids become abundant. However, their preservation is an essential part of a long-term integrated pest management program for aphids. If aphids or honeydew cannot be tolerated and insecticide applications are deemed necessary, choose materials that are least toxic to natural enemies. Treat only in spots where aphids are most abundant to preserve natural enemies elsewhere. Insecticidal soap and narrow-range oil kill aphids and other

insects on contact. In comparison to other materials (Table 4-6), they have low residual toxicity to natural enemies that move onto plants after sprayings. Use baits or sticky barriers to control honeydew-seeking ants because ants can disrupt biological controls by protecting aphids from their natural enemies. A forceful stream of water dislodges aphids from plants, and many of these will die. Wash plants early in the day so they dry before night.

Biological Controls. Lady beetle larvae and adults and the larvae of lacewings and many syrphid and midge flies are common aphid predators. Many small wasps, including *Aphelinus, Aphidius, Ephedrus, Praon,* and *Trioxys* species, are also important aphid natural enemies. These parasites reproduce by laying their eggs in aphids. The immature wasp feeds inside and kills its host, causing the aphid to "mummify" or become slightly puffy and turn tan or black. A round hole can be observed where the adult parasite has chewed its way out of the aphid mummy (see Figure 4-5). As an example, *Aphelinus mali* is a tiny wasp that often causes populations of the woolly apple aphid to crash.

Many aphid predators and parasites are aided in their search for aphids by the presence of honeydew, which attracts them and also provides a food source. Plant nectar-producing flowers to further increase the food supply for adult lacewings, parasitic wasps, and syrphid flies. Avoid using persistent, broad-spectrum, contact insecticides. These provide only temporary aphid control and are likely to kill more of the active natural enemies in comparison with the more sessile aphids; aphid populations may resurge after an application and become more of a problem than before they were sprayed. Control

PLANT SPECIES __Tulip Tree__   MONITORING DATE __6 June 93_____

MONITORING TIME __11am-3pm__ PERSON MONITORING __Jan Doe_____

Area of each monitoring card = length x width = __3 x 2 = 6 sq. inches_____

Tree Location	Card Quadrant (or No.)	Total Drops	Card Area	Total Drops / Card Area =	Average for Each Card
4th & Main	E	68	6		11.3
	N	49	6		8.2
	W	71	6		11.8
	S	92	6		15.3
				Sum of Averages	46.6

Number of cards __4__   Sum of averages / Number of cards = Overall average = __11.7 drops/sq. in.__

Figure 4-9. Example of a honeydew monitoring record form for one tree. An actual record-keeping form should include space for more than one tree.

ants, which may prevent predators and parasites from controlling pests.

Aphids are very susceptible to fungal disease when it is humid. Look for dead aphids that have turned reddish or brown and have a fuzzy, shriveled texture unlike the smooth, bloated mummies formed when aphids are parasitized. Fungus-killed aphids sometimes have fine, whitish mycelium growing over their surfaces.

Resident natural enemies frequently provide sufficient biological control. Some managers supplement these populations on small plants by releasing commercially available aphid predators; there is little information on their effectiveness, and conserving resident beneficials is likely to be more effective and economical than releasing purchased species.

The convergent lady beetle, *Hippodamia convergens*, is commonly sold for release to control aphids (see Suppliers). Although resident lady beetles are important predators, the commercial *Hippodamia* are collected in the Sierra Nevada where they overwinter in large aggregations. After overwintering, beetles inherently fly and most will soon leave the site where they are released, even if food is plentiful.

Releasing sufficient numbers of lady beetles may temporarily reduce aphid numbers on small plants; there is no research-based information on how many beetles to release and how often. Purchased lady beetles are often thirsty; spraying them with sugar water before release may increase their survival. If beetles are stored in the refrigerator (don't freeze them) and some are released periodically, warm beetles weekly to room temperature and feed them sugar water. Wetting plants first, and releasing beetles on the ground near the trunk and under plants in the late evening when it's cooler, may reduce beetle dispersal.

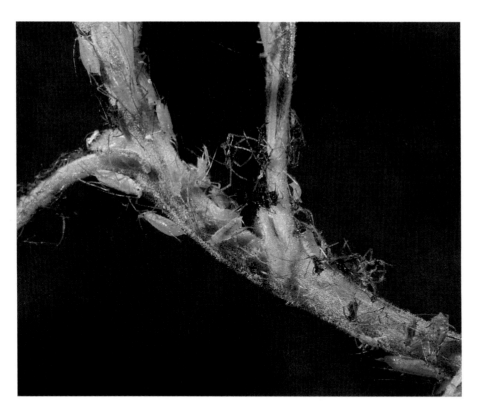

Orange gall midge larvae, *Aphidoletes* sp., are feeding on willow aphids, *Chaitophorus* sp.; the black, shriveled aphids have already been consumed.

In a futile effort to repel the *Metasyrphus* sp. syrphid larva grasping it, a rose aphid is secreting a droplet of noxious liquid from its cornicle. See the Predaceous Flies section earlier in this chapter for an adult photograph.

A convergent lady beetle, *Hippodamia convergens*, eating a green peach aphid. This aphid predator is named for the two converging white bars behind the adult's head; individuals vary in the number of black spots and some have no spots.

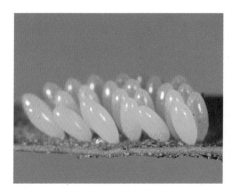

Convergent lady beetles lay their oblong, orangish eggs on their ends in a group.

CONVERGENT LADY BEETLE

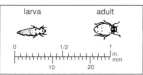

larva   adult

0   1/2   1 in.
mm
10   20

The ashy gray lady beetle, *Olla v-nigrum* or *O. abdominalis*, is an important aphid predator. Here it's feeding on the black eggs of a sumac psyllid, *Calophya californica*, infesting sugarbush.

An orange convergent lady beetle pupa and several larvae among whitish cast skins of aphids.

Green lacewings, *Chrysoperla* (or *Chrysopa*) *carnea* and *Chrysoperla rufilabris,* can be purchased as oblong, green to grayish eggs or as tiny alligatorlike larvae (see Suppliers). Lacewing larvae are effective aphid predators, but it takes practice and imagination to distribute sufficient numbers of predators in plants. Holding eggs at room temperature until the larvae begin hatching, then sprinkling them on plants, may be most effective. Releasing prefed lacewing larvae may be more effective than using eggs.

Insufficient research has been conducted to allow specific release recommendations. Predators are more likely to be effective if several releases are made at about weekly intervals beginning when aphid populations are still low. Foliage should be dry so that lacewings don't get stuck and drown in water droplets. High aphid populations can be reduced with a nonpersistent insecticide, such as horticultural oil or soap, followed by predator introductions the next day. Control aphid-tending ants as they prey on released predators. Green lacewing adults tend to disperse before laying eggs, so only the insects you release as eggs or larvae, and not their progeny, are likely to provide any control. See the section earlier in this chapter on effectively releasing natural enemies.

Cultural and Physical Controls.
Populations of most aphids are highest on plant parts with high nitrogen levels, such as new growth or foliage that will soon drop. High levels of nitrogen fertilizer also favor aphid reproduction. Never apply more nitrogen than necessary and use slow-release materials.

Severe infestations on only a portion of the plant may be pruned out and disposed of. Pruning is especially appropriate for *Cinara* species if they are infesting only a few branches, or for gall-making species. Thinning especially dense inner tree canopy foliage may lower aphid numbers, but may also stimulate new growth flushes, which aphids favor.

Insecticides. Narrow-range oil and insecticidal soap provide temporary control if applied to thoroughly cover infested foliage. They provide no residual control, so applications may need to be repeated. Because aphid predators and parasites often become abundant only after aphids are numerous, applying nonpersistent insecticides like soap or oil may provide more effective long-term control because they do not kill natural enemies that migrate in after the spray. These and other insecticides with only contact activity are generally ineffective in preventing damage from aphids that gall or distort foliage.

Oil applied during the delayed dormant season kills overwintering aphid eggs and may require a smaller volume of spray than treating leafy plants. If aphids were a problem the previous season and the pest species is known to overwinter as eggs on bark rather than on alternate hosts, apply narrow-range oil after buds have swollen but before they burst into leaf.

Several organophosphate, carbamate, pyrethroid, and other broad-spectrum insecticides can be applied to foliage to control aphids. However, these can reduce long-term control by killing natural enemies. Some insecticides are ineffective because populations of some species, such as the green peach aphid, have developed resistance to them. Systemic insecticides applied by implants or injection may control aphids without directly affecting natural enemies. Injections or implants avoid the environmental contamination of sprays, but are expensive and damage trunks or roots. Do not inject or implant

Aphid mummies, the crusty skins of aphids killed by parasitic wasps, are commonly tan or black. Round holes are chewed by the adult wasp that emerges after consuming the aphid and pupating inside.

Rose aphids vary in color from green to red. However, the orangish, fuzzy aphids seen here have been killed by a naturally occurring fungal disease.

trees more than once a year. For specific insecticide recommendations see *Insect Pest Management Guidelines for California Landscape Ornamentals* (UC Publication 3317).

ADELGIDS

Adelgids, family Adelgidae, are small aphidlike insects that suck plant juices. They feed only on conifers, including Douglas fir, fir, hemlock, larch, pine, and spruce. There are about 14 adelgid species in the U.S. in two genera, *Pineus* and *Adelges*.

DAMAGE

Adelgids cause white cottony tufts on the bark, branches, twigs, needles, or cones of their host plants. Cone-shaped galls or swollen twigs may also appear on infested spruce or fir. High adelgid populations cause yellowing and early drop of needles and the drooping and dieback of terminals. The galls on spruce can be unsightly, but are unlikely to seriously harm trees. High populations of the non-gall-forming stages can retard or kill trees, although vigorous plants tolerate moderate adelgid populations.

IDENTIFICATION AND BIOLOGY

Most adelgid species alternate generations between two different conifers. Adelgids commonly form galls on spruce, which are considered the primary host on which these insects undergo sexual reproduction and overwinter. Pines are the alternate host for *Pineus* species, and *Adelges* species feed on Douglas fir, fir, hemlock, or larch as their alternate host. Adelgids on their alternate hosts are recognized by the cottony white or grayish material secreted by colonies of females on the trunk, limbs, cones, twigs, or needles. Heavily infested trees may seem covered with snow. The adelgids themselves are beneath this material and are small, dark, soft-bodied insects, somewhat pear-shaped like aphids.

Most adelgids have a complex life history similar to that for the species detailed below. The conifer species serving as the primary or secondary host is not known for all adelgids,

and some populations apparently don't migrate between hosts. The insects can look different depending on the host, and each species typically has several different kinds of egg-laying adults. Most species overwinter as eggs under cottony masses or as early-stage immatures under bark or bud scales.

Cooley Spruce Gall Adelgid
Adelges cooleyi

The Cooley spruce gall adelgid occurs throughout the U.S. It alternates generations between spruce and Douglas fir. Nymphs on spruce overwinter

The pine needle adelgid secretes a whitish, waxy material and causes stunting of pine needles.

Pine bark adelgids produce a whitish gray material on pine bark.

under buds or bark. These move to the base of needles in the spring and begin to suck plant juices. This initiates the formation of a gall, which eventually encloses the insects. The galls are from ½ to 3 inches long, and are light green to purple. About midsummer, the nymphs emerge and molt into winged adults. The now-empty galls harden, turn brown, and may persist for years. Galls on spruce in California are seldom seen, except along the north coast or in mountainous areas.

The emerged adults feed and reproduce on spruce, or migrate to Douglas fir. Adults that migrate settle on needles, shoots, or cones. They give birth to wingless nymphs and produce white cottony tufts. This generation overwinters on Douglas fir and can damage trees in the spring when feeding resumes and high populations cause needles to become distorted, spotted, and drop prematurely. Some of these adelgids develop wings and migrate back to spruce. There the migrants produce males and females that mate, and the females lay eggs. Feeding by the ensuing nymphs causes galls to form, and the insect's two-year life cycle begins over.

Pine Bark Adelgids
Pineus spp.

The pine bark adelgid, *Pineus strobi* (also called the pine bark aphid), and two similar but less common species, *P. pinifoliae* (the pine leaf adelgid) and *P. similis* occur throughout the U.S. Most pine bark adelgids form harmless but sometimes unsightly galls on spruce. Their alternate hosts are pine, or pine and spruce in the case of *P. pinifoliae*. Adult females are purplish black, soft-bodied insects. Females and yellowish pink masses of eggs occur in cottony, wax-covered

colonies on pine. Crawlers resemble tiny pepper grains on the cottony egg masses. The adelgids overwinter as eggs and have several generations a year.

MANAGEMENT

Adelgid galls on spruce are usually harmless and can be ignored unless the trees are young or galls become very abundant. To restore the plant's aesthetic quality and provide some control, clip and dispose of infested foliage when the galls are green and before the insects have emerged. Avoid excess fertilization and quick-release formulations, which can promote adelgid populations. Replace some spruce with other tree species to reduce adelgid populations that alternate hosts.

Many predators feed on adelgids, including several species of small dark lady beetles, lacewings, and the maggotlike larvae of some small flies in the Cecidomyiidae and Chamaemyiidae families. Predators are especially important in natural forests, where most adelgids are uncommon. Except for the balsam woolly adelgid, *Adelges piceae*, a serious pest of fir in the Northwest and Northeast, there has been little research on adelgid natural enemies, especially in landscapes.

A forceful stream of water directed at the cottony masses on conifers, especially on trunks, dislodges and kills many adelgids. High populations, especially on young trees, can be controlled by applying narrow-range oil or another broad-spectrum insecticide in the spring when crawlers are abundant. Oil may cause spruce foliage to change color, and carbaryl can cause an increase in mite populations unless a miticide is added. Insecticides are more effective when a wetting agent is added and applications are made with high-pressure equipment so that the spray pen-

etrates the insects' waxy secretions. For specific insecticide recommendations see *Insect Pest Management Guidelines for California Landscape Ornamentals* (UC Publication 3317).

PSYLLIDS

Psyllids, family Psyllidae, resemble miniature cicadas and are sometimes called jumping plantlice. Over 100 species occur on both native and introduced landscape plants in the U.S., but each kind of psyllid feeds on only one plant or closely related species. For example, the boxwood psyllid, *Psylla buxi*, occurs only on boxwood, causing terminal leaves to become cupped. About a dozen species of *Pachypsylla* occur only on hackberry, and more *Psylla* species occur on willow than any other host.

DAMAGE

Psyllids suck plant juices. Some secrete a white wax and all produce honeydew, sometimes in pelletized or crystallized form, on which blackish sooty mold may grow. High populations reduce plant growth or cause terminals to distort, discolor, or die back. A few species cause galls on leaves or buds. Many native shrubs planted as ornamentals, such as manzanita and sugar bush or lemonade berry, can host native psyllid species. These are hardly ever problems and even if psyllids are abundant, most plants tolerate extensive psyllid feeding. However, several introduced plants support exotic psyllids that can be pests.

IDENTIFICATION AND BIOLOGY

Adults hold their wings rooflike over their bodies, and at maturity are ⅒ to ⅕ inch long. They are related to aphids, but psyllids have strong jumping legs and longer antennae. Don't confuse psyllids with similar looking psocids, which feed on fungi, including sooty mold growing on psyllid honeydew. Mature psyllids commonly jump when disturbed, while psocids run or fly away. Unlike psyllids, psocids have a distinctly swollen, bulbous area in front of the head between the widely spaced antennae, which can be distinguished with a hand lens. Psocids also lack sucking mouthparts and do not damage plants.

Psyllids on deciduous trees overwinter as eggs or young nymphs in or around bud scales. Nymphs emerge in the spring and feed on developing buds, flowers, and new leaves. On evergreen plants in mild-climate areas, all stages may be found year-round. Populations are usually highest when new plant growth is abundant, but high temperatures may reduce populations of some species.

MONITORING

Because psyllid damage is primarily aesthetic, tolerance varies among people and with the species and location of plants. Set thresholds appropriate to your local situation by monitoring insect populations and recording when psyllids become a problem. During subsequent seasons, take control action if populations or damage approach the levels that you previously found to be intolerable. Keep in mind that foliar damage is caused primarily by nymphs. However, for effective treatment timing, you must monitor adults and spray to kill eggs or newly hatched nymphs before damage occurs. Therefore, you must base your decision on the adult populations occurring several weeks before damage became intolerable. You may discover an annual cycle to psyllid abundance; population increases are typically associated with the availability of tender new growth.

Monitor psyllids by visually inspecting and counting the insects on 4 to 8 or more leaves, new growth tips, or branch terminals on each of several plants. Leaves should be of the same age at each sampling. Use a hand lens or microscope and clip samples to facilitate their inspection. Because counting the small immature psyllids is tedious, sampling adults is an efficient alternative.

Adult psyllids are easily monitored with yellow sticky traps or by beating branches to dislodge them. Branch beat monitoring, as discussed earlier in this chapter, may be best for some species like acacia psyllid, because it allows important predators to also be monitored. When using beat samples, count and record separately the number of adult (winged) psyllids and psyllid-feeding predators that are dislodged. Be sure that you distinguish psyllids from psocids as discussed above. Sample every 1 or 2 weeks beginning before psyllids become a problem, typically in the spring. Sample until plants stop producing new flush and populations decline.

MANAGEMENT

Reduce irrigation and avoid fertilizing plants when new growth is occurring. Reducing water and nutrients discourages excessive flush of succulent foliage that promotes increased psyllid populations. Minimize shearing or trimming terminals to provide a smooth, dense canopy surface for ornamental purposes as shearing stimulates new growth preferred by psyllids.

Lady beetles, lacewing larvae, small predaceous bugs, and parasitic wasps are important in controlling psyllids,

An adult psocid (on top) has longer antennae, a more narrow "neck" or separation between head and thorax, and chewing mouthparts (not visible here) in comparison with adult psyllids, which have tubular, sucking mouthparts. Psocids, which do not damage plants, may be confused with adult psyllids, such as the acacia psyllid shown below it. See Minute Pirate Bug section for an acacia psyllid nymph photograph.

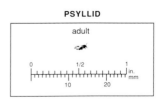

PSYLLID

adult

and University researchers are introducing new beneficial species that attack psyllids that are currently pests. Because beneficials often do not become abundant until after psyllids are common and weather has warmed, supplemental control may be desirable, even for those species with effective natural enemies.

Psyllids are difficult to control effectively with sprays because most species reproduce all year and have many annual generations. Systemic insecticides or pyrethroids can kill the highest percentage, but applications must be repeated, have negative effects on natural enemies, and may stimulate plant growth that favors psyllids. If psyllids are too abundant to tolerate, narrow-range oil or insecticidal soap applied to foliage gives adequate short-term control of many species. The low residual toxicity of soap or oil does not kill natural enemies that migrate in after plants have been sprayed, but the application may need to be repeated in several weeks if populations rebound.

Time applications to kill eggs and young nymphs before foliage is damaged; monitor when adults become active and treat soon after a sharp increase in adult numbers is observed in sticky traps or beat samples. Continue monitoring after treatment. If predators as well as psyllids become abundant, delay reapplication and monitor again later to determine if populations have declined and spraying can be avoided.

Spraying for psyllids, unless done frequently, may not greatly reduce foliage damage. Sprayed plants may tend to grow more, and this new flush is the most susceptible to damage by any psyllids that survive the spray or migrate in from untreated plants. No treatment restores damaged foliage; it remains distorted until trimmed or replaced by new growth.

Acacia Psyllid
Acizzia or
Psylla uncatoides

Acacia psyllid was accidentally introduced from Australia or New Zealand in the 1950s and occurs in Arizona, California, and Hawaii. The small adults are mostly green or brownish. They often appear darker during cooler weather. The tiny eggs and the orange to green, flattened nymphs are found primarily on growing tips, new leaves, or flower buds. Psyllids are most abundant in the spring when temperatures warm and host plants produce new growth flushes. All stages and reproduction occur throughout the year.

Avoid planting susceptible acacia species (see Table 4-9) and consider replacing problem acacias. Acacia psyllid is often kept under control by natural enemies, including a small black lady beetle, *Diomus pumilio*, introduced from Australia, and a purplish minute pirate bug, *Anthocoris nemoralis*. Natural enemies usually do not become abundant until after psyllid populations have increased and weather warms in the spring. Tolerate psyllids until predators provide control or temporarily reduce high populations with spot applications of soap or oil.

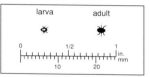

DIOMUS PUMILLO

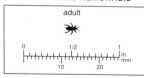

ANTHOCORIS NEMORALIS

An adult lady beetle, *Diomus pumilio*, feeding on acacia psyllid eggs.

TABLE 4-9

Resistance of *Acacia* Species to the Acacia Psyllid, *Acizzia uncatoides*, in Northern California.[a]

NOT INFESTED OR SLIGHTLY INFESTED (<0.5 NYMPHS/TIP)
aspera, podalyriifolia, baileyana,[b] *pravissima, craspedocarpa, armata, karoo, cardiophylla, giraffae, dealbata, gerardii, albida, collettioides*
SLIGHTLY TO MODERATELY INFESTED (0.5-1.1 NYMPHS/TIP)
cultriformis, decurrens, robusta, mearnsii, cunninghami, iteaphylla, cyanophylla, triptera
MODERATELY TO SEVERELY INFESTED (>2 NYMPHS/TIP)
salingna, obtusata, spectobilis, pendula, implexa, cyclops, longifolia, penninervis, melanoxylon, retinodes

a. From: C.S. Koehler, W.S. Moore, and B. Coate. 1983. J. Environ. Hort. 1: 65-67.
b. Infested by the baileyana psyllid, *Acizzia acaciaebaileyanae*.

Eucalyptus Psyllids

Several species of eucalyptus-feeding psyllids from Australia and New Zealand have been introduced into California. The blue gum psyllid, *Ctenarytaina eucalypti*, damages *Eucalyptus pulverulenta* foliage grown for floral arrangements and also infests young foliage on some eucalyptus species in landscapes. Pairs of adult blue gum psyllids mate tail-to-tail and may look like a grayish moth, unless examined more closely. The pale yellow to cream-colored eggs are laid in crevices between buds and young leaf petioles or openly on young leaves. Young nymphs are orangish, becoming mostly grayish with olive green as they mature. Because there are several hundred species of psyllids on eucalyptus in Australia, it is likely that more of these will be introduced into California, and some may become pests.

With the possible exception of young plants, no control is needed in landscape situations where mature plants are not harmed. Where eucalyptus is grown commercially for use in cut flower arrangements, reductions in fertilizer and irrigation may help, but pesticide applications may be warranted.

Eugenia Psyllid
Trioza eugeniae

The eugenia psyllid was introduced into California from Australia in 1988. Adults are mostly dark brown with a white band around the abdomen. The tiny golden eggs are laid primarily along the edges of young leaves, where the yellowish crawlers with orange-red eyes settle and feed. As it forms a feeding pit, the nymph resembles a soft scale insect

White, waxy material produced by blue gum psyllids on juvenile *Eucalyptus globulus* foliage.

Psyllid nymphs are commonly flattened, such as these blue gum psyllids.

and appears flat when viewed from the lower leaf surface. Populations are highest when new foliage is produced in the winter and spring, but reproduction and all psyllid stages occur the year around. A parasitic wasp, *Tamarixia* sp., has been introduced from Australia and may provide biological control of this pest. If damage is intolerable, applying insecticide to kill eugenia psyllid nymphs as flushes of new growth occur can improve the appearance of foliage produced over the next several weeks. Spray after adults become abundant in samples or when golden eggs are common on the edge of succulent tips. To be effective, spraying may need to be repeated every several weeks during the growth flush season; repeated insecticide spraying may itself damage foliage, cause outbreaks of other pests, and prevent parasites from becoming abundant and providing biological control.

The adult eugenia psyllid has a white band around its dark brown abdomen.

Eugenia psyllid nymphs feed in pits on the leaf underside, causing the foliage upperside to redden and distort.

Tiny golden eugenia psyllid eggs cause the edges of new eugenia leaves to glisten.

Peppertree Psyllid
Calophya rubra

The peppertree psyllid was accidentally introduced from South America into California in about 1984. It feeds only on the California pepper tree, a plant that despite its common name is native to South America and was introduced into California by Spanish settlers. Adults are greenish or tan and somewhat pear-shaped. Females deposit their tiny eggs on growing tips throughout the year. The orangish nymphs feed on any succulent plant part, causing the plant to form a pit around where each nymph settles. One psyllid generation requires only a few weeks during warm weather. Reproduction and all life stages occur throughout the year.

Improve the ability of pepper trees to tolerate psyllids by providing proper cultural care. Pepper trees are adapted to well-drained, sandy soil and summer drought. Planting trees in heavy clay soils or in summer watered landscapes, such as lawns, promotes root disease and causes

trees to decline and die. Avoid problems by planting other species. For example, *Agonis flexuosa*, *Pittosporum phillyraeoides*, and *Geijera parviflora* are relatively drought-tolerant and have a similar weeping appearance but are not affected by the peppertree psyllid. A *Tamarixia* species wasp that parasitizes pepper tree psyllid has been introduced from South America by University scientists and may reduce psyllid populations over the long run.

When adults are abundant and terminals are growing (usually winter), a systemic insecticide applied as a foliar spray or through injection or implants can provide temporary control. However, implants and injections damage trunks and generally no control is necessary unless aesthetic damage cannot be tolerated.

WHITEFLY

pupa   adult

0   1/2   1
in.
mm
10   20

Peppertree psyllid nymph feeding pits and distorts California pepper tree foliage.

WHITEFLIES

Whiteflies, family Aleyrodidae, are not true flies, but are related to psyllids and aphids in the order Homoptera. Many different species of whiteflies occur on landscape plants, but most are uncommon because of natural controls such as parasites and predators. Whiteflies are pests primarily in greenhouses and outdoors in mild-winter areas.

DAMAGE

Whiteflies suck phloem sap and high populations cause leaves to yellow, shrivel, and drop prematurely. The honeydew excreted by nymphs collects dust and leads to sooty mold growth. Honeydew attracts ants, which disrupt the biological control of whiteflies and other pests.

IDENTIFICATION AND BIOLOGY

Whiteflies usually occur in groups on the underside of leaves. They derive their name from the mealy white wax covering the adult's wings and body. Adults are shaped like a tiny moth or house fly and most species are very similar in appearance. They have yellowish bodies and whitish wings, and some species have blackish wing markings. Tiny, oblong eggs are usually laid on the underside of leaves. Eggs hatch into barely visible, oblong, yellowish nymphs or crawlers. Crawlers wander for a few hours, then insert their mouthparts and remain settled until adulthood. After the first molt, the semitransparent nymphs become flattened, oval, covered with a waxy secretion, and look like tiny scale insects. Most species have several annual generations with all stages present the year around on evergreen hosts in areas with mild winters. The time required for whiteflies to complete a single generation can vary from several months during the winter to a few weeks in the summer.

Whitefly metamorphosis differs from most homopteran because mature nymphs become temporarily inactive during the last instar. This stage is commonly called a pupa, even though whiteflies have incomplete metamorphosis and do not have a true pupal stage. The appearance of these pupae, the location and pattern of egg laying, and the species of host plant help one to distinguish among whitefly species. Depending on the species, the pupal cover may be covered with smooth or curly whitish to transparent wax. For species with a clear cover, the yellow to black, sometimes patterned insect body helps to identify the whitefly. Most adult whiteflies leave a T-shaped slit in the pupal case from which they emerged; parasites generally leave a small rounded hole.

Six of the most common species in landscapes are described and pictured here. For additional species, consult Color-Photo and Host Keys to California Whiteflies listed in References.

MONITORING

Inspect the underside of shriveled and yellow foliage and nearby healthy leaves for whiteflies. Most species prefer to feed on new plant growth. A cloud of tiny mothlike adults appears when you shake heavily infested foliage. Sticky traps are useful for detecting the presence of adult whiteflies and for estimating seasonal changes in their abundance as discussed at the beginning of this chapter.

MANAGEMENT

Most whitefly species are satisfactorily controlled by natural enemies, unless these beneficials are disrupted by ants, dust, or insecticide sprays. Minute pirate bugs, lacewings, lady beetles, and bigeyed bugs are impor-

Adult whiteflies like this ash whitefly are covered with a mealy white wax and are difficult to distinguish from other whitefly species. Ash whitefly pupae have a characteristic broad band of whitish wax down the back and a fringe of tiny tubes, each with a liquid droplet at the end.

Yellow sticky traps, like this one full of citrus thrips, are also a good way to detect adult whiteflies. Cover them with clear plastic to preserve insects before collecting traps.

Small lady beetles are important whitefly predators; this Delphastus pusillus is feeding on a sweetpotato whitefly nymph.

An adult wasp, Encarsia formosa, parasitizing a greenhouse whitefly nymph.

tant predators. Parasitic wasps, such as *Amitus, Encarsia,* and *Eretmocerus* species, control many whiteflies. To conserve these natural enemies, control ants, which disrupt beneficials, by using enclosed insecticide baits or sticky material barriers as discussed in the Ants section. Plant ground covers to reduce dust, which interferes with natural enemies. When managing many whitefly-infested plants, trim only a portion of the plants at a time. Mature foliage provides a refuge for natural enemies, which can migrate to attack whiteflies that are more common on new growth.

Some natural enemies of whiteflies are also commercially available. *Encarsia formosa,* a parasitic wasp, is effective in controlling greenhouse whitefly when released in greenhouses, but has not been shown to be effective when released outdoors.

An insecticidal soap or narrow-range oil spray can provide temporary control; however, whiteflies are difficult to manage with insecticides. Thorough coverage on the underside of leaves is essential. Applications made primarily to the upper leaf surface kill many beneficial insects while

missing whiteflies and thus do more harm than good. Persistent pesticides are generally not recommended. They are often more toxic to the actively searching beneficial insects than to whiteflies, which settle on the lower leaf surface where they are somewhat protected from insecticides. Whiteflies also have developed resistance rapidly to many broad-spectrum insecticides. A forceful stream of water applied to plant surfaces washes away honeydew, which is often the most bothersome aspect of whiteflies.

Adult whiteflies are attracted to bright yellow surfaces. Sticky yellow cards are used primarily for monitoring adult populations and should be deployed during the time of year when adults are active. Standard size or extra large sticky traps may also help to control whiteflies where many traps can be deployed around smaller, relatively isolated hosts.

CLITOSTETHUS ARCUATUS

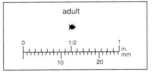

Ash Whitefly
Siphoninus phillyreae

Ash whitefly occurs in the U.S. in California, Arizona, Nevada, and New Mexico. It may occur on many hosts, including ash, citrus, pear pomegranate, redbud, and toyon. Mature ash whitefly nymphs have a broad band of whitish wax extending lengthwise down the back and a fringe of tiny tubes around the periphery of the body. A tiny liquid droplet collects on the end of each tube. Unlike many whitefly species that occur primarily on new growth, immature ash whiteflies can be found on any age of leaf, usually in clusters on the lower surface.

Soon after it was first discovered in southern California in 1988, high populations appeared on host plants. Honeydew and black sooty mold were abundant and infested trees defoliated prematurely. Enormous numbers of adults become active on warm days, resembling swirling snowflakes, with the greatest numbers occurring during the late summer and fall.

Ash whitefly is now rarely a pest. It is under good biological control by two natural enemies introduced from Europe and North Africa. These are *Encarsia partenopea,* a tiny black and yellowish parasitic wasp, and *Clitostethus arcuatus,* a small, mostly brownish lady beetle. Conserve these natural enemies by controlling ants and dust and by avoiding the use of broad-spectrum insecticides. Tolerate local outbreaks; they are likely to be temporary because natural enemies soon provide control. Insecticides are not very effective because of the many generations of this insect each year. Insecticidal soap and narrow-range oil kill whiteflies on contact, but they provide no residual control

Parasitized whitefly nymphs commonly darken and develop round emergence holes (left). Adult whiteflies leave a characteristic ragged or T-shaped slit (right), as shown here for ash whitefly.

and must be frequently reapplied. Commercially available *Encarsia formosa* parasites are not effective against the ash whitefly, and there is no benefit from purchasing and releasing *E. formosa* against this pest.

Citrus Whitefly
Dialeurodes citri

Citrus whitefly eggs are laid randomly on the underside of full-sized leaves. Pupae lack a visible waxy covering and have a distinct Y-shaped mark on the back. This insect is primarily a pest of citrus in the southern states and California, but occurs on many plants including ash, *Ficus*, and pomegranate. No special control should be necessary in landscapes.

Citrus whitefly pupae lack a visible waxy covering and have a Y-shaped pattern on their back.

Crown Whitefly
Aleuroplatus coronata

Crown whitefly occurs in California on oak and chestnut. Adults appear only during the spring and may become a nuisance on warm days when enormous numbers may emerge, resembling swirling snowflakes. These adults soon disappear and can be ignored because they apparently do not damage plants. Tiny white to pink eggs are attached by a short stalk to the lower leaf surface. Oval nymphs and pupae are black, but become mostly covered with broad, white waxy plates that spread out from the insects' sides, somewhat resembling a minute crown. Crown whitefly overwinters as a pupa and has one generation a year. Although high populations can be unsightly, trees are apparently not harmed and generally no control is recommended.

Crown whitefly occurs in California on oak and chestnut. Nymphs blacken as they mature. Pupae have broad, white waxy plates spreading from their sides. The similar Stanford whitefly, *Tetraleurodes stanfordi*, occurs on oaks and chiquapin.

A fringe of filaments protrudes around the perimeter of the upperside of greenhouse whitefly pupae.

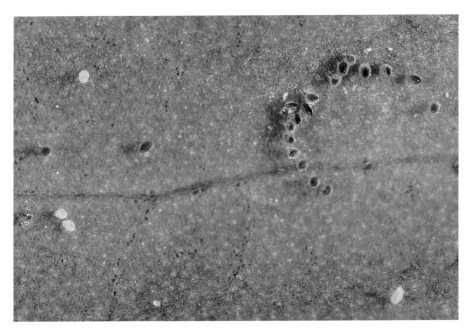

Greenhouse whitefly eggs are scattered or laid in partial or full circles on the leaf underside.

Greenhouse Whitefly
Trialeurodes
vaporariorum

Greenhouse whitefly eggs are whitish yellow when laid and turn dark black, green, or gray before nymphs emerge. Tiny eggs are laid in circles, half circles, or scattered groups of 30 to 40 on the undersurface of leaves. Pupae have a transparent cover and are oblong with vertical sides. A fringe of filaments protrude around the perimeter of the upper edge of the pupa. Greenhouse whitefly is a pest throughout the U.S. primarily on annuals, especially vegetables and flowers, but it can occur on many woody landscape species.

Conserve important natural enemies of the greenhouse whitefly by controlling dust and ants and avoiding the use of broad-spectrum insecticides. If whitefly populations are high and cannot be tolerated, apply insecticidal soap or narrow-range oil. *Encarsia formosa* and other parasitic wasps are important greenhouse whitefly natural enemies. Female *Encarsia* feed on all immature whitefly stages and lay eggs in third-and fourth-instar whiteflies. Eggs hatch into larvae that feed inside and kill the whitefly. Parasitized immature whiteflies look like brownish or black scales, in contrast to the whitish or yellowish green color of healthy whitefly nymphs. *Encarsia* chew a round hole in whiteflies and leave black deposits in the host, in contrast to the mostly clear skin left by emerging whiteflies. *Encarsia formosa* are sold through the mail and are effective when released in warm, humid greenhouses; however, there is no information that releases control greenhouse whitefly in landscapes.

Greenhouse whitefly pupae turn black when parasitized by *Encarsia* formosa, in comparison with unparasitized (right) and emerged (lower left) pupae.

Sweetpotato whitefly nymphs produce little or no whitish wax and pupae have few or no protruding filaments.

Sweetpotato or Silverleaf Whitefly *Bemisia tabaci*

Sweetpotato whitefly (or strain A), and silverleaf whitefly (strain B) may be two different, almost identical-looking species. They damage many different plant species in greenhouses and hot, interior areas of California. Herbaceous species are most severely affected, but some woody ornamentals can be heavily infested, including citrus, crape myrtle, hibiscus, lantana, orchid tree (*Bauhinia* spp.), rose, and willow.

Discolored and distorted foliage, copious honeydew, sooty mold, and premature defoliation are common damage symptoms. Nymphs and pupae are round to oval and yellowish. Unlike most other common species, they do not produce whitish waxy material and they have few or no tiny filaments or setae protruding from around their edge.

Adults are attracted to yellow sticky traps, which are used primarily for monitoring populations. Control is difficult, and University scientists are introducing natural enemies in an effort to provide biological control. Spraying lower leaf surfaces with a forceful stream of water daily during warm weather can provide control. Soap or oil applied to thoroughly cover lower leaf surfaces temporarily reduces populations.

Woolly Whitefly
Aleurothrixus floccosus

Woolly whitefly eggs are laid in circles or partial circles on the lower surface of mostly full-sized leaves. Nymphs and pupae are covered with fluffy, waxy filaments. Woolly whitefly is common in Gulf states and California on citrus and eugenia.

Parasitic wasps, including *Amitus spiniferus* and *Cales noacki*, provide complete biological control of woolly whitefly in California unless disrupted by ants, dust, or pesticides. Conserve these natural enemies and avoid spraying broad-spectrum insecticides. A bright reddish fungus, *Aschersonia aleyrodis,* has been reported in Florida as effective in controlling the woolly whitefly and some other whiteflies under warm, moist conditions.

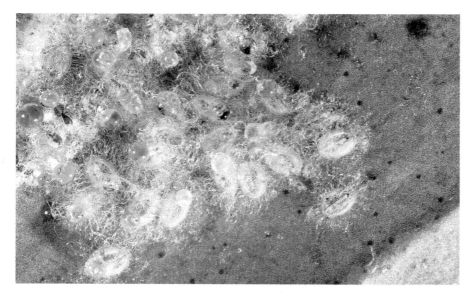

Woolly whitefly is common on eugenia and citrus in California and states along the Gulf of Mexico. Nymphs and pupae are covered with fluffy, waxy filaments.

MEALYBUGS

Several hundred mealybug species occur in the U.S., and most plants are susceptible to one or more of these. Some species, like the citrus mealybug and obscure mealybug, occur on many different hosts throughout mild-winter areas.

DAMAGE

Mealybugs tend to congregate in large numbers, forming white, cottony masses on plants. High populations slow plant growth and cause premature leaf or fruit drop and twig dieback. Honeydew production and black sooty mold are the primary damage caused by most mealybugs. Low populations do not harm plants. High populations can cause plant decline, and young plants may be killed.

GROUND MEALYBUG

adult female

0		1/2		1	
		10		20	in. mm

IDENTIFICATION AND BIOLOGY

Most adult female mealybugs are wingless, soft-bodied, grayish insects about $\frac{1}{20}$ to $\frac{1}{3}$ inch long. They are usually elongate and segmented, and may have wax filaments radiating from their body, especially at the tail. Most females can move slowly and are covered with whitish, mealy or cottony wax. The cypress bark mealybug is somewhat atypical; it looks more like a scale insect than a mealybug.

Woolly aphids, adelgids, and cottony cushion scales may sometimes be confused with mealybugs because they also produce a whitish, waxy material. The white, fluted egg sac of cottony cushion scales erupts from the female's body, which is usually bright orange, red, yellow or brownish. Underneath the loose, cottony, waxy covering, the bodies of most aphids and adelgids appear pear-shaped. Some of the aphids or adelgids in a colony may have wings, while only male mealybugs and scales have wings and males are rarely seen. Male mealybugs are tiny and delicate; their body is commonly yellow or red with two long whitish tail filaments. For help with identification, consult *Color-Photo and Host Keys to the Mealybugs of California* listed in References.

Most female mealybugs lay tiny yellow eggs in a mass intermixed with white wax called an ovisac. Mealybug nymphs are oblong, whitish, yellowish, or reddish and may or may not be covered with waxy filaments. Most species feed on branches, twigs, or leaves. Depending on the species, host, and climate, they may overwinter only as eggs or females, or as all stages. Most mealybugs have several generations each year.

Large numbers of mealybugs, like these on mimosa, can form white, cottony masses.

An obscure mealybug colony on grape; adults have distinct filaments around the body.

A bark plate on Monterey cypress has been removed to reveal these cypress bark mealybugs, which are round, bright red or orangish, and surrounded by white wax.

Cypress Bark Mealybug
Ehrhornia cupressi

The cypress bark mealybug, some-times called cypress bark scale, occurs beneath bark plates on cedar, cypress, and juniper in Pacific Coast states. Foliage on infested plants becomes yellow and red and eventu-ally may die. Heavy populations cause dieback at the treetop, which gradually extends down the tree and may kill it.

Cypress bark mealybug nymphs and adults are round, bright red or orangish, and are surrounded by a ring of white wax. They do not move after settling as crawlers, and have one generation a year.

Obscure Mealybug
Pseudococcus affinis

The obscure mealybug occurs in warm areas of the U.S. on many hosts including cactus, fruit trees, magno-lia, oak, oleander, and willow. The light gray to white adults are covered with a powdery wax and have distinct filaments around the body. All stages occur year-round on bark, twigs, and leaves. One generation requires about 6 weeks during warm weather, and there are four to five annual generations.

This adult mealybug destroyer is an important predator of exposed mealybug species.

Longtailed Mealybug
Pseudococcus longispinus

The longtailed mealybug can occur on almost any plant species in areas with mild winters, but is commonly a pest only on nursery stock and indoor ornamentals. It is distinguished by its two tail filaments, which are longer than its body. Its biology also differs from most species because it gives live birth to nymphs, therefore no egg masses are found in longtailed mealybug colonies.

Citrus Mealybug
Planococcus citri

Citrus mealybug is a pest of citrus in coastal California and infests many different hosts in greenhouses and indoor ornamental plantings. It has short, waxy filaments of about equal length all around its margin; one dark, longitudinal stripe may be visible down its back.

MANAGEMENT

Provide proper cultural care so that plants are vigorous and can tolerate moderate mealybug feeding without being damaged. Naturally occurring predators and parasites provide good control of many mealybug species, unless these beneficials are disrupted. For instance, the parasitic wasps *Anarhopus sydneyensis* and *Arhopoideus peregrinus* help to keep longtailed mealybug populations at low levels outdoors. *Leptomastix dactylopii* is an important parasite of citrus mealybug.

Conserve natural enemies by controlling dust and avoiding persistent pesticides. Insecticidal soap, narrow-range oil, or a forceful stream of water can be applied to reduce populations with minimal harm to natural enemies that may migrate in later. Control ants that tend mealybugs by placing enclosed pesticide baits such as ant stakes at the base of infested plants or trim branches to eliminate ant bridges and apply sticky material to trunks as discussed in the Ants section. Populations of cypress bark mealybug can be reduced by thoroughly spraying infested bark with narrow-range oil in August and again in September; however, dense foliage makes it difficult to thoroughly spray bark.

An important predator of the citrus mealybug and other exposed species is the mealybug destroyer, *Cryptolaemus montrouzieri*. This small, mostly blackish lady beetle has a reddish brown head and tail. Mealybug destroyer larvae are covered with waxy white curls and look like mealy-

Mealybug destroyer larvae are covered with waxy white curls and look like mealybugs. This one is feeding on orangish grape mealybug, *Pseudococcus maritimus*, eggs laid within a cottony sac.

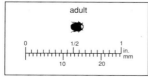

CRYPTOLAEMUS

adult

bugs, except that the lady beetle larvae are larger and more active. Both adult and larval lady beetles feed on all mealybug stages. The beetle has about four generations a year and lays its eggs into mealybug egg masses.

The mealybug destroyer survives poorly over the winter in California and cold areas and may need to be reintroduced locally in the spring to provide control. Some citrus growers purchase *Cryptolaemus* from commercial suppliers and release them in the spring before exposed mealybugs that feed on bark or leaves become abundant; there is no research showing if this is effective in landscapes.

Another commercially available natural enemy is the parasite *Leptomastix dactylopii,* which controls only the citrus mealybug. This yellowish brown wasp lays its eggs in late-instar nymphs and adult mealybugs, preferring hosts in warm, sunny, humid environments. At warm temperatures, *Leptomastix* can complete one generation in about 3 weeks. It has been released in combination with the mealybug destroyer to successfully control citrus mealybug in greenhouses. *Leptomastix* was reportedly effective when several hundred parasites were released on each shrub infested with citrus mealybug in interior plantscapes that

The ground mealybug, *Rhizoecus falcifer,* does not have obvious filaments along its sides or tail.

were not previously sprayed with persistent insecticides. There is no available information on its effectiveness when released in landscapes.

Ground Mealybugs
Rhizoecus spp.

Ground mealybugs commonly live in the soil and feed on the roots of many different plants, including *Abutilon,* acacia, boxwood, citrus, grape, palm, pine, *Prunus* spp., spruce, and *Syringa.* Several native and introduced ground mealybug species occur throughout the U.S.; *Rhizoecus falcifer* is apparently the most common in California. High populations can cause a general decline of the plant and kill young plants. Ground mealybugs may be covered with white wax and their short antennae and legs may be visible, but they do not have obvious filaments along their sides and tail.

Minimize ground mealybug damage by providing adequate summer and fall irrigation to prevent drought stress. If populations are extremely high, a soil-applied insecticide may be effective. Some insect growth regulators can be applied to control ground mealybugs; check pesticide labels for permitted uses. Insecticidal soap in warm water poured on soil around small plants as labeled may reduce ground mealybug populations.

SCALES

Scale insects, order Homoptera, are common and damaging pests. They are easily overlooked because they are small and immobile most of their lives and do not resemble most other insects.

DAMAGE

Scales feed by sucking plant juices, and some may inject toxic saliva into plants. When numerous, scales weaken a plant and cause it to grow slowly. Infested plants appear water stressed, leaves turn yellow, and foliage and fruit may become black from sooty mold or drop prematurely. Branches or other plant parts that remain heavily infested die; if they die quickly, the dead brownish leaves may remain on branches giving them a scorched appearance. Several years of severe infestations may kill young plants.

The importance of infestations depends on the scale species, the plant species, cultivar, or variety, environmental factors, and natural enemies. Plants are not harmed by a few scales. However, populations of some scales can increase dramatically within a few months, especially when honeydew-seeking ants protect scales from their natural enemies. Scale-infested plants may become sticky from honeydew and foliage may blacken from the resulting sooty mold growth. Sticky and blackened foliage may be bothersome to people even when scale populations are too low to harm the plant.

IDENTIFICATION
AND BIOLOGY

Adult female scales are circular to oval in outline, wingless, and lack a separate head or other easily recognizable body parts. Adult males are tiny, delicate, white to yellow insects with one pair of wings and a long tail filament. Males are rarely seen, do not feed, and live only a few hours. Females of many scale species reproduce without mating.

Eggs are commonly protected beneath the cover of the female. The newly hatched scale nymphs, called crawlers, emerge and walk along branches or are spread by the wind or inadvertently by people or animals. Scale crawlers are usually pale yellow to orange and about the size of a period. After one to a few days, crawlers settle and insert their strawlike mouthparts to feed on plant juices. After settling, armored scales (see below) secrete a waxy covering and remain on the same plant part for the rest of their lives; nymphs of soft scale species can move a little, usually from foliage to bark before leaves drop in the fall.

Most scale species are one of two types: armored or soft. Armored scales, family Diaspididae, are less than ⅛ inch long and have a platelike shell. This cover usually can be removed from the scale body. Armored scales, such as the San Jose, oystershell, and greedy scale, do not excrete honeydew. The life cycle of a typical armored scale is illustrated in Figure 4-10. Female unarmored or soft scales, family Coccidae, may be smooth or cottony, and are ¼ inch or shorter. The surface is the actual body wall of the insect and cannot be removed. Soft scales, including black and brown soft scale, are prolific honeydew excreters. Most immature soft scales retain their barely visible legs and antennae after settling and are able to move extremely slowly. The following discussion and photographs and Tree and Shrub Pest Tables at the back of this book will help you to identify and manage common scales on landscape plants. Most of the species discussed here occur throughout the U.S. Color photographs and descriptions for some scale species not detailed here may be found in *Pests of the Garden and Small Farm* (UC Publication 3332), *Color-Photo and Host Keys to the Armored Scales of California*, *Color-Photo and Host Keys to the Soft Scales of California*, and *Insects That Feed on Trees and Shrubs*, listed in References.

THRESHOLDS AND MONITORING

Monitor scales by inspecting plants for crawlers, mature females, or scale-associated ants. No action thresholds have been established for scales on landscape plants. Develop thresholds for your local situation. Monitor and record scale densities and use the density that caused damage (dieback or unacceptable honeydew) as your preliminary control action threshold. Refine this threshold over time as you gain more information and experience.

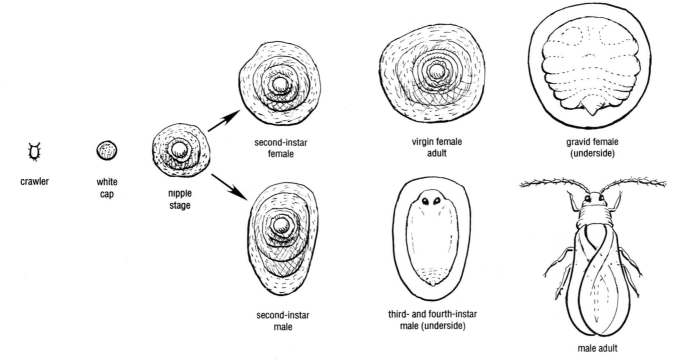

crawler   white cap   nipple stage   second-instar female   virgin female adult   gravid female (underside)   second-instar male   third- and fourth-instar male (underside)   male adult

Figure 4-10. Life cycle of a typical armored scale, California red scale. Eggs hatch into tiny crawlers which soon settle and secrete a cottony (white cap) cover and later a more solid cover (the nipple stage). After the first molt, males begin to develop an elongated scale cover whereas female covers remain round.

Females molt three times. The final stage is the mated female, a rounded scale cover with a legless, wingless, immobile female beneath. Males molt four times. They develop eyespots, which can be seen when scale covers are turned over in the third and fourth instar. The adult male has legs and two wings.

Monitor crawlers with sticky tape, or inspect plants on at least two dates several weeks apart when mature females are expected to be present (usually in the spring). Examine portions of the plant (leaves, fruit, or one-foot branch terminal segments) where mature females occur as described for each species. Count and record the number of mature female scales, on each of 4 to 8 shoots on each of several plants. Also record the number of parasitized scales; these can be recognized by one or more holes chewed in the scale cover by the emerging adult parasites or by the darker color of parasitized nymphs. Estimate the average number of parasitized and unparasitized scales per sample by totaling the number of insects counted, and dividing by the number of samples inspected. Compare the average scale density on your samples to the density during previous years to determine if scales are increasing and to evaluate whether any treatment during the last year

was effective. Compare your samples from the same year to see if the percentage of parasitized scales is increasing.

An alternative to counting each scale is determining the percentage of samples with scales. This presence-absence sampling is quicker but less precise than counting each scale, and it is difficult to estimate parasitism.

Inspect trunks for columns of ants, which may indicate a soft scale infestation. If the descending ants have swollen, almost translucent abdomens, they are probably feeding on honeydew produced by scales or other insects that suck plant juices.

Sticky Tape Traps. If insecticide application is needed, apply oil during the dormant season where possible. If application is necessary during the spring or summer, use sticky tape

traps to monitor and effectively time a foliar insecticide application against crawlers, which are the stage most susceptible to insecticides.

Choose several twigs or small branches for monitoring on each of two or more plants. Before crawlers begin to emerge in the spring, tightly encircle each twig or branch with transparent tape that is sticky on both sides (this tape is available at stationery stores). Double over the loose end of the tape several times so you can pull the end to easily unwind it. Place a tag or flagging near each tape so you can readily find it. Change the tapes at regular intervals, about weekly. After removing the old tape, wrap the twig at the same location with fresh tape. Preserve the old sticky tapes by sandwiching them between a sheet of white paper and clear plastic, such as an overhead projector acetate

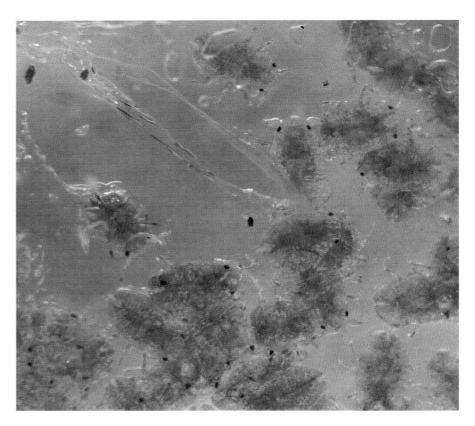

Wrap double-sided sticky tape tightly around twigs to monitor when scale crawlers are active. Double over the end so you can grasp and easily unwrap tapes to check them.

European fruit lecanium scale crawlers caught in a sticky tape trap.

or a plastic bag. Label the tapes with the date, location, and host plant from which they were collected.

Scale crawlers get stuck on the tapes and appear as yellow or orange specks. Examine the tapes with a hand lens to distinguish the crawlers (which are round or oblong, orangish, and have very short appendages) from pollen and dust. Use a hand lens to examine the crawlers beneath mature female scales on bark or foliage to be certain of crawler appearance. Other tiny creatures including mites and springtails may also be caught in the tapes.

Visually compare the tapes collected on each sample date. If a spring or summer foliar insecticide application is planned, spray after a sharp increase in crawler production occurs or after crawler numbers have peaked and begin to decline. The number of crawlers caught on each tape can be counted and the average number of crawlers per tape on each date can be plotted using graph paper or a computer graphics software program. This is more time-consuming than

just making visual comparisons among tapes, but this more precise information can improve the effectiveness of your management decision-making. Pheromone traps, in combination with degree-day monitoring, can be used to time California red scale and San Jose scale controls when managing many high-value plants.

MANAGEMENT

Biological Control. Scales are often controlled by natural enemies, including many species of small, dark lady beetles. *Hyperaspis* species are tiny, shiny, black lady beetles with several red, orange, or yellow spots on the back. *Rhyzobius lophanthae* is a lady beetle that has a reddish head and underside and a grayish back densely covered with tiny hairs. The twicestabbed lady beetle, *Chilocorus orbus*, is shiny black with two red spots on its back, and reddish underneath. The larvae of certain predaceous lady beetles can be found under the covers of female soft scales feeding on scale eggs and crawlers.

Many parasitic wasps are important natural enemies, including species of *Aphytis, Coccophagus, Encarsia,* and *Metaphycus*. Estimate parasite activity by checking scale covers for the round exit holes made by emerging adult parasites and flip armored scale covers and examine beneath them for immature parasitoids. Plant flowering species near scale-infested trees and shrubs to help augment natural enemies. Adult parasitic wasps live longer, lay more eggs, and kill more scales when they have nectar or honeydew to feed on. Natural enemies are commercially available for release against black scale and California red

The adult twicestabbed lady beetle, *Chilocorus orbus* or *C. stigma*, has two red spots on its shiny black body. *Chilocorus kuwanae* looks almost identical.

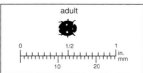

TWICESTABBED LADY BEETLE
adult

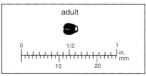

RHYZOBIUS
adult

An adult *Rhyzobius lophanthae* on the underside of a toyon leaf infested with European fruit lecanium scale nymphs.

scale (see below). However, conserving resident natural enemies is a more efficient and longer lasting strategy.

Avoid using persistent, broad-spectrum insecticides for scales or other pests because these disrupt natural enemies. Apply narrow-range oil instead, preferably during the dormant season. Prevent excessive dust and control honeydew-seeking ants, (see Ants section) to enhance the biological control of scales.

Insecticides. Dormant season applications of specially refined narrow-range oils, labeled "supreme" or "superior" oil, are effective against many scales on landscape plants. Avoid oils called dormant oil or dormant oil emulsions, which are more likely to injure plants. When applied as a delayed dormant spray, just before buds break, narrow-range oil treatment also kills a portion of overwintering mite, aphid, and caterpillar eggs on bark. Do not spray oils when plants are drought-stressed or if temperatures are over 90°F or under 32°F.

Narrow-range oils are also effective in spring or summer against scale eggs and crawlers. A foliage season application may require more spray volume than a dormant season spray to deciduous plants because foliage as well as bark must be thoroughly covered. Do not apply oil to the foliage of sensitive plant species as identified in *Managing Insects & Mites with Spray Oils* (UC Publication 3347).

In addition to narrow-range oil, insecticidal soap and several organophosphate and carbamate insecticides are registered as foliar sprays for scale control. Monitor scale crawlers with sticky tape to effectively time an application during spring or summer. Foliar sprays of the more persistent, broad-spectrum insecticides cause more disruption of biological control than oil or soap because persistent residues kill natural enemies migrating in after the application (Table 4-6). See *Insect Pest Management Guidelines for California Landscape Ornamentals* (UC Publication 3317) for specific insecticide recommendations.

ARMORED SCALES

California Red Scale
Aonidiella aurantii

The hosts of California red scale include acacia, boxwood, citrus, eugenia, euonymus, magnolia, mulberry, palm, podocarpus, privet, and rose. The roundish, reddish orange females are difficult to distinguish from yellow scale, *Aonidiella citrina*, which has a similar biology and management. Red scale is more common because it attacks more plant species and apparently is not as well controlled by natural enemies.

The minute, yellow crawlers emerge from beneath females and settle in small depressions on twigs, fruit, or leaves. They begin feeding and secrete cottony filaments to form a circular cover. As the scales grow, they develop a more solid cover with a nipple near the center. Midway

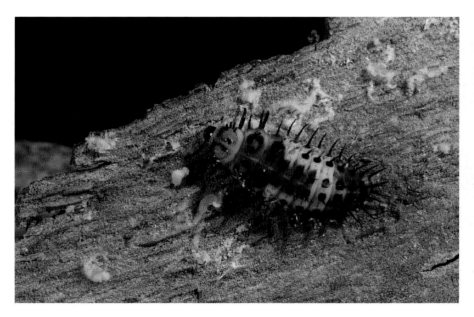

A twicestabbed lady beetle larva feeding on sycamore scale eggs and nymphs on the underside of a sycamore bark plate.

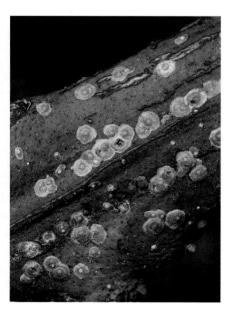

Female California red scales are round with concentric rings on their cover.

through the second instar, females and males begin to look different (Figure 4-10). An elongated cover forms over immature males, which later develop wings. Females remain round and develop distinct concentric rings on their cover, the number of rings increasing as the scale grows. Maturing females produce a sex pheromone to attract males. After mating, the female's body expands to fill the scale cover and is securely attached to the leaf, twig, or fruit. All stages overwinter, although cold weather often kills the early instars. Red scale has two to five generations a year. Oil effectively controls red scale; spray deciduous plants if needed during the dormant season or time a foliar application by monitoring crawlers. Pheromone-baited traps can also be used to time controls when managing a large number of high-value plants, as detailed in *Integrated Pest Management for Citrus* (UC Publication 3303).

Biological Control. Several tiny, yellow to brownish parasitic wasps attack California red scale, including *Aphytis melinus*, *Aphytis lingnanensis*, *Encarsia perniciosi*, and *Comperiella bifasciata*. *Rhyzobius lophanthae* and *Chilocorus orbus* are important predaceous lady beetles.

Aphytis melinus, the most important parasite, kills scales by puncturing them and feeding on the exuding

Aphytis melinus is an important parasite of California red scale.

fluid or by laying an egg under the scale cover, where the immature parasite feeds. *Aphytis* leaves a flat and dehydrated scale body beneath the scale cover where the parasite's cast skin and fecal pellets may be observed. The adult wasp may emerge through a small, round exit hole in the scale cover or push out from beneath the scale cover, so that parasitized scales often slough off. *Aphytis* prefers to parasitize the adult virgin females, which have a wide, gray margin extending beyond the insect body, and the scale cover and body can be readily separated. The short life cycle of *Aphytis* (10 to 20 days) allows two to three parasite generations for each scale generation. Naturally occurring populations of *Aphytis* are more effective in controlling California red scale in south coastal areas than in the Central Valley of California. The female scales susceptible to parasitization by *Aphytis* are more continuously present in mild-climate areas than in hot areas where there is less overlapping of scale life stages.

Releasing commercially available *Aphytis melinus* (see Suppliers) can reduce red scale populations in citrus orchards, but the effectiveness of releases in landscapes has not been researched. Based on work in citrus, for a 20-foot tree it may be effective to make several releases each of at least 200 *Aphytis* every 2 weeks beginning when most scales are in the virgin female stage. April and May are usually the best release times, but inspect leaves and new twigs with a hand lens to determine whether the wide, gray margined scale stage (virgin females) preferred by *Aphytis* are present. Control dust and ants and avoid using persistent pesticides before releasing any parasites. Consult the beginning of this chapter for guidelines on effectively introducing natural enemies.

San Jose Scale
Quadraspidiotus perniciosus

San Jose scale has many hosts including acacia, aspen, citrus, cottonwood, fruit trees, maple, mulberry, poplar, pyracantha, walnut, and willow. Although named for San Jose, California, where this species was first described, the scale is originally from China. Mature female San Jose scales have a smooth, yellow body beneath the round, grayish cover. San Jose scale looks like olive scale, *Parlatoria oleae*, which is found on many of the same hosts, except that the female olive scale's body beneath its cover is purple. Walnut scale, *Quadraspidiotus juglansregiae*, is also similar, except that under its cover, the margin of the yellow female body has indentations. Heavy scale infestations can be recognized on deciduous plants by the brown foliage that remains on infested branches after most deciduous plants have dropped their leaves in the fall.

The minute, bright yellow crawlers of San Jose scale that emerge from beneath females are motile for about a day. After settling on bark, crawlers secrete a white, waxy covering (called the white cap) and sometimes cause a red halo to form on young wood or fruit where they feed. After about a week, a band of dark wax appears around the periphery of the white cap, marking the beginning of the black cap stage in which most San Jose scales overwinter.

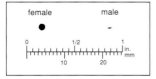

SAN JOSE SCALE

female   male

0   1/2   1
|||||||||||||||| in.
                  mm
        10   20

Scales resume growth and molt in the spring; females and males then become distinguishable. Females form a round cover for the remainder of their lives. Males form an elongate cover under which the minute, yellow, two-winged adult develops. Males begin emerging in March and April. Females mature then and produce a sex pheromone, which attracts flying males. About a month after mating, eggs laid by females begin hatching into crawlers. These usually first appear in May. The scale has two to five generations a year.

The twicestabbed lady beetle, a dark, pinhead-sized nitidulid beetle (*Cybocephalus californicus*) and several tiny parasitic wasps, including *Aphytis* and *Encarsia* species, are important natural enemies of San Jose scale. Apply narrow-range oil during the dormant season if a pesticide application is necessary on deciduous plants. Oil or other insecticides may also be applied when crawlers are abundant (about May), but this disrupts natural enemies. If spraying is necessary during the foliage season, monitor scale crawlers beginning in April with double-sided sticky tape. Spray 2 to 3 weeks after the bright yellow, pinpoint-sized scale crawlers are first observed on the tapes. The precise treatment timing is 200 to 300 degree-days above 51°F accumulated after crawlers are first observed.

Pheromone-baited traps can detect the flight of each male generation, which occurs in about June, July-August, and September-October. Traps and degree-day monitoring can be used to time scale treatments more precisely when managing a large number of high-value trees, as described in *Integrated Pest Management for Almonds* (UC Publication 3308).

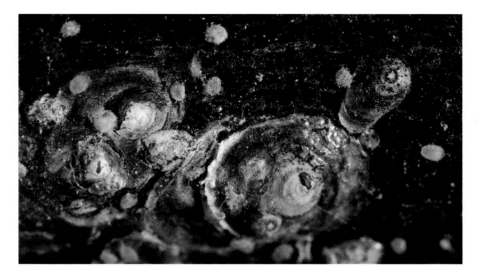

San Jose scale females and crawlers. Lift the female cover to distinguish this species from olive scale and walnut scale, as discussed in the text.

Greedy Scale
Hemiberlesia rapax
and Latania Scale
Hemiberlesia lataniae

Greedy scale is so named because of its many hosts, including acacia, bay, boxwood, cactus, ceanothus, fruit trees, holly, laurel, magnolia, manzanita, palm, pepper tree, pittosporum, pyracantha, redbud, strawberry tree, and willow. Latania scale has a similarly broad host list and in California may be the more common of these two very similar looking species. Female scales are circular and convex with an off-center yellow

Greedy scales are usually tan with an off-center yellow or brown nipple, like these infesting acacia.

or brown area or nipple. Latania scales are usually white or tan while greedy scales are usually gray. Males apparently do not occur in California. Distinct concentric rings often form on the cover as the scales grow. The scales are found on leaves, stems, and fruit. Crawlers first appear in the spring, and the scales have several generations per year.

Prune out heavily infested branches. Apply oil if necessary during the dormant season or when monitoring indicates that crawlers are active in the spring.

Oleander Scale
Aspidiotus nerii

Oleander scale infests acacia, bay, boxwood, cactus, holly, laurel, magnolia, manzanita, maple, mulberry, oleander, olive, palm, pepper tree, sago palm, *Taxus*, redbud, yew, and yucca. Oleander scale is tan to yellow and flat, but otherwise appears very similar to greedy scale. Oleander scale is lighter colored, less globular, and the brown nipple is more nearly centered on the cover in comparison to greedy scale. Scales are found on bark, foliage, and fruit. Several generations occur each year.

Prune out heavily infested branches. Apply oil if necessary during the dormant season or when monitoring indicates that crawlers are active in the spring.

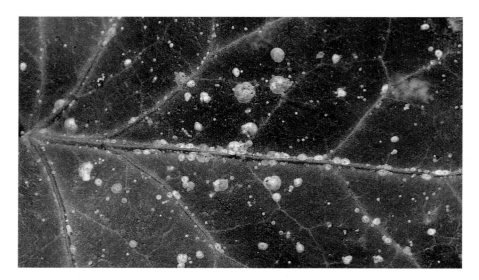

These oleander scales infesting ivy are tan to yellow and flat. They are lighter colored and less globular in comparison with greedy scale.

Oystershell scale females on Lombardy poplar bark. This species does not attack citrus, which may be infested with a similar looking species, purple scale.

Oystershell Scale
Lepidosaphes ulmi

Oystershell scale feeds on alder, aspen, box elder, boxwood, ceanothus, cottonwood, fruit trees, holly, maple, poplar, sycamore, walnut, and willow. Mature, gray to dark brown elongated scales look like miniature oysters and are found on bark, usually in clusters. Oystershell scale does not attack citrus, which may be infested with a similar looking species, purple scale, *Lepidosaphes beckii*. Oystershell scale overwinters as whitish eggs, about 50 to 150 of which can be found under the cover of mature females. Crawlers emerge

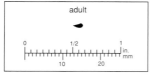

OYSTERSHELL SCALE

adult

in the spring after buds have burst, and walk across the bark for several hours before settling to feed. Oyster-shell scale usually has one generation a year in northern California and two generations in southern California.

Prune out heavily infested branches. An oil spray, if necessary, is apparently most effective if applied when monitoring indicates that crawlers are active in the spring.

Euonymus Scale
Unaspis euonymi

Yellowish or brownish spots on euonymus leaves indicate a euonymus scale infestation. The immature male is a felty or fuzzy white and elongated with three longitudinal ridges. The female is wider, oyster-shell-shaped, slightly convex, and brown to black. Both sexes have brownish yellow areas on the narrow end of their covers. Scales overwinter as mature females. Eggs develop beneath these scales and, in spring, hatch into orangish crawlers, which emerge over a several week period. Euonymus scale has two or three annual generations.

Replace, and do not plant, *Euonymus japonica*. It is extremely susceptible to euonymus scale. *Euonymus kiautschovica* (or *E. sieboldiana*) tolerates scales. *Euonymus alata* remains nearly scale-free even when heavy infestations occur on nearby susceptible hosts. A predaceous lady beetle, *Chilocorus kuwanae,* is being introduced for euonymus scale control and it appears to be effective in the eastern U.S. Like the twice-stabbed lady beetle, *Chilocorus orbus* or *C. stigma, Chilocorus kuwanae* is shiny black with two reddish spots. Narrow-range oil controls euonymus scale; time any application by monitoring crawlers.

Minute Cypress Scale
Carulaspis minima

Colonies of minute cypress scale cause yellow or brown encrustations on arborvitae, cypress, or juniper foliage, which may discolor and die. Other pests beside these scales, such as the juniper twig girdler and cypress tip miner, may cause the foliage of junipers and related plants to turn yellow or brown and die, so use a hand lens to inspect discolored foliage for scales. The mature female is circular, convex, and whitish with a yellow center. The tiny male is elongate, oval, felty with longitudinal ridges, and is yellow on the terminal of its mostly whitish cover. Crawlers emerge in spring, and the scale has one to two generations a year.

Apply oil if necessary or use another insecticide on oil-sensitive species when monitoring indicates that crawlers are active.

Cycad Scale
Furchadaspis zamiae

Cycad scale is a common pest of bird-of-paradise and cycads such as sago palm. Scales are white, oval, and convex with a darkened area (exuviae) at one end. Males are unknown. Oil applied during the dormant season or when crawlers are active can provide control. Some palms may be sensitive to oil; make a test spray on an out-of-the-way portion of the plant first and observe this area for damage for a week before spraying further, or use another insecticide against crawlers.

Euonymus scale males are elongated and white, females are wider and darker, and nymphs are tiny and yellowish.

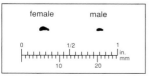

EUONYMUS SCALE

female	male

0   1/2   1 in.
                mm
     10   20

SOFT SCALES

Black Scale
Saissetia oleae

Among the black scale's many hosts are aspen, *Baccharis*, bay, citrus, cottonwood, fruit trees, holly, maple, mayten, oleander, olive, palm, pepper tree, pistachio, poplar, privet, and strawberry tree. Adult female black scales are about ⅕ inch in diameter, dome-shaped, and dark brown or black. Each female produces up to

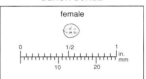

BLACK SCALE

female

0   1/2   1 in.
              mm
     10   20

1,000 to 2,000 pearly white to reddish orange eggs beneath her hard shell body, mainly during May and June. The tiny emerging crawlers are light brown. Crawlers settle and feed mostly on leaves. During the late second instar, a ridge develops on the scale's back and later expands into an H-shape. After the second molt, young scales migrate to twigs where they become dark mottled gray and leathery. Once egg laying starts, the scales become darker and harder and the H-shaped ridge may become difficult to see. Black scale has two generations a year along the coast and one generation inland in California.

Metaphycus helvolus, a parasitic wasp, kills young black scales by laying eggs in them or by feeding on their body fluids. Parasite activity can be recognized with a hand lens by inspecting scale covers for the round exit hole chewed by the emerging adult parasite. *M. helvolus* is one of several *Metaphycus* species that

attacks and emerges from immature scales. Another wasp, *Scutellista cyanea,* emerges from mature scales. Commercially available *Metaphycus* can be released when young scales with an H-shaped ridge are present, but there is no research on the effectiveness of parasite releases in landscapes. Monitor for scale crawlers using double-sided sticky tape and begin making any *Metaphycus* releases after crawler activity declines and young nymphs begin to settle and feed. Consult the beginning of this chapter for general guidelines on effectively introducing natural enemies.

Conserve resident and introduced natural enemies by controlling ants, reducing dust, and avoiding persistent, broad-spectrum insecticides. Prune to open up tree canopies in warm-climate areas such as the Central Valley of California. This increases heat mortality and helps control black scale. Narrow-range oil controls black scale; spray deciduous plants during the dormant season if needed, or time a foliar application by monitoring crawlers.

Black scales have a characteristic H-shape on the back. The feature is most visible here on the flattened, brownish nymphs in the center. The dark, bulbous black scales are adult females.

Brown Soft Scale
Coccus hesperidum

Brown soft scale has many hosts, including aspen, citrus, cottonwood, fruit trees, holly, manzanita, palm, poplar, strawberry tree, and willow. Immature scales are a mottled yellow brown and rounded. Nymphs are found primarily on leaves and then move back onto twigs to mature. Mature females are yellow to dark brown, somewhat flattened, and look similar to citricola scale (see below). Brown soft scale has three to five annual generations, which overlap so that multiple life stages are usually present at once. Populations are usually highest from mid-summer to early fall.

The wasp *Metaphycus luteolus* is an important parasite of brown soft scale, leaving one to several exit holes in larger nymphs or mature scales. Immature scales are also parasitized by several *Coccophagus* species wasps. The small, oblong scales parasitized by *Coccophagus* are black, in contrast to the normal yellowish color of brown soft scale nymphs. *Chilocorus cacti*, a small, mostly black lady beetle, also preys on brown soft scale.

Control honeydew-seeking ants and conserve beneficials. Prune out heavily infested branches. Apply oil if necessary during the dormant season or when monitoring indicates that crawlers are active in the spring.

Citricola Scale
Coccus pseudomagnoliarum

Citricola scale occurs on citrus, elm, hackberry, pomegranate, and walnut. It is mottled dark brown to gray. Citricola scale may be confused with brown soft scale, but the mature brown soft scale is smaller and yellow or dark brown, not gray. Citricola scale has only one generation a year, so most individuals are about the same size. Because brown soft scale has several generations a year, different-sized life stages commonly occur at the same time.

Citricola scale is apparently controlled by parasitoids in south coastal California, but not in California's Central Valley; conserve these natural enemies where they are present. Apply oil if necessary during the dormant season or when monitoring indicates that crawlers are active in the spring.

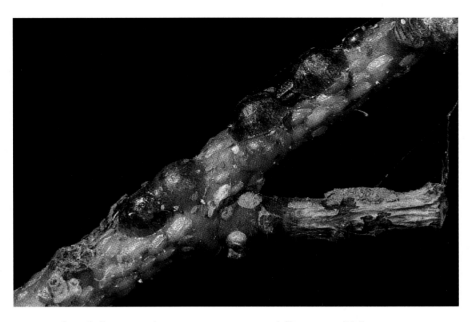

Brown soft scale has several generations a year, so different-sized life stages commonly occur at the same time. Shown here are tiny yellow crawlers, yellow first instars, and orangish to dark brown females.

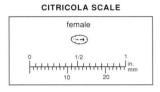

BROWN SOFT SCALE	CITRICOLA SCALE
female	female

Citricola scale females are larger and grayer than similar-looking, mature brown soft scales. Maturing citricola scales are all about the same size because the insect has only one generation a year. Note the tiny crawlers on the branch.

Oak lecanium scale, *Parthenolecanium quercifex*, looks like European fruit lecanium and frosted scale. *Chilocorus bipustulatus*, a reddish to brown scale-feeding lady beetle with three lighter spots on each wing cover, is visible atop the two left most scales.

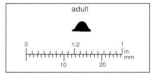

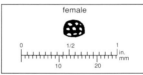

These calico scale females on box elder are typically mottled white and black or brown.

European Fruit Lecanium *Parthenolecanium corni* and Frosted Scale *Parthenolecanium pruinosum*

European fruit lecanium, also called brown apricot scale, commonly feeds on alder, aspen, cottonwood, elm, fruit trees, pistachio, poplar, toyon, and walnut. Frosted scale, sometimes called globose scale, occurs on ash, birch, elm, fruit trees, laurel, locust, pistachio, rose, sycamore, and walnut. Females of both species have a shiny dark brown, oval-domed shell, often with several ridges along the back. The scales' life cycles are similar, except that unlike European fruit lecanium, the frosted scale female produces a white, waxy, frostlike cover in spring that weathers away by early summer. In spring, the female produces up to 2,000 ovoid, translucent white eggs beneath its cover. The yellow to brown nymphs emerge from May to July and feed on twigs and leaves. They have one generation a year.

Control ants and dust and conserve natural enemies by avoiding persistent pesticides. Prune out heavily infested branches. Apply oil if necessary during the dormant season or when monitoring indicates that crawlers are active in the spring.

Calico Scale *Eulecanium cerasorum*

Calico scale occurs on box elder, liquidambar, maple, and walnut. The mature female is relatively large, globular, and has a typical white and brown or black mottled or "calico" pattern. Scales begin to mature on twigs in late winter. The tiny crawlers emerge in early spring and move onto leaves. Before leaves drop in fall, scales move back onto twigs to over-winter.

Calico scale nymphs are covered with thick, elevated, waxy plates. Nymphs are larger and more elongated than frosted scale nymphs, which are flat. Unlike calico scale, the mature frosted scale has a frostlike or powdery covering in spring that

weathers away by early summer. Both scales have one generation a year.

Calico scale populations are rarely abundant enough to warrant control. If populations cannot be tolerated, apply narrow-range oil after leaf drop, but before mid-January when scales begin to mature and become less susceptible to treatment. Oil or another insecticide can be applied when monitoring shows that crawlers are numerous in late spring or early summer, but spraying then may be more disruptive of natural enemies.

Irregular Pine Scale
Toumeyella pinicola

Irregular pine scale overwinters as females on pine branches, typically in blackened and honeydew-encrusted colonies on 1- or 2-year-old shoots. The yellowish, gray, and brown female is robust, dimpled, and roughly circular. The late-instar immature male scale is elongate and flattened with a raised central ridge. Male nymphs resemble grains of rice and may be observed in large numbers on needles.

A female irregular pine scale produces up to 2,000 crawlers. Crawlers are distinctly flattened, oval, orange to yellow, and visible as they move over shoots and needles. Crawlers appear from February through May in southern California, and from late April through June in the San Francisco Bay Area. One generation occurs each year.

If populations are damaging, monitor crawlers with sticky tape or inspect foliage weekly with a hand lens beginning in February in southern California or in April in northern California. Apply oil when crawlers first become abundant and spray again 2 or 3 weeks later if populations are especially high. Some more persistent insecticides (such as carbaryl) to which a commercial spreader-sticker has been added are effective but may cause a spider mite outbreak unless a miticide is also added.

Irregular pine scale males look like grains of rice on these Monterey pine needles. Brownish, females encrusted with sooty mold infest the twig; one dead female has parasite emergence holes. Monterey pine scale, *Physokermes insignicola*, looks very similar but it is uniformly spherical and black.

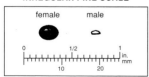

IRREGULAR PINE SCALE

female   male

0   1/2   1
|⊦⊦⊦⊦⊦⊦⊦⊦⊦|⊦⊦⊦⊦⊦⊦⊦⊦⊦|⊦⊦⊦⊦⊦⊦⊦⊦⊦| in.
                                    mm
        10   20

OTHER COMMON SCALES

Cottony Cushion Scale
Icerya purchasi

Cottony cushion scale, family Margarodidae, is most common on acacia, boxwood, citrus, magnolia, *Nandina*, olive, pittosporum, and rose. The female is bright orange, red, yellow, or brown and is distinguished by its elongated, fluted, white cottony egg sac, which contains from 600 to 800 eggs. Eggs hatch in a few days during warm weather, but take up to two months to hatch in winter. Crawlers are red with dark legs and antennae. First- and second-instar nymphs settle on twigs and leaves, usually along veins. The third instar is covered with a thick, yellow, cottony secretion, which disappears after it molts. The minute, red, winged male is rarely seen; it seeks a secluded place on the tree or ground to form a loose, white cocoon.

Cottony cushion scale has several generations a year. It is usually well controlled by two introduced natural enemies. The most famous is the vedalia beetle, *Rodolia cardinalis*. This red and black lady beetle was introduced from Australia in the 1890s and saved California's fledgling citrus industry from destruction by the prolific scales. Adult beetles feed on scales and females lay their eggs underneath the scale or attached to scale egg sacs. The young reddish larvae move into the egg masses and feed; more mature larvae feed on all scale stages. The other important natural enemy, the parasitic fly *Cryptochaetum iceryae,* deposits its eggs inside the scale body. The larvae feed within the scale; later their dark, oblong pupal cases may be seen there. This tachinid fly produces up to eight generations per year.

Conserve natural enemies by controlling ants and dust and by avoiding use of persistent insecticides. If scales cannot be tolerated until natural enemies become abundant, apply narrow-range oil to deciduous hosts during the dormant season or spray foliage when the tiny reddish scale crawlers are active.

Sycamore Scale
Stomacoccus platani

Sycamore scale, family Margarodidae, occurs only on sycamore. Infested leaves have numerous small yellow spots. Leaves become distorted and may drop prematurely or turn brown, die, and then drop. Nymphs and eggs overwinter on and beneath bark plates. They resume development in spring, and at maturity are yellow to

Cottony cushion scale females and nymphs on grevillea bark.

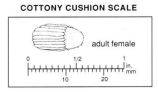

COTTONY CUSHION SCALE

adult female

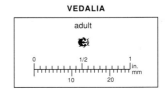

VEDALIA

adult

Black predominates on some vedalia, while some others have more red.

brown. The mature female is easily recognized by the cottony white tufts of developing eggs that emerge from beneath the body and protrude from bark cracks and crevices. Each female produces from 50 to 100 eggs and the emerging immatures move onto foliage. As they mature, most scales on foliage move back to the trunk and limbs and produce eggs, yet some females and eggs occur on leaves in summer. Sycamore scale has several generations a year.

Sycamore scale damage is most obvious during the late spring when leaves may be severely spotted, but foliar sprays are not recommended. It is difficult to spray the underside of leaves thoroughly where scales feed. The lower leaf surface of native *Platanus racemosa* has dense mats of tiny hairs, which entwine scales and repel liquids. If scales are abundant and damage cannot be tolerated, apply 1% narrow-range oil, insecticidal soap, or another insecticide during the delayed dormant season. Inspect trees regularly beginning in late December and spray at bud break; scales are in the highly susceptible immature stage at bud break. Applying oil too late, after buds open and before leaves fully flush, may cause phytotoxicity and be less effective. Thoroughly spray branch tips and use a high-pressure sprayer to reach scales under the bark plates on trunks and large limbs.

Sycamore scale severely spots sycamore leaves. Infested young leaves distort as they develop.

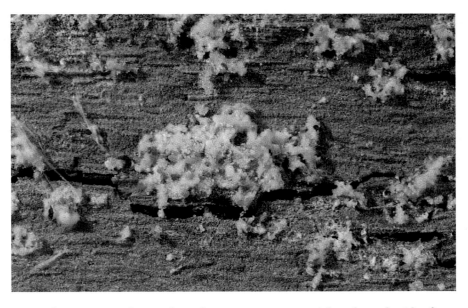

Orangish sycamore scale nymphs and eggs in cottony material on the underside of a sycamore bark plate.

European Elm Scale
Gossyparia spuria

European elm scale, family Eriococcidae, occurs only on elm. The conspicuous mature female is a dark red, brown, or purple oval surrounded by a white cottony wax fringe on the sides of the body. They encrust bark at the crotches of twigs and on the lower surface of limbs. Scales overwinter as yellow to brown nymphs on bark. The immature male in the spring looks like a tiny, elongate, whitish cocoon. Females mature during spring and early summer and crawlers begin emerging in late spring; some settle and feed on the underside of leaves before returning to bark in the fall. The insect has one generation a year.

Keep trees healthy so they tolerate feeding by scales and other insects. European and American elms are adapted to frequent summer rains; provide adequate irrigation in areas of

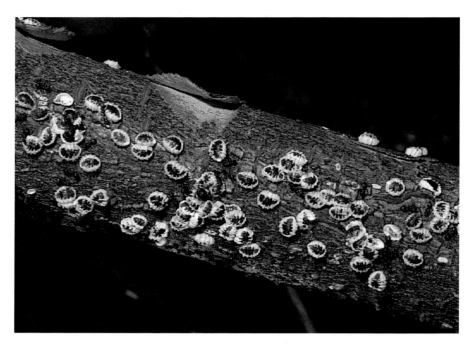

Purplish, white-fringed, mature female European elm scales on Chinese elm tended by Argentine ants.

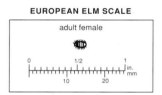

EUROPEAN ELM SCALE

adult female

0   1/2   1
in.
mm
10   20

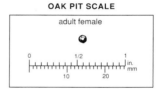

OAK PIT SCALE

adult female

0   1/2   1
in.
mm
10   20

Golden oak scale, *Asterolecanium variolosum*, and pits made by scales that have dropped from this California black oak twig. Some scales have parasite emergence holes.

prolonged summer drought. Several introduced parasites, primarily *Coccophagus insidiator* and *Trichomasthus* sp., attack European elm scale at some locations in California. If parasites are present, as evidenced by round emergence holes in mature female scales, increase the effectiveness of biological control by controlling honeydew-seeking ants.

European elm scale can be controlled on smaller or individual trees by using a hydraulic sprayer to thoroughly apply a forceful stream of water to twigs, branches, and crevices from at least three directions. Spray after the soft-bodied females have begun maturing in spring, but before elm leaves unfold to obstruct the water. Foliage usually begins pushing out when the clusters of seeds (fruit) have matured and start to drop. If populations are intolerable, narrow-range oil can be applied in spring or early summer as timed by monitoring crawlers.

Oak Pit Scales
Asterolecanium spp.

Oak pit scales, family Asterolecaniidae, feed on oak, causing ring-shaped depressions in bark. Dead twigs and leaves are apparent in winter on infested deciduous oaks. Heavy infestations cause branch dieback and distorted terminal regrowth. *Asterolecanium minus* and *Asterolecanium quercicola* in California prefer native valley oak (*Quercus lobata*) and blue oak (*Q. douglasii*) and also occur on coast live oak (*Q. agrifolia*) and California black oak (*Q. kelloggii*). *Asterolecanium variolosum* prefers English oak (*Q. robur*). Mature scales are brown, gold, or green, flattened, circular, immobile insects about the size of the head of a pin. Crawlers emerge from beneath the female from

April through October, primarily in April through June. When scales are abundant, their feeding pits coalesce giving twigs a roughened, dimpled appearance.

Narrow-range oil provides control if applied to cover all bark and branch tips thoroughly in the delayed dormant season, just before buds open. To get control after leaves have fully flushed, combine oil with a compatible botanical, organophosphate, or carbamate insecticide and apply it with high-pressure commercial spray equipment. Make this spray when inspection with a hand lens or monitoring with double-sided sticky tape indicates that crawlers are abundant (April to June). One annual application of either treatment during several consecutive years may be necessary to reduce high populations to a low level.

LEAFHOPPERS

Several hundred species of leafhoppers, family Cicadellidae, suck the juice from various landscape plants, but most kinds feed on only one or several closely related plant species. Leafhopper feeding causes leaves to appear stippled, pale, or brown, and shoots may curl and die. Some leafhopper species transmit plant diseases, but this is important mostly among herbaceous crop plants. A few species secrete honeydew on which foliage-blackening sooty mold grows.

Most adult leafhoppers are slender and ¼ inch or shorter. Some species are brightly colored, while others blend with their host plant. Leafhoppers are active insects, that walk rapidly sideways or readily jump when disturbed. Adults and nymphs and their pale cast skins are usually found on the underside of leaves.

Females insert their tiny eggs in tender plant tissue. The wingless nymphs that emerge molt four or five times and mature in about 2 to 7 weeks. Leafhoppers overwinter as eggs on twigs or as adults in protected places such as bark crevices. Most species have two or more generations each year.

Ignore these insects as they rarely if ever cause serious harm to woody plants. Insecticidal soap or narrow-range oil can be applied to infested foliage to reduce high populations of leafhopper nymphs; thorough coverage of leaf undersides is important. It is very difficult to effectively control adults and no control is recommended.

TREEHOPPERS

Treehoppers, family Membracidae, suck plant juices. This feeding damage is slight, although the honeydew produced by treehoppers supports the growth of sooty mold, which may blacken leaves and twigs when treehoppers become numerous. Treehop-

Oak treehopper adults on coast live oak. Tiny bark punctures are visible where eggs were laid.

OAK TREEHOPPER

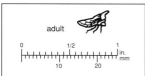

LEAFHOPPER

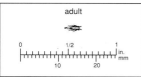

An adult leafhopper on *Myoporum*.

pers injure plants primarily by making numerous small slits or crescent-like punctures in bark where they lay their eggs. These egg punctures cause bark to appear roughened, and twigs may die back. Mature woody plants tolerate extensive egg-laying damage, but the growth of heavily infested younger plants may be retarded.

Treehopper adults are commonly greenish to brown and ½ inch long or shorter. They have an expanded hood covering the body, which may be formed into hornlike projections. Nymphs have numerous spines on the back of the abdomen, and both immatures and adults readily jump.

The oak treehopper, *Platycotis vittata,* is common in the spring throughout the U.S. on the lower branches of deciduous and live oaks

The white frothy material on this rose bud petiole conceals an immature spittlebug sucking on plant tissue.

and occasionally on birch, chestnut, or other broadleaf trees. Adults are olive green to bronze with reddish bands and their surface is covered with tiny pits. They often scurry to the opposite side of the twig or leaf when approached. Females usually remain with their eggs and the nymphs after they emerge. The nymphs are black with yellow and red markings. The spring generation is colorful and usually gregarious; individuals typically aggregate in rows on twigs.

The buffalo treehopper, *Stictocephala bisonia,* is common in landscapes throughout the U.S. Its hosts include ash, elm, fruit trees, hawthorn, locust, poplar, and many herbaceous plants. Adults are bright green or yellowish with a yellowish underside. Nymphs are green with prominent spines on the back.

If treehopper populations were high on deciduous trees the previous season and damage cannot be tolerated, narrow-range oil can be applied during the dormant season to kill overwintering eggs. To control species known to feed on many different plants, removing some of these alternate hosts may reduce treehopper populations feeding on more valued plants. High populations of nymphs and adults may be reduced by spraying exposed insects with insecticidal soap, narrow-range oil, or another insecticide as recommended in *Insect Pest Management Guidelines for California Landscape Ornamentals* (UC Publication 3317).

SPITTLEBUGS

Spittlebugs or froghoppers, family Cercopidae, suck plant juices. They occur throughout the U.S. and can at least occasionally be found on almost any plant. Heavy infestations distort

plant tissue and slow plant growth, but this is primarily a problem on herbaceous species. The obvious and occasionally abundant masses of white foam on cones, foliage, or stems may be annoying, but the spittlebugs do not seriously harm established woody plants.

Adult spittlebugs are inconspicuous, often brownish insects, about ¼ inch long. They look like leafhoppers and readily jump or fly when disturbed. Females lay small eggs in rows in hidden parts of the plant, such as the sheath between leaves and stems. The presence of immature spittlebugs is readily recognized by the frothy white mass that nymphs surround themselves with on plant tissue where they feed. Nymphs undergo about five molts, and may be orange, yellow, or green. More than one nymph may be found in a single spittle mass.

The meadow spittlebug, *Philaenus spumarius,* is found throughout the U.S. It feeds primarily on herbaceous plants, but also occurs on conifers and young woody deciduous plants. Adults are robust and tan, black, or mottled brownish. Females lay white to brown eggs in rows at plant nodes. Nymphs are yellow to green and hidden beneath a foaming mass of spittle.

The western pine spittlebug, *Aphrophora permutata,* is one of several *Aphrophora* species that feed on conifers and their understory shrubs. Western pine spittlebug occurs on Monterey pine and other pines, Douglas fir, fir, hemlock, and spruce. Pine spittlebug eggs are tiny, pale yellow to purple, slightly curved and tapered. Eggs are laid in a row on pine needles or may be partially or completely submerged in needle tissue. Nymphs are dark greenish, brown, or black, sometimes with lighter spots or a pink abdomen. Adults are brownish orange to dark brown and may have an indistinct diagonal white line across the back. Overwintering occurs as eggs, and pine spittlebugs have one or two generations a year in California.

Ignore spittlebugs on woody plants or wash nymphs off of plants with a forceful stream of water. Spittlebugs are more likely to become abundant on woody plants when they migrate from nearby herbaceous species. Cut weeds or wash spittlebugs off of these alternate hosts in the spring, before the insects mature and can spread.

PLANT BUGS, LACE BUGS, BOXELDER BUGS, AND OTHER TRUE BUGS

Plant bugs, lace bugs, boxelder bugs, lygus bugs, and chinch bugs are in the order Hemiptera, the only group of insects that entomologists call bugs. More than 600 true bug species occur just in California. Many are aquatic or semiaquatic, and most of these are predaceous. Many terrestrial true bugs feed on plants, although some species such as assassin bugs, damsel bugs, bigeyed bugs, and minute pirate bugs are important predators.

DAMAGE

Plant-feeding true bugs suck juices from leaves, fruit, or nuts. A pale white or yellow stippling forms around feeding sites and plant tissue may become distorted. True bugs do not seriously harm established woody plants; however, activities of some species can be undesirable. For instance, lace bugs leave dark specks of excrement on the underside of leaves. Large numbers of boxelder bugs (and occasionally other species like assassin bugs) can be a nuisance when they enter houses to overwinter.

IDENTIFICATION AND BIOLOGY

Bugs usually have thickened forewings with membranous tips. When they rest, the dissimilar parts of their folded wings overlap. Nearly all true bugs can be recognized by the characteristic triangle or X-shape on the back formed by their folded wings. Hemipterans have sucking mouthparts, which on plant-feeding species point downward, perpendicular to the plane of the insect's body. The mouthparts of predaceous bugs can be extended forward when attacking other insects. Depending on the species, eggs are laid exposed on foliage or bark or inserted in plant tissue. The flightless nymphs gradually change to winged adults without any pupal stage (Figure 4-3).

MANAGEMENT

True bugs rarely cause serious harm to established woody plants. Provide proper cultural care so plants are vigorous. Damaged foliage can be pruned out. Consider replacing especially susceptible plants with resistant species. Spraying for bugs is generally not recommended. Extreme populations may be reduced by applying an insecticide to foliage when nymphs are abundant in the spring; systemic insecticides are the most effective. No treatment will restore stippled foliage, which remains until replaced by new growth. See *Insect Pest Management Guidelines for California Landscape Ornamentals* (UC Publication 3317) for specific insecticide recommendations.

Lace Bugs
Corythucha spp.

Many kinds of lace bugs, family Tingidae, feed on landscape plants throughout the U.S. *Corythucha* species are common and each species feeds on only one or a few closely related plants, including alder, ash, *Baccharis*, birch, ceanothus, fruit trees, photinia, poplar, sycamore, toyon, walnut, and willow. Leaf stippling caused by lace bugs usually appears late in the summer and can be distinguished from feeding by mites by the dark specks of excrement that lace bugs deposit on the

Bleached foliage caused by lace bugs feeding on photinia. Other true bugs, thrips, and mites cause similar leaf stippling.

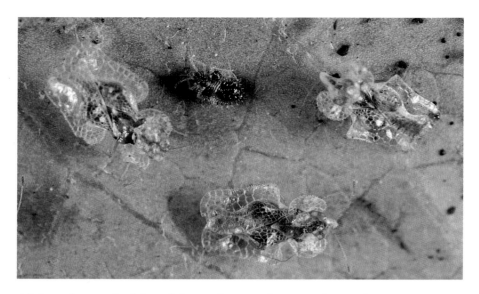

Adults and a nymph of the California Christmas berry tingid, *Corythucha incurvata*, a common lace bug species on toyon.

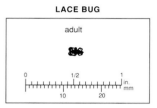

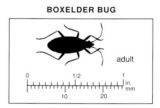

lower leaf surface. Greenhouse thrips also produce both leaf stippling and dark excrement, so you must examine the lower leaf surface for insects to distinguish these pests.

Most adult lace bugs are about ⅛ inch long and flat. The body is concealed beneath an expanded, lacelike or reticulated thorax and forewings. Females insert tiny eggs partly in plant tissue, often hidden under excrement. The wingless nymphs commonly have long body spines. All stages occur in groups on the underside of leaves. Most species overwinter as adults under bark plates and have several generations a year.

Tolerate lace bug damage as it does not seriously harm plants. Provide adequate irrigation and other care to improve plant vigor. Prune out damaged foliage, as insecticides do not restore undamaged appearance. Narrow-range oil or insecticidal soap can be applied to lower leaf surfaces infested by adults and nymphs to lower their abundance.

Boxelder Bugs
Boisea spp.

Boxelder bugs, family Rhopalidae, occur throughout the U.S. *Boisea trivittata* is probably the most common species. Boxelder bugs usually become abundant only on female box elder trees, *Acer negundo,* but can also occur on maple and fruit trees. Boxelder bug feeding causes leaf stippling, but this is apparently harmless to trees. Boxelder bugs are a pest because high populations are annoying to people. In the fall, adults often aggregate in large numbers on sunny surfaces, such as the south side of trees or buildings. Swarms of adults then fly to sheltered places to overwinter, often inside homes.

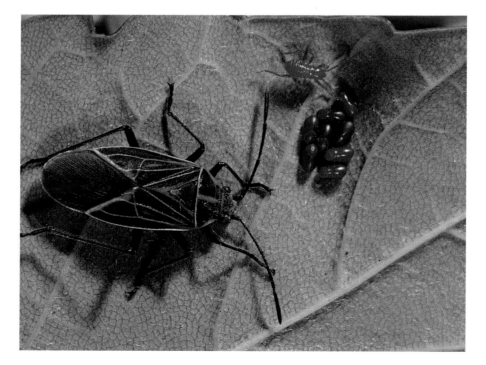

Boxelder bugs like this adult, nymph, and eggs, are most common on female (pod-bearing) box elder trees.

Boxelder bugs are grayish brown to black with conspicuous red lines on the body. Females lay oblong red or orange eggs in the spring in bark crevices or on foliage. Nymphs are gray and bright red, and develop black marks as they mature. Boxelder bugs have one generation a year.

Replace, and do not plant, the pod-bearing female box elder trees; they support high boxelder bug populations. Eliminate debris and litter near homes, especially around foundations, to reduce the shelter that boxelder bugs need to successfully overwinter. Vacuum up bugs that enter the home. Seal exterior cracks in the house and screen windows and doors to prevent bugs from entering the home. No pesticides are recommended.

Ash Plant Bugs
Tropidosteptes spp.

Ash plant bugs are in the plant bug family Miridae. Ash plant bugs occur throughout the U.S. on ash and may occasionally feed on nearby plants if ash becomes heavily infested and defoliated. *Tropidosteptes illitus* and *T. pacificus* are pests in the West, especially in the warm interior valleys of California. *T. illitus* nymphs are light brown, and adults are yellow and brown or black. *T. pacificus* adults are brown, and the nymphs are green with black spots. Nymphs and adults suck plant juices from ash leaves, twigs, flowers, and seeds. Ash plant bug damage usually consists of leaf stippling. Tiny, dark spots of excrement may be visible on foliage. Extreme infestations can defoliate trees.

Ash plant bugs overwinter as eggs in twig bark. These hatch in February or March and the nymphs feed until they mature in April or May. The adults feed until June or July when they lay eggs. Ash plant bugs have one or two generations a year.

Trees apparently tolerate ash plant bug damage; it is rarely severe enough to cause defoliation or warrant control. Severe defoliation of ash is usually due to anthracnose fungus or drought. If damage cannot be tolerated, insecticidal soap or narrow-range oil may be applied to thoroughly cover leaf undersides infested with nymphs in the spring.

Lygus Bugs
Lygus spp.

Lygus bugs, family Miridae, feed on many different broadleaf plants, including rose, *Prunus* species, and the fruit of trees. *Lygus hesperus* is the most common species. Adults are green, straw yellow, or brown with a conspicuous yellow or pale green triangle on the back. Lygus bug eggs are inserted into plant tissue and are not easily observed.

Lygus bug feeding causes discolored bumps or depressions on fruit, but without the white pithy areas beneath that are characteristic of stink bug feeding. Lygus bugs are most likely to damage fruit when nearby herbaceous vegetation on which they feed dries up or is cut, prompting the bugs to move into trees. Control is generally not recommended on woody ornamental plants. If damage cannot be tolerated, reduce movement by controlling weeds and reducing nearby herbaceous vegetation before young fruit appear

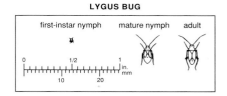

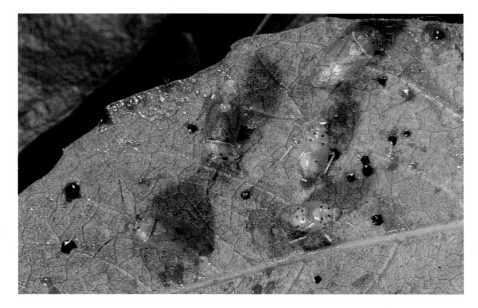

Brown adults and green nymphs of the Pacific ash plant bug, *Tropidosteptes pacificus*, leave varnishlike excrement on the underside of ash leaves.

The adult lygus bug, *Lygus hesperus*, has a distinct yellow or pale green triangle behind its head.

Unless blemished fruit cannot be tolerated, this consperse stink bug and related species do not harm woody plants. Its white, barrel-shaped eggs are at left.

STINK BUG

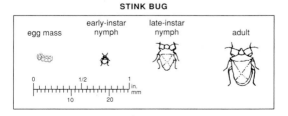

on trees. Alternatively, keep nearby vegetation lush so that bugs are not induced to move.

Stink Bugs

Stink bugs, family Pentatomidae, are shield shaped with a large scutellum or triangle on their backs. They are wider than most other true bugs (Figure 4-3) and are named because of the offensive-smelling defensive chemical some species give off when disturbed. Stink bug eggs are barrel shaped with distinct circular lids and are usually laid in groups of 10 or more on leaf surfaces.

Most stink bugs are pests of vegetable or herbaceous plants; a few species are beneficial predators. The consperse stink bug, *Euschistus consperus,* attacks stone fruit and pear trees, causing discolored depressions, blemishes, or dark pinpricks on fruit. Damaged areas beneath spots on fruit become white and pithy but remain firm as fruit ripen. Except for fruit, woody plants are not harmed by stink bug feeding, and control is generally not recommended. If damage cannot be tolerated, manage nearby herbaceous vegetation to reduce movement as discussed above for lygus bugs.

Chinch Bugs

Chinch bugs, family Lygaeidae, damage the fruit and flowers of some landscape trees, but are primarily pests of herbaceous plants. *Blissus* species are the most common pests; these adults are small, slender, blackish bugs with reddish or yellowish brown legs. Wings may be white with brown spots or brown with white tips.

Replanting turf or other nearby herbaceous plants with species less preferred by chinch bugs can reduce populations that may build up and move to attack woody ornamentals. Tolerate damage or manage nearby herbaceous vegetation to reduce movement, as discussed above for lygus bugs.

THRIPS

Thrips, order Thysanoptera, are tiny, slender insects that feed on tissue surfaces with their sucking mouthparts. Most species feed in flowers, buds, or other hidden areas of growing plant parts such as central terminals. Most thrips are relatively harmless to plants and some, such as the sixspotted thrips, are beneficial predators.

DAMAGE

Thrips feeding can stunt growth and cause leaves to become stippled, papery, and distorted. Infested terminals may discolor, become tightly rolled, and drop leaves prematurely. Thrips can cause dead spots or blotches to appear on flowers, and high populations of some species cover the lower surface of leaves with black, varnishlike specks of excrement. Thrips are poor fliers, so that damage may first appear in one location then slowly spread over the plant. Infestations reduce the aesthetic quality of landscapes but usually do not seriously harm or kill woody plants.

IDENTIFICATION AND BIOLOGY

Adults are narrow, less than $\frac{1}{20}$ inch long, and have long fringes on the margins of their wings. Adults are commonly yellowish or blackish and

Toyon thrips, *Rhyncothrips ilex*, feeding distorted these toyon terminals.

Greenhouse thrips caused this leaf stippling on viburnum. Damage often begins in one area and gradually spreads throughout the entire plant.

shiny. Nymphs are translucent white to yellowish. Females lay tiny eggs within leaf tissue or in the curled or distorted foliage caused by feeding nymphs and adults. Thrips have several generations a year.

THRIPS

adult

0   1/2   1
|++++++++++|++++++++++| in.
                              mm
       10   20

MANAGEMENT

Healthy woody plants usually tolerate thrips damage, which is mostly aesthetic. Provide proper cultural care to keep plants vigorous. Prune and destroy injured and infested terminals when managing a few small specimen plants. Avoid shearing plants. Shearing—clipping the surface of dense foliage to maintain an even surface on formal hedges—stimulates susceptible new growth. New growth increases populations of Cuban laurel thrips and other species, resulting in more damage. Prune by cutting plants just above growing points such as branch crotches and nodes instead of shearing off terminals.

Resident populations of predaceous arthropods including spiders, minute pirate bugs, and mites help to control plant-feeding thrips. Some natural enemies of thrips are commercially available, including a parasitic wasp (see greenhouse thrips), several *Amblyseius* species of mites, and the minute pirate bug, *Orius tristicolor* (see Suppliers). Little or no research has been conducted on the effectiveness of releasing additional thrips predators or parasites in landscapes. Conserving naturally occurring populations of beneficials by controlling dust and avoiding persistent pesticides is the most important way to encourage biological control of thrips.

Most thrips are difficult to control effectively with insecticides because they reproduce year-round in areas of California with mild winters and are protected from sprays by leaf curls or other plant parts that surround them. Because several applications of a systemic insecticide during the growing season may be required to provide control, and because spraying also kills natural enemies, insecticides are generally not recommended. Certain plant growth regulators may be applied to prevent the formation of the new growth preferred by thrips; growth regulators can damage plants and label directions must be strictly followed. Monitor plants for thrips before any spraying because damage remains after insect populations have declined or disappeared.

Monitor for thrips by branch beating or shaking foliage or flowers onto a sheet of paper and counting the thrips. Adult populations can be monitored using bright yellow sticky traps, as discussed earlier in this chapter. Blue sticky traps are most effective against western flower thrips and can be used when this species is of primary interest.

Predators like this adult minute pirate bug, *Orius tristicolor*, help to control many thrips species.

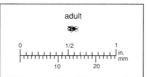

MINUTE PIRATE BUG

adult

An adult predatory mite, *Euseius tularensis*, is eating this yellow citrus thrips nymph.

Cuban Laurel Thrips
Gynaikothrips ficorum

Cuban laurel thrips occurs in Gulf Coast states, Hawaii, and in southern California where it is especially abundant on *Ficus microcarpa*. All thrips stages occur the year around in tightly rolled, podlike leaf terminals of *Ficus* species. Adults are black, nymphs are yellow, and eggs are white. Galled foliage is formed from mid-summer through fall, and thrips populations are highest from about October through December.

Cuban laurel thrips does not seriously harm *Ficus*, so no control is needed if distorted foliage can be tolerated. Several predators occur in galls, most commonly larvae of the common green lacewing and adults and nymphs of a minute pirate bug, *Macrotracheliella nigra*, which is dark reddish brown to black and less than ⅛ inch long. Pruning and disposing of infested terminals can provide effective control. Winter may be the best time to prune off tips because more galled tissue generally does not form until next summer and relatively few thrips can survive outside of the protection provided by the rolled leaves.

Flower Thrips
Frankliniella spp.

Flower thrips occur throughout the U.S., and overwinter as adults in debris or on herbaceous plants. Western flower thrips, *Frankliniella occi-*

Rolled, podlike *Ficus microcarpa* terminals caused by Cuban laurel thrips feeding.

dentalis, is the most common pest species. Adults are mostly yellowish with a brown or blackish abdomen. Flower thrips feed primarily on herbaceous plants, but high populations occasionally damage continuously or late blossoming flowers on woody plants such as roses. This aesthetic damage is of concern on exhibition blooms and in greenhouse production, but damage is usually not important in landscapes, so control is generally not recommended.

Greenhouse Thrips
Heliothrips haemorrhoidalis

Greenhouse thrips attacks many landscape plants throughout the U.S. Adults are mostly black, except for the tip of the abdomen, which is reddish brown. Unlike most thrips species, greenhouse thrips feeds openly on leaves in dense colonies of

The adult western flower thrips is mostly yellowish, often with a darker abdomen.

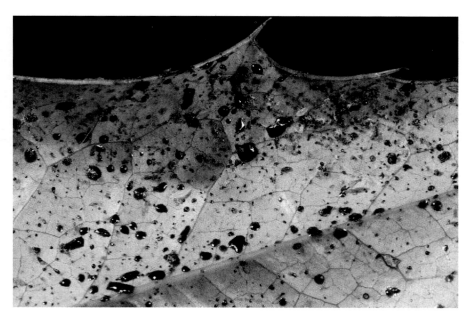

Unlike most thrips species, greenhouse thrips feed openly on leaves. They have produced much black excrement on the underside and bleached this mahonia leaf.

adults and immatures. There are five to seven annual generations in California.

Where practical, frequent spraying of infested surfaces with a forceful stream of water controls greenhouse thrips. Populations can also be reduced by applying insecticidal soap or narrow-range oil when insects and damage first appear. Because of their short persistence, oil or soap sprays are less disruptive of natural enemies. These beneficials include the wasp *Thripobius semiluteus,* a parasite recently imported from South America and Australia that attacks only greenhouse thrips.

Thripobius releases in greenhouses and southern California avocado orchards have been effective in controlling greenhouse thrips. The tiny wasp lays its eggs in young thrips nymphs, which become swollen around the head as they mature.

About 2 weeks before the wasp's emergence, parasitized nymphs turn black, in contrast to the yellow color of unparasitized nymphs. Unlike healthy black mature thrips, the black parasitized nymphs are smaller and do not move.

Thripobius develops from egg to adult in about 3 weeks when temperatures average 70°F, so many generations can occur each year in warm areas. *Thripobius* is commercially available (see Suppliers), but no specific release recommendations have been developed for landscape plants. Based on research in avocado orchards, releasing several hundred wasps per 15-foot-tall tree when young thrips nymphs are first observed may reduce greenhouse thrips populations and damage. See the beginning of this chapter for general guidelines on effectively releasing natural enemies.

Citrus Thrips
Scirtothrips citri

Citrus thrips can occur on most fruit trees, California pepper tree, and pomegranate. It usually causes damage only on citrus, where it scars the rind surface but does not damage the fruit inside. Flower thrips can occur on the same plants and is difficult to distinguish from citrus thrips. Flower thrips often (but not always) has a dark abdomen while adult citrus thrips is entirely yellowish. A citrus thrips infestation is indicated by the yellow to brownish scabby feeding scars that form on fruit, often in a ring on the rind around the citrus stem.

Do not spray for citrus thrips unless you are marketing fruit; thrips damage does not harm trees or the internal fruit quality. If you do spray, this cosmetic damage can be reduced by spraying only the outside of the canopy where thrips are most abundant. Sabadilla, a botanical pesticide, is recommended because it does not affect most natural enemies, including *Euseius tularensis,* a tiny, drop-shaped mite that is an important predator of citrus thrips. *Euseius* nymphs and adults are shiny and translucent to tan. This predator often remains unnoticed because it is small and most abundant on the underside of leaves in the interior of trees.

GALL MAKERS

Galls are distorted, sometimes colorful swellings in plant tissue caused by the secretions of certain plant-feeding insects and mites. These unusual growths may be found on leaves, flowers, twigs, or branches. Galls are

A yellow and black *Thripobius semiluteus* adult (center) and black pupae of this parasite among yellowish greenhouse thrips nymphs.

caused by many different invertebrates, including sawflies on willow, adelgids on spruce, aphids on poplar, cottonwood, and manzanita, and eriophyid mites on aspen, alder, beech, cottonwood, elm, fuchsia, linden, maple, poplar, and walnut. However, most galls are caused by cynipid wasps or gall midge flies, which are discussed here. The stem galls on ceanothus caused by a moth are also included in this section.

Gall development is poorly understood, but larval secretions apparently induce abnormal growth of cells in the plant. Many galls harbor a single, legless larva. Other galls may harbor several larvae, some of which may be different species that are predators or parasites of the gall maker.

Most galls are not known to harm trees. Prune and dispose of galls if they are annoying. This may provide control of some species if pruning is done when the immatures are in plant tissue and before the adults begin to emerge.

Oak Gall Wasps

Hundreds of species of gall wasps, family Cynipidae, occur in the U.S. Galls caused by these hymenopterans are especially abundant and varied on oak. The size, shape, and color of the galls formed vary greatly depending on the species of wasp and the part of the host plant where the egg is laid. Adult gall wasps are small, stout, shiny insects. They have very few wing veins, and the body is usually purple or black. The female deposits an egg in plant tissue and a gall begins forming several weeks or months after the white larva has hatched and started to feed.

Many gall wasps exhibit a complex life history; the appearance of galls

CARLTON S. KOEHLER

An oak stem gall made by *Callirhytis perdens* wasps on California black oak.

Pink spined turban galls made by *Antron douglasii* wasps and reddish oak cone galls made by *Andricus kingi* wasps on the underside of valley oak leaves.

and wasps may vary with the season and the part of the plant attacked. Most cynipid species occur on just one or several related host species. Species identifications are more easily based on their galls than on descriptions of the tiny wasps. Gall wasps do not seriously damage oaks, so no management is necessary.

OAK CONE GALL

SPINED TURBAN OAK GALL

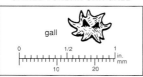

Gall Midges

Hundreds of species of gall midges (also called gall gnats or gall flies), family Cecidomyiidae, occur in the U.S. Not all of these dipteran species form galls. The larvae of some gall midges feed on fungi or dead organic matter or are important predators of small insects. Each gall-forming species feeds inside only one or a few related hosts, including *Baccharis*, dogwood, fir, oak, pine, and willow.

Adult gall midges are tiny, delicate flies, often with long, slender antennae. They lay their minute eggs on foliage. Eggs hatch into tiny white, yellowish, reddish, or orange maggots, which in gall-making species bore into plant tissue and feed inside the galls that form. Most species have several annual generations.

Honeylocust Pod Gall Midge *Dasineura gleditschiae*

Feeding by larvae of the honeylocust pod gall midge causes honey locust leaflets to form galls, each containing one to several small pinkish white maggots. Heavily infested foliage turns brown and drops prematurely, leaving parts of branches leafless. Galls are most apparent early in the growing season; by mid-summer the midges enter diapause and become inactive. This fly has 8 to 10 generations a year.

Because the honeylocust pod gall midge has many generations annually and larvae are protected from sprays, this insect is not effectively controlled with insecticides. Established trees are rarely if ever killed, so damage, while unsightly, can be tolerated. Consider planting alternative species or varieties in landscapes where the plant aesthetic value is high. The 'Shademaster' variety of honey locust appears less susceptible, and black locust is not attacked by this midge. Where damage cannot be tolerated, avoid the 'Sunburst' variety of honey locust, which has bright yellow spring foliage. 'Sunburst' is very sensitive to gall midge damage and defoliates in response to drought or temperature changes as well as gall midge damage.

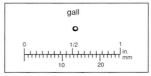

JUMPING OAK GALL

gall

The jumping oak gall wasp, *Neuroterus saltatorius*, causes discolored spots on the upperside, and these seedlike deformations on the underside, of valley oak leaves. Galls drop from leaves in summer. Huge numbers may be seen hopping an inch or more above the ground because of movement by a tiny wasp larva inside each gall.

Young oak apple galls are green. Galls turn reddish or brown, then black after the tiny *Andricus californicus* wasps inside mature and leave the galls.

Distorted terminals infested with honeylocust pod gall midge larvae.

Swollen stems infested with ceanothus stem gall moth larvae causing dieback (bottom) and stunted terminal growth (top).

Ceanothus Stem Gall Moth
Periploca ceanothiella

The ceanothus stem gall moth, family Cosmopterigidae, probably occurs throughout the U.S. wherever *Ceanothus* species occur, but the moth is apparently a pest only in California. The small, dark moths lay eggs on buds and flowers; eggs hatch into tunneling larvae. The spindle-shaped swellings on stems caused by the larvae stunt plant growth and reduce blooming. Overwintering is as larvae in galls. Adults emerge during the spring and early summer. They have one generation a year. Prune and dispose of galled shoots. Do not plant and consider replacing *Ceanothus* species most susceptible to the ceanothus stem gall moth (see Table 4-10).

TABLE 4-10

Relative Susceptibility of *Ceanothus* Species and Cultivars (cv.) to the Ceanothus Stem Gall Moth.[a]

NOT INFESTED
americanus, cuneatus, foliosus, gloriosus, gloriosus exaltatus, jepsonii, impressus, insularis, masonii, megacarpus, papillosus, parryi, prostratus, purpureus, ramulosus fascicularis, rigidus Albus, spinosus, verrucosus, cv. Blue Cloud, cv. Lester Rowntree
LIGHTLY INFESTED
aboreus, diversifolius, integerrimus, lemmonii, leucodermis, lobbianus oliganthus, cv. Concha, cv. Mary Lake, cv. Mountain Haze, cv. Royal Blue cv. Sierra Blue, cv. Treasure Island
MODERATELY INFESTED
cyaneus, thyrsiflorus, cv. Marie Simon, cv. Ray Hartman
SEVERELY INFESTED
griseus, griseus horizontalis

a. From: J. A. Munro. 1963. J. Res. Lepid. 1: 183-190.

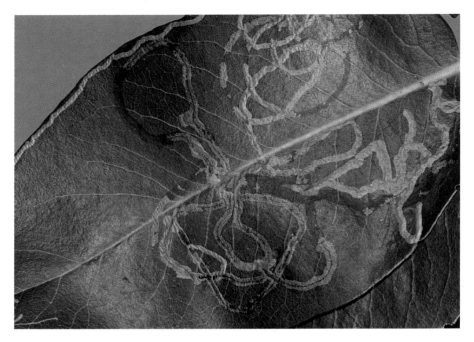

Sinuous trails caused by the madrone leaf miner, *Marmara arbutiella*. A yellowish moth larva is visible in its mine at the right edge of the leaf

This juniper is brown because cypress tip miner larvae are feeding inside foliage.

FOLIAGE MINERS

Many kinds of non-gall-forming insects feed inside succulent plant tissue, including some species of moths, beetles, flies, and sawflies. The larvae of several different families of small moths are the most common foliage-mining pests in landscapes. These insects feed inside of leaves, needles, shoots, or buds and are called leafminers and tipminers, casebearers, and shield bearers. Larval stages of some species also feed externally and skeletonize the surface of leaves, buds, or other plant parts. Mature larvae may pupate inside of leaves or in cocoons on foliage or bark.

Several hundred foliage miner species occur in the U.S. Each kind feeds on only one or several closely related plants. The host species and characteristic form of the larva's damage help to identify the insect species. The cypress tip miner, Nantucket pine tip moth, oak ribbed casemaker, and shield bearers are discussed here.

Foliage-mining insects cause off-color patches, sinuous trails, or holes in leaves. Portions of a leaf or patches of foliage may turn yellow or brown and die back. Tiny larvae may be seen dropping from foliage on silken threads. Severe infestations can slow plant growth, but established woody plants tolerate extensive foliage mining and are rarely if ever killed by these insects.

Provide proper cultural care to keep plants vigorous. Prune out and dispose of foliage infested with immature leafminers to restore the plant's aesthetic appearance and provide some control. Plant resistant species or varieties to avoid damage by some foliage miners. Other species can be effectively controlled by natural enemies; conserve these beneficials by avoiding broad-spectrum, persistent insecticides.

Cypress and Arborvitae Foliage Miners
Argyresthia spp.

The cypress tip miner, *A. cupressella,* is the most common *Argyresthia* pest of arborvitae, cypress, juniper, and redwood in coastal areas of the West. Several arborvitae leafminers, especially *A. thuiella,* infest arborvitae and eastern red cedar in the East. Infested foliage turns yellow in early winter, brown by late winter or early spring, then recovers its green color during the spring and summer. The silvery tan adult moths appear in southern California from March through May, in northern California during April and May, from May to June in Oregon, and from mid-June to mid-July in the East. Females lay scalelike eggs on green tips. These hatch into yellow or green larvae, which feed in branch tips until late winter or spring. The larvae then spin slender, white, silken cocoons between the twiglets. The moth has one generation a year.

Consider replacing plants especially susceptible to the cypress tip miner (see Table 4-11). High cypress tip miner populations and damage can be reduced on established plantings by applying a broad-spectrum, persistent insecticide when adult moths are active. Beginning in early spring, examine foliage tips for the cocoons. When these appear, vigorously shake foliage and watch to see if silvery tan, tiny moths fly up then settle back on the foliage. One application to foliage can be made when a large number of tip moths appear, between March and May, in California. This reduces foliage browning next season.

TABLE 4-11

Susceptibility of Juniper (*Juniperus* spp.) and Other Cupressaceae in California to the Cypress Tip Miner.[a]

LEAST SUSCEPTIBLE, ½ TO 2½ TIP MINERS[b]
Juniperus chinensis var. *sargentii* cv. Glauca, *Thuja plicata,* *J. scopulorum* cv. Erecta Glauca, *J. chinensis* cv. Kaizuka
MODERATELY SUSCEPTIBLE, 5 TO 8 TIP MINERS[b]
J. sabina cv. Tamariscifolia, *J. virginiana* cv. Prostrata, *J. sabina* cv. Arcadia, *J. chinensis* cv. Pfitzerana Aurea
MORE SUSCEPTIBLE, 13 TO 19 TIP MINERS[b]
J. virginiana cv. Cupressifolia, *J. chinensis* cv. Pfitzerana, *J. chinensis* cv. Robust Green, *Chamaecyparis lawsoniana* cv. Allumii
MOST SUSCEPTIBLE, ABOUT 40 TIP MINERS[b]
Thuja occidentalis

a. From: C.S. Koehler and W.S. Moore. 1983. J. Environ. Hort. 1: 87-88.

b. Numbers are tip miners per 100 grams of foliage.

This silvery tan adult cypress tip miner emerged from the silken cocoon at the base of the dead twiglet.

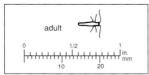

CYPRESS TIP MINER

Brown patches on coast live oak caused by oak ribbed casemaker larvae feeding inside and under the leaf.

Oak ribbed casemaker first-instar larvae leave round webbing as they change from feeding inside to feeding on the underside of leaves. The white pupal cocoons are elongate with distinct longitudinal ribs.

OAK RIBBED CASEMAKER

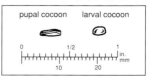

Oak and Birch Casemakers and Skeletonizers *Bucculatrix* spp.

The oak ribbed casemaker, *Bucculatrix albertiella,* feeds on deciduous and live oaks throughout California. Its common name refers to its white, cigar-shaped cocoons, which have distinct longitudinal ribs. Several similar *Bucculatrix* species occur in the eastern states: The oak leaf skeletonizer, *B. ainsliella,* feeds on oak and chestnut. The birch skeletonizer, *B. canadensisella,* damages birch. *B. pomifoliella* occurs on hawthorn and flowering fruit trees, especially apple, crab apple, and cherry.

Bucculatrix cocoons occur on host tree bark, leaves, and nearby plants and objects. Adults are mottled white, brown, and black. First-instar larvae mine inside the leaf. Later instars feed externally on the lower leaf surface. Damaged foliage between leaf veins appears translucent. Mature larvae are olive green with rows of pale spots. There are two generations a year for each species, one each in the spring and summer, except for *B. canadensisella,* which has one generation.

No control is generally warranted for *Bucculatrix* in landscapes. Intolerable populations may be reduced by a foliar insecticide application that thoroughly covers the lower leaf surface when larvae are observed feeding there. For specific pesticide recommendations see *Insect Pest Management Guidelines for California Landscape Ornamentals* (UC Publication 3317).

Shield bearers
Coptodisca spp.

Shield bearer larvae feed entirely within the leaves of plants, including apple, cottonwood, crape myrtle, oak, madrone, manzanita, poplar, and strawberry tree. Before pupation, each shield bearer larva cuts a round or oval area of mined foliage from the leaf approximately one-fourth inch long. This portion of the leaf drops to the ground or is carried by the larva and fastened to bark. High shield bearer populations cause leaves to develop numerous holes, like those made with a paper punch.

The madrone shield bearer, *Coptodisca arbutiella,* attacks the foliage of madrone, manzanita, and strawberry tree in Pacific Coast states. The tiny silvery female moth emerges in the early spring and lays eggs in leaves. Eggs apparently remain inactive until the fall, when they hatch and the larvae begin mining. In the late winter, the mature black larva cuts an elliptical disk of foliage from the leaf, inside which the larva pupates. The madrone shield bearer has one generation a year. Other species, such as the resplendent shield bearer, *Coptodisca splendoriferella,* on apple, have two generations a year. Pick and dispose of infested leaves on small plants if damage cannot be tolerated.

Spraying for shield bearers is not recommended. Much of their life cycle is spent within plant tissue protected from insecticides. Spraying disrupts the parasites that may help to limit shield bearer outbreaks to a short duration.

Elliptical holes in manzanita foliage caused by the madrone shield bearer.

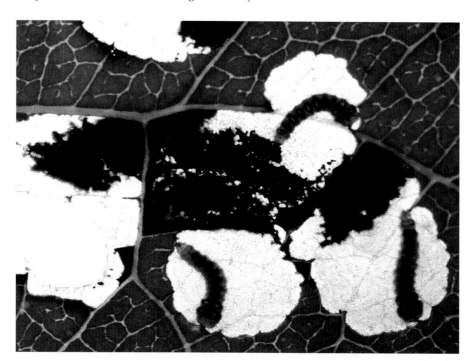

Poplar shield bearer, *Coptodisca* sp., larvae feeding in poplar leaf mines.

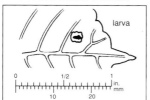

POPLAR SHIELD BEARER

larva

Nantucket Pine Tip Moth
Rhyacionia frustrana

The Nantucket pine tip moth occurs throughout the U.S. on most species of two- or three-needle pines. In southern California it is a pest primarily of Monterey pine planted away from the coast. Tip moth damage to the central growing terminal can significantly alter tree shape, reducing the marketability of Christmas trees.

The adult moth is reddish brown with silver-gray markings; it begins emerging in southern California in January. After mating, the female lays tiny eggs singly on the new growth

The adult Nantucket pine tip moth is reddish brown with silver-gray markings.

tips. The eggs hatch in 1 to 2 weeks and the young larvae feed on or in the base of needles or buds. More mature larvae are yellow to pale brown with a dark head. They cover shoot tips with webbing, which becomes covered with pitch as the larvae bore into the shoots and feed for 3 to 4 weeks. Summer-generation larvae pupate in the tips; overwintering pupae commonly occur in the litter. The annual generations range from one in Massachusetts to about four in the southern U.S., including southern California.

Management. Do not plant pine species particularly susceptible to the Nantucket pine tip moth if little or no damage can be tolerated (see Table 4-12). Consider replacing susceptible species like Monterey pine if their performance is unacceptable in the landscape or tolerate damage; pines appear to be less affected as they mature. Provide trees with proper cultural care, especially appropriate

NANTUCKET PINE TIP MOTH

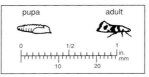

| pupa | adult |

irrigation, to increase their tolerance to damage. An ichneumonid wasp, *Campoplex frustranae*, parasitizes pine tip moth pupae and has reduced moth populations in many locations in southern California, resulting in improved vigor and appearance of infested Monterey pines.

Prune infested tips from October through January to prevent overwintering moths from emerging. If pines must be pruned during other times, monitor adults with pheromone-baited traps and prune between the peaks representing each generation of moth flights. Avoid pruning when moths are active because they are attracted to newly trimmed trees. Remove and dispose of clipped foliage to eliminate developing larvae and pupae on pruned tips.

High Nantucket pine tip moth populations can be reduced by applying a broad-spectrum insecticide to foliage to kill young larvae soon after moths are observed flying during each generation and before larvae enter tissue. However, pines tolerate extensive tip moth feeding and natural enemies often provide acceptable control in landscapes. The repeated spraying necessary to provide good control is not justified unless trees are of especially high aesthetic value, such as in Christmas tree plantations. Insecticide applications kill natural enemies, which can provide substantial biological control. Spraying for tip moth can also cause spider mite outbreaks, so monitor treated plants for this problem.

Insect activity varies with weather, so spraying is more effective if it is timed by monitoring insects instead of calendar dates. Pheromone-baited traps can be used to monitor moth flights from January through September when managing large numbers of susceptible pines. Hang one trap chest high in the outer canopy of each of two trees at least 50 feet apart.

A Nantucket pine tip moth pupa exposed in the terminal where it fed as a larva.

On properties with extensive pine plantings, deploy additional traps at approximately 500-foot intervals. Inspect each trap daily. Remove any debris and count, record, and remove any moths in the traps. Replace traps when the sticky surface becomes dirty and replace the pheromone lure every 4 weeks. If treatment is needed, spray a persistent insecticide 10 to 14 days after the beginning of an overall decline in the number of first-generation moths caught. Spray 1 week after the peak number of each subsequent generation of moths, a total of four applications per year in southern California. If applications are planned, thorough coverage of all branch tips and the treetop is important.

The most precise and effective application timing uses degree-day monitoring and moth traps. Where damage cannot be tolerated, spray 1,233 degree-days after the beginning of each moth generation, using a lower development threshold temperature of 42°F and an upper threshold of 99°F. The first generation begins in the spring when the first moth is caught. Subsequent generations start when moth catches first begin increasing after a dramatic decline in numbers from the previous peak.

TWIG, BRANCH, AND TRUNK BORING INSECTS

The adult or larval stages of some insects bore in wood, xylem, or phloem tissues beneath bark. Holes in bark, stains or oozing liquid on trunks or limbs, and sawdustlike powder in bark crevices and around trunks are common damage symptoms caused by borers. Foliage may discolor or drop prematurely because of borer activity. Wood-boring insects can become serious landscape pests

TABLE 4-12

The Relative Susceptibility of Pines (*Pinus* spp.) in California to the Nantucket Pine Tip Moth.[a]

NOT INFESTED
armandii, attenuata, bungeana, canariensis, caribaea, coulteri, edulis, gerardiana, monophylla, montezumae, mugo, nigra, palustris, pinaster, pinea, thunbergiana, torreyana
UNDER 25 PERCENT OF TIPS INFESTED
flexilis, halepensis, jeffreyi, oocarpa, ponderosa, rigidia, taeda
ABOUT 30-40 PERCENT OF TIPS INFESTED
brutia, cembroides, muricata, patula, pseudostrobus, roxburghii, sabiniana, sylvestris
ABOUT 50-85 PERCENT OF TIPS INFESTED
contorta, densiflora, echinata, glabra, insularis, radiata, resinosa, virginiana

a. From: G.T. Scriven and R. F. Luck. 1980. J. Econ. Entomol. 73: 318-320.

A sapsucker, *Sphyrapicus varius*, caused these horizontal rows of holes in spruce bark. Do not confuse woodpecker feeding with damage from boring insects.

because they weaken limbs and trunks and can kill branches or entire plants. However, many wood borers are secondary pests that develop because trees lack proper care or are injured or dying from other causes.

Boring insects discussed in this book include bark beetles, flatheaded borers, roundheaded borers, clear-wing moths, carpenterworm, juniper twig girdler, and carpenter ants. Carpenter bees, termites, horntails or woodwasps, and some other insects also can infest wood, but are relatively uncommon in landscapes and are not covered in this book; for information on these see *Wood Preservation* (UC Publication 3335).

Boring by adult bark beetles often results in pitch tubes; this one was caused by red turpentine beetle attacking Monterey pine.

Sawdustlike frass in lower bark crevices, spiderwebs, or on the ground indicates bark beetles. Red turpentine beetles are attacking this Monterey pine.

BARK BEETLES

Bark beetles, family Scolytidae, are common pests of conifers, and some species attack woody nonconiferous plants. Several hundred species occur in the United States. Bark beetles commonly infesting arborvitae, California buckeye, cedar, cypress, elm, fir, fruit trees, oak, pine, redwoods, spruce, and other hosts are discussed here.

DAMAGE

Some species live in cones or roots, but most bark beetles mine between the bark and sapwood (the phloem-cambial region) on twigs, branches, or trunks of trees and shrubs. This boring activity often starts a flow of tree pitch or sawdustlike boring dust called frass. Frass created by boring higher in the tree may drop and be visible in lower bark crevices, on the ground, or in spiderwebs. Bark beetles commonly attack trees weakened by other factors, such as drought stress, disease, injuries, or lack of proper cultural care. Beetles can contribute to the decline and eventual death of trees.

IDENTIFICATION AND BIOLOGY

Adults are small, cylindrical, hard-bodied beetles about the size of rice grains. Most species are dark red, brown, or black. Their antennae are elbowed and the outer segments are enlarged and clublike. When viewed from above, the head is partly or completely hidden by the thorax. They have strong, scooplike jaws (mandibles) for boring.

Small, oval, whitish eggs are laid in the tunnel that is constructed by adults at the interface of the bark and wood. After the eggs hatch, mining larvae form branching tunnels. Larvae of most species are cream or white, robust, grublike, and may have a dark head. At first the larval mines are very small, but they gradually increase in diameter as the larvae grow. Pupae are usually whitish and occur within or beneath bark. A buckshot pattern of holes may be apparent where the new adults have emerged. Depending in part on the beetle species' preference for stressed or dying trees and the condition of the plant, emerging adults may disperse to attack other trees rather than laying eggs on the same tree that they emerged from.

The species of tree attacked and the location of damage on bark helps in identifying the bark beetle species present. For example, engraver beetles usually attack pines beginning near the treetop, while red turpentine beetle attacks pine trunks near the ground. Peeling off a portion of infested bark also aids in identifying the beetle species present by revealing beetle tunnels. For example, *Dendroctonus* species adults usually pack at least part of their egg-laying tunnel with boring dust; these packed adult galleries distinguish *Dendroctonus* species from engraver beetles that maintain open adult tunnels. Larval galleries of all species are packed with frass (Figure 4-11).

Red Turpentine Beetle
Dendroctonus valens

The red turpentine beetle occurs throughout the U.S. It bores into the base of pine and, on rare occasions, spruce and fir trees. This bark beetle's presence is indicated by pinkish brown to white pitch tubes, a mixture of pitch and beetle boring dust that appears on the lower trunk. Reddish or white granular material or brown frass may accumulate at the tree base or in bark crevices. Red turpentine beetle is usually not a serious pest, but weakened trees attacked by this

With all bark beetles, the larval galleries radating from the central tunnel are packed with frass.

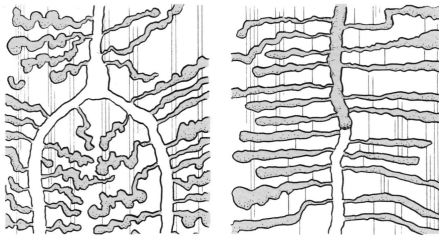

Wishbone-shaped galleries made by adult *Ips* species are largely free of frass.

Dendroctonus species bark beetles pack at least part of their central egg-laying gallery with frass.

Figure 4-11. Bark beetle adults bore a tunnel or gallery in which they lay eggs at the interface between bark and wood. Larvae hatch and bore side tunnels. The pattern of adult and larval galleries helps to identify the species of bark beetles.

beetle may die, especially Monterey pines under stress from other factors. Vigorous trees can survive a few beetles boring, and only a small area of the tree cambium may die.

Red turpentine beetle adults are reddish brown and larger than most other bark beetles. Pairs of male and female beetles bore through the bark together. They usually attack the trunk no more than 6 to 8 feet above ground. Pitch tubes observed higher on the trunk are probably caused by other species of beetles or, if tubes are much larger, by the sequoia pitch moth.

Red turpentine beetle adults excavate a gallery ½ to 1 inch wide and a few inches to several feet long in the phloem tissue beneath the bark. The female lays 100 or more white eggs along the side of this groove; these hatch into white larvae with brown heads. When fully grown in 2 or more months, the larvae are about ⅜ inch long and collectively have killed a few square inches to more than a

An adult red turpentine beetle.

RED TURPENTINE BEETLE

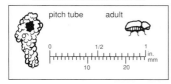

square foot in the phloem-cambial area. The beetle overwinters beneath bark and may have several generations each year.

Western Pine Beetle
Dendroctonus brevicomis

Western pine beetle attacks pines stressed from old age, severe drought, root rot, or other stress factors. More vigorous trees may be attacked if nearby trees are stressed and attacked and large numbers of beetles emerge from them. Inconspicuous pitch tubes and boring dust appear on the main trunk of successfully attacked trees, often on the main trunk well above ground. Adult galleries are much branched and run both laterally and longitudinally, crossing other galleries in a mazelike pattern. *Dendroctonus* spp. bark beetles pack at least part of the central egg-laying gallery with frass.

Engraver Beetles
Ips spp.

Ips jeffreyi, I. mexicanus, I. paraconfusus, and *I. pini* are important engraver beetle species, especially in Monterey pine planted outside its native coastal range. When pines are infested, their tops fade from their normal bright green color to lighter green, then to tan, red, and brown; this fading may occur within a few weeks or over several months or longer. In contrast to the normal shedding of interior needles, this fading extends to the branch tips and gradually progresses down from the treetop. The treetop, and sometimes the whole tree, dies.

The adults are dark brown, cylindrical beetles. *Ips* are distinguished from other bark beetles by the conspicuous cavity on the wing covers (elytra) at the rear of the body. There are three to six spines on each lateral margin of this cavity, depending on the species. *Ips* beetles prefer to bore at the treetops, although Monterey pine is often attacked along the entire trunk. Males attack first and produce an attractant that draws other attacking male and female beetles of the same species. Engraver beetles also breed in freshly cut pine wood or trimmed branches. When bark is removed, galleries can be observed in the cambium where adults lay their eggs and larvae bore (Figure 4-11). The pattern of boring in wood can help identify the pest species. The wishbone-shaped gallery made by adult *Ips* spp. is largely free of frass. As with all bark beetles, the larval galleries radiating from the central tunnel are packed with frass.

In southern California beetles can attack any time of year; in colder areas, beetles overwinter beneath the bark and begin to emerge in the late winter or spring. *Ips* have two to four generations a year depending on location.

Cedar or Cypress Bark Beetles
Phloeosinus spp.

Several *Phloeosinus* bark beetles attack arborvitae, *Chamaecyparis,* cypress, and redwoods in the western U.S., especially in Pacific coast states. Arborvitae, cedar, cypress, and juniper are common hosts in the East. Cedar and cypress bark beetles kill twigs, resulting in dead tips or "flags" hanging on the tree. This twig damage does not threaten tree survival. Beetles also attack the limbs and trunk of stressed or injured trees, which may become girdled and die; vigorous trees are rarely if ever attacked.

Phloeosinus are the only species of bark beetles commonly found in arborvitae, *Chamaecyparis,* coast redwood, and cypress. Adults are small, reddish brown to black beetles. The wing covers are roughened, and are convex with short, stout, sawtooth-like spines at the posterior end. Adults feed by mining twigs for a distance of about 6 inches back from their tips. The egg-laying female is attracted to the trunk and major limbs of unhealthy and declining trees. It bores through the bark and, depending on the species, tunnels

California fivespined ips, *Ips paraconfusus,* larvae exposed in their tunnels in wood just beneath bark.

parallel or perpendicular to the grain at the interface of the bark and wood. The eggs laid in these tunnels hatch into larvae that tunnel across the grain. When the bark is peeled back, these adult and larval engravings resemble a centipede on both the inner bark surface and on the wood. Pupation occurs in enlarged chambers at the ends of the larval tunnels. Adults emerge any time of the year, primarily in late spring, and again in late summer to early fall, when most of the twig mining occurs.

Oak Bark Beetles
Pseudopityophthorus **spp.**

Several bark beetle species attack oaks throughout the U.S. In Pacific coast states the most common oak bark beetle, *Pseudopityophthorus pubipennis*, also attacks California buckeye. Eastern species may occur in beech, birch, chestnut, hickory, and maple as well as oaks.

Bleeding or frothy material may bubble from tiny holes in the trunk or limbs of infested trees, or holes may be dry and surrounded by a pile of fine boring dust. Oak bark beetles rarely if ever kill trees, but their attack indicates that trees are unhealthy and may succumb to a combination of stresses if proper cultural care is not provided.

Adult oak bark beetles are cylindrical, dark reddish brown to black, very small beetles. They are attracted to the trunk or branches of stressed, fallen, or recently dead trees, or the dead branches of otherwise healthy trees. The adults bore through the bark to its junction with the sapwood and create two horizontal tunnels that are not plugged with frass, one on each

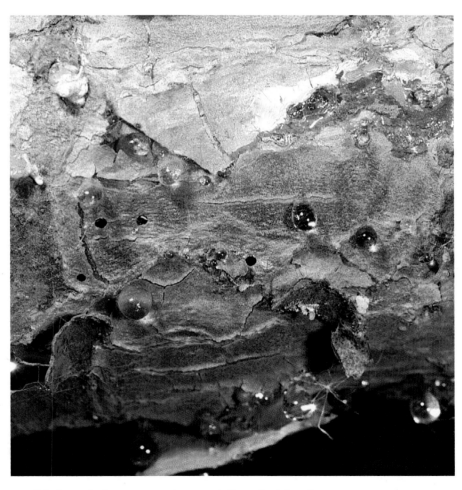

Cypress bark beetle feeding caused these dead terminals or flagging; this twig damage does not threaten tree survival.

Small holes in bark, some weeping sap, indicate bark beetles.

side of the entrance hole. Eggs are laid along these lateral tunnels. After hatching, each whitish larva tunnels perpendicular to the adult gallery. The mature larvae bore to just beneath the bark surface and pupate. The new adults gnaw through the bark, creating many tiny shot holes in the bark when they emerge. The beetles overwinter beneath bark and two or more generations occur each year.

Shothole Borer
Scolytus rugulosus

The shothole borer is a small bark beetle that attacks damaged trunks of many tree species throughout the U.S., including English laurel, fruit trees, and hawthorn. The many tiny holes that appear in the bark of heavily attacked trees resemble holes made by buckshot and give rise to this insect's common name. These dark

The female European elm bark beetle bores a linear tunnel where bark meets wood. The frass-filled side tunnels were made by larvae.

brown or black cylindrical beetles attack trees weakened by root diseases, sunburn, insufficient irrigation, or infestations of other pests. Adults first appear from April through June, and may be found crawling on bark. After boring a tiny hole through the bark, the mated female excavates a tunnel about 1 to 1¼ inch long in the cambium just beneath the bark and deposits her eggs along this tunnel. Beetles overwinter as immature stages beneath the bark and have two or more generations a year. Although the beetles typically attack weakened or injured trees, high populations may then move to attack nearby healthy limbs or trunks.

European Elm Bark Beetle
Scolytus multistriatus

The European elm bark beetle was accidentally introduced from Europe and occurs throughout the U.S. This beetle and the native elm bark beetle, *Hylurgopinus rufipes*, which has similar biology and management but occurs only in the eastern states, spread the Dutch elm disease fungus and are serious pests of elms. Although *Scolytus multistriatus* occurs throughout California, the Dutch elm disease fungus in California is limited to the San Francisco Bay area and around Sacramento (see Dutch Elm Disease, Chapter 5).

The adult European elm bark beetle is shiny dark brown to black. It lays its eggs in the limbs and trunk of injured or weakened elms or recently cut elm wood. Before doing so, it may fly to other elms to feed on twig bark, occasionally causing twigs to die and drop. If the adult emerges from infected elm wood, its body is contaminated with Dutch elm disease spores. The beetle then infects the

healthy elms with the Dutch elm disease fungus during feeding.

After feeding, the female bores through the bark of a dead or dying elm and makes a straight tunnel 1 to 2 inches long parallel to the grain of the wood, except that on Chinese elm the gallery is more meandering. She lays several dozen eggs along this gallery. These hatch into larvae, each of which bores a tunnel at right angles to the parent gallery. This tunneling is at the juncture of the bark and sapwood and when these are separated, both appear engraved with a distinctive centipedelike pattern. The beetle overwinters as larvae, pupae, or adults beneath bark. The European elm bark beetle has about two generations each year, depending on location.

MANAGEMENT

Plant only species properly adapted to the area. Learn the cultural requirements of plants and provide proper care to keep them growing vigorously. Healthy plants are less likely to be attacked and are better able to survive the damage from a few boring insects. Appropriate irrigation is particularly important; plants are seriously damaged by too much or too little water. Irrigate near the outer portion of the canopy, not near the trunk.

Prevention is the most effective method of managing wood-boring insects, in many instances it is the only available control. Avoid injuries to roots and trunks as discussed in Chapter 3 and protect trees from sunscald and other abiotic disorders as detailed in Chapter 6. Except for general cultural practices that improve tree vigor, little can be done to control most boring insects beneath bark once trees have been attacked.

Do not pile unseasoned, freshly cut wood near woody landscape plants. Freshly cut wood or trees that are dying or recently dead provide an abundant breeding source for some wood-boring beetles. Tightly seal firewood beneath clear plastic in a sunny location for several months to exclude attacking beetles and to kill any beetles already infesting the wood. Properly prune off infested limbs and remove and dispose of dying trees so that boring insects do not emerge and attack other nearby trees. Replace old declining trees so that future generations may enjoy mature trees. Plant resistant species where bark beetles have been a problem. *Ips* and red turpentine beetle do not attack redwoods or atlas or deodar cedar.

Especially valuable trees may be protected from further bark beetle attacks by spraying bark with a persistent insecticide in the spring, but do not substitute insecticide applications for proper cultural care. Unless trees are monitored regularly so that borer attack can be detected early, any spraying is likely to be too late and ineffective. Systemic insecticides injected through the bark do not control or prevent attack by bark beetles or other wood borers. For specific insecticide recommendations see *Insect Pest Management Guidelines for California Landscape Ornamentals* (UC Publication 3317).

FLATHEADED BORERS

Most woody landscape plants can be attacked by flatheaded borers, also known as metallic wood borers, family Buprestidae. Injury by flatheaded borers can cause sap to exude and form a wet spot around affected bark. Portions of the bark may crack and die. Limbs or entire trees, especially young trees, may be killed. Most flatheaded borers do not attack vigorous plants.

Adult flatheaded borers are often rather metallic—coppery, blue, black, or green—particularly on their lower surface and upper abdomen. Their streamlined bodies are flattened, elongate or oval, and typically have longitudinal grooves on the wing covers. Females lay their eggs in bark crevices. After hatching, the larvae bore tunnels beneath the bark and sometimes into the wood. Tunnels are often winding and filled with frass. Larvae of many species are broad and flat in the front and narrow and tapered toward the rear.

Prevention, as detailed above for bark beetles, is the most effective management for flatheaded borers. Correctly plant species that are well adapted to that location and provide them with proper care. Protect trees from injury. Remove and dispose of dying limbs and dead trees. Do not pile fresh-cut wood near trees; beetles may emerge from it and attack nearby plants.

Larvae of some of the larger, shallow boring species sometimes can be killed by inserting a sharp wire and probing tunnels. This method is practical only in a small infestation, and it is often difficult to know whether the wire has penetrated the tunnel far enough to reach and kill the larva. Insecticides are not effective against larvae beneath bark.

Pacific Flatheaded Borer *Chrysobothris mali* and Flatheaded Appletree Borer *Chrysobothris femorata*

Both the Pacific flatheaded borer and flatheaded appletree borer are attracted to diseased, stressed, or injured trunks or limbs of more than 70 woody landscape plants including

ceanothus, cotoneaster, fruit trees, manzanita, maple, mayten, oak, *Rhaphiolepis*, rose, sycamore, toyon, and willow. The flatheaded appletree borer is found throughout the U.S. and is especially abundant in the East. The Pacific flatheaded borer occurs only in the western states.

The adult Pacific flatheaded borer has a dark bronze or gray body and mottled coppery wing covers. The flatheaded appletree borer is greenish blue to grayish bronze. Adult beetles may feed at the base of twigs and partially defoliate young trees. Females lay their eggs in bark wounds caused by disease or injuries such as sunscald, pruning cuts, staking wounds, or the area where rootstock and scion are grafted. Larvae excavate just beneath bark in the cambial area and may bore deeper into wood as they

Rough, broken bark on a young apple tree trunk caused by Pacific flatheaded borer larvae.

mature. Sap, which is sometimes frothy white, may exude around boring sites and bark may become cracked. Mature larvae are pale yellow. The thorax is enlarged just behind the head. Larvae form creamy

PACIFIC FLATHEADED BORER

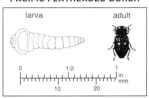

white to dark pupae just under the bark surface in the spring. Adults emerge and fly from April through August. Both species have one generation a year.

Provide proper cultural care to keep trees vigorous and resistant to attack by borers. Protect trees from injuries (see Chapter 3) and prevent sunscald and other damage from abiotic causes (see Chapter 6). Prune out and dispose of dead limbs and remove dead and dying trees where borers breed.

Flatheaded Alder Borer
Agrilus burkei

The flatheaded alder borer attacks only alders in the western U.S., primarily white alder, *Alnus rhombifolia,* in poorly irrigated landscapes. Its biology and management is similar to that of many other *Agrilus* species infesting landscapes, including several eastern species: the bronze birch borer, *Agrilus anxius,* infesting birch; the twolined chestnut borer, *Agrilus bilineatus,* which attacks oak and chestnut; and the bronze poplar borer, *Agrilus liragus,* infesting *Populus* spp. Wet spots, dark staining, and gnarled, ridged growth often appear on the bark of infested hosts. Adult emergence holes, often D-shaped and about ⅛ inch in diameter, are left in bark. Infested limbs die and trees can be killed.

The metallic blue adult of the flatheaded alder borer emerges from infested alders in April and May. The adult feeds on foliage, although the slight damage it causes is usually not apparent. In the late spring, the female lays whitish egg masses on the trunk and main branches of alders, especially stressed or declining trees. Several days later, the larvae emerge through the bottom of the egg mass and bore into the bark, making long winding tunnels through cambial tissue. Pupation occurs beneath the bark in late winter. There is one generation each year.

The adult Pacific flatheaded borer is dark bronze, gray, or a mottled coppery color.

The Pacific flatheaded borer larva is broad and flat in the front and narrow and tapered toward the rear.

FLATHEADED ALDER BORER

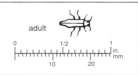

MANAGEMENT

Provide proper cultural care and protect trees from injury, as detailed above for bark beetles. Flatheaded borers rarely attack vigorous trees. Provide white alders, *Alnus rhombifolia,* with frequent irrigation throughout their lives; these trees are native to sites near permanent water. Alders grow poorly in western landscape areas where summer drought prevails and become very susceptible to borer attack. Do not plant alders unless you can provide frequent irrigation. Consider replacing problem trees and planting Italian alder, *Alnus cordata,* which is resistant to the borer. During late summer or fall when adult beetles are not active, prune out and dispose of all branches showing bleeding, swelling, dieback, or other evidence of larval infestation. Avoid pruning hosts for at least a month before and during the season when adults are active. Do not prune white alder anytime between March and the end of May as egg-laying adult beetles are apparently attracted to recent pruning wounds.

Properly timed insecticide sprays may reduce beetle attacks, but do not substitute insecticide applications for proper cultural care or trees are still likely to die. If an application is planned, beginning the first of April inspect leaves for adult feeding holes and look for adult beetles during mid to late afternoon by examining foliage and branch beating. Foliage and wood can be thoroughly sprayed with a persistent insecticide when adults are active, usually one time about mid-April and again about 3 to 4 weeks later. Insecticides are not effective against larvae beneath bark.

Wet spots and dark staining on this alder trunk are characteristic of flatheaded borer damage.

Oak Twig Girdler
Agrilus angelicus

Oak twig girdler is a flatheaded borer that attacks oaks throughout California, especially live oaks in southern California. The adult beetle is dark brownish copper and emerges around June in coastal areas and in May further inland. The tiny eggs are laid singly on the bark of young twigs. The whitish larva bores through the bark and spends 3 to 6 months chewing a linear mine several inches long in the direction of older twigs. It then begins to girdle or mine spirally around the twig, causing terminal foliage to die and turn brown. During the next season, it extends its mine a foot or more down the branch, causing more extensive patches of foliage to die. It bores into the center of the branch, then mines back out toward the terminal it has killed and pupates in wood near the surface of the twig. About 24 months after being laid as an egg, the adult gnaws through the bark and emerges.

An oak twig girdler infestation is first indicated by scattered patches of whitish brown leaves throughout the canopy. Leaves are dead, but have not been chewed and exhibit no surface scraping. These symptoms of twig girdler damage may be confused with oak twig blight and branch dieback diseases (Chapter 5). To distinguish the twig girdler from disease, peel back the bark of the larger twig at the junction of live and dead foliage. A flattened, spiral tunnel, possibly containing coarse, dark brown frass and a larva, should be visible in twig girdler-infested oaks. Unlike the boring into limbs or trunks that occurs only on damaged or weakened trees, the twig damage can be unsightly, but does not significantly harm trees.

MANAGEMENT

Native California oaks are adapted to drought; avoid planting turf or irrigated ground covers under them as frequent irrigations during warm weather makes the oaks susceptible to oak root disease. However, drought-weakened trees are especially prone to twig girdler attack and urbanization often reduces the natural availability of soil moisture. It may be appropriate to irrigate urban oaks once every 1 to 2 months during the warm dry season. Allow the water to soak deeply into the soil. Irrigate near the outer part of the canopy, not close to the trunk.

Prune infested branches to restore the oak's aesthetic quality. At least six species of parasitic wasps attack oak

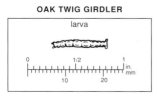

OAK TWIG GIRDLER

larva

0   1/2   1
|||||||||||||||||||||||| in.
             mm
   10   20

twig girdlers; however, their importance in biological control has not been documented. Because damage by this pest does not affect tree survival and spraying kills natural enemies, further management should not be necessary. However, where twig girdling has been extensive and damage cannot be tolerated on trees of high aesthetic value, adults and eggs in California may be killed by one insecticide application to outer canopy foliage in about early June on the coast or about early May inland. Precise timing is very important because, except for the few weeks as adults and eggs, these borers spend most of their two-year life cycle as larvae beneath bark and are protected from insecticides. To better time an application, monitor for adults by branch beating. Alternatively, enclose several infested branches with flexible screening on at least two locations on the sunny or warmer part of the canopy in the spring. Every few days, vigorously shake the caged foliage, then inspect the cage for dislodged beetles. Make a single application of a persistent insecticide when adult borers are first observed.

The adult eucalyptus longhorned borer has a yellowish or cream-colored zigzag-shaped band across its wing covers. The hole was made by an adult emerging from wood.

These dark trails were made by eucalyptus longhorned borer larvae tunnelling just under bark after they hatched from an egg mass. Each trail ends where a larva bored deeper down into the wood.

ROUNDHEADED BORERS

Most injured or stressed broadleaf deciduous trees are attacked by one or more species of roundheaded borers or longhorned beetles, family Cerambycidae. One important species in California landscapes, the eucalyptus longhorned borer, is detailed here. Other common longhorned beetles include *Ergates*, *Necydalis*, *Prionus*, and *Saperda* species, which occur throughout the U.S. For example, the poplar borer, *Saperda calcarata*, attacks aspen, cottonwood, poplar, and willow. Adults are robust, elongate, grayish green beetles with yellow stripes and spots on the back. Other *Saperda* species attack apple, ash, basswood, cotoneaster, hawthorn, linden, and poplar.

DAMAGE

Holes in bark and stains or oozing liquid on limbs or trunks are common roundheaded borer damage symptoms. Foliage may discolor and wilt, limbs may die back, and branches or entire plants may be killed. However, roundheaded borers attack mostly damaged or dying plants. Vigorous trees are rarely attacked.

IDENTIFICATION AND BIOLOGY

Adult roundheaded borers are medium to large, elongate, cylindrical beetles that are often brightly colored. They have long antennae, so are sometimes called longhorned beetles. Adult females of most species lay eggs in bark crevices. The larvae bore beneath the bark and sometimes into the wood on tree limbs, trunks, and main roots. Roundheaded borer larvae are creamy white, elongate, and cylindrical in cross section.

MANAGEMENT

Plant species that are well adapted to each location and provide them with proper cultural care. Protect trees from injuries. Remove dead limbs or trees promptly and do not store freshly cut wood near trees; beetles may emerge from it and attack nearby plants. Prevention as detailed above for bark beetles is the only effective strategy for avoiding roundheaded borer attacks. Pesticide applications to bark have not been found to be effective. Injected or systemic insecticides do not provide control.

Larvae of some of the larger, shallow boring species sometimes can be killed by inserting a sharp wire and probing tunnels. This method is practical only in a small infestation, and it is often difficult to know whether the wire has penetrated the tunnel far enough to reach and kill the larva.

Eucalyptus Longhorned Borer
Phoracantha semipunctata

The eucalyptus longhorned borer was introduced in California in the 1980s. Both this beetle and its host trees are native to Australia. Attacked trees may produce copious amounts of resin, and the treetops, branches, or entire trees may be killed. Resprouting may occur from the tree base. The relative susceptibility of eucalyptus species to attack by the borer is not well known, but *Eucalyptus diversicolor, E. globulus, E. nitens, E. saligna* and *E. viminalis* are susceptible, while *E. camaldulensis, E. cladocalyx, E. robusta, E. sideroxylon* and *E. trabutii* are resistant. Trees that receive proper cultural care, especially appropriate irrigation, are not readily attacked.

The adult is shiny blackish brown with a yellow to cream-colored, zigzag-shaped band across the wing covers. The antennae are as long as or longer than the body, and the antennae of the male have prominent spines. Several nights after emerging and mating, the female begins laying eggs in groups of 3 to 30 under loose bark of eucalyptus trees. Females may live from one to several months and lay up to 300 eggs, which hatch in 10 to 14 days. The larva often leaves a distinct dark trail, 1/4 inch to several inches long, on the bark before boring into the living cambial tissue beneath bark. The gallery formed by each large, dirty white to yellow larva widens as the insect feeds. A single gallery can extend several feet and

EUCALYPTUS LONGHORNED BORER

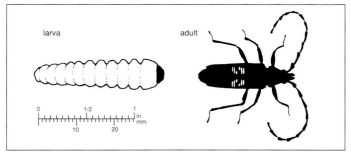

larva   adult

A mature eucalyptus longhorned borer larva exposed in wood.

PAVEL SVIHRA

can girdle a tree. Larvae require about 70 days to develop in fresh logs, and up to 180 days in dry logs. During the spring and summer, the beetle requires 3 to 4 months to complete its life cycle, but in the fall and winter it may require up to 9 months.

MANAGEMENT

Natural enemies of the eucalyptus borer are being introduced from Australia and may provide a long-term solution. By reducing beetle populations to a lower level, natural enemies may reduce borer damage because vigorous trees can survive a few attacks.

Map the location of high-value trees and inspect them regularly for stress, such as damage from *Phytophthora* or *Armillaria* root disease. Stress symptoms include a sparse canopy, leaf color changes (usually yellowing), and sprouting from inactive buds on the main trunk. Appropriate irrigation greatly reduces or eliminates eucalyptus longhorned borer attacks. Consider providing supplemental water about once a month during prolonged dry periods, particularly if seasonal rainfall has been below normal. Irrigate around the outer canopy, not near the trunk. Avoid frequent watering as this promotes root disease.

Prune dead branches and remove dead trees immediately; conduct other pruning during December and January when adult beetles are inactive. Eucalyptus logs, such as firewood, and dead branches and trees are the primary beetle breeding sites. Bury or, where permitted, burn dead wood. Alternatively, remove the bark from felled logs or seal the wood in a sunny location under an ultraviolet-resistant, clear polyethylene tarp for at least 6 months. This prevents new beetles from attacking or resident beetles from emerging and flying to nearby living eucalyptus.

CLEARWING MOTHS

Several species of clearwing moths, family Sesiidae, are important wood-boring pests in landscapes. Species commonly found in ash, birch, fir, oak, pine, poplar, sycamore, willow, and some other hosts are discussed here.

DAMAGE

Clearwing moth larvae feed beneath the bark, sometimes destroying the plant's food- and water-conducting tissue. Larvae typically produce copious sawdustlike frass, which collects on bark plates as the insects clean their tunnels. With some species, such as those attacking sycamore and pine, this feeding is tolerated by trees and apparently causes no serious harm. Larval feeding by some other species causes girdling and the dieback of plant parts so that limbs may drop and sometimes entire plants die.

IDENTIFICATION AND BIOLOGY

Clearwing moth adults are recognized by their narrow, mostly clear

Scattered dead branches may indicate a clearwing moth infestation. Ash borer larvae infest this Raywood ash.

wings and, on the male, the many fine hairlike projections along the antennae. Unlike some similar-appearing species of tiger moths (Arctiidae) and hawk moths (Sphingidae), the clearwing moths have interlocking forewings and hindwings. They are day-flying moths and resemble paper wasps. The two sexes usually have different amounts of clear wing area and are differently colored, often with yellow, orange, or red on black.

Adult moths may feed on nectar and live about 1 week. Soon after emerging from the host tree, female moths emit a pheromone that attracts the males. After mating, the female deposits her eggs in cracks, crevices, or rough areas on bark. Within several days, eggs hatch into larvae, which bore in the bark, cambium, or heartwood. The whitish larvae usually have brownish markings around the thorax. Just before adults emerge, the mobile pupae move to the bark surface where their protruding pupal skins may remain.

MONITORING

The ash borer, sycamore borer, western poplar clearwing, and many other clearwing moth larvae expel sawdust-like frass from bark surface openings. The activity of these species with larvae that maintain open tunnels can be monitored from spring through fall by brushing away the frass, plugging tunnel entrances with rope putty or grafting wax, and spraying the plug with brightly colored paint. Check the plug one week later and if it's gone, a larva is still feeding beneath the bark. This method can also be used to determine if an application of nematodes has provided control as discussed below. Monitor to determine adult emergence by regularly inspecting trunks for protruding empty pupal cases.

Pheromone Traps. Pheromones are available (see Suppliers) to attract adult male ash borers and some other species, including two species with similar biology and management that occur only in the East: the rhododendron borer, *Synanthedon rhododendri*, which infests rhododendron and occasionally azalea and laurel, and the oak borer, *Paranthrene simulans*, which infests oak and elm. Pheromone-baited traps are useful for

Adult clearwing moths: A) sycamore borer male, B) sycamore borer female, C) western poplar clearwing male, D) western poplar clearwing female, E) sequoia pitch moth female, F) ash borer male from the western U.S., G) ash borer male from the eastern U.S., H) Douglas-fir pitch moth male, I) peachtree borer male from the eastern U.S., J) peachtree borer female from the eastern U.S., K) pitch mass borer (*Synanthedon pini*) from the eastern U.S., L) peachtree borer male from the western U.S., M) redbelted clearwing male, and N) oak borer (*Paranthrene simulans*) from the eastern U.S.

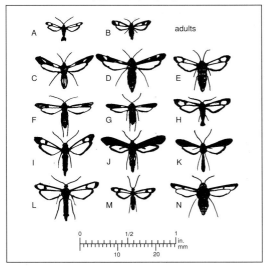

CLEARWING MOTHS

capturing moths for species identification and for determining when egg-laying adults are active to effectively time insecticide applications to kill adults. Pheromone-baited traps are generally not useful for estimating population densities, in part because a trap's attractiveness to a particular species varies depending on the exact blend of volatile compounds and type of dispenser used.

When the weather warms in the spring, hang a trap about shoulder high on each of two or more trees spaced at least several hundred feet apart. Because moths may be attracted from great distances, traps need not be located in infested trees, but may be placed where they are more convenient to monitor. Covered or wing type traps (for example, Pherocon 1C) are preferred. The pheromone dispenser is inserted on the top inside of the trap. Once each week, check traps for moths and identify whether any are a species that might attack your plants; commercial pheromones attract more than one species of clearwing moth. Remove moths from the sticky material after identifying them and reapply

sticky material or replace the trap as needed. Replace the pheromone dispenser monthly or check with your supplier for its longevity.

Although clearwing moths may be captured in traps almost any time during the growing season, each species typically flies in numbers during only a few weeks or months each year. Ash borer adults in California fly in April and May. Sequoia pitch moths fly from about mid-May to mid-August. Western poplar clearwing adults are active primarily from May through July. Male moths emerge first, and they fly primarily around dusk. Females are ready to mate and lay eggs almost immediately after they emerge. Eggs require about 7 to 10 days to hatch.

When using pheromone traps for spray timing, it is important to correctly distinguish the adults of the species that are a pest of your plants from the adults of other clearwing moth species that may be caught. Use the photos, Tree and Shrub Pest Tables at the end of the text, and adult male descriptions to help identify the moths. You may also take the trap containing your moths to your

county Cooperative Extension office for identification. Save the identified moths for comparison when additional moths are captured.

MANAGEMENT

Mature woody plants usually tolerate and can recover from the attack of a few clearwing moth larvae. However, the presence of this pest is a good indicator that plants require extra cultural care. Many species prefer to attack plants that are newly planted, have been injured, or are poorly cared for. Prevention is the best strategy. Protect roots and limbs from injuries and provide good cultural care as detailed in Chapter 3. Prune and dispose of infested and dying limbs. Heavier infestations may warrant treatment with insecticides or beneficial nematodes. Use selective methods whenever possible to help preserve natural enemies, including the woodpeckers and parasitic wasps that attack most species of clearwing moths.

Biological Control. Larvae of clearwing moth species that maintain a tunnel open to the outside can be controlled with an insect parasitic nematode, *Steinernema carpocapsae*, formerly known as *Neoaplectana carpocapsae* (see Suppliers). These nematodes carry mutualistic bacteria and together they kill the host insect. Nematodes have been shown to control the redbelted clearwing, sycamore borer, and western poplar clearwing in landscape trees in the western states and the dogwood borer, *Synanthedon scitula*, and peachtree borer, *Synanthedon exitiosa*, in the East.

Apply nematodes with a squeeze bottle applicator or 20-ounce oil can at a concentration of 1,000,000 or more invasive-stage nematodes per ounce of distilled water. First clear

Placing a clearwing moth pheromone lure in a wing type trap.

the tunnel entrance, then insert the applicator nozzle as far as possible into each gallery. Inject the suspension until the gallery is filled or liquid runs out another hole, then plug the tunnel entrances with rope putty or grafting wax. Agitate the applicator frequently to keep nematodes suspended in the liquid. Adding 2 percent red or orange latex pigment marks treated tunnels. Nematodes can also be sprayed onto bark, but spraying is less effective because nematodes die when they are exposed on dry surfaces.

Applications may be made during warm weather from spring through fall. Application is most effective when larvae are feeding most actively and tunnel openings are largest. Nematode-treated larvae continue to feed and push frass from their tunnels for about 1 week before dying. One week after application, check that the opening of each gallery is plugged, replug any that have been opened, then spray the plugged openings with bright-colored paint. Wait another week and check to see if these plugs are intact. If the gallery opening is no longer covered with paint, the larva has not died. Retreat the gallery.

Insecticides. Attack by some borer species, including the ash borer, sycamore borer, and western poplar clearwing, can be prevented by applying a persistent insecticide to the trunk when egg-laying adults are active; proper timing is critical or spraying is not effective. Insecticides have not been found effective for the sequoia pitch moth.

If a pheromone is available for the clearwing borer of concern, use pheromone-baited traps to properly time applications. Spray bark with insecticide on the trunk and lower limbs 10 to 14 days after catching the first pest moth. If moths continue to be caught for longer than about 3 to 4

A cluster of white cocoons left by *Apanteles* sp. wasps that killed a sycamore borer larva.

weeks after the application, spray again. Insecticide injections or implants do not control borer larvae and are not recommended. For specific pesticide recommendations see *Insect Pest Management Guidelines for California Landscape Ornamentals* (UC Publication 3317).

Western Poplar Clearwing
Paranthrene robiniae

The western poplar clearwing, also called the locust clearwing, is a native moth found throughout warm, low-elevation sites in the West. In southern California and the Central Valley of California it is a pest of birch, poplar, and willow, usually in stressed trees.

The adult moth greatly resembles a hornet or vespid wasp. The forewings are an opaque pale orange to brownish; the hindwings are clear. The thorax is black with a yellow hind border and the abdomen is yellow with three broad black bands. The body of the

desert form of this insect is entirely pale yellow.

Adults emerge primarily from May through July. Larvae emerge from eggs laid singly on bark and bore into the trunk or limbs where they feed, producing sawdustlike frass visible on the bark. The grublike larva is whitish with a reddish brown head and two hornlike spines on the back. Pupation occurs beneath bark in the early spring, but before adult emergence the pupa works its way to the bark surface. After the adult emerges, the cast pupal skin is left protruding from the gallery opening. The insect requires 1 or 2 years to complete a generation.

Management. Provide trees proper cultural care and protect them from injury as detailed in Chapter 3. Poplar clearwing larvae are often attacked by a braconid wasp, *Apanteles paranthrenidis*. Parasitized larvae have many small, oblong, white cocoons adhering to their surface. A minute blackish brown wasp emerges from each cocoon after the larva dies. The importance of parasites and

A western polar clearwing pupal cast skin (lower left) and a frass-covered larval tunnel entrance on a young poplar trunk.

Frass around tunnel entrances and gnarled bark produced by ash borer larvae infesting Raywood ash.

predators in reducing clearwing moth populations has not been documented, but avoid disrupting natural enemies whenever possible.

Research on western poplar clearwing infesting birch and poplar shows that the boring larvae can be controlled by applying parasitic nematodes in the spring or fall, as discussed above. A persistent insecticide applied to bark when adult moths are active also provides control, but selective methods are preferable.

Ash Borer
Podosesia syringae

The larva of the ash borer, also known as the lilac or lilac-ash borer, mines the wood of ash, lilac, olive, and privet. This clearwing moth occurs throughout the U.S., but varies in appearance and behavior depending on location. In the East, two similar species occur, *Podosesia aureocincta* and *P. syringae*. In the West, the male ash borer resembles a paper wasp. It has very long brownish legs and a black body with narrow yellow bands. In California, the ash borer occurs primarily in the Central Valley, where it attacks the tree trunk and small limbs, mostly within about 5 or 10 feet of the ground. Infestations most often occur at sites on the tree where bark has been injured, such as by improper staking, lawn mowers, string trimmers, or previous generations of *Podosesia*.

Throughout the U.S., adult *P. syringae* emerge from April to early June and deposit eggs on the bark of host trees. The boring larva is creamy white with a brown head. It periodically returns to the bark surface to expel sawdustlike frass, which accumulates around the exit hole. There is one generation a year.

The redbelted clearwing, *Synanthedon culiciformis*, is common around Sacramento, California. It infests red and white ash and also occurs in birch and alder. The adult is mostly brownish black with an orangish red band on the anterior of the abdomen. Its biology and management is similar to that of the ash borer.

Provide trees proper cultural care and protect them from injury as detailed in Chapter 3. A persistent insecticide applied to bark when moths are active can prevent further attacks. If spraying is necessary, time the application using pheromone traps as discussed above. Nematodes squirted into tunnels may kill boring larvae, but their effectiveness against ash borer has not been documented.

Sycamore Borer
Synanthedon resplendens

The sycamore borer occurs in the Southwest. It is prevalent in sycamore and also infests oak and ceanothus. Adults emerge from May through July after overwintering as larvae or pupae in tunnels in bark. Adults resemble yellowjacket wasps. The male is mostly yellow with a brownish black head and black bands on the body. Its legs are yellow, except for black along the margins on the portions nearest to the body. The wings are mostly clear with orangish to yellow margins. Adults display wasplike behavior by intermittently running while rapidly fluttering their wings.

Eggs are laid on bark, and the grublike larva is pink to white with a reddish brown head. When mature, it tunnels near the bark surface and leaves a paper-thin layer of outer bark through which the pupa protrudes just before adult emergence. Borer larvae cause bark to appear rough, and sawdustlike material sometimes

Rough bark and sawdustlike frass in crevices and around the tree base due to a sycamore borer infestation.

The sycamore borer larva is whitish to pink with a reddish brown head.

accumulates around the tree base. The insect has one generation a year.

Sycamores tolerate extensive boring by this insect, and generally no control is recommended. Parasitic nematodes can be applied to kill larvae and are most effective in spring when tunnel openings are largest. A persistent pesticide applied to bark when adults are active also provides control, but this is generally not recommended unless trees are of such high aesthetic value that damage cannot be tolerated.

Sequoia Pitch Moth
Synanthedon sequoiae

The sequoia pitch moth is found in pines throughout California, primarily in Monterey pine in urban areas of northern California. Infestations are

Sequoia pitch moth larvae cause unsightly but generally harmless gummy masses on Monterey pine bark.

recognized by the unsightly masses of gummy white, yellow, or pink pitch on the trunk and limbs. Pitch masses may be from one to several inches in diameter and protrude from the bark. This damage is primarily aesthetic and generally does not harm trees.

The adult moth's wings have bluish black margins with some yellow at the base. The male's head and thorax are brownish black, except for some yellow along the sides. The abdomen is broadly banded yellow. The legs are mostly bright yellow. Adults are active in the summer when the females lay their eggs on bark, especially around pruning wounds and other injury sites on bark. The dirty white or creamy larvae excavate shallow cavities just below the bark and typically do not girdle the trunk or limb. Larvae pupate in a brown, paperlike case, which can often be found protruding from the pitch masses.

Another species, the Douglas-fir pitch moth, *Synanthedon novaroensis*, infests pines, spruce, and Douglas fir from northern California to Alaska. Its biology and life history are similar to the sequoia pitch moth. Instead of yellow, the markings on the Douglas-fir pitch moth are bright orange.

Provide trees with proper cultural care and protect them from injury as detailed in Chapter 3. Moths are attracted to lay eggs on bark near pruning wounds and other injury sites. If pines must be pruned, prune only from October through January so that injuries begin closing before the egg-laying female Douglas-fir pitch moths and sequoia pitch moths appear in the spring. Larvae can be found and killed by scraping away fresh pitch masses. No other control except minimizing injuries is recommended as pines apparently are not seriously harmed by this insect. Insecticide applications have been found not to be effective.

OTHER WOOD-BORING MOTHS

Carpenterworm
Prionoxystus robiniae

The carpenterworm, family Cossidae, is a pest of deciduous trees throughout the U.S., including ash, aspen, cottonwood, elm, locust, oak, poplar, and willow.

DAMAGE
Sawdustlike frass around the tree base and discolored or bleeding limbs or trunk are indications of carpenterworm activity. The trunk of attacked trees becomes irregular and gnarled. Continued attacks over several years can cause branch dieback and some trees may die, although vigorous trees can apparently tolerate some carpenterworms.

IDENTIFICATION AND BIOLOGY
The adult is a large, mottled grayish moth. The male has orange to red margins on the front of the hind wings. Adults emerge in the evening during the spring and early summer. After mating, the female lays small, ovoid eggs in clumps of about two to six on roughened areas of the bark. Eggs change from a dirty white or greenish when first laid to dark brown before hatching. The newly hatched larva immediately bores through the bark and does most of its feeding in the heartwood. Its ½-inch-diameter gallery is mostly vertical and 6 to 10 inches long. Larvae occasionally come to the surface of the trunk or limb to clear their tunnels, spilling frass onto the trunk or ground. The large, mature larva is white or pinkish with a dark head and has brown spots

F OR ESPECIALLY VALUABLE TREES, U.S. Forest Service entomologist H.E. Burke recommended enclosing the lower 10 feet of the trunk in a wood-framed cage with wire screen walls, roof, and a door. He installed such a cage around an old oak in Los Gatos, California, from May through July, beginning in 1918. Burke captured and killed the large moths, which tend to rest on the screen late in the afternoon after emerging from the trunk. Because males and females commonly emerge at different times, and are not immediately ready to mate, there was little danger of reinfestation from within if the cage was checked and moths removed once a day.

Because carpenterworms take 3 to 4 years to complete a generation, trunk caging must be repeated for at least 3 to 4 years after the last moth is captured and until boring dust production is no longer observed. A well-made cage will last many years, and Burke suggested protecting the tree every year until the cage wears out. Perhaps he should have built a permanent screen house with room for a picnic table and barbecue?

at the base of groups of prominent hairs. It forms a shiny dark brown pupa, which has a double row of spines. Mature pupae wriggle to the surface of the bark where the adults emerge, leaving the empty pupal skins protruding about two-thirds of the way out of the bark. Carpenterworms require up to 3 to 4 years to complete one generation; most of this time is spent as wood-boring larvae.

MANAGEMENT

Provide trees with proper cultural care and protect them from injuries as detailed in Chapter 3. Appropriate irrigation is especially important; for example, California native oaks are adapted to summer drought and are stressed or killed from frequent irrigation of nearby turf. Trees are better able to tolerate a few carpenterworms if they are kept vigorous.

Based on research in fig orchards infested with carpenterworms, parasitic nematodes injected into tunnel openings as described above for clearwing moths can provide biological control. Larvae can sometimes be killed by inserting a sharp wire and probing tunnels. This method is practical only in a small infestation, and it is often difficult to know whether the wire has penetrated the tunnel far enough to reach and kill the larva. Insecticides are not effective against larvae beneath bark.

Juniper twig girdler caused these scattered dead canopy patches.

Juniper Twig Girdler
Periploca nigra

The juniper twig girdler, family Cosmopterigidae, infests juniper throughout the U.S., but apparently is a pest only in California, primarily in the south and the warm interior valleys.

DAMAGE

The smaller limbs of infested junipers become yellow, then turn brown and die. This branch "flagging" is most apparent in the late summer and causes a checkerboard of green and brown limbs and retarded plant growth. Twig girdler feeding does not kill entire juniper plants.

Don't confuse twig girdler damage with that caused by disease or other insects such as cypress tip miner or juniper scales. Look for larvae and tunnels under twig bark to confirm the presence of this insect. Dying juniper branches may also be caused by mice or root rot fungi. Bark chewed away in bands from lower parts of branches is symptomatic of rodent feeding. If you don't find insect damage or rodent chewing, the dieback may be caused by soil fungi, which thrive when soil moisture is high for prolonged periods. Twig dieback at the edges of plantings may be the result of dog urine, which can be diagnosed by the characteristic odor.

IDENTIFICATION AND BIOLOGY

The small, shiny, brownish black twig girdler moth is not often observed; it flies primarily from May through June in the San Francisco Bay area and March through May in southern California. The adult female lays tiny, shiny eggs on the woody stems of juniper. The eggs hatch into larvae, which tunnel in the stems for about 8 or 9 months. To confirm twig girdler damage, peel the bark from the area of the branch between dead or dying and living tissue. Inspect the wood for the characteristic girdling tunnels and the presence of larvae. The mature larva is cream colored with a brown head. By the time the larva matures, it often has girdled the twig, although the twig may live for several years before dying. The shiny black to brown pupa occurs beneath bark and the adult emerges in the spring. There is a single generation per year.

MANAGEMENT

To improve plant appearance, prune out and dispose of affected branches. Tam juniper, *Juniperus sabina* 'Tamariscifolia,' and Hollywood juniper, *J. chinensis* 'Torulosa,' are extremely suseptible to damage; avoid planting these and consider replacing existing plantings with more resistant junipers.

If damage cannot be tolerated, it can be reduced by throughly spraying foliage with a persistent insecticide twice annually. Insecticide kills adult moths and prevents them from laying eggs, but boring larvae are not affected and spraying does not restore the appearance of damaged foliage, which remains brown until new growth occurs. In southern California spray in late March and early May; in northern California spray in early June and mid-July. See *Insect Pest Management Guidelines for California Landscape Ornamentals* (UC Publication 3317) for specific pesticide recommendations.

MITES

Mites are common in landscapes, but in most situations they are not serious pests. Most are plant feeders, but some are beneficial predators. Mites are not insects but arachnids, belonging to the same class as spiders and ticks. Mites often go unnoticed because they are tiny and natural controls such as weather and predators frequently keep their populations low. Their damage to plants can usually be observed before you notice the mites themselves.

DAMAGE

Mites puncture plant cells with their mouthparts, then suck the exuding fluid. This causes leaves to appear stippled or flecked with pale dots where tiny areas of leaf tissue have been killed. Mite feeding on fruit appears as a silvery or brownish sheen called russeting. Some mites cover leaves, shoots, or flowers with large amounts of fine webbing; other species cause plant tissues to become distorted, thickened, or galled. Prolonged heavy infestations slow plant growth, cause leaves or fruit to drop prematurely, and young plants may die. Severe infestations often result because natural controls such as predators are disrupted by pesticide applications or excessive dust. Vigorous plants tolerate extensive stippling or tissue distortion with little or no loss in plant growth or fruit yield.

Spider mite feeding causes foliage to become flecked with pale dots. Many spider mite species cover plants with fine webbing.

Inspect foliage with a hand lens when mite presence is suspected. Hold the lens close to your eye and move the object being viewed until it is in focus.

Eriophyids are wormlike or wedge-shaped with four legs, which appear to be coming out of their head; these are greatly enlarged pearleaf blister mites, *Phytoptus pyri.*

IDENTIFICATION AND BIOLOGY

Mites, unlike insects, do not have antennae, segmented bodies, or wings. Most mites pass through an egg stage, a six-legged larval stage, and two eight-legged nymph stages before becoming an eight-legged adult (Figure 4-4). In most of California and the southern U.S., all stages of mites may be present year-round. In cold winter areas, mites overwinter as adult females or eggs on bark or in litter. At moderate temperatures, some species can complete a generation in 1 or 2 weeks.

If stippled or distorted plants are observed, inspect damaged foliage and nearby healthy plant parts with a hand lens to determine if mites are present. Stippled and distorted foliage can be caused by other pests, including thrips, lace bugs, and plant bugs, but these other pests often leave specks of dark excrement on lower leaf surfaces and they do not make webbing. Many mites prefer the lower leaf surface, so remove and turn some leaves over and inspect them. You can also sample spider mites and predaceous mites by branch beating; hold a sheet of paper beneath the plant and tap the foliage sharply. Inspect the paper for any dislodged mites; to the naked eye they look like moving specks. Some of these mites may be beneficial predators helping to control pest mites.

Because of their tiny size and diversity, most mites can be positively identified to the species level only by an expert. Identification of families is usually sufficient because mites within these groups have a similar life cycle and management. The most common pest groups are the spider mites and red mites (family Tetranychidae) and eriophyid mites (family Eriophyidae). Common predatory mites are in the family Phytoseiidae.

Adult and immature eriophyid mites have four legs, which appear to be coming out of the head. They are wormlike or wedgeshaped, and commonly are yellow, pinkish, or white. Eriophyids are minute and can be just barely seen with a 10x hand lens; a microscope is required to clearly distinguish them. Eriophyids include the fuchsia gall mite and *Eriophyes* spp. gall mites, bud mites, rust mites, and blister mites.

Spider mite and red mite adults have eight legs and tiny, globular or spherical bodies that are translucent or colored. Female spider mites hibernating over winter are usually orange or red. Most tetranychid mites have long bristles on their body and produce silken webbing from which the name spider mite is derived.

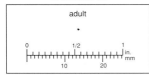

SPIDER MITE

Twospotted Spider Mite *Tetranychus urticae* and Pacific Spider Mite *Tetranychus pacificus*

The twospotted and Pacific spider mites are often pests on fruit and nut trees, especially almond, citrus, pear, and walnut. They feed on many other nonconiferous plants including azalea, fuchsia, maple, and rose. Immatures and adults are yellowish or greenish with irregular dark blotches on the sides of the body. Overwintering females may lack blotches and are often red to orange. Eggs are translucent and spherical and look like tiny drops on the leaf. Colonies are most abundant in pockets on the underside of leaves during summer and, especially in the case of Pacific spider mite, are surrounded by webbing when populations are high. Pacific spider mites occur on both sides of leaves while twospotted mites occur more on the leaf underside.

Twospotted spider mites are yellowish or greenish with irregular dark blotches on the sides of their body.

An adult citrus red mite. European red mite looks similar, except it has a white spot at the base of each hair on its back.

European red mite eggs. Citrus red mite eggs look similar, except they have 10 to 12 threads radiating from the tip of the vertical stalk protruding from each egg.

Citrus Red Mite *Panonychus citri* and European Red Mite *Panonychus ulmi*

Citrus red mite occurs on many plants, especially on citrus in the southern U.S. and California. The European red mite occurs throughout the U.S., especially on apple, *Prunus* species, and fruit trees. It is less common on ash, elm, locust, rose, and other plants. Mobile stages of both species look similar, except that the European red mite has white spots at the base of the hairs on the back. Adults and nymphs are red, oval, globular, and pinpoint size or smaller. Unlike most other tetranychid mites, red mites produce little or no webbing.

Citrus red mite females deposit eggs on both sides of leaves; European red mite eggs are usually on the lower leaf surface. The tiny red egg of both species has a distinct whitish, vertical stalk; the citrus red mite egg also has 10 to 12 threads radiating from the tip of this stalk to the leaf surface.

Red mite populations tend to be higher on young trees; one generation requires about 2 weeks when temperatures are moderate. Hot weather reduces citrus red mite populations; cold weather slows both species' development.

Pine and Spruce Spider Mites *Oligonychus* spp.

Several spider mites are pests of conifers in the western states *Oligonychus subnudus* and *O. milleri* occur on pines, especially Monterey pine. The spruce spider mite, *O. ununguis*, feeds on arborvitae, *Chamaecyparis*, Douglas fir, giant sequoia, juniper, redwood, spruce, and occasionally pine. The adults of each species are green, pink, or brown, and occur mostly on older needles. *O. ununguis* produces webbing, especially around the base of needles. Neither *O. subnudus* nor *O. milleri* produce obvious webbing. These mites overwinter as eggs or motile stages. Nymphs and adults are readily dispersed by wind. *Oligonychus subnudus* are most common in spring. *O. ununguis* populations tend to be highest in the spring and fall. *O. milleri* can be abundant anytime from spring through fall.

Sycamore Spider Mite
Oligonychus platani

The sycamore mite is common in hot, dry areas of California and the southwestern U.S. This green to black mite feeds on the upper surface of sycamore leaves and other hosts including loquat, oak, and pyracantha. Many other *Oligonychus* species, which are commonly brown or reddish, feed on the upper surface of broadleaf plants.

Gall Mites
Eriophyes spp.

Eriophyid mites cause blistered leaves or galled twigs on many landscape plants including alder, aspen, beech, elm, grape, linden, maple, and walnut. The cottonwood gall mite, *Eriophyes parapopuli,* is common throughout the U.S. and causes warty, woody swellings on twigs near the buds of cottonwoods and poplars.

The live oak erineum mite, *Eriophyes mackiei,* causes green to brown, raised blisters on the leaves of live

oak species in California. The mites occur in yellow to orange felty masses in depressions on the underside of blistered leaves, which may become curled or grossly distorted. This damage is harmless to oaks, and no control is known or needed. Oak leaf blister fungus, *Taphrina coerulescens,* causes similar blisters on oak leaves.

Fuchsia Gall Mite
Aculops fuchsiae

Fuchsia gall mite was accidentally introduced from South America in the 1980s. This mite causes leaves and shoots to become thickened and distorted, sometimes forming irregular galls. Fuchsia gall mites occur on growing tips year-round and in flowers during the blooming period. Because fuchsias grow best where summers are cool, this mite is a particular problem in coastal California.

The walnut blister mite, *Eriophyes erinea,* caused these harmless growths on California black walnut leaves.

Live oak erineum mites feed in yellow to orange felty masses in depressions on the underside of these coast live oak leaves; the top of infested leaves looks blistered.

Fuchsia gall mites caused these *Fuchsia magellanica* leaves to thicken and distort.

MANAGEMENT

Mite damage is usually not as serious as it looks. Plants tolerate extensive leaf stippling or distorted tissue without being seriously harmed. Citrus, for example, one of the best studied trees, generally tolerates an average of 8 citrus red mites per leaf without reductions in tree growth or yield. No controls are known or recommended for most eriophyid (gall and blister) mites. Eriophyids cause aesthetic damage and may reduce fruit yield, but most do not seriously harm woody landscape plants and can be tolerated. When mites are abundant, the most important actions are to conserve and augment natural enemies and to provide proper cultural care to keep plants vigorous.

Avoid using broad-spectrum pesticides to prevent disrupting important biological controls. Some organophosphates, pyrethroids, and carbaryl can increase spider mite populations even though the labels may say they control mites. Insecticides applied for other pests during hot weather appear to have the greatest effect on mites, sometimes causing dramatic outbreaks within a few days. If spray-ing is necessary, use selective pesticides or materials with a low residual toxicity, such as narrow-range oil or insecticidal soap (Table 4-6). The release of commercially available predaceous mites may be helpful in some situations after a soap or oil application.

Provide plants with adequate irrigation to prevent stress. Plants that are drought-stressed may be more likely to experience mite outbreaks and are less able to tolerate pest feeding. Regular overhead sprinkling helps control some mites. Sprinkling reduces dust that interferes with some predators and can alleviate drought stress and dislodge some mites.

Spider mite populations can be reduced with a forceful stream of water directed at the lower leaf surfaces. If rapid control of high populations of spider mites or red mites is necessary, insecticidal soap or narrow-range oil may be thoroughly sprayed on infested foliage, usually the underside of leaves. Sulfur is very effective in reducing populations of some spider mites, but this dust can disrupt predaceous mites.

Control dust and ants; they also disrupt natural enemies. Plant ground covers or other herbaceous plants to reduce dust and provide habitat for some overwintering predaceous mites. Ants protect honeydew-producing insects from natural enemies and can disrupt predators that feed on mites on the same plants. Control ants by placing ant stakes or other enclosed pesticide baits at the tree base or by trimming branches to eliminate ant bridges and applying sticky material to tree trunks.

High foliar nitrogen levels can favor outbreaks of some mites by increasing their reproduction and allowing their populations to grow more rapidly than their natural enemies. Do not apply more nitrogen than necessary and use less soluble forms. Urea-based "time released" formulations and most organic fertilizers generally release nitrogen more slowly.

To reduce problems with fuchsia gall mite, plant only resistant fuchsias (Table 4-13) and consider replacing susceptible plants. Prune or pinch off and destroy infested terminals. If damage cannot be tolerated, pruning may be followed with two applications of a miticide, applied 2 to 3 weeks apart. Soap or oil sprays provide some control, but in comparison with exposed-feeding pests, are less effective than synthetic miticides against eriophyid mites enclosed in distorted plant tissue.

Biological Control. Natural enemies frequently provide adequate control of mites with little outside assistance. The most important natural enemies of plant-feeding mites are predaceous mites, including *Euseius tularensis*, *Amblyseius hibisci*, *Phytoseiulus persimilis*, and the western predatory mite, *Metaseiulus occidentalis*. These predators are commonly found on the underside of leaves in the interior of

Predaceous mites are the most important natural enemies of plant-feeding mites. This western predatory mite is attacking a twospotted spider mite.

trees. Other important predators include the spider mite destroyer lady beetle, *Stethorus picipes,* the sixspotted thrips, *Scolothrips sexmaculatus,* and brown and green lacewings. Mite outbreaks often occur because natural enemies have been disrupted. Avoid using broadspectrum pesticides for mites and other pests.

Naturally occurring viral diseases sometimes control mites. For example, when citrus red mite populations reach about 3 or 4 mites per leaf, populations are often rapidly reduced by a viral disease harmless to people. Virus-infected mites walk stiffly, curl up, then die of diarrhea. In dry weather, the dead mites quickly dry up and blow away, and under humid conditions, they leave reddish brown to black, watery spots on leaves or fruit.

Most predaceous mites are long-legged, pear-shaped, and shiny. Many are translucent, although after feeding they often take on the color of their host and may be bright red, yellow, or green. Predaceous mite eggs are colorless and oblong in comparison with the eggs of plant-feeding mites, which are commonly

TABLE 4-13

Susceptibility of *Fuchsia* Species or Cultivars to Fuchsia Gall Mite Damage in California.

LOW SUSCEPTIBILITY OR RESISTANT[a]
Baby Chang, Chance Encounter, Cinnabarina, *F. boliviana, F. minutiflora, F. microphylla* subsp. *hindalgensis, F. radicans, F. thymifolia, F. tincta, F. venusta,* Isis, Mendocino Mini, Miniature Jewels, Ocean Mist, Space Shuttle

MODERATE SUSCEPTIBILITY[b]
Dollar Princess, Englander, *F. aborescens, F. denticulata, F. gehrigeri, F. macrophylla, F. procumbens, F. triphylla,* Golden West, Lena, Macchu Picchu, Pink Marshmallow, Postijon, Psychedelic

HIGH SUSCEPTIBILITY[c]
Angel's Flight, Bicentennial, Capri, China Doll, Christy, Dark Eyes, Display, Firebird, First Love, *F. magellanica,* Golden Anne, Jingle Bells, Kaleidoscope, Kathy Louise, Lisa, Louise Emershaw, Manrinka, Novella, Papoose, Raspberry, South Gate, Stardust, Swingtime, Tinker Bell, Troubadour, Vienna Waltz, Voodoo, Westergeist

a. No control needed.

b. Merely pruning off galled tissue whenever it occurs provides adequate control.

c. Pruning galled tissue followed by spraying may be necessary every several weeks to provide high aesthetic quality.

Phytoseiulus persimilis eating a twospotted spider mite egg.

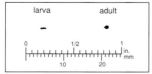

STETHORUS

larva	adult

A spider mite destroyer lady beetle eating a European red mite.

Sixspotted thrips, named for the three dark spots on each wing, is an important mite predator.

TABLE 4-14

Commercially Available Predatory Mites.

PREDATORY MITE	ATTRIBUTES
Metaseiulus occidentalis	Tolerates hot climates if relative humidity is at least 50%
Phytoseiulus persimilis	General predator active at 60-90% relative humidity and 70-100°F
Amblyseius californicus	Commonly used in greenhouses and at temperatures up to 85°F, needs relative humidity of at least 65%, survives when pest populations are low

spherical and colored to opaque. One way to distinguish plant-feeding mites from the predaceous species is to observe mites closely with a good hand lens. Predaceous species appear more active and move faster than plant-feeding species; they stop only to feed.

Many predaceous mites feed not only on all stages of plant-feeding mites, but also on insects such as thrips and scale crawlers or on pollen and fungi. *Phytoseiulus persimilis*, an orangish predator, and the light-colored western predatory mite, *Metaseiulus occidentalis*, are commercially available and can be released to control Pacific spider mite, twospotted mite, and some other species if resident predators are insufficient (see Table 4-14). However, no specific recommendations have been developed for releasing predaceous mites in landscapes. It is more efficient to conserve resident natural enemies by controlling dust, ants, and avoiding pesticide applications.

SNAILS AND SLUGS

Snails and slugs are mollusks and have a similar biology and structure, except that snails have a conspicuous spiral shell. Snails and slugs glide along on their muscular "foot." This muscle constantly secretes mucus, which later dries to form the silvery "slime trail" that is a clue to the presence of these pests.

DAMAGE

Snails and slugs feed on many species of plants. They chew irregular holes with smooth edges in leaves and can clip succulent plant parts. They can also chew fruit and young plant bark. Because they prefer succulent foliage near the ground, they are primarily a pest of seedlings, herbaceous plants, and other low-growing vegetation. The brown garden snail, *Helix aspera*, is a frequently observed species that was introduced from Europe because some people consider it to be a culinary delicacy. The strategies described here for its management are effective against most other snails and slugs in landscapes.

IDENTIFICATION AND BIOLOGY

Dried silvery trails on and around foliage, as well as chewed plants, indicate snail and slug activity. Search protected places as described below to find snails and slugs during the day or inspect plants at night using a flashlight. Snails and slugs are most active during mild, damp periods during the night and early morning. In mild-winter areas such as southern California and coastal locations, young snails are active throughout the year. During cold weather, snails and slugs hibernate in the topsoil. During hot, dry periods, snails seal themselves off with a parchmentlike membrane and often attach themselves to tree trunks, fences, or walls. Adult brown garden snails lay about 80 spherical, pearly white eggs at a time into a hole in the topsoil. They may lay eggs up to six times a year.

MANAGEMENT

Use a combination of methods to control snails and slugs. Avoid overwatering and irrigate early in the day so surfaces dry by evening; high snail and slug populations are promoted by wet, humid conditions. Reduce the places around susceptible plants where snails and slugs can hide during the day: boards, stones, debris, weedy areas around tree trunks, leafy branches growing near the ground, and dense ground covers such as ivy. Reducing these hiding places allows fewer snails and slugs to survive. The survivors congregate in the remaining shelters, where they can more easily be located and controlled.

During the rainy season, or year-round in well irrigated locations, regularly inspect for snails and slugs hiding in shelter that cannot be eliminated, such as low ledges under fences or decks, water meter boxes, and near the ground on walls adjacent to vegetation. Hand picking can be effective (wearing rubber gloves may be desirable). Wooden squares about 12 inches on a side, raised off the ground by 1-inch runners, can be used to monitor and trap snails. Place one or two trap boards beneath each tree or group of shrubs. Check the boards and other hiding places every evening the first week, every second evening the second week, every 3 to 4 days the third week, and weekly thereafter. Crush or dispose of these pests.

Barriers. Copper flashing or screen can be placed around planting beds to exclude snails and slugs. Other barrier materials have been investigated, including diatomaceous earth, wood ashes, and sand. Though effective, these barriers do not provide long-term control.

Use a 6-inch vertical copper screen buried several inches deep in the ground to prevent slugs from crawling through the soil beneath it. Prune lower branches that touch the ground or other objects and apply a copper

Snails and slugs are primarily pests of seedlings and low-growing herbaceous plants, but they also chew young woody plant bark or fruit. The brown garden snail is shown here on citrus.

Copper foil or screen wrapped around planting boxes, headers, or trunks will repel snails for several years.

barrier or other trunk treatment to keep snails out of trees. Copper foil (for example, Snail-Barr) can be wrapped around planting boxes, headers, or trunks to repel snails for several years. When banding trunks, wrap the copper foil around the trunk, tab side down, and cut it to allow an 8-inch overlap. Attach one end or the middle of the band to the trunk with one staple oriented parallel to the trunk. Overlap and fasten the ends with one or two large paper clips to allow the copper band to slide as the trunk grows. Bend the tabs out at a 90° angle from the trunk. The bands may need to be cleaned occasionally.

Instead of copper bands, Bordeaux mixture (a copper sulfate and hydrated lime mixture) can be brushed on trunks to repel snails. One treatment should last about a year. Adding a white latex house paint or a commercial spreader may increase the persistence of Bordeaux mixture through two seasons. Sticky material (such as Stickem Green, which contains copper) applied to trunks excludes snails, slugs, ants, and flightless species of weevils.

Biological Controls. Snails and slugs have many natural enemies, including ground beetles, pathogens, snakes, and birds. These agents alone may not provide effective control, but avoid the use of broad-spectrum pesticides to help improve natural enemies' contribution to pest control. The predatory decollate snail, *Rumina decollata,* consumes young to half-grown brown garden snails and has been very effective in controlling snails in citrus orchards. However, because they also feed on succulent young plants to a limited degree, decollate snail releases may not be desirable in landscapes.

This natural enemy is native to North Africa and southern Europe and was introduced in southern California in the 1970s. Do not release decollate snails in northern California. Decollate snail introductions in California are currently permitted only in the counties of Imperial, Los Angeles, Orange, Riverside, San Bernardino, San Diego, Santa Barbara, Tulare, and Ventura. Releases in other areas are illegal because they might decimate native snail and slug populations of ecological importance in natural areas. Check with your local wildlife protection agency to

A predatory species, the decollate snail, can effectively control brown garden snails in southern California. However, it is illegal to import it into other areas of the state because it attacks ecologically important native snails and slugs.

determine if decollate snail introductions are permitted in your area. For more information on releasing decollate snails, see *Integrated Pest Management for Citrus* (UC Publication 3303).

Pesticide Baits. Baits can provide effective, temporary control of snails and slugs, but should not be necessary where the recommended integrated program of reducing hiding places, using barriers, and biological control has been employed. Baits are toxic to the decollate snail and may poison pets.

The time of any baiting is critical; it should be during a cool, damp period—when snails are most active—before dry, warm weather begins. Irrigate before applying bait to pro-

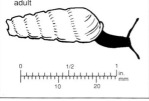

mote snail activity. Make spot applications instead of widespread applications. Apply bait in a narrow strip around sprinklers or in other moist and protected locations. Plant-eating snails and slugs are drawn to these locations, but predaceous snails are less affected than when bait is widely dispersed because decollate snails are not as mobile as other species.

CHAPTER FIVE

Diseases

MICROORGANISMS and environmental stresses can cause disease symptoms on any plant part. Diseased roots may be enlarged, stunted, or rotted. Sap may drip from infected branches or trunks. Leaves or stems may become spotted, stunted, swollen, discolored, distorted, or wilted, or they may die. The severity of symptoms expressed by affected plants depends on the interaction among the plant, its environment, and the pest or causal agents (Figure 5-1). Biotic or living causal agents include nematodes or tiny roundworms (discussed in Chapter 8), as well as the bacteria, fungi, and viruses discussed in this chapter. Nonliving (noninfectious or abiotic) causes such as overwatering or underwatering, toxins, and environmental stresses that can lead to disease are discussed in Chapter 6.

Disease diagnosis is often difficult. Symptoms of different diseases may be similar to each other or they may be difficult to distinguish from other causes, such as damage by certain insects. The organisms or abiotic conditions causing disease are often not visible to the naked eye and may not be readily apparent at the time disease symptoms develop. Disease symptoms are often variable, there are commonly several contributing factors, and many of the organisms involved are microscopic. Professional help and laboratory tests may be needed to positively identify the cause of a disease.

Types of Pathogens

Microorganisms that cause diseases are called pathogens. Fungi, bacteria, viruses, and nematodes (see Chapter 8) are the most common pathogens causing diseases of plants. Although pathogenic microorganisms feed on living organisms, many fungi, bacteria, and nematodes are beneficial; they attack and kill pests or feed on dead organic matter and help to decompose dead plants and animals so that nutrients become available for plant growth.

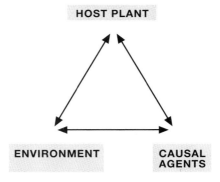

HOST PLANT

ENVIRONMENT

CAUSAL AGENTS

Figure 5-1. Infectious disease results from the interaction among the host plant, its environment, and pests or causal agents.

Pathogenic *fungi* cause many different symptoms, including leaf spots, wilts, curled leaves, dieback, enlargements, and stunted or dead plants. Some fungi are visible in forms—called signs—such as rusts, mildews, and sooty molds. Fungi are usually composed of fine, threadlike structures (hyphae) that form a network or mass (mycelium) growing on or through their host. Fungi can spread through rhizomorphs, sclerotia, or tiny, seedlike structures called spores. Rhizomorphs are rootlike or cordlike masses of hyphae that can contaminate soil and plant parts. Sclerotia are compact masses of hyphae that can persist for relatively long periods.

Fungal spores can be spread by wind, water, soil movement, machinery, insects, or other things with which they come in contact, including people. Sclerotia, rhizomorphs, and some types of spores may survive for long periods in or on plants or soil. When and where conditions such as temperature, moisture, and the presence of a host plant are suitable for growth, they produce new fungal hyphae. If they are large enough to be seen with the naked eye or a hand lens, signs such as

mycelium, masses of spores, and spore-forming structures such as mushrooms help in identifying fungi.

Bacteria are microscopic, one-celled organisms that feed in or on plants or other organic matter. Common symptoms of disease resulting from bacterial infection are shoot blight, leaf spots, soft rots, scabs, wilts, cankers, and galls on branches, twigs, stems, and roots. Unlike fungi, plant pathogenic bacteria generally do not produce spores that can survive adverse environmental conditions; they must usually remain in contact with a host plant or plant debris to survive. Plant-infecting bacteria generally require warmth and moisture to multiply, and are usually not a problem during dry summer weather, except where there is overhead irrigation. Bacteria are commonly spread by splashing water, but are also dispersed by insects or by moving infested plants, soil, or equipment.

Viruses are submicroscopic particles that can infect plants and lead to stunting, discoloring, deformation, or

death of leaves, stems, fruit, or entire plants. Viruses rarely kill woody plants, and some infected plants exhibit no symptoms. Viruses require a living host cell in which to reproduce, and generally do not survive for very long outside of living tissue. Many viruses are spread by aphids, leafhoppers, or other plant-feeding insects. Some viruses are spread by nematodes, budding or grafting, or the movement of infected seeds, plants, plant parts, or infested equipment. Once a plant is infected by a virus, it usually remains infected during its entire life.

Monitoring and Diagnosing Diseases

All infectious diseases involve a complex interaction among the host plant, pathogen, and the environment (Figure 5-1). Disease symptoms and damage are influenced by the disease-producing ability of the causal organism, the plant's genetic char-

Many fungal diseases are caused or aggravated by poor irrigation practices. Do not allow water to pond around trunks; this causes root and crown diseases.

acteristics, and stage of growth and vigor of the host plant at the time of infection. Environmental conditions such as humidity and temperature and other stresses on the plant influence disease development. If conditions are poor for pathogen development and plants are otherwise healthy, many pathogens have little or no effect on their host. The same pathogen can be devastating when conditions are favorable for the pathogen or host plants are stressed.

It is often too late to provide effective control once disease symptoms appear or become severe. Learn what diseases the plant species in your location are prone to, and prevent the conditions that allow those diseases to develop. The Tree and Shrub Pest Tables at the back of this book list common diseases in California organized according to the landscape plants they affect. Checking plants for conditions that promote disease (overwatering, soil compaction, injuries, and so on) is often more important than looking for disease symptoms. Action may be required before damage becomes apparent.

Check plants regularly for symptoms of stress, improper cultural care, and disease symptoms and signs.

Check plants regularly, preferably at least weekly, for symptoms of stress, improper cultural care, and disease symptoms and signs. Record when disease outbreaks are observed. Note the current and past environmental factors that may have contributed to the problem, including humidity, temperature, pesticide use, injuries, soil conditions such as drainage, and the presence of free water. Rain, dew, irrigation, and other water sources are especially important because many pathogens require water for germination of spores and infection.

Compare symptoms that appear in the field with the illustrations and descriptions in this chapter, which are grouped according to the portion of the plant most obviously affected. Consult the Problem-Solving Guide and Tree and Shrub Pest Tables at the end of this book for lists of common damage symptoms and their causes. Examine as many affected plants or parts of the same plant as possible. Look for plants with different stages of disease to determine how symptoms change as the disease progresses. Plant parts in the early stage of disease development often show more characteristic symptoms because later, secondary organisms or other factors that obscure symptoms may later become involved. Do not rely on a single symptom; the observation of several different symptoms is usually needed to identify a disease-producing agent. Look at all affected plant parts. Some aboveground symptoms like wilt and twig dieback are caused by root diseases; when these symptoms occur, you should expose and inspect the roots to see if they are diseased.

A notebook, hand lens, pocket knife, and shovel are essential for diagnosing many diseases. A soil-sampling tube and plastic bags for preserving samples frequently are

useful. It is not always possible to identify diseases with certainty in the field. Many can be confirmed only through special laboratory techniques performed on the diseased plants, surrounding soil, or nearby apparently healthy plant tissue. Contact the Cooperative Extension office in your county for a list of private laboratories that test for diseases.

Disease Management

Prevention is the most important method of disease management; for many diseases, prevention is the only effective option. Learn the cultural and environmental requirements of your plants and provide them with proper care. Pathogens frequently kill plants that are poorly cared for, so keep valued plants vigorous. Avoid conditions stressful to plants. Stresses include repeated insect defoliation; soil that is kept continually too wet, too dry, or compacted; overfertilization; and improper pruning, especially at bud break or during early growth flush. Physical damage to roots and trunks, changes in soil grade, excessive herbicides or salts, use of injections or implants, and planting species that are poorly adapted for local conditions also cause stress. Most pathogens require specific conditions to spread and infect plants. Learn the conditions that promote diseases common to your plants and avoid creating those situations. Read Chapters 3 and 6 in this book to learn how to care for plants to prevent disease.

Resistant Varieties. The species or cultivar planted often determines whether certain diseases are likely to develop or can be avoided. Resistant varieties either cannot be infected by certain pathogens or are not seriously damaged if they do become infected. Landscape plants that are resistant to certain insects and diseases, including anthracnose, root rots, powdery mildew, and vascular wilts, are listed in Table 3-2. Check with the Cooperative Extension office in your county or a certified nurseryperson for the most recent recommendations and use the information provided here to choose resistant species and varieties that are well suited to local conditions. If you select a more susceptible variety because of other preferred horticultural characteristics, be prepared to accept disease damage or devote the effort and resources required to manage it.

Quality Planting Material. Many diseases can be transmitted in nursery stock, transplants, or seeds. Select

Prevent conditions stressful to plants. Paving around established trees reduces oxygen and moisture availability to roots and changes temperature.

certified virus-free nursery stock when available. Examine young plants for symptoms of root disease, crown gall, and virus diseases before purchasing and planting. Expose roots to be sure they are not diseased or excessively kinked or restricted by the planting container. Examine bark for wounds and galls. Avoid plants that have been improperly pruned, as they are unlikely to develop good structure. Use high-quality planting stock obtained from a reputable supplier. See Table 3-1 for a checklist of what to look for when purchasing nursery stock. A relatively small initial investment in higher quality plants can pay great dividends in improved aesthetic quality and lower maintenance costs.

Planting Site and Design. Select plants that are adapted for your location. Some species require full sun while others do well in shady areas. Some diseases, such as powdery mildews, are more prevalent in shady areas; sunscald occurs when sensitive plants are planted at bright sites. Improve poorly drained soils before planting to avoid root diseases. Group plants according to their water requirements; do not plant drought-adapted species near plants requiring frequent light watering. Do not plant grass or other ground covers around tree and shrub trunks; keep the soil bare or use mulch. Keep mulch thin around the trunk or 6 inches back from the trunk to avoid promoting crown diseases. When replanting where diseased trees or shrubs have been removed, use species resistant to the disease-producing agent that occurred there. See Chapters 2 and 3 for more discussion on landscape design and planting to prevent disease development.

Irrigation and Fertilization. Provide adequate water for your plants as dis-

cussed in Chapter 3. Overwatering or irrigating during the wrong time of year promote the development of root diseases. Avoid overhead watering or water early in the day or before sunrise so foliage on disease-prone shrubs can dry quickly. Use soil or plant tissue tests where available to determine the nutrient needs when maintaining many plants or especially valued specimens. Inadequate or excess fertilizer promotes certain disease-producing organisms and other pests as discussed in Chapters 3 and 6.

Learn what pattern of moisture your plant is adapted to and provide proper watering. Most plants native to the eastern U.S., northern Europe, and eastern Asia require summer irrigation or rainfall. Conversely, except during establishment, avoid summer irrigation of plants adapted to summer drought, such as California native oaks. When needed during years of below-normal rainfall, these species should generally be irrigated during the normal rainy season. Irrigation at 1 or 2 month intervals during the dry season may also be appropriate for drought-adapted species in disturbed urban soils, as discussed in Chapter 3.

Irrigate when needed near the drip line, never around the trunk (Figure 5-2). Do not let water stand around trunks. If you have irrigation water basins around trunks, break down the mounded soil during the rainy season so that water can drain away. Provide good soil drainage by gently grading soil surfaces, installing subsurface drains or sumps (Figure 3-4), breaking up compacted soil layers, or sloping the base of compacted subsoils before planting. Instead of planting in a low-lying area, plant in raised beds or on a ridge or mound of soil (Figure 5-3). Prevent soil compaction, for example by avoiding traffic under plants.

If plants become damaged by root rot, reduce irrigation. Surface drains can be installed in established landscapes. It may help in some cases if the irrigation method is changed from flooding or sprinklers to a drip system. Temporarily remove soil within several feet of the base of diseased plants to expose roots and promote drying. Protect newly exposed tissue from direct sun or excessive temperature changes. After drying, cover roots to the same level with the same soil, which has been air dried. Do not wet or compact the earth. Alternatively, cover roots around the crown with pea gravel, which provides good drainage and aeration. Consider reducing the humidity beneath plants by thinning dense lower canopies and eliminating weeds or ground covers beneath plants. Once severe damage symptoms appear, little can be done to save the plant. Remove and dispose of dying trees, which may become hazardous. Correct any soil or water conditions promoting disease and replant with resistant species.

Pruning. Consider pruning out and disposing of localized areas of diseased plant tissue as soon as they appear. Pruning to remove infected tissue can stop the spread of some diseases, such as fireblight. Make pruning cuts in healthy tissue, well below the diseased or infected area. Dispose of diseased prunings away from susceptible plants. Removing some branches, especially in the lower canopy, can reduce the incidence of certain diseases, such as brown rot of fruit, by improving air flow and reducing the splashing of spores from the ground to the canopy by rain or irrigation. See Chapter 3 for more discussion on proper pruning.

Sanitation. Keep implements clean to avoid spreading contaminated soil

Figure 5-2. Do not water established trees and shrubs near the trunk, this promotes root and crown disease. Water plants when needed around the drip line and beyond. Adjust sprinklers or install deflectors to prevent wetting of trunks. Move drip emitters away from the base of the trunk after plants are established.

or disease organisms from infected plants. Sterilize pruning shears and other equipment with a commercial disinfectant after working on or around plants suspected of infection by fireblight or bacterial gall. Rinse, dry, and oil tools following this treatment to prevent rusting. Clean soil particles and plant parts off of shoes and garden tools and wash your hands before moving to another area after working with diseased plants.

Weed and Insect Control. Control weeds, turf, and ground covers near trunks by properly using mulch or by maintaining bare soil. Weeds, turf, and ground covers compete with desirable plants for moisture and nutrients and can increase humidity beneath woody plants, thereby promoting certain diseases. Infrequent or light-to-moderate damage by foliage-feeding insects can be tolerated by many landscape plants. However, repeated heavy insect damage that occurs more than once in a growing season or during consecutive years, such as total loss of foliage, should be prevented as this can weaken plants and increase their susceptibility to disease.

Soil Solarization. Some soil pathogens can be destroyed or their populations reduced by solarization before planting. Cover moist, bare

Figure 5-3. Avoid planting in a hole or a low-lying area, except when planting in sandy soils. Plant in raised beds or on a ridge or mound of soil several inches high and several feet across in areas where drainage is poor or soil is highly amended and plants will settle as organic matter in the soil decomposes.

soil with clear plastic for 6 weeks to 2 months during the sunny, warm, dry part of the year to reduce pathogen numbers near the soil surface as detailed in Chapter 7; this method is primarily used for annual and shallow-rooted plants.

Biological Control. Many naturally occurring organisms kill or retard the growth of pathogens. However, despite their importance, little is known on how to manipulate these beneficial microorganisms. For example, *suppressive soils* contain microorganisms that improve plant growth when added to pathogen-infested soil. Unfortunately, there are no general recommendations on effectively using suppressive soils in landscapes.

One beneficial microorganism is commerically available for use in preventing disease, as discussed later in this chapter. Prevent crown gall from developing in nurseries by dipping roots for 30 seconds in a protective suspension of the biological control agent *Agrobacterium radiobacter* 'K-84'.

Beneficial Microorganisms. Many soil-dwelling microorganisms improve plant growth in ways other than the ability to control pathogens. Many fungi and bacteria break down organic and inorganic matter in soil so that nutrients become available for new plant growth. Mycorrhizae are beneficial associations between plant roots and fungi as discussed in Chapter 3. They improve plants' ability to absorb nutrients and may aid in water uptake. Soil-dwelling bacteria convert nitrogen into forms that plants can use. Some species of these nitrogen-fixing bacteria form nodules on roots, especially plants in the legume family. Determine whether symptoms such as galls on roots are the result of beneficial or harmful organisms before taking control action.

Pesticides. With careful cultural management, at least some cultivars of most landscape plants can be grown at a high level of aesthetic quality using little or no pesticides to control pathogens. Proper management to prevent diseases is generally the most effective strategy; many diseases cannot be effectively controlled once symptoms develop or become severe. However, synthetic and organically acceptable pesticides are available to control certain plant pathogens, primarily fungi. Fungicides require careful timing to be effective.

Fungicides acceptable in California for use on organically grown crops include sulfur, fixed copper including Bordeaux mixture—a mixture of bluestone (copper sulfate) and lime (calcium hydroxide)—and fungicidal soap sprays. Sulfur is available in several forms. Elemental sulfur or sulfur formulated as a wettable powder is applied to prevent powdery mildew. Micronized sulfur provides better coverage and easier handling than conventional sulfur to control

pathogens and mites. Fixed copper compounds protect plants from damage by certain fungi, including shot hole fungus, peach leaf curl, and bacterial canker. Most copper fungicides resist weathering because they are only slightly soluble in water and have an ionic attraction to plant surfaces.

Organically acceptable fungicides generally only prevent the infection of healthy, spray-covered tissue and do not act systemically to kill existing pathogens, therefore repeated applications may be necessary during critical growing stages. Bordeaux mixture, fixed copper, and sulfur also can be damaging to some plants, particularly during warmer temperatures.

Several synthetic fungicides, most commonly chlorothalonil, captan, triadimefon, and triforine, are available for disease control in landscapes as directed on the product labels. Some synthetic fungicides have systemic activity. They are often easier to apply, more effective, provide control at lower rates, and are less likely to damage some plants when compared

These white *Ganoderma* sp. basidiocarps or conks are a sign of disease.

with organically acceptable materials. For specific fungicide recommendations, see *Foliage and Branch Diseases of Landscape Trees* (UC Leaflet 2616).

SYMPTOMS ON LEAVES, TWIGS, AND STEMS

Many pathogens and environmental conditions cause leaves, twigs, or stems to discolor, wilt, or die. Some of these diseases, such as sooty mold, many leaf spots, and some powdery mildews, are aesthetically displeasing but usually do not cause serious, long-term harm to plants. On the other hand, wilt and root diseases, wood-boring insects, and other pests that affect the plant's water and nutri-ent conducting tissue also cause symptoms on leaves and stems; plants with these problems often die. Leaf spots (Table 5-1), cankers (Table 5-3), and other symptoms can have many different causes. It is important to identify the cause of your unhealthy plants and to take action if the problem is serious.

Anthracnose

Anthracnose, often called leaf, shoot, bud, or twig blight, is a group of diseases resulting from fungi, including *Cryptocline, Discula, Glomerella,* and *Gnomonia* species. Anthracnose pathogens infect trees and shrubs throughout the U.S.

Terminal dieback and partly killed Modesto ash leaves due to ash anthracnose, *Discula aridum.*

TABLE 5-1

Some Common Causes of Leaf Spots.

CAUSE	COMMENTS	SEE PAGE NO.
Air pollution	Aggravates other causes if air quality is poor	224
Anthracnose	Many hosts, promoted by moisture during new growth	185
Bacterial blight	Dieback, cankers, and oozing twigs are associated symptoms	197
Chewing or boring insects	Insects present usually help to identify	63-91, 146
Entomosporium leaf spot	Rosaceae plants in Pomoidea group are affected	188
Eriophyid mites	Tiny, wormlike mites may barely be seen with a hand lens	173
Leaf blisters	Oak leaves affected by *Taphrina* fungus if spring is moist	
Mineral deficiency	*Prunus* species are most commonly affected	217
Pesticide injury	Commonly herbicides, but other pesticides can be the cause	12, 221
Rusts	Orangish or yellowish spore masses, often on leaf underside	195
Scabs	Dark, circular, scabby or velvety, spots on many hosts	188
Scale insects	Unlike disease causes, scales can usually be scraped off	117
Septoria leaf spot	Spots mostly older leaves, cankers may develop on poplars	187
Shot hole	Almond, apricot, plum, and other *Prunus* species are affected	187
Spider mites or red mites	May be webbing, tiny mites present	170
Sucking insects	May be dark excrement of thrips, lace bugs, or plant bugs	135-142
Sunburn	Yellow or brown area beginning between leaf veins	222
Viruses	Streaked, discolored, or distorted foliage	212
Water deficiency	May begin as yellow or brown area between leaf veins	32, 215

Sycamore anthracnose, *Apiognomonia veneta*, kills sycamore shoots and causes leaf tissue to die beginning along veins.

Black leaf spots on Chinese elm leaves caused by Chinese elm anthracnose, *Stegophora ulmea*.

DAMAGE

Anthracnose damage is commonly limited to conspicuous spots or irregular dead areas on leaves and twigs, which may cause foliage to become distorted and drop prematurely. Anthracnose does not seriously harm plants unless defoliation occurs repeatedly or branch dieback or cankering is extensive. Twigs and branches can die on the more susceptible hosts, including some species of ash, elm, oak, and sycamore. Cankers—dead areas that may or may not be surrounded by callus tissue—can form on twigs or small branches, causing them to become girdled and die. The resulting regrowth from lateral buds can give trees a gnarled or crooked appearance. Chinese elm anthracnose, also called black leaf spot, produces especially large cankers, which can weaken, girdle, or kill limbs and trunks as discussed in the section on canker diseases.

IDENTIFICATION AND BIOLOGY

Small tan, brown, black, or tarlike spots appear on infected leaves of some hosts, including oak or walnut. Dead leaf areas may be more irregular on other hosts such as ash, birch, elm, or redbud. Maple and sycamore anthracnose lesions typically develop around the major leaf veins. If leaves are very young when infected, they may become curled and distorted with only a portion of each leaf dying. Affected leaves may look like they have been damaged by frost.

Anthracnose fungi overwinter primarily in lesions on infected twigs on the tree. On evergreen species such as Chinese elm, the fungus can occur year-round on leaves. Spores are produced in the spring and are spread by splashing rain and windborne rain to new growth. If it is moist during the new growth season, these spores germinate and infect new twigs and foliage. More spores are produced and are readily spread to nearby foliage by raindrops or overhead irrigation.

MANAGEMENT

In areas where prolonged spring rains or foggy conditions are common, avoid planting especially susceptible species, including Modesto ash, California sycamore (*Platanus racemosa*), and American sycamore (*P. occidentalis*). The London plane tree (*P. acerifolia*), especially the 'Bloodgood' variety; privet varieties 'Amur,' 'Iobota,' and 'Regal'; and ash varieties 'Moraine' and 'Raywood' are more resistant to anthracnose than other varieties. Avoid planting the 'True Green' and 'Evergreen' cultivars of evergreen Chinese elm, which are susceptible to anthracnose; plant the resistant 'Drake' cultivar.

Prune out and dispose of infected twigs during the fall or winter to help control anthracnose. Fungicides have not been found to be effective in controlling anthracnose on elm or sycamore, but some fungicides provide some control of anthracnose on Modesto ash if thoroughly sprayed on all new growth as buds begin to open in the spring. If moist weather prevails, additional applications may be needed at intervals of about 2 weeks to protect newly exposed growth. Repeated fungicide applications for anthracnose control usually are not appropriate on other hosts. See *Foliage and Branch Diseases of Landscape Trees* (UC Leaflet 2616) for specific fungicide recommendations.

Shot Hole
Wilsonomyces carpophilus

Shot hole, also called coryneum blight, affects *Prunus* species, such as almond, apricot, and plum. It causes discolored spots on buds, leaves, shoots, and fruit. Holes can appear in affected leaves and foliage may drop prematurely. Concentric lesions may develop on branches. Severe mineral deficiency, injuries, insects, chemical damage, and viruses can cause similar symptoms on some *Prunus* species such as Japanese flowering cherry (Table 5-1). However, most holes in leaves are caused by chewing insects (see Chapter 4).

Shot hole first appears in the spring as reddish, purplish, or brown spots about 1/10 inch in diameter on new buds, leaves, and shoots. The spots expand and their centers turn brown. Tiny dark specks, visible only with a hand lens, form in the brown centers, especially on buds; these dark specks, the spores of the fungus, help to distinguish shot hole from other diseases. Spots on young leaves have a narrow, light green or yellow margin and their centers often fall out as leaves expand, leaving holes. Leaves may fall from the tree. Fruit spotting may occur, usually on the upper surface.

The disease is most severe following warm, wet winters and when wet weather is prolonged in the spring. The fungus survives the dormant season inside infected buds and in twig lesions. Spores are spread by splashing rain or irrigation water, which also promote spore germination.

MANAGEMENT

Sprinklers or overhead irrigation that wets foliage increase the severity of shot hole. Use low-volume, drip irrigation systems instead. Alternatively, keep water pressure low, redirect nozzles, use sprinkler deflectors, and prune off lower branches to prevent foliage from getting wet.

Prune out and dispose of infected tissue as soon as it appears. After leaf drop, inspect plants carefully and prune out varnished appearing (infected) buds and twigs with lesions. Diligent sanitation and water management can provide adequate control where the incidence of shot hole is low. Bordeaux mixture or fixed copper can be applied where disease incidence or plant aesthetic value is high. When applying a copper-containing compound, make one application of a material that is at least 50% copper after leaf drop and before fall rains begin. Additional treatments may be necessary if prolonged wet weather occurs in the spring. Some synthetic fungicides are also effective and avoid potential copper damage to plants.

Septoria Leaf Spot
Septoria spp.

Several dozen *Septoria* species occur in the U.S. Each causes round, angular, flecked, sunken, or irregular spots on mostly older leaves on a dif-

Leaf veins limit the spread of the Septoria leaf spot fungus, *Mycosphaerella populorum*, so some of these dead patches on poplar have angular edges.

Discolored spots on fruit and holes in this apricot leaf are characteristic of shot hole fungus, which is promoted by moisture.

ferent group of closely related hosts. Aspen, azalea, cottonwood, hebe, and poplar are commonly infected. Cankers may develop on the branches of certain severely infected *Populus* species. The biology of *Septoria* is similar to that of anthracnose. Prune out and dispose of infected wood in the fall. Reduce humidity and splashing water as described for anthracnose.

Entomosporium Leaf Spot *Entomosporium mespili* or *E. maculatum*

Entomosporium spots the leaves of plants in the Pomoideae group of the rose family, including apple, flowering crab apple, evergreen pear, hawthorn, pear, photinia, pyracantha, quince, *Rhaphiolepis*, serviceberry, and toyon. Tiny reddish spots, sometimes surrounded by a yellow halo, appear on the leaves of infected plants, usually on older growth. These spots darken and enlarge as the leaves mature. Spore-forming bodies eventually appear in the center of the spots; these cream-colored specks may appear to be covered with a glossy membrane, beneath which white masses of spores are visible.

Fungi infecting deciduous plants overwinter mainly as spores on fallen leaves or as mycelia within tissue. On evergreen hosts, the fungi may remain on leaves year-round. Fungi are spread from infected tissue or contaminated leaf litter to healthy leaves by splashing raindrops or overhead irrigation. The pathogens are most severe during wet weather, especially when it coincides with new plant growth.

Remove and dispose of spotted leaves that are on plants or have fallen. Do not water overhead as this spreads the fungus spores and favors infection. Reduce humidity around plants by providing adequate space between plants and by pruning lower branches. Consider removing ground covers beneath shrubs and mulching or maintaining bare soil instead.

Entomosporium causes reddish spots, sometimes surrounded by a yellow halo; spots darken and enlarge as leaves mature, like these on *Rhaphiolepis*.

Circular, scabby spots on toyon leaves caused by *Spilocaea photinicola*.

Scabs *Spilocaea* and *Venturia* spp.

Fungal scabs affect many hosts. *Spilocaea* spp. commonly infect apple, pear, pyracantha, and toyon. *Venturia* spp. infect coffeeberry and cotoneaster in California and maple, poplar, and willow in the midwestern and northeastern United States. Olive green to black, circular, scabby or velvety spots appear on infected leaves, which may yellow or redden and drop prematurely. Scabby spots, often more sunken, may appear on fruit, which may crack or shrivel and drop. Shoots may die back if the disease is severe.

Scab fungi overwinter primarily on fallen leaves, but also on lesions on twigs in some hosts. Rain or irrigation during spring splashes spores from leaf litter onto developing foliage or fruit, which become infected. Mild temperatures and high humidity promote disease development, which is arrested by hot, dry weather.

Remove and dispose of fallen leaves in the fall. Fall foliar fertilizer (urea) applications on deciduous hosts hasten leaf drop and promote leaf decomposition, reducing the number of spores in spring. Avoid overhead sprinkling, which splashes spores onto the plant, or irrigate early in the day so that foliage dries more quickly. Sulfur applied about weekly to foliage during wet weather before disease develops or some synthetic fungicides can prevent the disease, but chemical control is generally not warranted except where the disease is severe on apple or pear fruit. Vigorous plants tolerate extensive leaf scabbing, so provide plants with proper cultural care.

Oak Branch Dieback
Diplodia quercina

Oak branch dieback occurs on several oak species in California, including coast live oak, valley oak, black oak, and English oak. It causes leaves to wilt and turn tan or brown. Infected branches die, and if the bark is peeled back, infected wood is usually dark brown to black. Unlike oak twig blight that causes dead white or tan leaves in scattered patches throughout the canopy (see below), oak branch dieback generally occurs in a

whole section of the tree while other parts of the plant appear healthy. Oak twig blight is associated more with wet conditions, while oak branch dieback is more prevalent during and after periods of drought. Both diseases may become more prevalent when trees are stressed from environmental conditions.

Prevent branch dieback by providing trees with proper cultural care. Drought stress appears to contribute greatly to this disease. Even drought-adapted species may require supplemental irrigation if rainfall has been below normal. However, irrigation of native oaks should generally be done during the normal rainy season to supplement inadequate natural rainfall. Oaks in disturbed urban soils may also benefit from irrigation around the drip line (not near the trunk) at 1 or 2 month intervals during the dry season. More frequent irrigation during the dry season promotes serious root diseases, as discussed later in this chapter. Prune out diseased and dead branches from November through January; new infections are least likely to occur

during that time. Fungicides generally do not provide effective control. The disease is not likely to be a problem most years and control is usually not needed, especially if trees are cared for properly.

Oak Twig Blight
Cryptocline cinerescens and *Discula quercina*

Oak twig blight affects primarily coast live oak, but also may occur on other oak species. It is sporadic in occurrence and is caused by two fungi, *Cryptocline cinerescens* and *Discula quercina*. Leaves and twigs from the current season's growth turn white or tan and remain on the tree, often in scattered patches throughout the tree canopy. Oak twig blight has been found to be more severe on trees infested with oak pit scale.

Provide infected trees with adequate cultural care, especially appropriate watering. Do not irrigate native oaks during the dry season; irrigate

Oak twig blight caused scattered patches of dead leaves on current season growth of this coast live oak.

during the winter if needed because rainfall has been below normal. Proper pruning can control the disease, but this may be economical only for a few small or specimen trees. Prune out all infected twigs during dry weather in the summer or fall; make pruning cuts properly (Figure 3-8) in tissue below infected twigs. Some systemic fungicides provide control if applied within one week after pruning. Fungicides alone are not as effective. Dead twigs and leaves remain on the tree for 2 or 3 years, and the tree's appearance does not improve until these drop or are pruned out. See *Foliage and Branch Diseases of Landscape Trees* (UC Leaflet 2616) for specific fungicide recommendations.

Fireblight
Erwinia amylovora

Fireblight is a bacterial disease that damages only plants in the pome tribe of the rose family, including apple, evergreen pear, hawthorn, loquat, pear, pyracantha, and toyon.

DAMAGE

Fireblight causes a sudden wilting, shriveling, and blackening or browning of shoots, blossoms, and fruit. Rapid infection of extensive portions of the plant gives it a scorched appearance with dead leaves remaining attached to twigs, hence the name fireblight. Cankers can form on twigs and branches, which may die back. Prolonged serious infections can kill some plants such as pear.

IDENTIFICATION AND BIOLOGY

Fireblight bacteria infect new growth through flowers during the spring. During warm, wet, or humid weather, brownish droplets containing the bacteria ooze from around cankers. These bacteria are spread to flowers by many species of flying or crawling insects. Once flowers are infected, bees and splashing water can spread the bacteria from one flower to another. Infection occurs through the blossoms and slowly spreads throughout twigs and terminal branches. The bacteria overwinter in

Fireblight caused this pear blossom and terminal to suddenly wilt, blacken, and die.

plant tissue around cracked, sunken cankers in bark. Diagnose fireblight by peeling back bark around cankers and newly infected twigs and branches; inspect the wood, which turns reddish brown when newly infected. Once tissue dies (which can happen quickly) it turns black.

MANAGEMENT

Plant 'Bradford,' 'Capitol,' or 'Red Spire' varieties, which are less susceptible to fireblight than some other ornamental pear trees. Eliminate fireblight by pruning diseased branches back at least 6 inches into healthy appearing tissue and removing and disposing of all infected tissue. To avoid spreading bacteria during pruning, sterilize pruning tools before each cut by dipping them in a commercial disinfectant. Dry and oil tools after use to prevent rust. A very weak (about ½ percent) Bordeaux mixture or other copper fungicide applied several times as blossoms open can reduce infections.

Verticillium Wilt
Verticillium dahliae

Many deciduous trees, shrubs, and herbaceous plants are susceptible to infection by Verticillium wilt fungi. Common hosts include ash, camphor, Chinese pistache, fuchsia, hebe, maple, olive, pepper tree, pistachio, and rose.

DAMAGE

Verticillium wilt, along with Fusarium wilt and Dutch elm disease as discussed in the next sections, affects the plant's vascular system, the network of phloem and xylem tissue that transports nutrients, food, and water among plant parts. By interfering with the plant's "bloodstream," these vascular wilt diseases cause foliage to turn faded green, yellow, or brown, and sometimes wilt in scattered portions of the canopy or on scattered branches. Shoots and branches wilt and die, often beginning on one side of the plant, and occasionally entire plants die.

Small plants may die from Verticillium wilt in a single season, but in larger plants the disease spreads slowly. Mature trees may take many years to die and may suddenly recover if conditions become favorable for plant growth and poor for disease development.

IDENTIFICATION AND BIOLOGY

The survival structures of Verticillium wilt fungus (microsclerotia) reside in the soil. When it is cool and roots are present, microsclerotia germinate and hyphae grow from them. Hyphae infect plants through roots, then spread upward in the current year's growth, blocking the plant's

Brown, dead foliage in scattered patches on one side of a Japanese maple due to Verticillium wilt.

ability to transport nutrients and water. In some but not all plants, peeling back the bark on newly infected branches may reveal dark stains following the grain on infected wood. Depending on the plant species, the stains are dark gray, black, brownish, or greenish. A laboratory culture from newly infected wood is often required to confirm the Verticillium wilt fungus. Infection can occur during the spring but not become apparent until warm weather, when plants are more stressed.

MANAGEMENT

Keep plants vigorous by learning and providing for their cultural require-

Verticillium wilt damages plants' vascular tissue; peeling back the bark on newly infected branches may reveal dark stains following the grain as seen on this almond wood.

ments. Provide infected trees with proper irrigation, modest amounts of slow-release fertilizer, and other appropriate care to promote new growth and increase their chances of survival. Chronic branch dieback may develop in surviving trees; prune out any dead wood. Regularly inspect for possible hazards; affected trees may need to be removed. Where Verticillium wilt has been a problem, plant only resistant species as listed in Table 5-2.

Solarization can reduce Verticillium and Fusarium fungi in the upper few inches of soil in areas with warm weather. Before replanting, cover bare, moist soil with clear plastic for about two months during hot, dry weather (see Solarization, Chapter 7). Because roots eventually grow outside the treated zone, this method is most effective for annual plants.

Fusarium Wilt
Fusarium oxysporum

Several types of *Fusarium oxysporum* infect landscape plants, causing rotting of tissue, twig dieback, branch cankers, and seedling death. Certain varieties of this fungus can kill conifer seedlings, palms, or hebe shrubs, but most varieties of this pathogen attack herbaceous plants. Each variety of Fusarium wilt fungus is specific to certain hosts and does not spread to other plant genera. Like Verticillium wilt, Fusarium wilt results from infection through roots by hyphae that germinate from long-lasting survival structures (chlamydospores) in the soil. Older leaves usually die first in infected plants, commonly followed by death of the entire plant. Cutting into infected wood may reveal that vascular tissue has turned brown, often all the way from the shoot to the soil line.

TABLE 5-2

Landscape Trees and Shrubs Resistant to Verticillium Wilt.[a]

COMMON NAME	SCIENTIFIC NAME
Apple and crab apple	*Malus* spp.[b]
Beech	*Fagus* spp.
Birch	*Betula* spp.
Box and boxwood	*Buxus* spp.
California bay	*Umbellularia californica*
Citrus	*Citrus* spp.
Conifers	*Pinus, Abies, Picea* spp.
Dogwood	*Cornus* spp.
Eucalyptus	*Eucalyptus* spp.
European mountain ash	*Sorbus aucuparia*
Fig, edible	*Ficus carica*
Hawthorn	*Crataegus* spp.
Holly	*Ilex* spp.
Hornbeam	*Carpinus* spp.
Katsura tree	*Cercidiphyllum japonicum*
Linden	*Tilia* spp.
Locust	*Gleditsia* spp.
Manzanita	*Arctostaphylos* spp.
Mulberry	*Morus* spp.
Oak	*Quercus* spp.
Oleander	*Nerium oleander*
Palms	All genera
Pear	*Pyrus* spp.[b]
Plane tree	*Platanus* spp.
Pyracantha	*Pyracantha* spp.
Sage-leaf rock rose	*Cistus salviifolius*
Sweet gum	*Liquidambar styraciflua*
Rock rose	*Cistus tauricus*
Walnut	*Juglans* spp.
Western sycamore	*Platanus racemosa*
White rock rose	*Cistus corbariensis*
Willow	*Salix* spp.

a. This list provides a guideline only; there is no guarantee that these plants won't be affected. New pathogen strains develop or are introduced. Disease incidence is greatly influenced by cultural care and environmental conditions. For a complete list see *Plants Resistant or Susceptible to Verticillium Wilt* (UC Leaflet 2703).

b. Apple, pear, and quince are susceptible to European strains of *Verticillium albo-atrum*.

Provide proper cultural care and management as described above for Verticillium wilt. Fusarium wilt fungi are host-specific; replant at that site using a plant species from a different genus. Avoid using undecayed organic amendments and excessive fertilizer, especially urea, which may promote *Fusarium*.

Dutch Elm Disease *Ophiostoma* or *Ceratocystis ulmi*

Dutch elm disease fungus in California killed about 3,000 elms in the San Francisco Bay area from 1975 to 1990 and fewer elms around Sacramento; millions of elms have been killed in eastern and midwestern states since 1930. The symptoms usually first appear in only one portion of the canopy, resulting in yellow or wilting foliage. The dead leaves curl and turn brown, but remain on branches. Peeling back the bark reveals brown to blackish streaks in the wood, which appear as dark concentric rings when infected branches are cut in cross section. Do not confuse disease symptoms with the leaf discoloring caused by the elm leaf beetle. Elm leaf beetle chews holes and skeletonizes leaves, which may then become discolored, often giving the tree a brown appearance when viewed from some distance. Elms suspected of being infected with Dutch elm disease should be reported to the County Department of Agriculture for confirmation of the disease.

Dutch elm disease is spread long distances primarily by the European elm bark beetle (see Chapter 4). Beetles emerge from dead or dying trees or from elm logs infected with the fungus, carrying spores that infect healthy trees when the adult beetles feed on young twigs. People inadvertently assist this spread by moving infected elm logs to disease-free areas. The fungus can also spread from infected elms through root grafts to nearby elms.

MANAGEMENT

American and European elm species are adapted to summer rainfall. Maintain tree vigor by providing adequate summer irrigation in areas with summer drought. Prune elms only from late fall through winter to avoid creating fresh wounds that attract disease-spreading elm bark beetles, which fly during the spring and summer. Bury or (where permitted) burn freshly cut elm wood. Alternatively, seal elm logs tightly under clear plastic in the sun through the warm season and for at least 7 months, after which they are no longer suitable for beetle breeding.

Plant resistant species to avoid Dutch elm disease. Hackberry (*Celtis* spp.) look similar to elms but are not attacked by Dutch elm disease or elm leaf beetle. The evergreen Chinese elm, Siberian elm, and zelkova are less often affected than other elms, and new resistant elm hybrids are being developed. When planting elms, use these species instead of American or European elms. Planting any elm species is prohibited in areas quarantined for Dutch elm disease, currently the San Francisco Bay area and around Sacramento in California.

Contact local agricultural or forestry agency officials if elms are suspected of being infected with Dutch elm disease fungus. Remove infected elms immediately to eliminate them as a source of the fungus, which otherwise will spread to nearby elms. Digging a 2-foot-deep trench around infected trees may prevent the fungus from being spread by root grafts to nearby elms.

The removal of recently diseased limbs may be an alternative in areas where quarantine regulations do not

require the removal of the entire tree. This "therapeutic pruning" can be effective only if done immediately during the first season when disease symptoms appear on a tree. Symptoms must be limited to one or a few limbs and at least 10 feet of healthy wood (free of visible disease streaking) must separate the infected wood from the pruning point on the main trunk. The trees must be otherwise vigorous and healthy.

Powdery Mildew

Many landscape plants are susceptible to one or more species of powdery mildew fungi, which usually appear as a grayish or white powdery growth on leaves and other succulent tissue.

DAMAGE

Some powdery mildews are unlikely to seriously harm certain plants, while others grow extensively into tissue and slowly debilitate their hosts. Infected leaves often drop prematurely and leaves and shoots may become distorted, dwarfed, and discolored, such as oak terminals that form "witches' brooms." The type and severity of symptoms vary depending on the species or variety of host plant, the age of tissue when infected, environmental conditions, and the specific pathogen involved. Deciduous species may be less severely damaged because they annually shed all leaves.

IDENTIFICATION AND BIOLOGY

Powdery mildew may develop on any green plant tissue or on flowers and fruits. Light-colored mats of fungal growth often appear on infected leaves. Spores are produced in these vegetative strands, and in some powdery mildews these spores form in chains and can be seen with a hand

Powdery mildew is growing on these rose leaves and sepals, but not on the flower petals.

Some euonymus varieties are highly susceptible to powdery mildew, which develops in white patches on infected leaves and causes premature leaf drop.

lens. Weblike russeting may appear on infected fruit. There are many powdery mildew species; some prefer new plant growth while others are more prevalent on old tissue. Some powdery mildew species have many different host plants, whereas others, such as *Sphaerotheca pannosa* var. *rosae* on rose and *Microsphaera euonymi-japonici* on euonymus, grow

This coast live oak shoot has become distorted, dwarfed, and discolored by a powdery mildew infection, giving it a witches' broom appearance.

only on host plants in one genus and are not known to spread to plant species in other genera.

Powdery mildew spreads as wind-blown spores. Spores do not need free water to germinate; they die in water. Powdery mildew survives only on plant tissue and in dormant buds and does not survive in the soil. It over-winters on senescent and fallen leaves as little round structures (cleistothecia) that look like grains of pepper with appendages. Powdery mildew grows best at moderate temperatures and in shade, but it occurs in humid, foggy areas as well as in dry locations. Rain and direct sunlight inhibit powdery mildew.

MANAGEMENT

Moderate levels of powdery mildew can be ignored on most plant species, but prevention and immediate control action should be taken to avoid damage to highly susceptible plants, such as some crape myrtle, euonymus, and rose varieties. Plant in a sunny location with good air circulation to reduce the incidence of powdery mildew. Use resistant varieties where powdery mildew is a problem. *Platanus acerifolia* 'Yarwood' is resis-

tant in comparison with other sycamores. Some crape myrtle varieties with Native American names, such as 'Catawba,' 'Cherokee,' and 'Seminole,' resist powdery mildew. Many euonymus and some rose varieties are resistant. Resistant rose varieties reportedly include all colors of 'Simplicity' and the 'Meidiland' series. Contact the Cooperative Extension office in your county or a certified nurseryperson for recommendations.

Prune out infected tissue and dispose of it away from plants. Do not prune during dry weather and avoid excessive fertilization or irrigation; these activities promote susceptible new growth. For example, witches' broom or powdery mildew, *Cystotheca* or *Sphaerotheca lanestris,* of oak often follows the stimulation of off-season growth resulting from summer irrigation or pruning.

Overhead sprinkling may reduce powdery mildew infection because spores cannot germinate, and some are killed, when plants are wet. Sprinkle plants in the mid-afternoon when most spores are formed; this allows plants to dry before nightfall, reducing the likelihood that sprinkling will promote other diseases. Sulfur or systemic fungicides can be applied to highly susceptible plants at the earliest signs of the disease. Once powdery mildew growth is extensive, it is generally too late for fungicide applications to be effective. Avoid applying sulfur during hot weather when it is likely to damage foliage.

Sooty Mold

Sooty molds are dark fungi that grow on plant surfaces that have become covered with insect honeydew. Sooty mold is generally harmless to plants and can be ignored, except when it is extremely abundant and prevents

Powdery mildew, *Microsphaera alni*, caused white patches and distorted these sycamore leaves, which may die back.

enough light from reaching leaf surfaces, causing plants to become stressed. Even if sooty mold is extensive, do not apply fungicides. Wash sooty mold from plants with a forceful stream of water. Control insects that produce the honeydew on which sooty mold grows. Insecticidal soap controls most exposed-feeding, plant-juice-sucking insects and helps to wash away honeydew and sooty mold.

RUSTS

Rusts infect many hosts, including birch, cottonwood, fuchsia, hawthorn, juniper, pine, poplar, rhododendron, and rose. These parasitic fungi are named for the dry reddish, yellowish, or orange spore masses or pustules that many species form on infected tissue, especially on the lower surface of leaves.

Moderate populations of rust pustules on lower leaf surfaces apparently do not harm plants. The upper surface of heavily infested leaves turns yellow or brown and infected leaves may drop prematurely. Orange, gelatinous masses appear on some infected evergreen hosts. Some species cause tissue swellings or galls, colorful spots on plants, or cankers on bark. These can cause branch dieback and occasionally kill the entire plant.

Rusts are spread primarily by windblown or water-splashed spores. In addition to orangish pustules, many species also form black over-wintering spores on leaves in the autumn, which start the disease cycle in the spring. Many species have complex life cycles, alternating generations between two host species. Others, such as the rose rust, *Phragmidium mucronatum*, are apparently restricted to one host species. Each

Blackish sooty mold on California bay infested with scale insects and aphids.

Rust formed dry, orangish spore masses on the underside and discolored the upperside of these rose leaves

type of rust is specific to certain hosts. Rust fungi infect under mild, moist conditions. Avoid overhead watering, which favors spore germination. Rake infected leaves or needles and clip and dispose of infected shoots and branches as soon as they appear; an exception is that roses should be pruned only during the fall dormancy period to avoid reducing bloom. Fungicides applied in the spring can reduce some rust diseases, but the frequent applications required to provide good control are generally not warranted in landscapes.

Western Gall Rust
Peridermium or *Endocronartium harknessii*

Western gall rust infects two-needle and three-needle pines in the western states, including Aleppo, Bishop, lodgepole, and Monterey pine throughout California. The disease causes round swellings or galls on branches. In spring, galls become covered with orange spores, which are spread from pine to pine by wind and rain and infect healthy shoots. Infection occurs only during spring and only if shoots are wet. Foliage beyond the galls discolors and becomes stunted and bushy. Sometimes galls become colonized by other fungi or insects, and plant tissue terminal to the gall may die.

Prune out and dispose of infected branches before spring. If western gall rust galls occur on the trunk where pruning is impractical, you can wrap galls with a sheet of plastic during spring through early summer to reduce spore dispersal and spread to other pines. Wrapping galls helps only in landscapes where trees are isolated from other pines, which may be infected. Large galls on major limbs or the trunk can lead to structural failure; consider removing and replacing hazardous trees as discussed in Chapter 3.

Gymnosporangium Rusts
Gymnosporangium spp.

Gymnosporangium rusts cause orange, gelatinous masses, galls, stunted and bushy branches, and stem dieback. They are uncommon in California, except for junipers in some urban areas and cedar, cypress, and juniper in the Sierra Nevada. Gymnosporangium rusts require a rosaceous plant such as fruit trees or hawthorn to complete their life cycle. Gymnosporangium rusts on these alternate hosts can cause swellings and colorful spots on leaves, twigs, and fruit. Infected plant parts may die.

Prune out and dispose of infested twigs in the fall, before spores are produced in the spring. Make cuts in healthy wood, beyond swollen, infected tissue. Avoid overhead watering. Eliminate nearby rosaceous species that serve as alternate hosts.

Pine Stem and Cone Rusts
Cronartium spp.

Pine stem and cone rusts are common throughout the Sierra Nevada and in the Lake Tahoe area of California. Initially they cause yellow or brown dead spots and blotches on pine needles. Later the infection spreads to twigs, where most species grow beneath bark and in wood. Infected wood becomes visible in the spring when yellow to whitish, blisterlike spore-forming bodies burst through the bark. More serious damage includes galls, cankers, and branch and trunk dieback on pines. Seriously infected trees may be killed.

Resin may stream down the trunk around cankerous areas of infected, roughened bark, as in the case of white pine blister rust, *Cronartium ribicola*. Sugar pines are most seriously affected by this introduced pathogen. Species of *Ribes*, such as currants and gooseberries, are required nearby as an alternate host for white pine blister rust to complete its development and reinfect pines. Remove all *Ribes* species within 1,000 feet to provide some control of white pine blister rust.

Pine Needle Rusts
Coleosporium spp.

Over 20 different needle rust species infect pines in the U.S. They alternate generations with other hosts, often in the Compositae family. Pine needle rusts cause yellow or brown spots or bands to develop on partially green or yellow needles. Tiny, whitish bubble-like or tongue-shaped spore-forming bodies may also appear on needles, usually in winter or spring.

Round western gall rust swellings, which in spring become covered with orange spores.

Coleosporium pacificum or *C. madiae* on Monterey pine is a common pine needle rust in California. Control it on pines by eliminating alternate hosts in the family Compositae within 1,000 feet of pines, especially *Madia* species such as Chile tarweed, coast tarweed, and gumweed.

Bacterial Blight
Pseudomonas syringae

Bacterial blight, or bacterial canker, damage varies depending on the host plant and strain of *Pseudomonas syringae* involved. The most common symptom is elongated lesions on twigs and infected tissue that oozes material during wet weather. Blossom and tip dieback, vein blackening, leaf spots, or stem cankers are common disease symptoms on oleander, pine, and poplar. On flowering fruit trees, bacterial blight commonly causes brown to black lesions on the flowers, fruits, and stems; branch cankers and brown streaks in the wood may also occur. Shoots, leaves, and stems commonly discolor and shrivel on lilac. *P. syringae* strains also promote ice crystal formation on leaf surfaces of many hosts, increasing frost or freeze damage, especially to plants that are less cold tolerant.

Prune and dispose of infected twigs and branches. Prune during the dry season when infection is less likely to occur. Do not wet foliage with overhead irrigation. Damage is usually not severe enough to warrant spraying. If damage during previous seasons has been severe, apply Bordeaux mixture or a copper fungicide in the spring as soon as leaves emerge.

Bacterial blight killed these apple shoots and blossoms.

Bacteria entered and killed this almond shoot and are causing the adjacent wet, gummy accumulation on bark.

Bacterial Gall
Pseudomonas syringae pathovar *savastanoi*

Bacterial gall affects oleander and olive. It causes galls or knots on stems and bark; leaves also become galled on oleander. Bacterial gall can cause twigs and branches to die back, but overall plant health is usually not seriously threatened.

Gall bacteria reproduce in fissured or galled bark and are spread by contaminated water, implements, or hands. Healthy tissue is infected through fresh wounds during wet weather. Susceptible wounds include frost cracks and any leaf scars on branches for several days after olive leaves have dropped.

Avoid overhead watering, which spreads the bacteria. Where practical, especially for small plants or in the nursery, prune out and dispose of infected tissue during the dry season. Whole branches may be removed on olive trees. If plants must be pruned during the rainy season, sterilize pruning tools before each cut using a commercial disinfectant. Severe infections on olive can be controlled by applying Bordeaux mixture or a cop-

per fungicide beginning in the fall and periodically spraying through the spring as new growth appears. Fungicide or bactericide applications do not provide adequate control on oleander.

Fasciation

Fasciation is an abnormal flattening of stems, often appearing as if several adjoining stems have fused. Leaves growing from distorted stems are abnormally abundant and undersized. The cause of most fasciations is not understood, but some may be genetic or caused by bacterial or viral infections. Avoid wounding plants, except to prune out and dispose of distorted tissue. Do not propagate or graft symptomatic plants.

SYMPTOMS ON TRUNKS AND BRANCHES

Damage to trunks and branches can be caused by many factors, including injuries, weather, wood-attacking

insects, and disease-producing organisms. Some diseases that affect roots or leaves also cause damage to trunks and branches, but are discussed elsewhere. Diseases causing cankers, galls on bark, and wood decay are discussed here.

Wood Decay in Trunks and Limbs

Several fungal diseases, sometimes called heart or sap rots, cause the wood in the center of trunks and limbs to decay. Almost all species of woody plants are subject to trunk and limb decay.

DAMAGE

Decay fungi destroy the plant's internal supportive tissue. Decay is not visible on the outside of the plant, except where the bark has been cut or injured or when the rot fungi produce reproductive structures. Wood decay makes trees hazardous because

Seashell-shaped brackets on bark and mushrooms growing near the trunk indicate decay in this alder.

Bacterial galls on an oleander stem and leaves.

trunks and limbs become unable to support their own weight and can fall, especially when stressed by wind, heavy rain, or other conditions.

IDENTIFICATION AND BIOLOGY

Many wood rot fungi can be identified by the distinctive shape, color, and texture of the fruiting bodies they form on trees. These structures, called conks or basidiocarps, are often located around wounds in bark. These fleshy or woody spore-forming bodies are commonly mushroom-shaped or form groups of seashell-shaped "brackets."

Fomes, Fomitopsis, Ganoderma, Laetiporus, Phellinus, Polyporus, and *Trametes* species are common wood decay-causing fungi. These fungi often are divided into brown rots and white rots. Brown rots decay primarily the cellulose (carbohydrate) in wood, leaving behind the brownish wood lignin. Wood affected by brown rot is usually dry and fragile, readily crumbles into cubes, and commonly forms a solid column of rot in wood. Brown rot is generally more serious than white rot. White rots destroy principally the lignin, but may attack cellulose, sometimes just in pockets, often causing rotted wood to appear white or yellow and stringy.

Fungi that decay limbs and trunks are spread by airborne spores, which infect trees through injuries and dead branches. Injuries are often caused by people and include pruning wounds, vandalism, or injuries from machinery or construction. Lightning, extreme temperatures, fire, snow, ice, boring insects, and some other animals also cause wounds through which decay fungi infect wood. Unlike most other decay fungi, Annosus root disease, discussed later in this chapter, infects principally the roots and can spread to nearby plants from the roots of infected hosts.

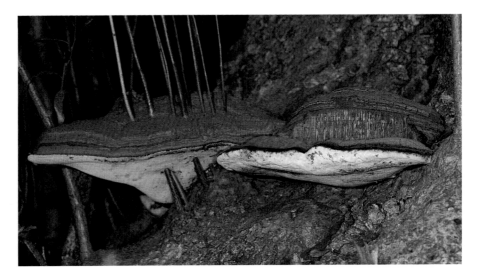

The white underside of these *Ganoderma applanatum* basidiocarps turns dark where touched; they're sometimes called artist's conks. Shoot growth through the conks demonstrates the tree is alive, but it has internal decay. Basidiocarps of another *Ganoderma* sp. are pictured near the introduction to this chapter.

MANAGEMENT

Prevent wood decay by protecting plants from injuries as discussed in Chapter 3. Provide proper cultural care to keep plants vigorous. Cut out dead or diseased limbs. Make pruning cuts properly; prune just outside the branch bark ridge, leaving a collar of cambial tissue around cuts on the trunk to facilitate wound closure, but avoid leaving stubs (see Figure 3-8). Make cuts so that rainwater will drain. Wound dressings are not recommended as they have not been found to hasten wound closure or prevent decay. Annosus root disease may be prevented by treating freshly cut stumps as discussed below.

Trees that may cause personal injury or property damage if they fall should be regularly inspected for signs of wood decay and other structural weakness. Hazardous trees may need to be trimmed, cabled, braced, or removed (see Chapter 3).

Avoid making large wounds. Fungi have entered where a large limb was pruned from this black walnut trunk, causing internal decay.

CANKER DISEASES

A canker is a sunken area containing dead tissue on a stem or branch. It may not be clearly visible, or it may be a well-defined infection on woody parts that often becomes surrounded by layers of callus tissue. Cankerlike wounds can be caused by injuries or sunscald as well as by disease-producing microorganisms (Table 5-3).

Cankers can cause foliage on infected branches to turn yellow or brown and wilt. Infected bark often discolors and may exude copious resin. Cankers are a serious concern because they can girdle and kill limbs or the entire plant. With the exception of Cytospora canker, the canker diseases discussed here can be identified largely based on the species of host plant they infect.

MANAGEMENT

Pine pitch canker, Chinese elm anthracnose canker, and Cypress canker of Leyland and Monterey cypress attack apparently vigorous trees. Planting other species or resistant cultivars is the primary strategy for managing these diseases. Cytospora canker and Botryosphaeria canker damage primarily debilitated plants. Avoid planting species that are poorly adapted for local conditions. Provide plants with proper cultural care to keep them vigorous and to limit these diseases.

Dark, reddish, resinous pitch on a Monterey pine limb infected with pine pitch canker.

TABLE 5-3

Some Common Causes of Cankers.

CAUSE	COMMENTS	SEE PAGE NO.
Anthracnose	Associated with leaf spots and distorted terminals	185
Bacterial blight	Bark oozes during wet weather, elongated twig lesions	197
Botryosphaeria canker	Oozing limbs and branch die back on many hosts	203
Chinese elm anthracnose	Affects only Chinese elm, *Ulmus parvifolia*	202
Cypress canker	Affects cypress and sometimes juniper	202
Cytospora canker	Many hosts, often causes sunken, elliptical lesions	201
Fireblight	Preceded by twig and leaf damage, affects Rosaceae plants	190
Injuries	Many causes	40, 215
Pine pitch canker	Pine branches also turn reddish, die back	201
Pine stem rust	Often spots needles, causes blistered pine bark	196
Pink rot	*Syagrus* spp. palms are affected	205
Pruning wounds	Caused by pruning large limbs or by improperly making cuts	37
Rusts	Reddish to yellow pustules on foliage common	195
Septoria leaf spot	Affects poplars, leaf spots present	187
Sunscald	Young or severely pruned trees commonly affected	222
Underwatering	Summer rainfall-adapted plants are most susceptible	32

Prune out dead and dying branches when they are first observed. Make the cuts in healthy wood beyond any apparent cankers. Once the main trunk is infected, pruning is of little value. Provide plants with moderate amounts of (preferably slow-release) fertilizer to improve plant growth, except for pines, which shouldn't be fertilized at all when suffering from cankers. Avoid heavy fertilization, which may promote disease.

Cytospora Canker
Cytospora spp.

Cytospora canker infects many plants including birch, ceanothus, Italian cypress, fir, fruit trees, maple, poplar, redbud, and willow. Cankers on major branches appear as slightly sunken, smooth, roughly elliptical, reddish brown areas. Cankers are somewhat restricted when new and usually have a sharp margin between healthy and infected bark. However, *Cytospora chrysosperma* on aspen and poplar causes sunken lesions that kill many small branches and twigs without forming any definite canker. Minute, pimplelike fungal fruiting bodies may appear imbedded in infected bark and produce yellow to red "tendrils" of spores during moist weather. *Cytospora* fungi can cause infected branches to turn brick-red in the spring, then fade to brown or tan by the fall.

Heat and drought stress combine to increase the susceptibility of many plants to canker disease development. Provide appropriate water for species adapted to summer rainfall or river-bank environments if these species are planted where summer drought prevails; irrigation should be deep and infrequent. Plant species that are resistant or not susceptible. 'Nor,' 'Easter,' 'Platte,' and 'Mighty Mo'

poplar hybrids show some resistance to *Cytospora*.

Pine Pitch Canker
Fusarium subglutinans

Pine pitch canker infects only pines. It occurs throughout the southeastern U.S. and in some locations in California.

Dark, reddish, resinous pitch on limbs or the trunk is a distinguishing symptom of pine pitch canker. Branch tips, entire branches, and the treetop or entire tree may die. *Pityophthorus* spp. twig beetles also kill pine branch tips, but this damage alone is usually not considered serious. Bark beetles, especially *Ips* spp., are a more common cause of pine treetop death than pitch canker. Bark beetles may act alone or in combination with pine pitch canker.

Dense pine plantings seem to be most severely infected by pine pitch canker. Symptoms are apparent most typically from autumn through spring. Pitch canker fungus is transmitted by insects that attack branch tips and developing cones. Pitch canker can also infect trees through wounds, such as those made by pruning tools and other equipment contaminated with spores.

Prune pines only during the winter, as insects that spread the causal fungus are less active then. After using tools on trees with resinous cankers, carefully clean and sterilize the tools with a commercial disinfectant before pruning healthy pines. Don't fertilize infected or nearby pines as the resulting rapid growth may promote the development of pitch canker. Avoid planting Monterey pine in hot areas, because even if not infected with the canker it typically declines and dies after about 20 to 30 years no matter how good the cultural care provided. Plant nonhost species or Brutia pine, *Pinus brutia*, which is resistant to pine pitch canker fungus.

Extensive branch dieback on Monterey pine infected with pine pitch canker.

ARTHUR C. McCAIN

Cypress canker causes resinous lesions and discolored bark.

Cypress Canker
Seiridium or
Coryneum cardinale

Cypress canker, also called
Coryneum canker, infects cypress,
especially Leyland cypress and Monterey cypress planted away from the
coast. It occasionally damages
junipers. A similar appearing
Coryneum species occasionally infects
coast redwood.

Resinous lesions form on infected
bark and cambium and the fungus
can girdle limbs. Infected branches or
treetops turn conspicuously yellow or
faded and then die. The fungus often
progresses until the entire plant is
killed. Coryneum canker fungi are
moved by the wind and are spread
within plants by splashing water.

Cypress cankers frequently become
colonized by larvae of the cypress
bark moth. These insects are secondary invaders attracted to the
cankers and their control is generally
not warranted. It is the fungus that
kills branches and trees, not the
insect.

Provide trees with proper care and
prune out diseased branches as discussed above. Plant species that are
well adapted to local conditions.
Leyland cypress, Italian cypress,
and Monterey cypress planted in hot,
inland areas will likely become
severely infected with cypress canker.
Cupressus arizonica, C. benthamii, and
C. lusitanica are less susceptible to
cypress canker.

Chinese Elm
Anthracnose Canker
Stegophora ulmea

The fungus that causes anthracnose
in Chinese elm as discussed earlier
also causes cankers on the limbs and

Yellow and brown branches on a Leyland cypress infected with cypress canker.

trunk. Even vigorous Chinese elms may become girdled and die. Irregular, black, tarlike spots on leaves, premature leaf drop, and twig dieback are common symptoms of this disease.

Excise small cankers on the trunk and major limbs before they become large by cutting about ½ inch into healthy wood, which should allow wounds to close. Do not make large wounds. Consider replacing severely infected trees. The 'Drake' cultivar of Chinese elm is resistant to anthracnose canker.

Botryosphaeria Canker and Dieback
Botryosphaeria dothidea

Botryosphaeria canker and dieback in California commonly affects giant sequoia. Many other plants in landscapes also can be affected, including incense cedar, coast redwood, and madrone. Scattered branches are commonly killed by *Botryosphaeria;* recently killed or dying branches are reddish brown and often exude drops of yellowish pitch. Branches with an older infection are grayish brown and mostly bare. Cankers can occur on large, infected limbs. *Botryosphaeria* typically infects giant sequoia that are drought-stressed or grown away from their native habitat. The fungus is spread primarily by splashing water in the spring and may develop slowly for many months before symptoms become visible.

Plant species that are well adapted to local conditions and provide them with proper irrigation and other care as discussed above. Giant sequoia planted in hot areas typically displays branch dieback due to *Botryosphaeria* throughout its life. No matter how good the cultural care provided, this species is not adapted to heat and does poorly where hot weather prevails.

Crown Gall
Agrobacterium tumefaciens

Agrobacterium tumefaciens bacteria cause galls principally on the root crown at the soil line or just below the soil surface. Galls sometimes also form on roots, limbs, and trunks of many woody plants, especially euonymus, fruit trees, *Prunus* species, rose, and willow. Some herbaceous plants, such as chrysanthemums and daisies, are also susceptible.

DAMAGE

Agrobacterium tumefaciens usually does not seriously harm woody plants unless galls occur in the root crown

These Chinese elm anthracnose cankers may grow, eventually girdling limbs and causing dieback.

Giant sequoia planted in hot areas typically displays branch dieback due to *Botryosphaeria* throughout its life, no matter how good the cultural care provided.

ARTHUR C. McCAIN

area when plants are young, then plants become stunted and subject to wind damage and drought stress. If galls are large, young plants can be girdled and killed.

IDENTIFICATION AND BIOLOGY

The crown gall bacteria stimulate the plant to produce actively growing, disorganized tissue, which originates in the cambium and appears on bark. Galls appear similar to damage caused by some woolly aphids or boring insects. Some boring insects may be attracted to gall tissue and colonize it, further complicating identification of the original causal agent. The surface of a crown gall is the same color as healthy bark and gall wood has the same color as normal wood. However, when cut with a knife, crown galls are softer than normal wood and lack the typical pattern

Trees infected with crown gall commonly have warty tumors on large roots near the crown. A tree as large as this walnut usually tolerates the growths; however, young trees planted near it may be seriously affected.

of annual growth rings. Galls can be tiny and smooth on young plants, but are commonly rough and sometimes massive on mature trees.

Crown gall is caused by bacteria that can survive for long periods in the soil. The bacteria enter plants through wounds, which are commonly inflicted by handling in the nursery or during transplanting. The bacteria can also enter established plants when soil enters growth cracks or wounds caused by cultivation, mowers, weed trimmers, or sucker removal. The bacteria stimulate infected tissue to grow rapidly and form galls, which may slough off and return some bacteria to the soil.

MANAGEMENT

Purchase and plant only high-quality nursery stock. Avoid injuring trees during transplanting. Dipping seeds or roots in a solution containing a biological control agent, the K-84 strain of *Agrobacterium radiobacter* (marketed as Galltrol) also reduces infection by most strains of pathogenic crown gall bacteria, but the strain commonly affecting grape is not prevented by this biological control agent. Solarization, covering moist, bare soil with clear plastic for several weeks during the hot dry season before planting, (as detailed in Chapter 7) may reduce crown gall bacteria in the soil.

Crown gall bacteria are especially abundant where previously infected plants have grown. Where crown gall has been a problem, plant only resistant species, including birch, cedar, holly, incense cedar, magnolia, pine, redwood, spruce, tulip tree, and zelkova. Take care not to injure trees, especially around the soil line. Existing galls may be excised by cutting into healthy wood around galls, then exposing the tissue to drying. Cut out galls only during the dry season and minimize the amount of healthy

tissue into which cuts are made. If galls encompass much of the crown area, so that excising them may cause such extensive wounds that plants develop other problems or die, consider tree replacement. A bactericide, Gallex, may provide control when painted onto galls as directed on the product label.

Wetwood or Slime Flux

Wetwood is caused by several species of bacteria; yeast organisms may also be involved. Wetwood is especially common in elm and poplar, but affects many other plants including box elder, hemlock, magnolia, maple, and oak.

DAMAGE

Trees affected with wetwood have stained areas of wood that exude fluid. Usually only trees about 10 years of age or older exhibit symptoms. Foliage wilt and branch dieback can occur on severely infected trees, but the disease rarely causes serious harm to trees. Although it can be unsightly, wetwood may be as strong as healthy wood.

IDENTIFICATION AND BIOLOGY

Wetwood causes a portion of the trunk or branches to appear discolored and watersoaked. A sour or rancid, reddish or brown fluid commonly seeps from infected bark cracks or wounds. Wetwood-causing microorganisms are common in soil and water. They infect trees through wounds, including sites where pesticides have been injected into trees. Alcoholic flux (see below) also causes wood to exude fluid, but only for a short time during the summer, and that fluid has a pleasant, fermentative odor.

MANAGEMENT

Prevent wetwood bacteria and yeasts from infecting trees by avoiding injuries to bark and wood. Control wetwood infections if they are small by opening wounds so they are exposed to the air and liquids do not accumulate; avoid making large wounds. To reduce the spread of bacteria and yeasts in an infected tree, drill a ¼-inch hole several inches long until fluid begins flowing, then install a copper tube to drain excess fluid and release the pressure of gases that form in infected wood. Don't insert the tube so far into the hole that the inside end becomes plugged. Leave the outside end of the tube protruding so that liquid drains away from the infected bark area. Check the tube opening regularly and clear it if it becomes plugged. Do not weaken the tree's structure by drilling drain holes at branch crotches.

Stained wood exuding fluid around the crotch of this Siberian elm is a result of bacterial wetwood infection.

Foamy Canker or Alcoholic Flux
Zymomonas spp.

Some species of bacteria cause a white frothy material to exude from cracks or holes in bark, commonly on elm, oak, sweet gum, or Victorian box. This foamy material appears for only a short time during warm weather, and has a pleasant alcoholic or fermentative odor, unlike the rancid smell of wetwood fluids. In severely infected trees, the cambium beneath the bark may become rotten, white, mushy, and eventually turn brown and die.

Preventing injuries to bark may help to prevent this disease. Prune out infected tissue when it is limited to a small area of the bark to allow wounds to close; avoid making large wounds.

This foamy canker material or alcoholic flux on almond has a pleasant fermentative odor, unlike the rancid smell of wetwood fluids.

Pink Rot
Gliocladium vermoeseni

Pink rot fungus can kill infected *Washingtonia* spp. fan palms, *Chamaedorea*, and other palm species. Pink rot is named for the pink mass of spores formed on infected tissue. Trunks can become severely deformed and split. Cankers form on the trunks of *Syagrus*. Dark material may ooze from wounds on severely infected tissue. Infection is most often observed around dying leaves, wounds, and, in the case of *Chamaedorea*, around the base of the plant near the soil. The disease is most serious on plants of low vigor and on palms planted near the coast.

Provide proper cultural care to keep plants vigorous. Excessive moisture apparently promotes pink rot. Avoid overhead watering, do not overirrigate, and provide good drainage. Avoid wounding plants when removing old fronds. Remove only dead or dying fronds. Sterilize pruning tools with a commercial disinfectant before cutting on each new plant. Reciprocating power saws or hand tools should be used because these can be easily sterilized, unlike chain saws. Cut out trunk cankers if the rot is not extensive; avoid making large wounds. Replace severely infected palms. Applications of a systemic fungicide can control the fungus, but should not be substituted for proper cultural care. For specific fungicide recommendations see *Foliage and Branch Diseases of Landscape Trees* (UC Leaflet 2616).

ROOT AND CROWN DISEASES

Several root and crown diseases commonly affect landscape trees and shrubs. These include Armillaria root rot, collar and crown rots, and Dema- tophora root rot. Because roots transport nutrients and water to the rest of the plant, any root disease is likely to affect other parts of the plant as well. Often the first observed symptoms of root disease are wilting or an apparent nutrient deficiency. In advanced stages, leaves discolor and die, then branches and the entire plant are killed. Several abiotic diseases (see Chapter 6), including too much or too little water, mineral toxicity, and herbicides, can also damage roots and cause symptoms that may be confused with root and crown diseases. Because of their propensity to fall, root-damaged trees can be hazardous and may need to be removed if they are located where their failure could injure people or damage property.

Most fungi that cause root diseases are continuously present in soils. The only effective control is to provide trees with proper cultural care to keep them vigorous and to prevent conditions that promote disease development. Proper planting, as detailed in Chapter 3, and appropriate irrigation, as summarized earlier in this chapter (see Figures 5-2 and 5-3), are the most critical aspects to controlling root diseases. Purchase only high-quality nursery stock (see Table 3-1). Root rot diseases commonly develop in nurseries because potted plants are watered frequently. Root rot fungi can then be introduced into landscapes on contaminated nursery stock.

In comparison with healthy hackberry trees of the same age across the street, the stunted tree on the left has yellow, sparse foliage and dead terminals at the treetop resulting from root and crown disease.

Armillaria root rot fungus forms characteristic white mycelial fans between bark and wood in the crown region of trees.

Armillaria Root Rot
Armillaria mellea

Armillaria root rot, also known as oak root fungus disease or shoestring fungus disease, affects many broadleaf trees and conifers. This native pathogen is most prevalent in landscapes established in areas of natural forests or where oaks or other native trees once grew, such as former riverbeds or areas subject to flooding.

DAMAGE

Armillaria infects and kills cambial tissue, causing major roots and the trunk near the ground to die. The first aboveground symptoms are often undersized, discolored, and prematurely dropping leaves. Branches begin dying, often first around the tops of deciduous trees or in the lower canopy of conifers. Eventually the entire plant can be killed. Young plants often die quickly; mature trees may die quickly or slowly, but can recover, at least temporarily, if conditions become good for tree growth and poor for disease development.

IDENTIFICATION AND BIOLOGY

Armillaria forms characteristic white mycelial plaques between the bark and wood. These distinctive white fans have a mushroomlike odor and are visible when the bark is removed from infected roots and the lower trunk. Dematophora root rot also causes white growths that may be confused with *Armillaria*, but *Dematophora* tends to occur in smaller patches and grows throughout the wood rather than just under the bark (see below).

During cool rainy weather, usually in the fall, clusters of mushrooms may form at the base of *Armillaria*-infected trees. The honey yellow to brown mushrooms range from 1 to 10 inches in diameter. They have a ring on the stalk just under the cap, and they shed white spores.

Armillaria frequently produces rootlike structures (rhizomorphs), which attach to the surface of roots or the root crown. These have a black to dark reddish brown surface. When pulled from their host or pulled apart in the hands, their cottony interior becomes visible. When similar sized roots are pulled apart for comparison, roots have a more solid, woody interior than rhizomorphs.

Armillaria thrives under moist conditions, for example when irrigated turf is planted around the roots of California native oaks. Plants become

During cool, rainy weather, clusters of mushrooms form around the base of *Armillaria*-infected trees.

infected through root contact with infected plants or rhizomorphs attached to infected roots. Armillaria root rot can develop slowly, and symptoms may not appear until the fungus is well established. The fungus can survive for many years in dead or living tree roots.

MANAGEMENT

Prepare the site well before planting and provide appropriate cultural care, especially proper irrigation as discussed in the introduction to this chapter and in Chapter 3. Plant only resistant species (Table 5-4) in locations where Armillaria root rot has been a problem, such as where floods occur. Because general tree health and care is so important in disease susceptibility, Table 5-4 provides only a guideline. Before replanting, remove as many roots (½ inch in diameter or larger) from the soil as possible because these can harbor *Armillaria*. Air-dry the soil before replanting.

TABLE 5-4

Landscape Plants Highly Resistant to Armillaria Root Rot.[a]

COMMON NAME	SCIENTIFIC NAME
Acacia	*Acacia longifolia, A. mearnsii, A. verticillata*
Ash	*Fraxinus oxycarpa, F. velutina, F. uhdei*
Bald cypress	*Taxodium distichum*
Bottle tree	*Brachychiton populneus*
Boxwood	*Buxus sempervirens*
Carob	*Ceratonia siliqua*
Catalpa	*Catalpa bignonioides, C. hybrida, C. ovata*
Cherry	*Prunus caroliniana, P. ilicifolia, P. lyonii*
Chinese elm	*Ulmus parvifolia*
Chinese pistache	*Pistacia chinensis*
Chinese wisteria	*Wisteria sinensis*
Coast redwood	*Sequoia sempervirens*
Cork tree	*Philodendron amurense, P. chinense*
Crab apple	*Malus floribunda, M. ioensis*
Cryptomeria	*Cryptomeria japonica*
Dawn redwood	*Metasequoia glyptostroboides*
Ellwood cypress	*Chamaecyparis lawsoniana*
Eucalyptus	*Eucalyptus camaldulensis, E. cinerea, E. grandis*
Hackberry	*Celtis australis, C. occidentalis*
Holly	*Ilex aquifolium, I. x aquipernyi, I. cassine, I. opaca*
Incense cedar	*Calocedrus decurrens*
Jacaranda	*Jacaranda acutifolia*
Leyland cypress	*x Cupressocyparis leylandii*
Madrone	*Arbutus menziesii*
Magnolia	*Magnolia grandiflora*
Maidenhair tree	*Ginkgo biloba*
Maple	*Acer macrophyllum, A. palmatum*
Mayten tree	*Maytenus boaria*
Oak	*Quercus ilex, Q. lobata*
Pine	*Pinus monticola, P. nigra, P. patula, P. sylvestris, P. torreyana*
Pittosporum	*Pittosporum heterophyllum, P. rhombifolium*
Privet	*Ligustrum tschonskii*
Sacred bamboo	*Nandina domestica*
Smoke tree	*Cotinus coggygria*
Sumac	*Rhus aromatica, R. copallina*
Sweet gum	*Liquidambar orientalis, L. styraciflua*
Tree-of-Heaven	*Alianthus altissima*
Tulip tree	*Liriodendron tulipifera*
White fir	*Abies concolor*

a. This list provides only a guideline. Many of the species listed may be attacked if soil is highly contaminated with infected roots and conditions are poor for plant growth and good for disease development. For a complete list see *Resistance or Susceptibility of Certain Plants to Armillaria Root Rot* (UC Leaflet 2591).

Dematophora Root Rot
Dematophora or *Rosellinia necatrix*

Dematophora root rot, or white root rot, is less common than the other root diseases discussed here, but it quickly kills plants when it occurs. Its hosts include ceanothus, cotoneaster, fruit trees, holly, poplar, privet, and viburnum. The fungus is active whenever hosts are growing, especially during mild, wet weather. It infects primarily through healthy roots growing near infested plants.

The initial symptoms of canopy decline caused by Dematophora root rot may be exhibited throughout the entire plant, or in just a portion of the canopy. Branches killed as a result of *Dematophora* often retain dry foliage. A white mycelial mat may be visible on the lower trunk or in soil over infected roots. Minute white growths may also be visible beneath bark. These whitish patches are much smaller than *Armillaria* mycelia and lack the characteristic mushroomlike odor produced by *Armillaria*. If the soil is excavated, white strands can be observed growing from infected roots into the adjoining soil. A dark crust may also form over dead roots or around the root collar.

When *Dematophora*-infected tissue is sealed in a moist chamber, such as a plastic bag or jar, it produces a distinctive white fluff within a few days. However, if *Dematophora* is suspected, it is best to seek an expert to confirm its presence. Minimize *Dematophora*-caused disease by preparing the site well before planting, using quality nursery stock, and providing appropriate cultural care, especially proper irrigation as discussed in the introduction to this chapter and in Chapter 3.

White, cobwebby patches of fungus in soil at the base of this apple tree are characteristic of Dematophora root rot.

Excessive irrigation of nearby turf and compacted, poorly drained soil is promoting *Phytophthora cinnamomi* in this Irish yew, resulting in branch dieback.

Collar, Foot, Root, and Crown Rots *Phytophthora* spp.

Several species of the *Phytophthora* fungi infect the roots or crowns of landscape plants. Hosts in California include many species or cultivars of acacia, ceanothus, cedar, *Chamaecyparis,* chestnut, citrus, cypress, daphne, dogwood, eucalyptus, fir, *Fremontodendron,* fruit trees, hemlock, holly, juniper, larch, oak, pine, *Prunus* spp., redbud, redwood, *Rhamnus,* rhododendron, walnut, and willow, as well as many other woody ornamental species.

DAMAGE

Phytophthora kills the roots and root crown area of infected plants. This causes plants to wilt and leaves to discolor, become stunted, and drop prematurely. Infected mature plants grow slowly and may gradually decline. Twigs and branches die back and the entire plant can be killed. *Pythium* can cause similar damage (see the next section on damping-off diseases) and may occur along with *Phytophthora.*

IDENTIFICATION AND BIOLOGY

The symptoms of a *Phytophthora* infection depend on the environment, the species of fungus, and the species of host plant. Often a vertical streak, stain, or canker becomes visible on infected trunks. Black or reddish sap may ooze from darkened areas of infected bark. To confirm the presence of *Phytophthora,* cut away the outer bark around the stain streaks or canker. The concentric margins between the healthy whitish or yellowish wood and the reddish or brown infected wood in the trunk look like they are soaked with water. Woody roots decaying from *Phytophthora* are firm and brittle. In contrast, roots destroyed by excess water are soft, although *Phytophthora*-infected roots eventually soften as a result of the action of secondary organisms.

All *Phytophthora* species require high soil moisture, but temperature requirements vary. *Phytophthora cinnamomi,* an important species in California, spreads, infects plants, and develops rapidly during warm, moist conditions. On the other hand, *P. cactorum* requires cool, moist weather.

Gumming or a vertical streak, stain, or canker is often visible on the trunk of *Phytophthora*-infected trees.

Brownish streaks in roots indicate a *Phytophthora* infection.

Phytophthora fungi can survive in the soil for many years and enter plants through the crown or roots. Depending on the species of fungus, *Phytophthora* may affect only small feeder roots or rootlets, major roots, or all roots and the crown.

Phytophthora species produce no fruiting bodies visible to the naked eye. Confirmation of *Phytophthora* requires taking a sample from suspected infections, culturing it on laboratory medium, then examining this under a microscope. Test kits that employ a serological technique called "ELISA" also are available. These can confirm the presence of *Phytophthora* in as little as 10 minutes with no need for specialized equipment or facilities. However, caution must be exercised when using test kits as several species of *Pythium* also react with the *Phytophthora* test kits. Samples must be collected from tissue with a viable

Confirmation of *Phytophthora* requires a laboratory test on tissue suspected of being infected or an ELISA test kit like this can confirm presence in about 10 minutes.

infection. Infected tissue is ground to a liquid suspension, a few drops of this liquid are added to a detector device, then another solution is added. If *Phytophthora* is present in the sample, a visible color-change reaction occurs.

MANAGEMENT

Prepare the site well before planting and provide appropriate cultural care, especially proper irrigation as discussed in the introduction to this chapter and in Chapter 3. Where Phytophthora root rot is a problem, such as where soils are compacted, drain poorly, or are usually damp, improve drainage and plant only species not reported to be susceptible. If you have identified *Phytophthora cinnamomi* as the cause of root disease, replant using species listed in Table 5-5. Some fungicides (for example, fosetyl-al and metalaxyl) can be effective in managing *Phytophthora*, and their use may be warranted on some high-value specimen plants.

Damping-off Diseases

Several soilborne fungi, including *Rhizoctonia* spp. and water molds such as *Pythium*, thrive under wet soil conditions. Infected roots become soft, mushy, darkened, and decayed. Water mold fungi also cause "damping-off," the death of seedlings that collapse at the soil line under damp conditions. More mature plants infected with *Pythium* grow slowly and may gradually decline, exhibit terminal dieback, and die.

Prevent damping-off diseases by preparing the site well before planting and providing appropriate cultural care, especially proper irrigation as discussed earlier in this chapter and in Chapter 3. Solarizing the soil before planting (see Chapter 7) can

TABLE 5-5

Trees and Shrubs Not Reported to Be Susceptible to *Phytophthora cinnamomi*.[a]

COMMON NAME	GENUS NAME
Albizia	*Albizia*
Alder	*Alnus*
Apple	*Malus*[b]
Ash	*Fraxinus*
Aspen	*Populus*
Baccharis	*Baccharis*
Box elder	*Acer*
Boxwood	*Buxus*
California bay	*Umbellularia*
California buckeye	*Aesculus*
Cotoneaster	*Cotoneaster*[c]
Cottonwood	*Populus*
Elm	*Ulmus*
Euonymus	*Euonymus*
Honey locust	*Gleditsia*
Linden	*Tilia*
Madrone	*Arbutus*
Magnolia	*Magnolia*
Maidenhair tree	*Ginkgo*
Manzanita	*Arctostaphylos*
Mayten	*Maytenus*
Oleander	*Nerium*
Photinia	*Photinia*
Podocarpus	*Podocarpus*
Poplar	*Populus*
Sweet gum	*Liquidambar*
Tamarisk	*Tamarix*
Toyon	*Heteromeles*
Tulip tree	*Liriodendron*
Zelkova	*Zelkova*

a. This list provides only a guideline; host vigor and environmental conditions are important in disease development. Some hosts are susceptible to other *Phytophthora* species. For additional information see *Plants in California Susceptible to Phytophthora cinnamomi* (UC Leaflet 21178).

b. Highly susceptible to *Phytophthora cactorum*.

c. Susceptible to *Phytophthora cryptogea* and *P. parasitica*.

reduce *Pythium* and *Rhizoctonia* fungi. Some fungicides (for example, fosetyl-al and metalaxyl) can be effective against *Pythium*, and their use may be warranted on some high-value, specimen plants.

Annosus Root Disease
Heterobasidion annosum or *Fomes annosus*

Annosus root disease can infect the roots or butt of many conifers and some hardwoods. It infects through roots and primarily affects conifers in areas where conifers grow naturally. Susceptible hosts, primarily pines, are often killed within several years. Other common hosts—true firs, Douglas fir, incense cedar, and hemlock—are usually not killed outright, but develop decay in heartwood that increases susceptibility to insect attack and wind damage.

The fungus can survive for several decades in the roots of dead hosts, so trees are often killed in a gradually expanding clump as nearby plants are infected through root contact. The fungus spreads long distances by airborne spores. Spores can germinate when they contact a freshly cut stump, creating a new infection center as the fungus spreads down through the stump into roots that contact nearby living trees.

Disease presence may be indicated by conks. These vary in form, often forming a small button, seashell-like bracket, or amorphous whitish, gray, or light brown growth, usually around the root crown. Bark may separate readily from wood in infected trees; the separated surfaces are light brown and the wood surface is often streaked with darker brown. Numerous silver or whitish flecks may also appear on the inner bark surface, and small whitish mycelial growths may

Pythium and overwatering are causing these rose shoots to turn brown and die.

occur between outer bark scales or on the bark surface.

Avoid wounding trees. Apply borax to freshly cut pine stumps in areas where pines grow naturally to prevent infection by *Heterobasidion annosum*, which can spread from stumps through roots to nearby pines.

VIRUSES

Viruses are submicroscopic particles that infect cells, changing some cell functions. Most viruses distort or discolor foliage. Four common viruses of *Abutilon,* camellia, *Nandina,* and rose are detailed here, but many other woody landscape plants may show similar viral symptoms on occasion.

DAMAGE

Viruses can slow plant growth, but most do not seriously harm woody landscape plants. Damage is usually noticeable only in foliage. Infected leaves may become spotted, streaked, discolored, distorted, or stunted. The variegation or other foliage changes that viruses cause are sometimes considered to be attractive.

IDENTIFICATION AND BIOLOGY

Viruses can be transmitted by insects feeding on plant sap or mechanically in sap that is spread by hand or grafting tools. Viruses also commonly spread in seed, pollen, or in vegetative parts of plants used for propagation through budding and grafting.

The names of most viral pathogens in landscape plants indicate their host plants and the primary type of damage they cause. For example, apple mosaic virus and elm mosaic virus cause an irregular pattern of discolored leaves on apple and elm, respectively. Hibiscus chlorotic ringspot and prunus necrotic ringspot cause small yellow or brownish spots or blotches on the leaves of hibiscus or plants in the rose family, respectively. Once a plant becomes infected with virus, it usually remains infected throughout its life.

Rose Mosaic Virus

Prunus necrotic ringspot virus and several other viruses may infect roses. Virus infection causes yellow to brownish lines, bands, rings, vein clearing or yellowing, oak-leaf patterns, or blotches on leaves, sometimes on only a portion of the plant. Virus-infected plants may grow more slowly, produce delayed or fewer flowers, and become more susceptible to frost damage. The severity of damage varies with the host variety, and some infected roses exhibit no damage. Rose mosaic viruses are not spread by insects or pruning tools and do not infect healthy roses except through grafting, budding, or rooting cuttings from infected plants.

Camellia Yellow Mottle Virus

Camellia yellow mottle virus causes an irregular yellow mottling of camellia leaves and a mottled whitish pattern in the blossoms. Camellia yellow mottle virus is sometimes deliberately introduced through grafting to produce an attractive leaf or flower variegation.

Nandina Virus

Nandina virus causes a mottled red discoloration of the new leaves of heavenly bamboo. Nandina virus is apparently the same as cucumber mosaic virus, a group of viruses that infect a variety of agricultural and ornamental plants and annual and perennial weeds. Nandina virus is spread by aphids, especially the melon and green peach aphids.

Vein clearing and yellow patterns on rose leaves caused by rose mosaic virus.

Camellia yellow mottle virus causes irregular yellow areas on foliage. Most viruses do not seriously harm woody landscape plants, unless foliage discoloring cannot be tolerated.

Some virus infections may be considered attractive, like this nandina virus that causes reddish, mottled leaves on heavenly bamboo.

Aphids ingest the virus while feeding on infected plants and winged aphids that fly to other plants transmit the virus when they feed.

Abutilon Mosaic Virus

Abutilon mosaic virus causes vein-limited yellow blotches on leaves of Chinese lantern or Chinese bell-flower. These leaf blotches are considered attractive; infected plants are commonly sold as variegated plants. The virus is naturally spread by the sweetpotato whitefly, *Bemisia tabaci*, or by grafting with infected stock. See the Action Thresholds and Guidelines section near the beginning of Chapter 3 for a photograph.

MANAGEMENT

There is no cure or treatment for virus-infected plants in landscapes and generally none is needed. Provide proper cultural care to improve plant vigor or replace infected plants if their growth is unsatisfactory. Purchase and plant only high-quality, certified virus-free, or virus-resistant nursery stock or seeds. Do not graft virus-infected plant parts onto virus-free plants unless you want to introduce the virus. Although certain viruses are spread by aphids and other insects that suck plant juices, controlling insects is generally not a recommended method of preventing virus infection in woody landscapes. It is very difficult to detect or control insects effectively at the low densities that can spread virus, especially insects like the melon and green peach aphids that spread nandina virus and feed on many different plant species.

CHAPTER SIX

Abiotic Disorders

Abiotic (nonliving or noninfectious) disorders are diseases induced by adverse environmental conditions, often the result of human activity. These causes include nutrient deficiencies or excesses, salt, cold, heat, herbicides or other pesticides, air pollution, or too little or too much water. Activities that compact soils, change soil grade, or injure trunks or roots also cause abiotic disorders. In addition to directly damaging plants, abiotic disorders can predispose trees and shrubs to attack by insects and pathogens.

Many abiotic disorders can be recognized by characteristic distorted, discolored, or dying foliage. To remedy the problem, you must distinguish abiotic causes from damage caused by insects, mites, and pathogens, which can produce similar symptoms. Many abiotic disorders develop from improper planting or care; proper cultural care is detailed in Chapter 3. Damage from nutrient deficiencies and excesses, pesticides, air pollution, light, heat, and other weather conditions is detailed here. Consult Table 6-1 to help you diagnose the cause of abiotic disorders based on symptoms.

Water Deficiency and Excess

Inappropriate watering is a common cause of landscape plant damage. Inadequate water causes foliage to wilt, discolor, and drop prematurely. Prolonged moisture stress results in smaller leaves, dieback, and susceptibility to wood-boring insects and other pests, which eventually can kill plants. Excessive moisture smothers and kills roots. As roots die, discolored and dying foliage appears in the aboveground portion of the plant. Read the important section on irrigation in Chapter 3.

Mineral Deficiencies

Certain nutrients, in relatively small amounts, are required for healthy plant growth. Deficiencies cause foliage to discolor, fade, distort, or become spotted, sometimes in a characteristic pattern that can be recognized to identify the cause. Fewer leaves, flowers, and fruit may be pro-

TABLE 6-1

Common Abiotic Disorder Symptoms and Their Causes.[a]

SYMPTOMS	POSSIBLE CAUSE	MANAGEMENT
Foliage wilts, droops, discolors and drops prematurely. Twigs and limbs may die back. Bark cracks and develops cankers. Plant may become attacked by wood-boring insects.	water deficiency	page 32 and Table 3-3
Foliage yellows and drops. Twigs and branches die back. Root crown diseases develop. Mineral toxicity symptoms develop.	water excess or poor drainage	page 32 and Table 3-4
Foliage is discolored, undersized, sparse, or distorted and may drop prematurely. Plant growth is slow. Limbs may die back.	mineral deficiency	page 215 and Table 6-2
Foliage turns brown, dry, and crispy. Limbs may die back. Odor of natural gas may be detectable.	natural gas line leak underground	Contact utility company immediately if a natural gas leak is suspected.
Foliage or shoots turn yellowish, undersized, or distorted. Leaves may appear "burned" with dead margins and drop.	pesticide toxicity	page 221
Yellow, brown, then white areas develop on upper side of leaves, beginning between veins. Foliage may die.	sunburn	page 222
Leaves or needles turn yellowish, brownish, or have discolored flecks. Foliage may be sparse, stunted, and drop prematurely.	air pollution	page 224
Leaves turn yellowish or brownish, especially along margins. Foliage may drop prematurely. Bark becomes corky.	mineral toxicity	page 220
Foliage is yellowish or pale. Shoots are long and spindly.	deficient light	page 223
Foliage is abnormally dark.	excess light	page 223
Excess growth of succulent foliage. Foliage may appear "burned" and die. Plant is infested with many mites, aphids, psyllids, or other insects that suck plant juices.	nitrogen excess	page 220
Shoots, buds, or flowers curl, darken, and die. Limbs and entire plant may die.	frost	page 223
Foliage, twigs, or limbs are injured. Cankers may develop.	hail or ice	page 224
Bark or wood dead, often in a streak or band.	lightning	page 224
Bark is cracked or sunken, often on south and west sides. Wood may be attacked by boring insects or decay fungi.	sunscald	page 222

a. Many of these symptoms can have other causes, including pathogens and insects.

duced, and these can develop later than normal and remain undersized. More severely deficient plants become stunted and exhibit dieback. Symptoms of common deficiencies are summarized in Table 6-2 and are detailed below.

NITROGEN

Uniform yellowing of entire, older leaves is usually the first symptom of nitrogen deficiency. Affected plants grow slowly, and in the spring produce fewer and smaller than normal leaves and shoots. Discolored foliage may drop prematurely.

Nitrogen (denoted by the symbol N) is provided to plants in nature by the decay of organic matter. Bacteria in soil or associated with roots also convert nitrogen from air into forms usable by plants. Also, people supplement the nitrogen supply by applying fertilizers. Nitrogen availability to plants is reduced when N is absorbed by weeds, used by other organisms such as soil microbes decomposing organic matter low in nitrogen, or is leached from the root zone by water. Nitrogen availability is influenced by irrigation, temperature, pH, and the organisms present in soil. Nitrogen fertilizer is commonly provided to plants as organic matter, as urea from either organic or synthetic sources, or as inorganic nitrate (NO_3^-) or ammonium (NH_4^+).

Ammonium sulfate is an inexpensive and widely used form of inorganic fertilizer. Ammonium is adsorbed onto the surface of soil particles and may not be immediately available to plants; it must generally be converted into nitrate by soil microorganisms before it moves down and can be taken up by roots. On the other hand, nitrate fertilizers are readily absorbed by plants. They are useful for quickly remedying a nitrogen deficiency and promoting rapid plant growth. However, quick-release fertilizers, such as nitrate, sometimes promote excess succulent growth. Succulent growth favors pests such as aphids and mites and promotes certain diseases. Nitrate fertilizers are more likely to be leached than ammonium or most organic fertilizers. Be sure that the soil is moist before and after applying nitrogen or else foliage may "burn," discolor, and die.

Organic sources of nitrogen include manures, blood, fish meal, cottonseed, sewage sludge, and compost. Most organic forms of nitrogen must decompose before being absorbed by plants. Decomposition

TABLE 6-2

Common Mineral Deficiency Symptoms.

SYMPTOMS	DEFICIENCY
Older leaves or needles are uniformly yellowish. New growth is sparse and undersized. Plants grow slowly and may drop foliage prematurely.	nitrogen
New foliage is undersized and yellowish, except for green along veins. Brown, dead spots may develop between veins. Leaves may dry and drop prematurely. Plants grow slowly and branches may eventually die.	iron or manganese
Leaves are uniformly yellowish, especially on new growth. Spring leaf flush and blossoming may be delayed. New leaves may be small, narrow, and grow in tufts. Foliage may turn purplish and die. Eventually, branches begin to die back.	zinc
Foliage is abnormally dark green, bluish, purplish, or may develop spots. Shoots are short and spindly, and plant grows slowly. Phosphorus deficiency is rare in landscapes.	phosphorus
Foliage growth is sparse. Older foliage is yellowish and may have brown tips and margins or brownish spots near leaf edge or between veins. Uncommon in most California soils.	potassium

Branch dieback on ash caused by insufficient water.

Relatively uniform yellowing of leaves may indicate nitrogen deficiency in this rhododendron. Iron deficiency may also be the cause.

takes weeks to months, depending on soil conditions. This slower availability of nitrogen is often desirable when growing woody plants as it is unlikely to promote excessive succulent foliage. Organic material added to soil also improves soil tilth, increasing its water- and air-holding ability and reducing compaction. However, manure and compost contain relatively little nitrogen. For instance, 100 pounds of chicken manure would have to be added to soil to gain the equivalent amount of nitrogen obtained by adding about 8 pounds of ammonium nitrate. Cattle manure is often high in salts, which can damage plants. Adding excessive amounts of undecomposed organic matter to soil may actually increase nitrogen deficiency in plants because decomposer microorganisms can use up most of the available nitrogen. Too avoid this problem, properly compost undecomposed organic matter before mixing it into soil and consider supplementing it with a more readily available form of nitrogen at a rate of about 1 pound N per cubic yard of organic matter.

Commercially formulated slow-release fertilizers are also available. They provide the easy handling of synthetic fertilizers and preferred slow-release characteristics of organic materials. Although more expensive than other preparations, these can be a good choice for adding nitrogen to nutrient-poor soils. For more information, see Fertilizing Woody Plants, Chapter 3.

PHOSPHORUS

Plants deficient in phosphorus (P) produce short, spindly shoots and grow slowly. Leaves can develop a bluish or purplish tint and lower canopy leaves may turn light bronze with purple or brown spots. Adding phosphoric acid or heavy applications of chicken manure to soil can remedy a deficiency, but phosphorus occurs in soil in adequate amounts for most trees and shrubs; adding phosphorus to soils is rarely beneficial to woody landscape plants.

POTASSIUM

Potassium (K) deficiency causes sparse leaf growth on shoots. Older leaves turn yellow and develop brown tips and margins or spots near the leaf edge. Potassium deficiency is uncommon in landscapes. It occurs primarily in fruit or nut trees grown in sandy soils or in palms.

To correct a deficiency when roots are near the surface, for example growing under mulch, apply potassium sulfate to the surface and water it in. Alternatively, apply potassium sulfate in holes bored in the soil or a trench dug near the drip line. Minimize any root damage by trenching in a line radiating out from the trunk, not perpendicular to the trunk. Potassium nitrate may also be used, but this may result in the application of excess nitrogen unless nitrogen deficiency is also a problem. Do not use potassium chloride where chlorine or salt toxicity is a problem. A slow-release NPK fertilizer (see below) with K in a ratio of 3-1-3 can be applied for palms.

NITROGEN, PHOSPHORUS, AND POTASSIUM (NPK)

So-called complete fertilizers contain nitrogen (N), phosphorus (P), and potassium (K), listed by percent weight in that order. Soil around landscape trees and shrubs is rarely if ever deficient in all three elements. Adding sufficient NPK fertilizer to provide the deficient element can result in an excess of other nutrients and may contribute to salinity problems and pollution. Plants should be fertilized in response to specific needs, and complete fertilizers are generally not recommended for woody landscape plants.

IRON

Iron deficiency causes new foliage to be undersized, pale, and chlorotic. Fading appears first around leaf margins, then spreads inward until only the veins are green. In contrast, nitrogen deficiency causes entire, older

Pinched, undulating leaf margins on a phosphorus-deficient pear tree.

leaves to turn yellow. Brown spots between leaf veins can develop in iron-deficient plants; leaves may later dry and drop prematurely.

Iron (Fe) is present in most soils, However, if the soil is alkaline (high pH, as is common in California), high in calcium content, or poorly drained or waterlogged, iron is less available; plants are unable to absorb iron under these conditions. Many plants, such as azaleas, citrus, gardenias, and rhododendrons are adapted to acidic (low pH), well-drained, aerated soils high in organic matter. These plants are especially prone to iron deficiency.

Amend soils to lower pH and increase organic matter before planting species adapted to acidic soils. If soil is alkaline, add 3 to 6 pounds of sulfur per 100 square feet of soil surface and rototill it in about 6 months before planting. Sulfur lowers soil pH and increases iron availability, but its effects may take several months. Alternatively, add organic matter that has been well composted and mix it into the top 1 to 2 feet of soil before planting. Be aware that some organic materials contain naturally occurring compounds that can be toxic to plants (see Chapter 7); properly compost these materials or leach them with a heavy irrigation before use. Amended soils also compact as organic matter decomposes, causing new plants to settle in the planting hole and become subject to root and crown diseases. Compost organic matter well before use, place the rootball on solid soil, or plant slightly above the soil line in amended soil.

Correcting iron-deficient soil around established plants is often a slow, gradual process. One quick method is to spread an iron chelate evenly over the soil beneath the plant canopy or apply it to foliage according to the product label; check and compare labels to determine percent iron before purchasing a product.

Alternatively, use a soil probe to create holes in the soil around the drip line, then fill the holes with sulfur.

Regularly placing composted organic matter as mulch on top of the roots of established plants will eventually remedy iron deficiency; iron is taken up by roots as soil becomes more acidic and organic matter decays. Conifer needle mulch is generally more acidifying than mulch from broadleaf plants. Allow fallen leaves to remain on the soil over plant roots or gather and compost leaves and other organic debris, then spread this mulch over the soil. Mulch provides many benefits in addition to nutrients.

MANGANESE

Manganese (Mn) deficiency produces pale, chlorotic leaves with only the smallest veins remaining green; dead spots can then develop on leaves. Discoloration from manganese deficiency usually occurs only in new foliage and is often nearly indistinguishable from iron deficiency. Manganese deficiency occurs primarily in alkaline soils and in certain plants, such as

palms. Leaf symptoms can be remedied before or after planting by lowering soil pH or increasing organic matter, as discussed above for iron deficiency. Manganese chelates can be applied as labeled to newly emerging foliage as a quick remedy.

ZINC

Zinc deficiency, sometimes called little leaf disease, is common in fruit and nut trees, usually those grown in sandy soils or old barnyards. A mild deficiency in zinc (Zn) resembles iron deficiency; leaves are pale between the veins and may be slightly undersized. Zinc deficiency symptoms are most apparent on new foliage in the spring. Severely deficient plants bloom and leaf out late, sometimes several weeks later than normal. When buds do open, leaves are small, mottled yellow, and may grow in tufts. Affected leaves may later turn purplish and die. When plants are severely affected, branches also die.

Drive several glazier points through the bark into the xylem to remedy zinc deficiency. Glazier points are small zinc-coated metal

Yellow new growth with distinctly green veins indicates an iron deficiency in this toyon.

wedges used to install glass in wooden window frames and are sold at hardware stores. Pound the glazier points into the bark so that their wide, flat surface is vertical and at a 90° angle to the ground, not parallel to the soil surface.

Alternatively, if needed, apply zinc sulfate or chelates once a year according to the label; methods include applying the material to soil beneath plants and watering it in thoroughly or applying it as a foliar spray to newly emerging leaves. Commercial laboratories can conduct a foliage or soil analysis to verify zinc deficiency.

Nutrient and Mineral Excesses

Nutrients, salts, and pesticides can be toxic to plants if present in excess amounts or if applied incorrectly. Toxicity symptoms include marginal leaf chlorosis, necrosis or "burn," branch dieback, and increased pest problems.

NITROGEN

Excess nitrogen kills small roots on plants and causes leaves to turn dark green, gray, or brown along the margins. Foliage may temporarily wilt or die. Plants given too much fertilizer grow excessively and develop succulent tissue, which promotes the development of certain pest problems as discussed in Chapter 3. Apply only moderate amounts of fertilizer when needed. Alleviate any drought stress before application and irrigate well after applying fertilizer. Use slow-release fertilizers where warranted.

BORON AND SALTS

Small amounts of boron (B) and some other nutrients are essential for plant growth, but high concentrations cause the margins of leaves or tips of needles to turn yellow or purplish brown and die. Foliage may drop prematurely and bark can crack or become corky. Severely affected plants die. Boron or salt toxicity affects plants irrigated with water high in minerals or plants grown in some soils, such as those common in the western side of the Central Valley of California, parts of the Mojave Desert, and some coastal areas in southern California. Toxicity caused by excess sodium or chloride commonly occurs along roadsides where salt is used to dissolve snow and ice on the pavement. Direct injury to foliage can occur from overhead irrigation with water high in sodium or chloride, such as reclaimed or swimming pool water.

Improve soil drainage to alleviate boron toxicity. Apply supplemental irrigation water that is low in minerals, such as rainwater, to leach minerals away from roots. Apply more water each time so minerals are leached deeper into the soil and away from and below roots; at the same time increase the interval between irrigations to avoid overwatering. Apply mulch around plants to reduce evaporation; evaporation concen-

Zinc deficient trees develop small, chlorotic leaves in tufts, like this almond.

Mineral toxicity is causing these maidenhair leaf margins to turn yellow, then brown and die.

trates minerals near the soil surface where most roots occur. Use other compounds instead of rock salt to de-ice pavement. Avoid increasing soil acidity as this makes boron more available to plants.

Pesticides and Phytotoxicity

Pesticides can cause undesirable damage to plants, called phytotoxicity. Herbicides are designed specifically to kill plants and can injure desirable species that are exposed to them. Nonherbicidal pesticides, such as insecticides and fungicides, also can cause plant damage. Pesticides may cause foliage or shoots to twist, distort, discolor, become spotted, and die. Foliage may be undersized and drop prematurely, stunting plant growth. Plants contaminated with certain herbicides in the fall or winter may not exhibit damage until months later when new growth occurs in the spring. Characteristic injury symptoms can often be used to determine the specific pesticide involved.

HERBICIDES

Each kind of herbicide causes characteristic damage symptoms. Injury is most likely when label directions are not followed, such as applying excessive rates. Twisted shoots and leaf petioles are caused by the phenoxy herbicides 2,4-D and MCPP. Dicamba causes foliage to become dwarfed, distorted, and discolored. These herbicides are contained in some lawn "weed and feed" products and can severely damage or kill broadleaf trees and shrubs growing near treated lawns. They also cause injury if droplets drift during application or when warm weather causes herbicides to vaporize after application. Spray equipment contaminated with

minute quantities of phenoxy herbicides can damage plants when used to apply insecticides, fertilizers, or other chemicals.

Glyphosate (Roundup) contamination on foliage or thin or green bark causes leaves to turn yellow or mottled green and sometimes die. Plants contaminated with glyphosate in the

fall may not exhibit symptoms until new growth appears in the spring. Plant growth is then retarded and leaves appear yellowish, undersized, puckered, and almost needlelike.

Atrazine, a preemergent herbicide, can persist for many months and can retard the growth of some species of plants transplanted into treated soils.

In comparison with normal foliage, sycamore leaves on the right are twisted and cupped from exposure to 2,4-D.

When glyphosate gets on trees in fall, symptoms the following spring include small, puckered needlelike leaves.

It causes leaf margins to turn brown and die, mostly on older foliage. It sometimes severely defoliates or kills nearby plants whose roots grow into treated soil.

Amitrole or aminotriazole causes new growth to become completely yellow or chlorotic because it interferes with the development of chlorophyll, the green plant pigment.

Oxyfluorfen can cause new growth to be distorted and flecked with dead spots.

Apply pesticides carefully as directed on the label. Do not spray herbicides during the fog. Do not allow spray or drift to contact desirable plants. Trunk wraps may help protect green bark from herbicide drift. Cardboard or other material can be used to shield desirable plants before spraying nearby weeds. Alternatively, special equipment such as wick type applicators (Tables 2-3 to 2-5) can be used to avoid drift.

INSECTICIDES AND OTHER PESTICIDES

Insecticides and fungicides occasionally cause leaves to discolor and die or appear burned. Damage is most common from applications during or just before hot (about 90°F) weather or if plants are stressed from drought or other factors. Emulsifiable concentrate (EC) formulations may be more likely to damage plants while wettable powder (W or WP) formulations are generally less likely to cause phytotoxicity. Some plant species are sensitive to certain insecticides, such as insecticidal soap or horticultural oil. For example, horticultural oil discolors or spots foliage on some arborvitae, maple, palm, and spruce species. Check label precautions against use on certain species; *Managing Insects & Mites with Spray Oils* (UC Publication 3347) lists landscape species that may be damaged by oil. When in doubt as to whether the plant species is sensitive to that pesticide, spray a small area of the plant and observe it for several days for any signs of damage before spraying any more of the plant.

Sunlight

Too much or too little sunlight can damage plants. The amount of light required to cause damage varies with the species of plant, environmental conditions, and whether adequate cultural care is provided. Sunburn, sunscald, and light deficiency are syndromes associated with improper light levels.

SUNBURN

Sunburn is damage to foliage and other herbaceous plant parts caused by a combination of too much light and heat and insufficient moisture. A yellow or brown area develops on foliage, which then dies beginning in areas between the veins. Although sunburn is often used to refer to damaged bark, the term sunscald is used here to denote bark damage.

Avoid sunburn by choosing plants that are adapted to the site where they are planted. Provide them with proper cultural care, especially appropriate water, to prevent sunburn. Appropriate irrigation can restore the color to sunburned foliage before it is killed.

SUNSCALD

Sunscald, also sometimes called sunburn, is damage to bark caused by excessive light or heat. Sunscald-damaged bark becomes cracked, sunken, and is susceptible to attack by wood-boring insects and rot fungi. Sunburned trunks and limbs can develop cankers, become girdled, and die.

Sunscald often occurs on young woody plants. Their bark is thin and may not tolerate exposed landscapes because before planting they were grown crowded together in nurseries where their trunks were shaded. Older trees are damaged when bark is newly exposed to the sun because of

Yellow and brown areas on sunburned euonymus leaves.

extensive pruning or premature leaf drop. Removing structures or trees that provided shade or adding pavement or structures that reflect light or radiate heat around established plants can also lead to sunscald. Even in soil that is saturated with water, sunscald may occur if plants are unable to absorb sufficient moisture when it is sunny or temperatures are hot or cold.

Prevent sunscald through proper planting and pruning. Encourage desired structure by properly pruning young plants and avoid removing more than about 20% of the plant canopy during any one year. Apply white interior (not exterior) latex paint, diluted 50% with water, to the trunks of young trees and to older bark newly exposed to the sun. Mulches can reduce or increase heat and light around plants, depending on the location and type of material used (see Chapter 7). Minimize the changes to a plant's environment and provide adequate irrigation.

EXCESS OR DEFICIENT LIGHT

Each plant is adapted to certain amounts of light, depending on its species and previous growing conditions. Plant growth can be retarded by either too much or too little light. Deficient light causes pale foliage and elongated, spindly shoots. Excess light can cause foliage to darken. Typical color returns when plants again receive normal light, but a prolonged light imbalance causes plants to become susceptible to other problems and possibly die. For example, artificial lights at night alter the response of some plants to seasonal changes in natural light, increasing their susceptibility to frost damage.

Plant only species that are well adapted to the amount of light available at that location. Avoid changing the environment in any way that significantly alters the amount of light received by established plants unless this is purposely done to remedy inappropiate light conditions.

Frost

Frost damage causes shoots, buds, and flowers to curl, turn brown or black, and die. Whole branches or entire plants may be killed. Frost damage to foliage resembles some leaf anthracnose diseases. Frost damage occurs when low temperatures cause the water in plant tissue or on plant surfaces to freeze. During cool, clear nights, dust or bacteria, including some strains of *Pseudomonas syringae*, serve as particles on which moisture from the atmosphere can condense and freeze. Plants that are gradually exposed to increasingly cool weather, such as during the fall, become acclimated and tolerate more cold than during other times of the year. Succulent plant tissue in the spring is especially susceptible to frost. However, by the summer new growth often replaces tissue damaged by spring frosts. Plants adapted to the local environment usually are not permanently harmed by frost.

Apply white interior latex paint, diluted 50% with water, to prevent sunscald to young trunks.

ROBERT D. RAABE

Camellias are adapted to partial shade. Excess light discolored this foliage.

To prevent frost damage, do not plant species adapted to mild climates in areas where freezing temperatures occur. Provide soil with adequate moisture to increase its ability to retain heat. When frost is expected, cover sensitive plants overnight to reduce heat loss to the atmosphere; remove covers during the day. Placing electric lights (household size or Christmas lights) in the canopy, especially if plants are covered, can generate enough heat to prevent plants from freezing. Be sure equipment is designed for outdoor use and not likely to create electrical shock or fire hazards. Operating sprinklers overnight to wet foliage can reduce frost damage because extensive cold is required to turn water to ice. Even if the water freezes, ice-covered plants may be somewhat insulated from cooling to temperatures much below freezing. Do not combine the use of outdoor lights and sprinkling.

Freezing weather killed this lemon foliage.

Hail and Ice

Hailstones injure leaves, twigs, and bark and in serious cases can girdle and kill branches. Hail injury to bark provides entry sites for some pathogens, such as fireblight bacteria that are usually present on the surface of susceptible species but normally infect plants only through blossoms. Where ice occurs on plants, limbs can break from the added weight. Prune out wood that is seriously damaged by hail or ice.

Lightning

Lightning most commonly strikes isolated, exposed, or tall plants. Lightning kills bark or wood in a long, vertical band and can cause plants to explode or burn. Lightning

Hail made many small scars on this citrus twig.

strikes can seriously damage roots even though the damage on the aboveground portions of the plant appears relatively minor. Lightning rods wired to the ground can be installed at the top of especially valuable, tall trees in areas where lightning is prevalent. Have an expert inspect lightning-struck trees for root damage that may cause the tree to fall.

Air Pollution

Air pollution damage is caused by mostly invisible gases, especially ozone and sulfur oxides. Nitrogen oxides, carbon monoxide, halogens such as chlorides or fluorides, and acidic deposition ("acid rain") also damage plants. Damage is especially prevalent when plants are located near sources of dirty air, such as freeways or industries, or where weather and topography concentrate local or distant sources of pollution in certain locations. Some pollutants develop through complex reactions among chemicals and light, such as peroxyacetyl nitrate (PAN) resulting from ultraviolet radiation acting on precursors in photochemical smog.

Air pollution damage is difficult to diagnose because many symptoms are similar to, and aggravated by, those associated with other stresses including drought, nutrient disorders, pathogens, and sucking insects and mites. Typical air pollution damage includes browning on the underside or margins of leaves or other discoloring, and dead and prematurely dropping leaves or needles. Symptoms may develop soon after short-term exposure to high concentrations of air pollutants, or after longer exposure to relatively lower pollution levels. The susceptibility of plants to air pollution damage varies greatly. Azalea, birch, fuchsia, pine, and sycamore are among the plants most readily damaged by air pollution.

OZONE

Ozone naturally occurring in the upper atmosphere shields plants and animals from harmful solar radiation; ozone near the ground damages plants. Ozone is produced when the nitrogen oxides and hydrocarbons emitted during combustion are exposed to sunlight and react with oxygen.

Ozone causes pale flecks or small dark patches to appear on needles and leaves. Discolored areas can enlarge and foliage may drop prematurely. Pine needle tips can turn brown and die or banding may appear on affected needles. Ozone retards growth and increases plants' susceptibility to diseases and insects.

SULFUR OXIDES

Sulfur oxides are produced by burning coal or oil, refining petroleum and some minerals, and by motor vehicles. Sulfur oxides cause tip dieback and yellow or brown bands on conifer needles. Broadleaf foliage bleaches and dies beginning between the veins. Affected foliage may be sparse, stunted, and grow in tufts.

Air pollution like this causes plant damage that is difficult to diagnose because many symptoms with other causes are similar to, and are aggravated by, air pollution.

Ozone pollution damage can be subtle, like the yellowish patches in these Japanese maple leaves.

Tips turn brown and die or banding may appear on pine needles affected by excess ozone levels.

MANAGEMENT OF AIR POLLUTION INJURY

Provide proper cultural care and control other causes of stress to keep plants vigorous and increase their tolerance to pollution. Grow more plants because plants help in several ways to reduce air pollution. Particulates become trapped by foliage and are washed by precipitation from foliage to the soil. Gaseous air pollutants are absorbed by bark and taken into plants through leaf stomata.

Plant tolerant species in areas where air quality is especially poor. Extensive lists of species especially susceptible or tolerant to pollution have been developed (see references in *Diseases of Trees and Shrubs*).

Air pollution is best controlled at its source. Reduce pollution by using alternative means of transportation and energy, properly maintaining vehicles and engines, conserving resources and materials, and supporting appropriate regulations.

CHAPTER SEVEN

Weeds

WEEDS ARE PLANTS that are out of place. The same plant species can be desirable in one setting and a weed in another situation. For example, turf and ground covers are widely planted, desirable species that often invade areas under trees and shrubs, where they become weeds.

There are several key concerns with weeds around trees and shrubs. First, turf, ground covers, and other low-growing species next to trunks are commonly trimmed with mowers or weed trimmers, which often injure trunks or roots around the crown; this damage makes plants susceptible to wood-boring insects, crown rot diseases, and other problems. Second, weeds compete with desirable landscape species for moisture and nutrients. Competition is especially detrimental to newly planted trees and shrubs, which can be stunted because of nearby competing vegetation. Third, herbaceous species around woody landscape plants can provide habitat for snails, rodents, and other pests and can contribute to the potential for disease development by increasing humidity and moisture

around trunks. Lastly, weeds can become eyesores in the landscape.

The focus of this chapter is on preventing and managing weeds directly under and around woody landscape plants. Management of weeds in turf, ground covers, and annual bedding plants is discussed in several publications listed in References at the back of this book.

Managing Weeds

The most critical time for effective weed management is before planting. Prevent weed problems through good landscape planning and design and proper site preparation before planting. If you wait for weeds to mature and become a problem in landscapes and then try to take curative actions, your management options will be more limited and results may be less satisfactory than if you take preventive measures or act when weeds first appear.

Remove weeds and amend, loosen, and grade the soil before planting to provide for good landscape plant growth. Choose species that are well adapted to local conditions. Group together plants that require similar cultural care and separate plants with cultural care needs or growth characteristics that are incompatible with nearby plants. Correctly plant and adequately care for trees and shrubs, as discussed in Chapter 3, so that desirable species outcompete, displace, and exclude weeds.

Prevent weed growth in established plantings by minimizing disturbance of the soil, using low-volume irrigation systems, and by carefully choosing, applying, and maintaining mulches. See Table 7-1 for a summary of weed IPM methods. If these actions are taken, regular hand-pulling or hoeing of occasional weeds is all that will be needed in many situations once landscape plants become established.

DESIGNING AND REDESIGNING LANDSCAPES TO AVOID WEEDS

Avoid inadvertently designing a new landscape that encourages weeds. Consider redesigning and replanting landscapes with chronic weed problems. Weed-prone landscapes include those that are frequently reinfested with undesirable species or that have adjoining plants with different irrigation or other cultural care needs. Select landscape species that are well adapted to local soils, moisture, temperature, and light. Choose plant species or varieties that resist common insect and disease problems as discussed in Chapter 3; plants that are appropriate for their location grow more vigorously and are less affected by competition from weeds.

Group together plants that have compatible cultural requirements; for instance, separate drought-tolerant and summer rainfall-adapted species. Avoid planting together species with incompatible growth characteristics.

TABLE 7-1

Summary of Weed IPM Methods.

DESIGN/REDESIGN SITES TO AVOID WEED PROBLEMS
Select species that are well adapted to local climate and soil conditions.
Group together plants that require similar cultural care, such as like requirements for water.
Separate plants with incompatible growth characteristics.
Plan on installing a low-volume irrigation system.
Consider using a professional landscape designer who is knowledgeable about pest prevention.
Select plants that develop an overlapping canopy to shade out weeds.

PREPARE THE SITE BEFORE PLANTING AND PLANT PROPERLY
Eliminate any established weeds, especially perennial species.
Grade and prepare the site for good drainage.
Loosen and amend or add topsoil if needed.
Provide for any needed irrigation.
Plant trees and shrubs properly.
Choose appropriate mulch and apply it correctly.

PROPERLY CARE FOR ESTABLISHED LANDSCAPES
Provide desirable species with proper cultural care.
Monitor regularly and frequently for weeds and keep written records of when different species appear.
Determine which weeds can be tolerated and when control is warranted.
Hand-pull or hoe weeds while they are seedlings.
Effectively operate and maintain a low-volume irrigation system.
Correctly maintain mulch.
Minimize any disturbance to the soil.
Use a preemergent herbicide or spot applications of a contact herbicide where appropriate.
Consider redesigning and replanting problem-prone landscapes.

For example, bermudagrass is a hardy and drought-tolerant turf grass, but because it spreads by rhizomes and stolons it can invade nearby shrubs. Do not plant spreading ground covers such as ivy or turf such as bermudagrass near trees and shrubs; if you do, minimize invasiveness by reducing the length of any borders between grass, ground covers, and shrubs. For instance, plant the same number of shrubs in one large group rather than several smaller groups, each bordered by turf. Install deep barriers or headers between turf and planted areas.

Headers. Separate shrub areas from invasive ground covers or turf by using sidewalks, driveways, or headers. Headers are wood, metal, or concrete dividers buried 8 or more inches deep and projecting 2 to 3 inches above the soil (Figure 7-1). Wide cement or brick headers serve as a mowing strip, which allows lawn mowers to cut all the way to the edge of the turf and beyond, thereby reducing the chance that turf can spread into shrub beds. Flexible plastic or other temporary barriers can be used, then moved as the landscape matures or when portions are replanted. Instead of planting a median strip or other pavement- or header-bounded area with a mixture of turf, ground cover, and shrubs, alternate plantings so that each area is entirely shrubs, ground cover, or turf.

Competitive Plantings. Competitive plantings of ornamental species are an excellent method of weed control. Vigorous, densely growing annuals or ground covers planted in bare spaces among trees and shrubs can rapidly grow together and shade out weeds. However, be aware that some aggressive ground covers can become weeds by crowding out and killing shrubs. Use species that have cultural requirements compatible with nearby plants. For example, Table 7-2 is a list of ground covers and perennials that require little or no irrigation after they are established and are therefore more compatible with native California oaks and other drought-adapted trees. Use enough plants so they are close together and exclude weeds; mulch any bare areas in between. Trim or remove some individual plants as they become older and crowded. Interplanted landscape is more attractive and easier to care for than bare soil between widely spaced landscape plants; bare soil is inevitably colonized by weeds and requires ongoing control action.

Avoid planting turf close to trees and shrubs. Do not plant irrigated ground covers too close to tree trunks. Turf, ground covers, or weeds near trunks can dramatically retard growth of young trees and shrubs. Watering turf near trunks can cause drought-adapted trees and shrubs to die from excess moisture and stem or root diseases. Conversely, summer rainfall-adapted woody plants may not get enough water and nutrients if turf and ground covers grow underneath them because these other

TABLE 7-2

Ground Covers or Perennials Requiring Little or No Irrigation and Suitable for Around Mature, Drought-Adapted Trees in the Central Valley of California.[a]

FULL SUN (SOUTH OR WEST EXPOSURE)	
COMMON NAME	SCIENTIFIC NAME
Yarrow	*Achillea millefolium*
Dwarf coyote brush	*Baccharis pilularis pilularis*
California buckwheat	*Eriogonum fasciculatum*
Nolina	*Nolina* sp.
Purple needle grass	*Stipa pulchra*
California fuchsia	*Zauschneria californica*
Island California fuchsia	*Zauschneria cana*
Yucca	*Yucca whipplei*
PARTIAL SHADE (EAST OR NORTH EXPOSURE)	
Maritime ceanothus	*Ceanothus maritimus*
Blue wild rye	*Elymus glaucus*[b]
Creeping wild rye	*Elymus triticoides*[b]
California fescue	*Festuca californica*[b]
Deergrass	*Muhlenbergia rigens*[b]
Evergreen viguiera	*Viguiera deltoidea parishii*
Yerba-de-selva	*Whipplea modesta*[b]

a. From UC Davis *Arboretum Review*, Winter 1992. For more information see *Compatible Plants Under and Around Oaks* and other publications listed in References.

b. These plants survive without summer water but look better if they are irrigated once a month in the summer.

A deep container may prevent this newly planted bamboo from spreading and becoming a weed.

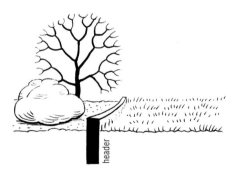

Figure 7-1. Separate shrub areas from invasive lawns or ground covers by using headers. Headers are narrow concrete, metal, or wood barriers extending 8 or more inches below ground and 2 to 3 inches above ground.

plants can be more efficient at capturing water and nutrients near the soil surface. Although competition can be partially reduced by providing additional irrigation and fertilizer, better growth will occur if you mulch or maintain bare soil for at least 4 feet from the trunks of young woody landscape plants. Consider using mulch as an attractive ground cover where appropriate.

Allelopathy. Some plants, such as black walnut, certain aromatic shrubs, and many desert species such as sagebrush, produce compounds that retard the growth of nearby plants. This chemical warfare among plants is called allelopathy. Mature plants usually tolerate allelochemicals (compounds produced by plants that inhibit other plants), but germination and growth can be reduced in seedling plants such as annual flowers or weeds. To date, little research has been conducted indicating how to effectively use allelochemicals in landscapes.

Applying some organic mulches may produce an effect similar to planting allelopathic species. In addition to preventing weed growth by excluding light, natural toxins leaching from uncomposted, fresh bark or foliage of certain species applied as mulch may temporarily retard young plants (weeds) but have little effect on mature, established plants. Composting the organic mulch or leaching it with a heavy irrigation before use reduces or eliminates any toxicity.

PREPARING THE PLANTING SITE

Prepare sites properly before planting as discussed above and detailed in Chapter 3. Eliminate established weeds and reduce future weed growth before planting, such as by using proper irrigation and cultivation, solarization, or herbicides. It is especially important to reduce or eliminate perennial species before planting or moving soil around the site. Loosen compacted soils and break up hardpan by ripping, chiseling, boring, or using other equipment. Soil may be amended by adding organic matter or changing pH if necessary, but the benefits are uncertain; it is better to choose species that are well adapted to conditions at that site. Properly grade soils so that water drains well around roots, which helps to prevent root disease.

Irrigation. Provide for any needed irrigation by installing drip irrigation or another efficient system that allows appropriate watering as discussed in Chapter 3. Unless the water source is high in minerals, subsurface irrigation systems, such as porous hoses or buried emitter heads, are especially good because they keep water away from weed seeds near the surface and place water below ground near desirable plant roots. By irrigating below ground, weed seeds near the surface are less likely to be wetted and germinate. Alternatively, use low-volume aboveground emitters to deliver water slowly near landscape plant roots. Sprinklers widely disperse water, much of which becomes available to weeds. Seasonally adjust irrigation schedules according to the weather and the plant's need for water.

Cultivation. Cultivation cuts, uproots, and buries weeds. Rototill or manually cultivate before planting to kill young annual weeds. Reduce weed seeds by irrigating the soil to promote germination, then cultivate again in about 1 to 3 weeks after seedlings emerge. Repeat these steps (water, wait, then cultivate) two or more times before planting. Make each subsequent cultivation shallower than the last so that deeply buried seeds are not brought to the surface. To minimize any subsequent soil disturbance, the area must already be at final grade and the irrigation system installed before beginning this water, wait, then cultivate system.

Although most effective against annuals, cultivation also controls perennial weed seedlings if it is conducted before they have stored much carbohydrate or produced tubers, stolons, or rhizomes. Mature perennial weeds also can be controlled by cultivating at frequent intervals. This repeated damage and disruption prevents perennial weeds from storing additional carbohydrate and requires them to continually draw on reserves, which are eventually depleted, killing the plant. Some established perennials in dry inland valleys can be controlled by cultivating every 1 to 3 weeks during the summer without any irrigation, then allowing the soil and weeds to dry. This regime can control johnsongrass, bermudagrass, kikuyugrass, and purple nutsedge, but not yellow nutsedge. Cultivation generally is required for more than one summer to control field bindweed. Cultivating perennials generally does not give effective control in coastal areas or in the inland valleys during cool, rainy weather. Cultivating perennials when soil is moist or followed by irrigation can increase the spread of these weeds.

Solarization. Solarization before planting can effectively control most annual and certain perennial weeds for about 6 months to one year (see Table 7-3). Solarization, tarping soil to retain the sun's heat, also reduces nematodes and many soilborne diseases. To solarize, you must cover bare, moist ground with clear (not black) plastic, 1.5 to 2 mils thick, during the hottest part of the year. Cover soil for at least 4 to 6 weeks during a period of intense sunlight

TABLE 7-3

Weed Species Susceptibility to Soil Solarization.

COMMON NAME	SCIENTIFIC NAME	RELATIVE SUSCEPTIBILITY
Annual bluegrass	*Poa annua*	S
Annual sowthistle	*Sonchus oleraceus*	S
Barnyardgrass	*Echinochloa crusgalli*	S
Bermuda buttercup	*Oxalis pes-caprae*	S
Bermudagrass	*Cynodon dactylon*	P
Black nightshade	*Solanum nigrum*	S
Cheeseweed	*Malva parviflora*	S
Common chickweed	*Stellaria media*	S
Common groundsel	*Senecio vulgaris*	S
Creeping woodsorrel	*Oxalis corniculata*	P
Field bindweed	*Convolvulus arvensis*	P
Hairy nightshade	*Solanum sarrachoides*	S
Henbit	*Lamium amplexicaule*	S
Johnsongrass	*Sorghum halepense*	S
Lambsquarter	*Chenopodium album*	S
Large crabgrass	*Digitaria sanguinalis*	P
Lovegrass	*Eragrostis* spp.	P
Prickly lettuce	*Lactuca serriola*	S
Purslane	*Portulaca oleracea*	P
Redmaids	*Calandrinia ciliata*	S
Redroot pigweed	*Amaranthus retroflexus*	S
Shepherd's-purse	*Capsella bursa-pastoris*	S
White sweetclover	*Melilotus alba*	R
Wild oat	*Avena fatua*	P
Yellow nutsedge	*Cyperus esculentus*	P

For more details see *Soil Solarization: A Nonchemical Method for Controlling Diseases and Pests* (UC Leaflet 21377).

S= Susceptible: proper solarization can control all of this weed for one season if soil is undisturbed.

P= Partially susceptible: many plants are killed, but some survival and regrowth may occur.

R= Resistant: little or no control.

Solarization before planting controls weeds and many soilborne diseases. To solarize, cover bare, moist, smooth soil with clear plastic for at least 4 to 6 weeks during hot, sunny weather.

ated by clods or air pores in dry soil are poor conductors of heat. Seal the tarp edges with soil to retain heat. Protect the tarp surface from punctures during solarization to achieve the highest soil temperatures. If holes form in the plastic while on the soil, seal them with clear patching tape. Plant soon after removing the plastic. After solarization, avoid deep cultivation. Working the soil deeper than about 3 inches may bring some weed seeds to the surface that were buried too deeply to have been exposed to temperatures high enough to kill them.

MULCHES

Mulching is one of the most effective and desirable methods of preventing germination and growth of annual weeds. Mulch is a layer of material covering the soil to exclude sunlight. Many seeds require light to germinate, and all green plants need light to grow. Although effective mulching can require a significant initial investment, it provides long-term aesthetic benefits and greatly reduces ongoing weed management costs. If you have properly prepared your planting site, killed or removed vegetative propagules of perennial weeds, and immediately applied an effective mulch, regular hand-pulling or hoeing of

with little wind (usually June through September in California). Solarization requires more time and is less effective in cloudy, windy coastal areas.

Clear any vegetation from the area to be solarized. Scrape vegetation off, mow weeds closely (to ½ inch tall) and rake the soil free of cuttings, or rototill no deeper than 4 inches.

Grade soil and otherwise prepare it so it is ready for planting and any subsequent disturbance is minimized. Irrigate soil thoroughly just before covering it. Lightly work the soil surface to even it, then irrigate again if the soil surface has dried. Be sure the ground is smooth and free of clods and trash so that the plastic lies very close to the soil surface. Air gaps cre-

TABLE 7-4

Organic Mulches.

MATERIAL	COMMENTS
Bark chips and ground bark	Attractive, slowly improves soil as it gradually decomposes. Can harbor earwigs, termites, sowbugs, and other pests. Often placed over plastics as a decorative material.
Wood chips	Sometimes inexpensive. May contain weed seeds. May not stay in place. May use soil nitrogen as it decomposes. Compost well first or add nitrogen to the soil.
Compost	Excellent source of organic matter, readily available or can be made. May harbor weed seeds if not properly composted. May promote crown disease if applied to contact trunk.
Grass clippings and leaves	Readily available, can be applied often. May contain weed seeds or bermudagrass stems. May mat and reduce water penetration if not dried first. Better if composted before use.
Peat moss	Increases water-holding capacity if mixed into the soil. Adds acidity to alkaline soils. Contains few or no weeds. Resists wetting when dry, expensive.
Hay and straw	Allows good water penetration. Looks good. Usually contains grain seed, which may germinate. May use soil nitrogen as it decomposes. Compost well before using or add nitrogen to soil.
Rice hulls	Benefits soil tilth, slow to degrade. May contain weed seeds unless composted or rolled to crush seeds. May use soil nitrogen as it decomposes. Compost well before using or add nitrogen to soil.
Leaf mold	Can add needed acidity to alkaline soils, attractive. Must be carefully prepared, purchased, or can be collected.
Newspapers (shredded)	Readily available, inexpensive, no weeds. Attracts earwigs and sowbugs. Not stable in windy conditions. Inks may be toxic, do not use around edible plants. Unattractive.
Pine needles	Adds acidity, readily available. Leachate helps stop weed growth, but it may be toxic to young plants. Suitable only for acidic soil-adapted plant species. Slow to break down.
Sawdust	Improves soil organic content. Inexpensive or free. Will mat and inhibit water penetration. May use soil nitrogen, blows away, and decomposes rapidly. Compost well before using or add nitrogen to soil. May contain organic compounds that can harm young plants.
Pressed heavy fibrous paper for mulching (e.g., Hortopaper)[a]	Good water and air penetration, easy application. Must be purchased. Tends to break or tear after transplanting or if walked on.

a. See Table 7-6 for how long this material remains effective.

weed seedlings and maintenance of the mulch may be the only weed management activities necessary. However, if perennials become established, other management practices such as herbicide use may be necessary.

Organic mulches include plant-derived materials such as bark, wood chips, and lawn clippings (Table 7-4). Effective nonorganic mulches include inorganic materials like crushed rock and synthetics such as landscape fabrics (Table 7-5). In many cases, a combination of two, such as a landscape fabric covered with bark or chip mulch, may provide the most practical mulch.

In addition to good weed control, mulches conserve soil moisture by reducing evaporation and reducing water use by weeds. Reduced evaporation reduces salt buildup in soils irrigated with water high in salts. Mulch also reduces compaction and erosion from irrigation, rainfall, and traffic.

Organic Mulches. Organic mulches have the major advantage of improving the soil. The minerals and organic matter gradually released from decaying mulch enrich deficient soils, replacing nutrients taken up by roots as plants grow, and often enhancing earthworm populations. Many organic mulches are attractive, contrasting nicely with foliage and flower colors and providing a pleasant "natural" appearance and aroma. Organic mulches moderate the soil wetting and drying cycle between irrigations and reduce summer soil temperatures around roots, thereby improving plant growth. Most organic mulches improve water penetration by reducing water runoff and increasing infiltration.

TABLE 7-5

Nonorganic Mulches.

MATERIAL	COMMENTS
Black plastic (polyethylene)[a]	Very effective, easy to handle. Not permeable to air and water. Usually needs drip irrigation. Warms soil somewhat. Breaks down in a few months and is unattractive unless a top mulch is applied. Weeds can grow readily through tears or holes.
Clear plastic (polyethylene)	Performs like black plastic, except that it encourages weed growth unless solarization procedures are followed. Cover with top mulch if not used for solarization. Weeds can grow readily through tears and holes.
Woven polypropylene and nonwoven polyester[a]	Very effective, long lasting. Allows air and water penetration. Expensive, may be unattractive without a top mulch. Brands differ in effectiveness.
Photodegradable plastic	May not need to be removed. Degradation may not be complete. Must be exposed to light to degrade. If exposed to light, not as long lasting as some other materials.
Crushed stone, gravel	Attractive as a top mulch for synthetics. Tends to become weed infested if used alone. May get too hot. Time consuming to remove, expensive.
Roofing/building paper	Long-lasting and durable. Unattractive unless a top mulch is applied, expensive.
Used carpet	Long-lasting and durable. Unattractive unless a top mulch is applied. May produce an unpleasant odor when wet.

a. See Table 7-6 for information on how long these materials remain effective.

If not properly selected or used, organic mulches have some disadvantages. Organic mulches gradually decompose; mulch must be periodically added to maintain a sufficiently deep layer (3 to 4 inches) to provide good weed control. Mulch may contain weed seeds or stolons; kill them by composting well before applying organic mulch that may be contaminated. Hand-pull or otherwise control weeds during the seedling stage if they begin to grow in mulch. Mulch can harbor snails and slugs, earwigs and other insects, and rodents. Apply copper bands around trunks or planting areas to exclude snails and slugs. Use wire or plastic guards to protect trunks from gnawing rodents. Maintaining bare soil within about 1 foot of trunks also can reduce problems with these pests.

Although most organic mulches improve water penetration and retention, thick applications of certain materials such as sawdust or fresh grass clippings can reduce water pen-

Organic mulches can provide a pleasant, natural appearance and improve plant growth as well as control weeds.

etration to roots. If sprinklers are used, apply more water during each irrigation so that moisture penetrates to soil and roots and increase the interval between irrigations to avoid overwatering. If water runs off, suspend irrigation for an hour to allow moisture to sink into the soil. Water penetration problems are avoided if a low-volume irrigation system is used.

Some bark, wood, and foliage contain naturally occurring toxic compounds (allelochemicals) that may damage young plants. The amount of these compounds varies depending on the plant from which they are derived. Plants also vary in their susceptibility to allelochemicals. Before applying organic materials around young plants that may be affected by allelochemicals, compost the material well or leach the organic mulch with a heavy irrigation. Do not allow the leachate to run off or drain into surface water or storm sewers. Alternatively, apply mulch with natural toxins only around older landscape plants, which are less affected by the leaching chemicals and may benefit from the extra weed control provided.

Nonorganic Mulches. Inorganic and synthetic mulches are sometimes easier to maintain than organic mulches. They do not improve soil quality, and most are unattractive unless a top mulch is applied. Some plastic materials traditionally used for mulching, such as polyethylene, require special irrigation procedures because they are waterproof and sprinklers cannot

be used to water plants. These waterproof mulches can also promote root rot fungi, especially if soils are poorly drained. Although more expensive, woven polypropylene and polyester mulches, also called weed barriers or landscape fabrics, are preferred because they allow air and water penetration to roots. These products are more durable and effective than conventional plastic sheeting and should be used on long-term plantings wherever possible.

Cover landscape fabrics with a layer of material such as crushed rock or bark to improve their appearance and prevent wind damage. Covering them also reduces breakdown by ultraviolet light, although many of the longer lasting polypropylene and polyester products contain ultraviolet inhibitors to resist photodegradation. Photodegradable mulches may be desirable where slow-growing shrubs or trees are expected to eventually shade out potential weed growth. These mulches must be left exposed

to sunlight (without a top mulch) for them to break down.

Synthetic mulches or landscape fabrics vary in how long they remain effective (see Table 7-6). Shorter lasting fabrics can be adequate where plants will soon grow together and shade the soil surface. Longer lasting materials are preferable for use under slow-growing plants or where mulch alone is used as a ground cover between more widely spaced plants.

Proper Mulch Application and Maintenance. Use mulch whenever possible. Mulch is not appropriate in all situations, but its drawbacks can be minimized through proper use. Keep organic mulch and waterproof synthetics several inches back from trunks, or apply only a thin layer of mulch near trunks to avoid promoting crown diseases. Where root rot disease is a problem or when overhead watering is used, avoid plastics that are not permeable to air and water. Before applying mulch, be sure

TABLE 7-6

Some Landscape Fabrics and the Approximate Length of Time They Remain Effective When Used as Weed Barriers Under 2 to 3 Inches of Redwood Chips.

MATERIAL	PRODUCT	APPROXIMATE LENGTH OF TIME EFFECTIVE (IN YEARS)[a]
Nonwoven polypropylene	Duon Weed Control Mat 2.5 oz[b]	3 to 5+
Nonwoven polypropylene	Soil-check[b]	3 to 5+
Nonwoven polypropylene	Terra Mat P	2+
Nonwoven polypropylene	Typar (DuPont)[b]	3 to 5+
Woven polypropylene	DeWitt Pro 5 Weed Barrier	3 to 5+
Nonwoven polyester	Terra Mat E	4
Nonwoven polyester	Warren's Weed Arrest[b]	5+
Polyethylene	Black plastic, 4 mil not permeable[b]	3 to 5
Polyethylene	Weed Block Landscape Fabric[b]	3 to 5
Peat moss and cellulose fibers	Hortopaper[b]	½ to 1

a. Results obtained from field trials in Davis, California. Efficacy may vary, for example due to local conditions or manufacturer changes in materials; + indicates that materials may last longer than indicated.

b. Material requires a top mulch to protect it from degradation by ultraviolet light and to provide the indicated longevity. If exposed to sunlight, these and some other materials may not last as long as indicated.

the soil is properly graded and weed-free and install any needed irrigation equipment. Smooth soil and remove any sharp objects before applying landscape fabrics. Dig and prepare the planting hole(s), lay down the fabric, cut out sections the same diameter as the planting holes, plant, then apply any top mulch.

Organic mulches must be applied at least 3 to 4 inches deep to prevent light from reaching soil and to assure suppression of most annual weeds. Organic mulches gradually break down and become mixed into the soil as they improve tilth, so additional mulch should be applied later unless plants grow together and shade the soil. Because decomposing organic mulch may temporarily reduce the nitrogen available to plants, consider adding nitrogen fertilizer to mulched soil. Regularly inspect mulch and remove any weeds soon after they germinate; weeds growing in a top mulch can damage the landscape fabrics underneath as their roots grow.

Availability, cost, ease of application and maintenance, appearance, stability, rate of decomposition, and penetration by water and air are considerations when selecting among the mulches available. The characteristics of some common, effective mulches are listed in Tables 7-4, 7-5, and 7-6. For more details on mulching, see *Arboriculture: Integrated Management of Landscape Trees, Shrubs, and Vines* listed in References.

CONTROLLING WEEDS IN ESTABLISHED PLANTINGS

Good planning, preparation, and planting and proper irrigation and use of mulch minimize the need for ongoing weed control. Weeds that do appear despite the above practices, can be controlled with hand-weeding, hoeing, cultivation, weed trimmers, mowers, flamers, herbicides, or a combination of these methods.

Never allow weeds to produce seeds. If weeds were not controlled before planting or during the seedling stage, take action before flowers appear and before weeds produce seeds. Once they are produced, seeds can remain viable in the soil for many years, especially if they become buried.

Preventing Weed Introductions. Evaluate the potential for introducing weeds before bringing materials into the landscape. Topsoil, plants in containers, mulch, manure, and many other organic soil amendments are often highly contaminated with weed seeds or plant parts (stolons, rhizomes, or tubers). Consider their weed potential before using these materials. Check to see if commercially obtained soil or mulches have been sterilized, such as by kiln-drying or steam treatment. Reduce weed contamination in organic materials by properly composting them before use.

Mowers and other implements are often contaminated with weed seeds or vegetative parts. Clean equipment well before moving it from one area to the next. Avoid planting nursery stock that has weeds growing in the container soil. Surface water (from ponds or rivers) is often highly contaminated with weed seeds; filter surface water to reduce seeds before using it for irrigation.

Water and Fertilizer Management. Provide sufficient but not excessive irrigation water and fertilizer; apply them evenly. A lack or an excess of nutrients can restrict growth or damage plants, resulting in more weed growth. Poor or excessive applications of water reduces growth of desirable plants and promotes weed germination and growth.

Install a low-volume irrigation system around trees or shrubs to minimize weed growth. Maintain the

irrigation equipment; several weed species can take advantage of extra moisture around leaky or improperly operating sprinkler heads. See Chapter 3 for more details on irrigation.

Hand-Weeding. Pulling weeds by hand is the oldest form of weed control and still is of great value in landscapes. Pull weeds when they are young; hand-weeding is easiest and most effective for small plants, especially when soil is loose or moist so that the entire root and crown are easily removed. Weed poppers, dandelion knives, and similar specialized hand tools are available for removing individual weeds and their roots while minimizing soil disturbance. To effectively control established perennial weeds, it may be necessary to dig up and destroy all underground stems and tubers that can grow into new plants.

Hoeing. Cut grass weeds slightly below the soil surface and sever broadleaf weeds at the soil surface using a hoe, such as a scuffle hoe or Hula-hoe. Keep the tool blade sharp so that weeds are easily cut. Do not use a hoe to cultivate or loosen earth by digging in soft soil. This disturbs the soil and exposes buried weed seeds, which may germinate. The best time to hoe is when soil is dry. Allow 3 to 5 days for weeds to fully dry out before irrigating again. Because perennial weeds can regrow from severed roots or stems, hoeing is most effective against annual species.

Cultivation. Cultivation as previously discussed controls weeds around established landscapes. If mulches or other preventive measures are not applied, it may be necessary to cultivate about weekly when landscape plants are young to provide adequate control. However, cultivation, especially with rototillers or other motor-

ized equipment, is generally not recommended in established plantings. Mixing and disturbing the top several inches of soil brings previously buried weed seeds to the surface where they can germinate in the freshly loosened earth. Cultivation or rototilling can also break up and spread vegetative parts of perennial plants, such as tubers, stolons, or rhizomes, which can develop into new plants. Cultivation also can injure surface roots of desirable plants. Consider methods other than cultivation if weeds appear in established landscapes.

Mowing. If you choose to tolerate grasses or other tall herbaceous vegetation around trees and shrubs, mow or cut them before they bloom and form seeds. Use a hand sickle or portable weed trimmer. Weed trimmers have a small motor that spins a short, flexible cord or hard plastic blade at high speeds to cut or break herbaceous species and small diameter woody plants. Avoid damaging desirable plants, especially young or thin-barked plants. Trunk damage from weed trimmers can girdle and kill young trees or promote attack by wood-boring insects. Place flexible

These photographs show the effectiveness of three weed control strategies in 15 by 15 foot plots of *Pittosporum tobira* 4 years after planting in Davis, California. Plants were drip irrigated, with no weed control except at the time of planting. The top plot received a single postplant preemergent herbicide (oryzalin) application to bare soil. In the center plot, redwood chip mulch (2–3 inches deep) was applied once after planting. Landscape fabric (woven polypropylene) was applied to the bottom plot and covered with 2–3 inches of redwood chips. All plots are surrounded by unmanaged weeds, but *Pittosporum* within the bottom plot are larger and weed-free in comparison with the other plots because of the superior weed control and greater moisture availability provided by landscape fabric covered with chips.

A covering layer of crushed rock can improve the appearance and protect landscape fabrics applied to control weeds.

Use a dandelion knife or other specialized hand tool to remove scattered weeds and their roots like this sowthistle while minimizing soil disturbance.

Cut weeds near the soil surface when soil is dry by using a sharp scuffle hoe.

metal or plastic shields around trunks before using a weed trimmer.

Flaming. Flaming is useful for controlling weeds in bare earth, along fence rows, in pavement cracks, and in certain mulched areas. Special hand-held flamers are available for weed control, usually fueled with propane or kerosene. Do not flame weeds to the point where they char and burn; only brief contact with high temperatures is needed to disrupt cells. Kill weeds by briefly touching the basal stem area of each plant with the tip of a hot flame. It is not necessary to flame the foliage, as all aboveground parts die if the basal stem is killed. Flaming is best done in early morning or late evening when winds are low and the flame is more easily visible.

Plants may wilt, change color, or appear unaffected soon after flaming.

Portable weed trimmers cut or break herbaceous species and small diameter woody weeds.

Use trunk guards to protect young trees and thin-barked species when using weed trimmers or mowers nearby.

Even if no change in the weeds is evident immediately, flaming causes plants to yellow and die within several days. Broadleaved annuals and seedlings are most susceptible to flaming; grasses or established perennials are only partially controlled and often regrow. Work at a slower pace when flaming grasses because their growing points are somewhat protected slightly below the soil surface.

When flaming these less susceptible plants, it can be more effective to treat them again about a week after the initial treatment. For best effectiveness, flame weeds when they are less than a few inches tall, especially the less susceptible species like grasses.

Use caution to avoid exposing young tree and shrub bark and foliage or structures to fire. Avoid flaming

Flaming kills weeds in bare soil, along fence rows, in pavement cracks, and in certain mulched areas like this, where weeds are being killed before reapplying mulch to an area where mulch is too thin.

mulches that may melt or burn, although flaming can be used with caution around coarse chip and bark mulch if the flame is only briefly held near the surface as recommended. Do not use flames in dry areas where fire is a hazard. Keep water or a fire extinguisher handy when using a flamer.

Biological Control. Many organisms feed on, parasitize, or kill weed seeds, seedlings, or established plants. These biological control organisms are present in most landscapes and include microorganisms, invertebrates, vertebrates, and even other plants. For example, microorganisms, seed-eating insects, birds, and other small animals feed on and destroy weed seeds remaining near the soil surface. Take advantage of these seed eaters by keeping seeds near the soil surface. Unless the purpose is to loosen compacted soils, avoid deeply turning soil, such as through spading, to prevent burying seeds where they cannot be attacked by seed predators and decomposers.

Introduced insects and diseases have been effective in controlling certain weeds, primarily aquatic and rangeland species (for instance, see Klamathweed beetle, Chapter 4). However, there are no biological control agents available for application to control most weeds in landscapes. Microbial herbicides (mycoherbicides) consisting of diseases that affect only specific weeds have been used in rice and other agricultural crops. There has been little or no research on controlling landscape weeds using these natural enemies.

Domesticated animals, including ducks, geese, and goats are used in some weed-control situations. Because of the difficulty in maintaining, protecting, and confining these animals, they have limited applications in landscapes. Goats are used to control weeds and create firebreaks, for example on steep hillsides that cannot be mowed or easily sprayed. Goats can also be used to clear weeds before planting new landscapes. They eat many different plants and prefer woodier species, including poison oak, bamboo, and blackberry. Goats may be rented and confined to a weedy location using portable fences or herd dogs. Goats are most commonly used by temporarily crowding them into a comparatively small area so they consume nearly all available vegetation before moving them to a new location. Provide goats with water and protection from dogs and vandals.

Chemical Control. Herbicides are a convenient and generally inexpensive way to control weeds in some landscape situations. They are frequently used in larger, institutional landscapes to save labor costs. Properly applied herbicides reduce competi-

tion from weeds and enhance desirable plant growth. They allow landscape plants to grow more vigorously and outcompete and eventually shade out weeds, especially during the establishment of new plantings.

A well-designed, mature landscape may require little or no ongoing use of herbicides. As a general rule, it is desirable to use nonchemical methods and to minimize herbicide use in landscapes. Repeated use of the same herbicide encourages buildup of species that tolerate certain herbicides. For example, common groundsel, bristly oxtongue, prickly lettuce, and bermudagrass tend to become more common where more susceptible species have been killed by repeated applications of dinitroaniline herbicides, such as trifluralin. In established landscapes, herbicides can damage desirable plants because of drift during application, runoff in irrigation or rainwater, volatilization and movement in air after application, or improper use. Examples of herbicide toxicity symptoms are illustrated in Chapter 6. Certain herbicides can persist in the soil and may injure species planted later or may damage nearby plants whose roots grow into treated soils. Furthermore, some herbicides may pose health and environmental risks.

Given the time and energy involved in training and supervising personnel, reading pesticide labels, deciding on the proper chemical, checking and calibrating sprayers, measuring out the proper amount of chemical to use, applying the herbicide, washing out equipment after use, and the potential problems associated with storage, clean-up, disposal, and record-keeping, herbicides often may not be the preferred method of weed control in landscapes. When used, herbicides should be integrated with the nonchemical methods described earlier. For exam-

ple, after spraying to kill weeds, apply mulch to reduce new weed growth or plant and care for desirable species to increase competition that reduces reinvading weeds.

Safe Use and Handling of Herbicides. If you decide to use herbicides, use them only where needed. Good landscape design, proper planting, and good management of desirable species can eliminate or at least reduce any need for herbicides. Persons who handle herbicides or other pesticides as part of their job must be trained and may need to be certified by the state.

Strictly follow the label instructions of any herbicide or other pesticide that you use; you are legally responsible. Avoid exposing other people and minimize exposing yourself when using pesticides. Wear proper protective equipment as indicated on the label; eye protective wear is required when handling or applying any pesticide in California. Avoid using pesticides or application methods that might injure nontarget organisms, property, or the environment.

Carefully read the label each time before you use a herbicide. Know how much to use, how and when to use it, how long it lasts, which ornamental plants or locations it is registered for, and what weeds it kills. Use accurate rates; overdosing even with "selective" herbicides may injure desirable plants. Keep children and pets out of treated areas until the herbicide is worked in, irrigated into the soil, or has dried. Do not use herbicide spray equipment to apply any other pesticides. Some herbicides (especially phenoxy herbicides) leave residues in spray tanks or hoses that can damage desirable plants. Purchase only the amount of herbicide needed. Store herbicides and other pesticides in their original labeled

TABLE 7-7

Checklist for Selecting the Appropriate Herbicide.

1. ALTERNATIVES
   Can some practical method other than herbicides be used?

2. SITUATION
   Is the weed problem at a planting site, new planting, or in an established landscape?

3. TIMING
   Use a preemergent herbicide if treating before weeds germinate, use a postemergent herbicide when treating after weeds emerge.

4. WEED SPECIES
   What weeds are causing the most problem? Most herbicides control only certain weed species. Monitor the site, list the weed species present, and compare the list to the label.

5. REGISTRATION
   Are the species or site(s) you plan to treat listed on the herbicide label? Read the label thoroughly before purchasing, mixing, or applying any herbicide to avoid injuring plants, people, or the environment.

6. RESIDUAL CONTROL
   What is the desired length of herbicide activity? Consult Table 7-8. Herbicides with a longer residual prevent weed germination for a longer period. They may also preclude desirable seedlings or young plants from being planted until the herbicide breaks down. What is the intended use for the site? Avoid using materials that may affect planned replantings.

7. SURROUNDINGS
   Could roots, green bark, or foliage of nearby trees and shrubs be affected if a nonselective herbicide is applied? A soil-applied, nonselective herbicide should generally not be applied in established landscapes. Avoid herbicide drift.

8. APPLICATION EQUIPMENT
   Do you have the necessary application equipment to apply the herbicide correctly? Some herbicides are available only as granular or wettable powder formulations and require special application equipment.

9. CALIBRATION
   Can you accurately measure and apply the correct amount of that herbicide? It is easier to measure certain formulations (such as granulars). Proper calibration is essential for safe and effective herbicide use.

10. ACTIVATION REQUIREMENTS
    Must the material be watered or mechanically incorporated into the soil?

11. EXPENSE
    How do costs compare? Certain formulations are usually less expensive than others; for example, wettable powders generally cost less than granulars.

container in a **locked** cabinet out of the reach of children and pets. Store herbicides separately from food, seeds, fertilizers, and other pesticides such as insecticides. Consult Table 7-7 or the local Cooperative Extension office for help in selecting the proper herbicide for your situation. See also Chapter 2 and *Residential, Industrial, and Institutional Pest Control, The Safe and Effective Use of Pesticides,* and other publications listed in References.

Types of Herbicides. Herbicides are classified according to when they are applied relative to plant growth, how they control weeds, and the method of formulation. *Fumigants* are applied to soil before planting the landscape to kill weeds such as yellow nutsedge, seeds, nematodes, and soilborne disease-causing organisms. Certain weeds may not be killed by fumigants, such as seeds of sweet clover. Roots of nearby desirable plants can be injured by fumigants and beneficial soil organisms may be killed. Solarization is an alternative to soil fumigation in certain circumstances.

Preemergence herbicides kill germinating weeds for several weeks or months after application. They must be applied before weed seeds germinate. Preemergence herbicides generally do not kill established weeds and are relatively safe for application around existing landscapes. However, some preemergence herbicides can retard the root growth of established plants, especially when plants are young. Because some materials are persistent (see Table 7-8), they may affect new plantings for up to a year or more after application.

Some herbicides must be mechanically worked into the soil to place them at the proper location to control weeds. Others may be placed on the surface and followed with sprinkler irrigation or rainfall.

Postemergence herbicides are applied to already emerged weeds. Under some circumstances, they may cause some damage (phytotoxicity) to established desirable plants. *Contact* postemergence herbicides usually kill only those green plant parts on which spray is deposited, so thorough coverage is important for good control. For example, saturated fatty acids, such as Sharpshooter, are effective against many weeds. These soaplike herbicides kill many young plants (including desirable species) on contact.

TABLE 7-8

Approximate Residual Control Provided by Some Preemergent Herbicides.[a]

HERBICIDE	APPROXIMATE PERSISTENCE IN MONTHS ON SUSCEPTIBLE WEED SPECIES
Benefin	1 to 2
Bensulide	8 to 10
DCPA	2 to 4
EPTC	1 to 2
Napropamide	2 to 8
Oryzalin	6 to 8
Oxadiazon[b]	4 to 6
Oxyflurofen[b] + oryzalin	4 to 8
Pendimethalin	6 to 8

a. Actual persistence is influenced by many factors, including soil, irrigation, rainfall, and weather.
b. These materials can be deactivated by cultivation.

Translocated (systemic) herbicides are taken up by green parts of the plant and are transported to roots and growing tips, so it may not be necessary to spray all of the plant to kill it. The principal advantage of translocated herbicides is that they can control perennial weeds. For best control, perennial weeds should be growing vigorously and have an abundance of mature leaves when they are sprayed. Depending on the season and stage of plant growth, the effect of some translocated herbicides may not be apparent until some time well after they are applied. For example, the effect of glyphosate (Roundup) may not be apparent until 2 or 3 weeks after application.

Microbial herbicides or mycoherbicides are also being developed for weed control. These are microscopic living organisms such as fungi or nematodes that kill certain plants. For example, fungus species are registered to control sickle pod and joint vetch. Mycoherbicides are relatively specific to certain weed species and have very low or no toxicity to animals and other plants; however, none are currently available for use in landscapes.

Selectivity. Some herbicides are *nonselective*; they can kill both weeds and desirable plants that are sprayed. Nonselective herbicides, such as glyphosate, are used where there are no desirable plants nearby or under certain circumstances where they can be applied selectively so that the material contacts only weeds and not the green bark or foliage of desirable plants. Do not apply nonselective contact herbicides around desirable landscapes unless you can apply them very carefully, such as with special equipment like a wick, wiper, or low-pressure applicator. Landscape plants may be damaged by direct spraying or from herbicides that reach plants through drift, volatilization after application, or by contacting roots in treated soils.

Selective herbicides kill only certain types of plants and can be used around some desirable plants as directed on the label. For example, sethoxydin or fluazifop can be used as directed to selectively control most annual grasses and bermudagrass without injury to trees or shrubs. Phenoxy herbicides like MCPA or 2,4-D are used in lawns because they kill broadleaf weeds but not grasses when used as directed. However, phenoxy herbicides can injure nearby trees and shrubs if the material drifts onto leaves or volatilizes after application and is moved by air.

Herbicides are available in different formulations, which may be appropriate for different situations or require different types of application equipment. Common formulations are granules that are typically applied dry then watered in and wettable powders, flowables, and emulsifiable concentrates, which are mixed with water and sprayed on.

TOLERANCE LEVELS AND MONITORING

One of the most important concepts underlying integrated pest management is that some level of weed infestation can be tolerated. Furthermore, it is rarely if ever possible to completely and permanently eliminate all weeds from landscapes. The landscape manager must determine what level is tolerable in each situation. For example, growth of young landscape plants can be greatly diminished by competition from weeds near trunks, so weeds should be well controlled in this situation. In older plantings, weed impact on plant vigor may be minimal, but there can be diminished aesthetic quality. Aesthetic impacts vary depending on the observer and the visibility of the location. Weeds under roses in a home garden or in front of City Hall are more bothersome than in less-used areas. People may disagree on what species are weeds and where and at what densities they are bothersome.

Inspect landscapes regularly for weeds to help you decide when and where weeds are a problem. Maintain

Monitor weeds among widely spaced plants or in mulched beds or turf by walking a straight line or transect through the landscape and recording the plant or substrate at the tip of your toe after each step.

careful records so that troublesome weed species can be controlled before they spread too much. Try to identify summer or winter annual species in the spring and fall when weeds germinate and are in their easier-to-control seedling stage. Establish tolerance levels by considering whether the species and abundance of weeds in an area are tolerable and when and where control is needed. Assess the potential of weeds to reproduce, spread, and cause problems. Perennial weeds should be controlled at lower thresholds than annual weeds, because they are more difficult to control.

Maintain written records of monitoring information, including species of weeds, age (seedling or established), location, density, when weeds occurred, what action you took, and the approximate size of any area treated. Weed species and their abundance tend to change in response to your management actions as well as seasonally. Written records allow you to determine whether particular weed species are increasing, decreasing, or remaining about the same from year to year or after control actions have been taken.

Landscape Maps. One monitoring method uses a landscape map. Draw a sketch of the landscape area and mark the location of landscape plants, mulch, bare soil, and other ground coverings at that location. Identify individual large plants or groups of smaller plants. You can refer to any detailed monitoring information corresponding to these areas on a separate sheet of paper. Survey the landscape periodically (such as every fall and spring and before and after control actions) and use a copy of the map to record the location, date, and severity of any weed problems. You can employ a qualitative rating of weed severity for each area as in Figure 7-2. For example, rate each different landscape area from 1 to 5, where 1 means very few weeds and 5 means a very heavy infestation. For greater detail, you can use the transect count method and assign quantitative values to these weed ratings.

Transect Counts. This monitoring method involves counting weeds at periodic intervals along a straight line or transect. Tie a stake or pole on each end of a cord or rope of appropriate length for the size of your landscape area. A suggested length is about one-half or one-quarter as long as the area you intend to sample. Mark the line with paint, tape, or a permanent marker at regular intervals, such as every 1 or 2 feet. You can also use a tape measure and evaluate the area at 1- or 2-foot intervals. Adjust the length of your cord, size of your sampling area, and number of samples to the time available for monitoring each landscape. Stake the cord in a straight line running through your landscape. Be sure to include all the different areas of your landscape to get a representative sample. Try to sample in approximately the same area or areas on each date that you monitor at that location, so that you can compare your results among sample dates.

Record the date, the species (weed or desirable landscape plant) or lack of vegetation (bare soil or mulch) and the age (seedling or established) of each plant touched by or underneath the mark on the cord. Percent cover of weeds is then determined by dividing the number of points with weeds by the total number of sample points and multiplying by 100. Another method for more widely spaced plants, mulched beds, or turf is to walk through the landscape and record the plant or substrate at the tip of your toe after each step or set number of steps. You may want to relocate your cord and take additional transect counts, especially if the sample area is large or the species counted are quite variable. Figure 7-3 is an example of a form for recording this monitoring information. You can use both a landscape map and transect method of monitoring weeds at the same location until you become experienced enough at estimating weed cover that you can dispense with actual counts. It may be best to put weed counts and notes on the back of the landscape map. Use a new copy of the map on each monitoring date.

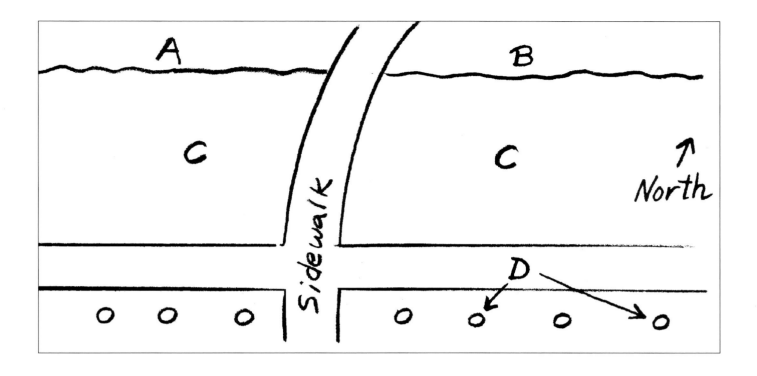

DATE 10 April 93   LANDSCAPE MONITORED BY   Jane Doe

LOCATION   400 Main St., City Hall

Weed Infestation Level Ratings:

| 1 = very light, less than 1% weed cover | 2 = light, 1–2% weeds | 3 = moderate, 3–4% weeds | 4 = heavy, 5–10% weeds | 5 = very heavy, more than 10% weeds |

Landscape Area	Weed Infestation Level	Management Actions Planned or Comments
A. Roses	2	Scattered annual weeds, hoe then apply more mulch
B. Roses	1	Apply more organic mulch
C. Turf	2	Dethatch, aerate, fertilize, overseed.
D. Young trees	5	Remove and maintain turf 2 feet back from trunks

Notes:
       Monitor again in May after completing control actions.

Figure 7-2. Landscape map method of recording weed infestations. Use a copy of your original map and record the above information each time you monitor as discussed in the text. Insects, diseases, or inadequate cultural care can also be recorded using landscape maps to document when and where these problems occurred.

DATE <u>13 Aug 93</u>   LANDSCAPE MONITORED BY <u>Joe Doe</u>

LOCATION <u>Community Park, Northeast shrub bed</u>

SAMPLE NO.	SUBSTRATE (SOIL, MULCH, ETC.) OR PLANT SPECIES	PLANT AGE (SEEDLING/ESTABLISHED) OR COMMENTS (e.g., CONTROL TAKEN)
1.	Rhaphiolepis	Mature Shrubs
2.	Mulch	
3.	Mulch	Mulch decomposing
4.	Spurge	
5.	Rhaphiolepis	
6.	Mulch	
7.	Euonymus	
8.	Mulch	
9.	Spurge	
10.	Euonymus	

NOTES: Low-growing spurge under mature shrubs is not very visible, tolerate or hand pull before seed production. Apply more mulch.

Total number of samples taken <u>10</u>

	Number	Percent[a]
Samples with desirable plants:	4	40
Samples with weeds:	2	20
Samples with bare soil, mulch, or other:	4	40

a. Percent is number of samples in that category, divided by total number of samples, multiplied times 100.

Figure 7-3. Keep records of your transect count weed monitoring using a form like this. An actual sampling program and record-keeping form should include more than ten samples.

TYPES OF WEEDS

Weed species are grouped according to their life cycle as annuals, biennials, or perennials. Annual plants begin each growing season as seeds and complete their life cycle in one year, often producing great quantities of seed before they die. Annual weeds are classified as summer annuals or winter annuals, depending on when they most commonly grow. Summer annuals germinate in the spring or early summer. They flower and produce seed in the fall before dying in the winter. Major species of summer annuals include crabgrass, pigweed, spotted spurge, and purslane. Winter annuals normally germinate in the fall, grow during the winter, flower and produce seed in the spring, and die by early summer. Annual bluegrass, annual ryegrass, sowthistle, and common groundsel are examples of winter annual weeds. In coastal areas with a moderate climate, winter annuals may germinate whenever water is present. Certain annuals such as annual bluegrass or cheeseweed can behave as biennials or short-lived perennials in areas of California with mild weather. Most annuals can be controlled in mature landscape plantings by an integrated program of mulching, hoeing, and hand-weeding or spot application of a herbicide.

Biennial weeds complete their life cycle in two growing seasons. They produce vegetative parts in the first growing season and flowers and seeds during the second year. Bristly oxtongue and milk thistle are biennials.

Perennial plants can live for three years or longer. Perennials may be woody, such as trees and shrubs, or they may be herbaceous. The aboveground portion of herbaceous perennials may die back during the winter then regrow during the spring or early summer from underground roots, tubers, or rhizomes (underground stems). Although they produce seeds, many of the weedy perennial species spread and reproduce primarily by vegetative parts, such as stolons (stems that creep along the ground) or rhizomes (see Figure 7-4). For example, a single tuber of yellow nutsedge can grow and reproduce so that hundreds of plants and several thousand tubers are produced within a year.

Common perennial weeds are kikuyugrass, bermudagrass, field bindweed, oxalis, blackberry, bamboo, poison oak, and nutsedges. Because of their underground food reserves, established perennials are usually more difficult to control than annual weeds. Preventing establishment of perennials should be an

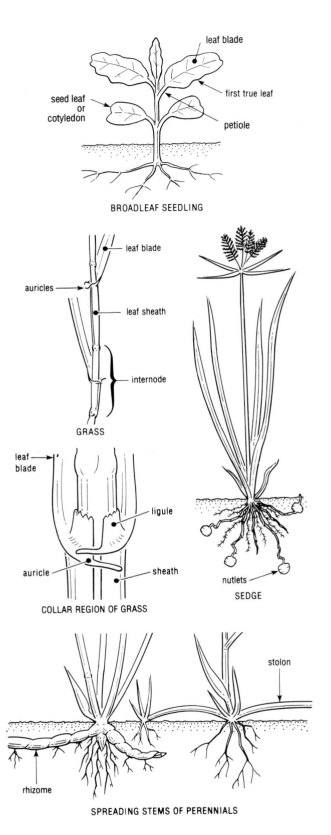

leaf blade

seed leaf
or
cotyledon

first true leaf

petiole

BROADLEAF SEEDLING

leaf blade

auricles

leaf sheath

internode

GRASS

leaf
blade

ligule

auricle

sheath

COLLAR REGION OF GRASS

nutlets

SEDGE

stolon

rhizome

SPREADING STEMS OF PERENNIALS

Figure 7-4. Vegetative parts of weeds and terms used in identification.

important focus of your weed management program.

WEED IDENTIFICATION

Learn the identity of plants in the landscape and determine which ones are weeds and what special problems are associated with their management. For example, some species spread aggressively and are difficult to control once they mature beyond the four- or five-leaf stage. Learn about the life cycle of particular weeds and consider available controls so you can choose effective and appropriate management methods should control action be warranted.

Proper species identification is essential if you use herbicides. Most herbicides do not control all species, so if weeds are not identified accurately, herbicide applications may be ineffective and wasteful. Some common troublesome weeds in landscapes are described below.

To obtain help in weed identification, contact the Cooperative Extension or Agricultural Commissioner's office in your county, a certified nurseryperson, or botanical garden. Consult References for weed identification publications.

Some troublesome or common weed species infesting woody landscapes are discussed here. Vegetative plant parts used in identifying weeds are illustrated in Figure 7-4.

Large crabgrass resembles bermudagrass, but it is an annual that grows from seed and does not spread from stolons or rhizomes. Branches of the flower head arise from two or more points along the stem.

Spotted spurge is named for the dark reddish area in the center of true leaves, visible in this seedling.

ANNUAL WEEDS

Large Crabgrass and Smooth Crabgrass
Digitaria spp.

Large or hairy crabgrass, *Digitaria sanguinalis,* commonly called crabgrass, is a pale green summer annual. It usually has many branches at the base and spreads from roots growing at swollen joints in the stem. Leaves are 2 to 5 inches long. Smooth crabgrass, *D. ischaemum,* is similar to large crabgrass but it is smaller and is not hairy. The bract covering the grain is brownish black compared with pale yellow in large crabgrass. Seeds begin germinating about February or March, when soil at 1 to 2 inches deep is 50° to 55° F for 3 to 7 days. Crabgrass inflorescences look like the long claws of a bird. Crabgrass thrives under hot conditions, often where there is overirrigation.

Manage crabgrass with a regular program of hand-weeding and cultivation or mulching. Vigilance is required as plants are difficult to remove once they grow and develop an extensive root system. Crabgrass seed is only partially controlled with solarization.

Petty Spurge
Euphorbia peplus
and Spotted Spurge
Euphorbia maculata

Petty spurge is a smooth, erect, yellow-green plant up to 7 inches tall. A whitish, reportedly toxic fluid exudes when stems are broken. Lower leaves are up to 1 inch long, ovate or round, and stalkless. Upper leaves are roundish, gently tapered toward the stem, and stalked. All leaves are somewhat crinkled. The greenish yellow flowers are very small, not showy. Fruit are a round, sharply three-angled capsule. Petty spurge prefers moist, shady locations and often occurs among shrubs and flower beds.

Spotted spurge is a widely spreading, many-branched, low-growing, mat-forming summer annual. Seed leaves are oval, about one and one-half to two times as long as wide, with a rounded tip and smooth margins. Seed leaves are bluish green, powdery or mealy on the upper surface, and have a reddish tinge underneath. Leaves on mature plants grow oppositely on short stalks. Spotted spurge has milky, sticky sap and small, inconspicuous flowers. The plant is named for the dark, reddish spots often found in the middle of the leaves. Seeds germinate around February or March. Each plant can produce 600 to 3,500 seeds, which can survive for up to 12 years.

Spotted spurge is tolerant to some common herbicides, so it often thrives in areas of mostly bare soil. It sprouts in cracks in pavement, along edges, and in bare spots where it survives even very close mowing. It is easy to pull; grasp a mat of stems and the whole plant, including its short roots, will be removed. Mulch to prevent seedling growth or apply a pre-emergent herbicide where infestations are heavy. Because it has a low-growing habit, some landscape managers tolerate more spurge growing under woody plants in comparison with more visible weed species, which can grow up through or over shrubs. However, spurge is capable of setting seed within a few weeks of emergence, and plants should be monitored regularly and removed before they produce seed.

Mature spotted spurge is low growing. Leaves grow opposite on short stalks, are finely toothed on the margin, and are covered with soft hairs.

PERENNIAL WEEDS

Bamboo

Bamboos, *Bambusa* spp. and others, are evergreen grasses that grow as woody perennials. Bamboo has stems divided into sections by obvious joints and is used as a desirable landscape plant. It reproduces via rhizomes. Some running species tend to spread beyond where they are desired unless they are regularly trimmed and their root zone is confined. Use only clumping bamboo species. If running species are used, provide a barrier to spreading bamboo rhizomes by planting only in areas bordered by pavement or fences that extend beneath the soil. Install headers (narrow concrete, wood, or metal barriers extending 8 inches or more below the soil surface) to help confine rhizomes.

Eliminate established clumps of bamboo or reduce their spread by

This running *Phyllostachys* species of bamboo is sprouting new plants from rhizomes that spread from the main clump into turf and shrubs.

cutting back aboveground parts to near the ground, digging up and removing underground parts, applying a registered herbicide to foliage or freshly cut stumps, or a combination of these methods. Persistent effort and repeated control action against any regrowth is needed to eventually provide good control.

Bermudagrass
Cynodon dactylon

Mature bermudagrass plants form a dense mat with spreading, branching stolons and rhizomes. Stems grow 4 to 18 inches tall. Bermudagrass has a conspicuous ring or fringe of short, whitish hairs at the base of each blade. Plants produce inflorescences consisting of three to seven slender spikes radiating from one point and reproduce from seeds as well as rhizomes and stolons.

Bermudagrass is used as a hardy turf species that is well adapted to drought and alkaline soils. It is common along roadsides, sidewalks, and in vacant urban lots, but is generally absent from valley and foothill slopes that are dry during the summer. Bermudagrass turns brown during the winter in cold areas and does not thrive in dense shade.

With persistant effort, bermudagrass can be controlled by consistently removing plants as they emerge and by preventing additional seeds and stems from being introduced. Roots are readily killed when turned to the sun so repeated cultivation can provide control; do not irrigate for about a week after cultivation to improve control. Although mulch can reduce growth, bermudagrass can grow through most types of mulch.

Proper solarization controls bermudagrass in warmer areas of California, but carry out the solarization for at least 6 weeks during the hottest time of the summer. Closely mow (to about ½ inch) bermudagrass and rake the soil free of cuttings and trash before irrigating and tarping. Alternatively, rototill then irrigate soil before tarping it. Do not rototill deeper than 4 inches, as deeper cultivation may bury rhizomes too deeply to be effectively controlled.

Glyphosate, fluazifop-butyl, or sethoxydim provide control if applied when bermudagrass has plenty of moisture and is growing actively, such as during blooming or soon after seed heads form. Follow all label instructions and prevent the herbicide from contacting desirable plants. Once you have removed bermudagrass, avoid reinfestation with infested soil, mulch, sod, compost, or contaminated mowers and tools.

Blackberries
Rubus spp.

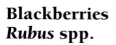

Blackberries have long, trailing, somewhat woody canes. Leaves are up to several inches wide and are compound with 3 to 5 leaflets. The blackberry species found in California produce white to reddish flowers and have thorny stems and leaves. The juicy, tasty, roundish, red to shiny black fruit are enjoyed by people and wildlife. Blackberry hedges can provide an effective barrier to restrict access by people and pets.

Keep desired hedges well pruned. Kill established clumps by repeatedly pruning stems until root reserves are exhausted. Alternatively, apply a herbicide as registered to foliage at bloom stage, before berries form.

Bermudagrass spreads as a mat of prostrate stolons and rhizomes. The slender spikes of flower heads usually branch from the same point on the stem.

Field Bindweed
Convolvulus arvensis

Mature field bindweed or perennial morningglory plants have slender, twining stems up to 5 feet long. Leaves vary greatly in shape, but are often rounded with a blunt tip and shaped like an arrow point. The white, pink, or reddish funnel-shaped flowers open only on sunny mornings. Seed pods are roundish and light brown. Plants produce abundant seed, which can remain dormant in the soil for many years. Field bindweed has an extensive root system growing to a depth of 10 feet or more and spreading several feet wide. Plants often occur in heavy soils, in hardpan or crusty soils, and less often in sandy soils.

Field bindweed can be easily controlled with cultivation while it is a seedling, before young plants develop beyond the five-leaf stage. Once plants begin to mature they are very difficult to control. Plants develop an

Blackberry leaflets grow in clusters of 3 to 5 on long, thorny, somewhat woody canes that can spread over shrubs like this flowering *Rhaphiolepis*.

Field bindweed seed leaves are nearly square with an indented tip. Petioles have a grooved upper surface. Cultivate seedlings before they mature beyond about 5 leaves; mature plants are very difficult to control.

This mature field bindweed infesting juniper has slender twining stems and white to reddish funnel-shaped flowers that open on sunny mornings.

extensive root system, which can develop into more new plants. Repeated cultivation at 3-week intervals for more than one year can provide control, but lack of persistence in cultivation only spreads the weed as it sprouts from severed pieces of root. Solarization for 6 to 9 weeks reduces, but does not eliminate, field bindweed. Rototill no deeper than 4 inches, then smooth and irrigate the soil well before tarping it. A systemic herbicide or soil fumigant may be necessary to provide good control. Glyphosate is effective if applied when bindweed is growing vigorously and has only a few flowers, before full bloom. Plants must be well irrigated and dust free for the maximum effect. Multiple treatments are often necessary to control a well-established infestation.

This young nutsedge resembles grass, but its leaves are thicker and stiffer than most grasses. Nutsedge leaves are V-shaped in cross section and grow from the base in sets of three; grass leaves are opposite in sets of two.

Nutsedges
Cyperus spp.

Nutsedges resemble grasses, but have solid stems that are triangular in cross section and leaves that usually radiate out in three directions from the stem. True grasses have hollow, round stems. Yellow nutsedge or yellow nutgrass, *Cyperus esculentus,* and purple nutsedge, *C. rotundus,* are the two most common species. Yellow nutsedge has tan or yellowish flowers and light brown seeds. Purple nutsedge has purplish flowers and blackish brown seeds. Nutsedges spread primarily from tubers or "nutlets" that form on rhizomes that grow as deep as 8 to 12 inches below the soil surface. Yellow nutsedge tubers are formed at the ends of rhizomes and have an almond taste when eaten. Purple nutsedge tubers are formed like beads on a chain and have a bitter taste. Tubers can remain viable for several years, even in dry soil.

Nutsedges are common weeds in the coastal valleys, Central Valley, and southern areas of California. They thrive in waterlogged soil, indicating that drainage is poor, irrigation is too frequent, or sprinklers are leaky. Irrigate properly, maintain irrigation equipment, and provide for good drainage.

Cultivate or hand-weed when plants are young. Control individual plants before they produce 5 or 6 leaves or when they are less than 6 inches tall; older, taller plants produce tubers from which they can resprout. Planting competing species that grow tall quickly can reduce the establishment of yellow nutsedge because it does not compete well in shade. Purple nutsedge can be controlled with repeated summer tillage of dry soil because its tubers are readily killed by drying. Tubers are not killed if soil is moist or has large clods. Mulching, solarization, or using the herbicides glyphosate or MSMA can reduce nutsedge populations somewhat, but generally do not provide good control.

Each nutsedge plant spreads to form a dense clump. Three long, leaflike bracts develop at the base of each flower head.

Bermuda Buttercup and Creeping Woodsorrel
Oxalis spp.

Bermuda buttercup or buttercup oxalis, *Oxalis pes-caprae*, and creeping woodsorrel, *O. corniculata*, have compound leaves, each consisting of three heart-shaped leaflets resembling clover leaves. Attractive flowers occur singly or in clusters on the ends of slender leaf stalks; each flower has 5 yellow petals. When seeds mature, pods open explosively, often spreading seeds 10 feet or more. *Oxalis* prefers shady situations, and Bermuda buttercup is sometimes grown as an ornamental.

Hand-pull young *Oxalis* plants before flowers form. Use shallow cultivation to kill young seedlings. A woven type of fabric mulch or other thick mulching material prevents most growth; *Oxalis* growing in the mulch can be hand-pulled. Solarization provides partial control of creeping woodsorrel. Application of a herbicide such as glyphosate may be needed to eliminate well-established creeping woodsorrel because of its tenacious root system.

Poison Oak
Toxicodendron toxicarium

Poison oak is an erect, deciduous shrub or vine that often climbs trees and shrubs. Poison oak leaves are green or light red in the spring, glossy green in late spring and summer, and yellow or red in the fall. Leaves are clusters of three leaflets, each 1 to 4 inches long and resembling an individual leaf. The most terminal or central leaflet has a petiole or stem; the side leaflets have no distinct stem. The leaves of true oaks

Bermuda buttercup flowers are attractive, but some people consider them a nuisance when they spread into shrubs like this juniper.

Oxalis spp., such as this purple leaf variety of creeping woodsorrel, have alternate, compound leaves, each consisting of three heart-shaped leaflets resembling clover. The large green leaves are *Rhaphiolepis*, which the creeping woodsorrel has invaded.

Poison oak has small, whitish flowers. Leaves are clusters of three leaflets, each 1 to 4 inches long and resembling an individual leaf. The most terminal leaflet has a stem; the side leaflets have no distinct stem.

grow singly, and each leaf has a distinct petiole.

Clusters of small white flowers are produced in the spring. These develop into white, waxy berries that are important food for birds and are eaten by other wildlife such as deer and rabbits. Poison oak usually occurs in disturbed areas, often along fence rows and under utility wires and trees where birds roost and excrete seeds.

Contact with poison oak or its oil, which rubs off onto clothing or pets, causes many people to develop a very bothersome skin rash. Poison oak in high-use areas warrants aggressive control action because of its severe skin hazard. However, because it can be an important wildlife food and control of established plants is difficult, consider tolerating poison oak in natural areas and locations not frequented by people or pets. Infested areas can be posted with a warning sign and description of the plant to educate people. Posted infestations can be used to restrict access to sites.

Goats can be very effective in reducing poison oak if they are confined in infested areas and are excluded from landscapes to prevent them from feeding on desirable plants. Physical removal can effectively control a few plants. Carefully cut and remove all top growth, then grub or dig out roots to a depth of 8 to 10 inches and remove horizontal runners. Wear tightly woven protective clothing, including washable cotton gloves worn over plastic gloves. Wash tools, rinse them in alcohol, then oil and dry tools to prevent rust. Separately launder all clothing thoroughly and shower immediately after working around poison oak; use a soap recommended for washing away poison oak. Do not burn poison oak; the smoke can be severely injurious if inhaled.

Poison oak can be controlled with triclopyr or glyphosate applied as a foliar spray to actively growing plants, but do not allow spray to contact desirable plants. Full foliage to flowering is the optimal time for a foliar spray; spraying anytime before leaves change color in the fall can be effective. However, the soil must be moist or control will be poor. Follow all label directions carefully.

Herbicides, grubbing, or a combination of chemical and physical control may be needed more than once on well-established clumps of poison oak. Once an area has been cleared of poison oak, plant and provide proper care to desirable species to exclude reinfestation. See *Poison Oak Control in the Home Yard* (UC Leaflet 2573) for further control measures.

Mistletoes
Phoradendron spp.

Large-leaf mistletoes are evergreen perennial plants that grow on woody plants, extracting moisture and nutrients from their host. *Phoradendron macrophyllum* infects many landscape plants, especially ash, but also alder, birch, black walnut, box elder, California buckeye, cottonwood, fruit and nut trees, locust, oak, and maple. *Phoradendron villosum* attacks only oaks. European mistletoe, *Viscum album*, resembles *P. macrophyllum*. *V. album* in the U.S. occurs only in Sonoma County, California, primarily on alder, apple, black locust, cottonwood, and maple. Dwarf mistletoes, *Arceuthobium* spp., attack primarily conifers in forests and are usually not a problem in landscape situations.

An otherwise healthy tree can tolerate a few mistletoes, but individual branches may be killed. Host plants can suffer reduced vigor or become stunted, especially if they are stressed by other problems such as drought or disease.

Large-leaf mistletoes have green stems and leaves. Leaves are thick and nearly oval. Plants often develop

Large-leaf mistletoes are evergreen. Roundish clumps of mistletoe infesting deciduous trees are most apparent during the host plant's dormant season.

Large-leaf mistletoe leaves are thick and nearly oval. The small, sticky, orangish to white berries are spread by birds or on tree-trimming equipment.

a roundish form up to 2 feet or more in diameter. Mistletoe seeds are dispersed by birds such as cedar waxwings, which feed on the plant's small, sticky, white to orangish berries and excrete the indigestible seeds. They also spread by sticking to birds' feet and beaks or on equipment people use to trim trees.

Some tree species appear resistant to mistletoe. Although resistance may vary among locations, resistant species should be planted in problem areas. Chinese pistache, crape myrtle, eucalyptus, ginkgo, golden rain tree, liquidambar, persimmon, sycamore, and conifers are rarely infested. Consider replacing severely infested trees with resistant species, although there is no guarantee that mistletoe could

not become a pest of these species in some locations.

The most effective control is to prune out infested branches as soon as mistletoe appears. Cut infected limbs 1 foot or more below the point of mistletoe attachment. Make pruning cuts properly, near crotches but leaving the branch collar intact (Figure 3-8).

Mistletoe infesting a main branch or trunk where it cannot be pruned may be controlled by cutting off the mistletoe flush with the limb or trunk of its host. Wrap the attachment point with several layers of wide, black polyethylene or landscape fabric. Tie it with twine or flexible tape to exclude light. Large-leaf mistletoes require light and die within a few

years after they are cut and wrapped. It may be necessary to repeat this treatment, especially if the plastic becomes detached. If mistletoe is cut but not covered, it grows back, but cutting is better than just leaving it alone because cutting can reduce the spread of mistletoe and may reduce damage to its host.

The plant growth regulator ethephon may be used as directed on the label to control mistletoe on some species of severely infested trees. However, spraying often only provides temporary control and mistletoe may soon regrow at the same point. Follow all label precautions carefully.

CHAPTER EIGHT

Nematodes

N EMATODES are tiny (usually microscopic) roundworms that feed on a wide diversity of organisms. Many species are free-living in soil or water and feed on bacteria and fungi. Others feed on plants or parasitize humans and animals (for example, hookworms, pinworms, heart-worms). Some nematodes are beneficial because they kill pest nematodes or insects. For example, nematodes in the genus *Monochamus* feed on other nematodes, and insect-parasitic species of *Heterorhabditis* and *Steinernema* nematodes can be purchased and applied to control certain insects that feed on roots or bore in wood.

Nematode species that damage plants may feed on or in roots, tubers, bulbs, leaves, or stems. With the exception of the pinewood nematode, which feeds inside branches and trunks, most species that are pests of woody plants feed on roots. These include root knot nematodes, cyst nematodes, root lesion nematodes, and dagger, pin, ring, stunt, and citrus nematodes.

Damage

The extent to which nematodes damage woody landscape plants is not well known. Their microscopic size, hidden feeding habits, and sometimes subtle damage makes it difficult to diagnose nematode infestations. Much of the information presented here is extrapolated from what is known about woody agricultural crops. Nematodes affect woody crops primarily by damaging roots, thereby reducing fruit or nut yields and slowing plant growth. These effects may not be a serious concern in landscapes. Most nematodes that are pests of woody landscape plants feed on and prune roots or disrupt vascular tissue and inhibit the plant's ability to obtain water and nutrients. Damage usually results only from heavy populations on the parasitized roots. Nematode damage symptoms include stunted plant growth or yellow foliage that may drop a few weeks prematurely. Plant tip dieback may be visible on infected trees and shrubs that are not regularly pruned.

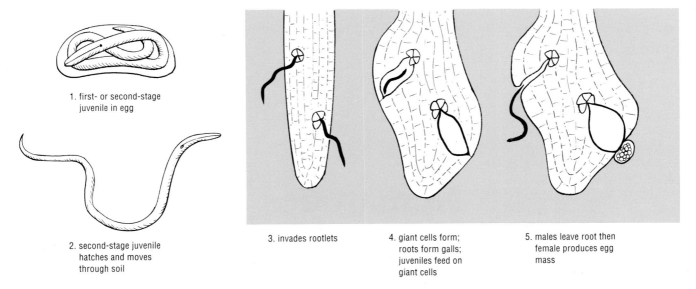

1. first- or second-stage
   juvenile in egg

2. second-stage juvenile
   hatches and moves
   through soil

3. invades rootlets

4. giant cells form;
   roots form galls;
   juveniles feed on
   giant cells

5. males leave root then
   female produces egg
   mass

Figure 8-1. Root knot nematodes spend most of their active life cycle in galls on roots. Second-stage juveniles invade new sites, usually near root tips, causing some root cells to grow into giant cells where the nematodes feed. As feeding continues, the plant produces a gall around the infected area.

Nematode feeding causes plant stress, but established woody plants are rarely killed by nematodes. However, if woody plants become heavily infected with nematodes, it may be difficult to grow some herbaceous and annual plants nearby because nematodes have become so prevalent in the soil.

Identification and Biology

Most plant-feeding nematodes are less than 1/20 inch long (about the thickness of a dime) and can be seen clearly only with a microscope. Pest species feed by inserting their body or spearlike or stylet mouth parts into plant tissue and consuming plant cell contents. Eggs are commonly laid in soil or in or near roots. Most nematode species develop through four juvenile stages and many species can develop through one generation in 3 to 6 weeks in warm, moist soil. In some, such as root knot nematodes, only adult males and second-stage juveniles are mobile in soil or roots (Figure 8-1); the other juvenile stages and adult females are immobile.

Nematodes require moist environments to feed and reproduce. During adverse conditions, such as dry soil, cold temperatures, or the lack of host plants, some species develop resistant stages. Resistant stages of cyst nematodes are typically eggs or first-stage juveniles within eggs, which become inactive and can survive for a year or more. Stem and bulb nematodes typically survive as second- or fourth-stage juveniles in a stage of arrested development that may last for several years, until conditions again become suitable for their growth.

Nematode infestations should be suspected whenever a general decline of a particular plant species is observed, including stunting or yellow leaves. Similar decline symptoms may be caused by root or vascular wilt diseases, insects that bore in wood or feed on roots, or a lack of proper cultural care, such as poor irrigation or fertilization practices. If no other causes for the unhealthy plant are obvious, try to remove soil from around some roots and examine them for signs of nematodes. Ease the roots out of the soil gently so that the smaller feeder roots are not broken off and can be examined. Signs include root galls or stubby, stunted, or proliferating roots. Roots that are darkened or have lesions and plants with fewer roots than normal can also indicate a nematode infestation.

Not all nematodes produce obvious symptoms on roots. To confirm a nematode infestation, collect roots from plants showing poor growth or portions of roots exhibiting symptoms; collect from several plants or several parts of one large plant. Seal these in a plastic bag along with a quart of soil collected from several locations in the root zone around affected plants. Soil can be dug with a shovel or collected using a soil sampling tube. Keep this material cool and moist and send it to a laboratory that can identify any nematodes present. Contact your County Cooperative Extension Office to locate a testing laboratory.

Root Knot Nematodes
Meloidogyne spp.

Root knot nematodes are the most commonly observed species attacking annual and perennial landscape plants. They are most commonly a pest in warm, sandy, irrigated soils. Woody landscape species occasionally stunted by root knot nematodes are listed in Table 8-1. Other exotic species may be attacked, but the host list is incomplete.

Root knot nematodes (Figure 8-1) cause galls or swellings on roots of many broadleaf plants, but some infected plants, especially annual grasses, may exhibit no galls. When roots infected with root knot nematodes are washed they may appear gnarled and restricted. Severely infected roots may become attacked by a variety of decay or disease organisms, including crown gall, wilt, and root rot.

Many common weeds also host root knot nematodes. One way to determine if soils are heavily infested with root knot nematodes is to dig up weeds growing around poor-growing landscape plants and examine their roots for infestation. Alternatively, you can plant several different species of quick-growing, susceptible annual plants underneath and around woody plants suspected of being infested; squash and tomatoes that are not resistant to nematodes (non-N or non-VFN) are good choices. Dig the plants up after they have grown for about 4 to 6 weeks in soil above 65°F. Wash or gently tap the soil from their roots, and examine the roots for swellings. Cut open any galls and use a hand lens to examine them for the presence of pinhead-sized, shiny white females that look like tiny pearls.

Beneficial nitrogen-fixing bacteria often form nodules on the roots of

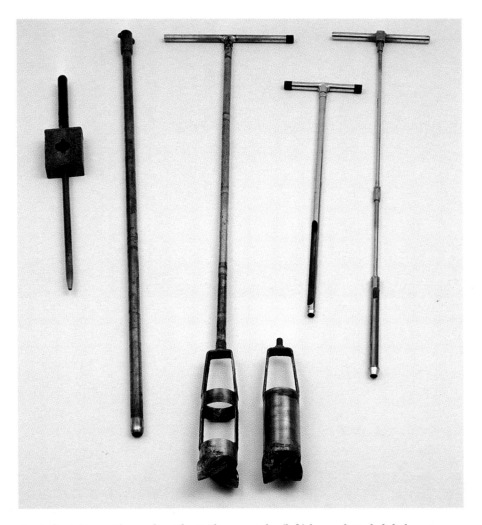

Tools for taking soil samples. The Veihmeyer tube (left) has a slotted slide hammer for driving the tube into the soil and removing it. Soil augers (center) are available with a variety of bits for different soil types. Oakfield soil tubes (right) are used for deeper sampling. These tools are useful for monitoring soil moisture and the Veihmeyer tube and soil augers are also suitable for sampling nematodes.

beans and other legumes, but these rub off roots easily, while galls caused by root knot nematodes are truly swellings on the roots. Also, a thumbnail can be pressed into a bacterial gall easily, but not into a root knot gall.

You can also confirm a root knot nematode infestation by collecting samples as described above and sending the material to a laboratory that can provide positive identification of the infesting species.

A heavy root knot nematode infestation has caused numerous galls. Beneficial nitrogen-fixing bacteria nodules also grow on some roots, but these rub off and a thumbnail can be pressed into them easily.

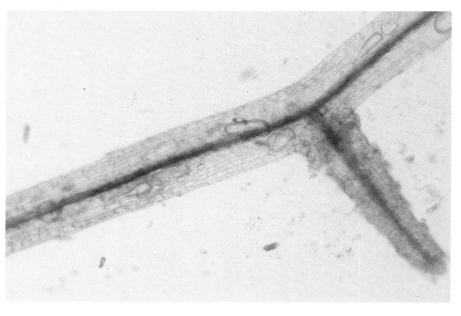

Adult root lesion nematodes are visible within this root.

Root Lesion Nematodes
Pratylenchus spp.

Damaging population levels of root lesion nematodes can occur on many plants (Table 8-1). In the early stages of infestation, a lack of small and large roots may be detectable. The lack of feeder roots and well-developed major roots can be seen if you remove soil around roots of healthy plants and compare these to roots from around unhealthy plants. On roses and some other hosts, infected plants are stunted, leaves are yellow, and roots are smaller and darker than on healthy plants.

Root lesion nematodes occasionally cause brown or black lesions to appear on roots. Lesions are usually apparent only on the larger roots of older trees, especially on walnut. Lesions, when present, become apparent when roots are scraped with a knife. However, apparent lesions can develop on walnut roots for other reasons unrelated to nematodes, for example if walnuts are given too much water.

Many plant species may be infected with high populations of root lesion nematodes without any evidence of necrosis (dead tissue) or lesions. A laboratory analysis of samples is the only sure method of diagnosing root lesion nematodes.

Dagger Nematodes
Xiphinema spp.

True firs (*Abies* spp.), grapes, and roses are reported to be damaged by dagger nematodes in California. Dagger nematodes may be a virus vector and can cause a sparseness of feeder roots, but this is difficult to recognize. Terminal galls can form on the

TABLE 8-1

Woody Landscape Plants Known or Suspected of Being Damaged by Nematodes in California.

HOST PLANT COMMON NAME	GENUS NAME	ROOT KNOT NEMATODES	ROOT LESION NEMATODES	RING NEMATODES	OTHER NEMATODES
Albizia	*Albizia*	•			
Alder	*Alnus*	•			
Almond	*Prunus*	•	•	•	
Apricot	*Prunus*	•	•	•	
Apple	*Malus*	•	•	•	
Azalea	*Rhododendron*				stunt nematode
Boxwood	*Buxus*	•			
Cactus	*Opuntia*	•			cyst nematode
Catalpa	*Catalpa*	•			
Cedar	*Cedrus*	•			pinewood nematode
Citrus	*Citrus*				citrus nematode
Euonymus	*Syzygium*	•			
Fir	*Abies*				dagger nematode
Grape	*Vitis*	•	•	•	citrus, dagger, and stubby root nematode
Hibiscus	*Hibiscus*	•			
Hydrangea	*Hydrangea*	•			
Juniper	*Juniperus*	•			
Larch	*Larix*				pinewood nematode
Lilac	*Syringa*				citrus nematode
Maidenhair	*Ginkgo*	•			
Mulberry	*Morus*	•			
Nectarine	*Prunus*	•	•	•	
Oak	*Quercus*	•			
Olive	*Olea*	•	•		citrus nematode
Palm	Several genera	•			
Peach	*Prunus*	•	•	•	
Persimmon	*Diospyros*				citrus nematode
Pine	*Pinus*				pinewood nematode
Pittosporum	*Pittosporum*	•			
Plum	*Prunus*	•	•		pin nematode
Poinsettia	*Euphorbia*	•			
Rose	*Rosa*	•	•		dagger nematode
Spruce	*Picea*				pinewood nematode
Tamarisk	*Tamarix*	•			
Walnut	*Juglans*		•	•	

roots of grapes, each with hundreds of dagger nematodes of the same species feeding on it. A laboratory analysis of soil surrounding affected roots is usually needed to confirm the presence of this pest, which mostly lives in soil and feeds from outside of roots.

Ring Nematode
Criconemella or *Criconemoides xenoplax*

Ring nematode is named for its annulated (ringed) body, which is visible under a microscope; most nematode species have a relatively smooth body. Ring nematode prunes the smallest roots on many woody plants. If extensive, this damage weakens trees and can predispose *Prunus* and occasionally *Malus* species to branch dieback and springtime death by bacterial canker disease.

Stunt Nematodes
Tylenchorhynchus spp.

Stunt nematodes cause roots and aboveground plant parts to grow slowly and be undersized. Azaleas are reportedly susceptible. Leaves may turn yellow, die back, or drop. Iron deficiency symptoms, primarily leaf yellowing, may be aggravated on infested plants.

Pinewood Nematode
Bursaphelenchus xylophilus

Pinewood nematode feeds in the vascular tissue of twigs, stems, and trunks. Pines are most seriously affected, but other conifers including cedar, larch, and spruce are also hosts. Branch dieback is the most common symptom in native pines infested with pinewood nematodes. Pinewood nematodes are widespread in exotic conifers, such as Japanese black pine, Japanese red pine, and Scotch pine, that have been introduced into the U.S. Infested pines are typically dead or dying, but it is uncertain whether nematodes are a major cause of this damage. The unhealthy trees in which they are found have typically been damaged from other problems, such as root disease or improper care, and the nematodes may be a secondary invader.

Pinewood nematodes are spread primarily by juveniles "hitchhiking" on adult roundheaded borers or longhorned beetles, including *Monochamus* spp. The beetles feed as larvae beneath bark and pupate in wood, then emerge from dead or dying trees as adults contaminated with nematodes. Before laying their eggs in unhealthy trees, adult beetles may fly to other pines to feed on foliage; nematodes can leave the beetles then and infect the new tree. If beetles feed on the foliage of healthy plants, the introduced nematodes may eventually contribute to the decline of that plant as they reproduce within the tree.

Pin Nematodes
Paratylenchus spp.

Several species of pin nematodes cause lesions and death of plum roots, resulting in poor plant growth. If good fruit yield is desired, avoid planting *Prunus* species in old orchard sites or former vineyards, unless the soil has been fumigated or kept bare for at least several years to reduce nematode populations. If trees are not performing as desired because of a nematode infestation, consider removing them and replanting with trees from another genus. See *Prune Orchard Management* (UC Publication 3269) and *Peaches, Plums, and Nectarines: Growing and Handling for Fresh Market* (UC Publication 3331) for more information.

Citrus Nematode
Tylenchulus semipenetrans

A citrus nematode infestation can reduce fruit size and number on infested host plants (Table 8-1). Serious infestations cause undersized leaves and twig dieback. Provide trees with proper cultural care so that they are better able to tolerate nematode feeding. Purchase trees from a nursery that sells nematode-free plants. Use resistant rootstock, especially when replanting in soil known to be nematode-infested. Trifoliate orange and certain other rootstocks are resistant to citrus nematode. Citrus nematode biology and management is detailed in *Integrated Pest Management for Citrus* (UC Publication 3303).

MANAGEMENT OF NEMATODES

Prevention, sanitation, and crop rotation where practical are the most important nematode management strategies. Avoid introducing nematode-infested plants into landscapes by using only good-quality plants obtained from a reliable supplier (see Table 3-1). Consider replacing severely infected plants; replant with species or varieties more tolerant of the specific nematodes present. Do not plant susceptible species in locations where nematodes have previously been a problem; for example, do not replant the same plant genera into the old site. Alternatively, reduce nematode populations greatly by keeping soil free of all plants for 4 years or more or treat the soil before replanting as discussed below. Remove and dispose of dead and dying conifers, which host pinewood nematodes and the wood-boring beetles that spread them.

Provide proper cultural care so that plants are vigorous and better able to tolerate feeding by nematodes and other pests. Increase the organic matter content of soil to improve water and nutrient availability to plants and to encourage greater numbers of nematode predators and parasites in soil. More frequent irrigation of drought-stressed plants can reduce damage caused by root knot nematodes, but does not reduce the population levels of nematodes. Do not allow irrigation water from around infested plants to run off onto healthy plants as this spreads nematodes. Do not transfer soil from around infested plants to healthy plants. Thoroughly wash soil and plant parts from all tools and equipment used around infested plants before working around healthy landscapes.

Solarization before planting, covering moist, bare soil with clear plastic for several weeks during hot weather (see Chapter 7), temporarily reduces nematode populations in the upper 12 inches of soil. Solarization before planting reduces nematode damage to annual plants and may help young woody plants to become established before nematode populations increase. Solarization is of little or no help to deeply rooted plants and any nematode control is temporary.

A soil fumigant can be used in certain situations to reduce nematode populations *before planting*. Before using a fumigant, be sure that nematodes or other soil pests are the cause of your problem by having a laboratory test performed or by having an expert examine your plants and soil. Consider alternatives before using a nematicide, such as planting species or varieties tolerant to the nematodes present at that location. Plant susceptible species only in locations where nematode populations are low and at sites where soil or conditions are not conducive to nematode buildup. Be sure the nematicide is registered for that plant and follow label directions strictly; improper application is not effective and may be hazardous. Preplant nematicides can damage or kill roots of nearby desirable plants that grow under or adjacent to the treated soil.

Postplant nematicides for use in soil around established plants can generally be purchased and applied only by certified applicators. These chemicals can be harmful to people and pets if not used properly. Employ other alternatives as discussed above and tolerate some nematode damage before considering postplant nematicides. Postplant nematicides are rarely used or warranted in established landscapes. Contact your Cooperative Extension Office for specific nematicide recommendations.

CHAPTER NINE

Problem-Solving Tables

THIS CHAPTER contains two complementary tables that **must** be used together when diagnosing problems. If you are uncertain of the cause of a problem and don't know which chapter to go to for solutions, consult the "Problem-Solving Guide". This briefly summaries damage symptoms that can occur on many woody landscape plants and directs you to the section(s) of the book that discuss these problems. "Tree and Shrub Pest Tables" are more extensive and are organized according to host plants. These list problems of over a hundred genera or related species of woody landscape plants, **excluding** common problems that affect many different species. To conserve space and avoid repetition, problems such as too little or too much water or root diseases that affect many different plants are included only in the "Problem-Solving Guide". Use **both** tables when diagnosing problems.

Check the index at the back of the book to find where in the Tree and Shrub Pest Tables the plant species of interest to you is located. The Tree and Shrub Pest Tables are organized alphabetically, usually by the common name of the plant. However, some plants have several common names and some related species or genera are grouped together. For example, non-fruiting ornamental pear and plum species are included in "fruit trees". Check the index for page numbers.

The Problem-Solving Guide and Tree and Shrub Pest Tables refer you to other parts of this book where you can get more information on identification, biology, and management. For those pests not covered elsewhere in the book, a brief description of management practices is provided in these tables. Because of the broad scope of this publication, its California emphasis, and because new plant and pest species are often introduced from elsewhere, some of the pests you may encounter are not pictured or described here. For vertebrate pests, see University of California Agriculture and Natural Resources Publication 21385, *Wildlife Pest Control Around Gardens and Homes.* Other sources of information are listed in References. Some pest problems can only be diagnosed reliably by experienced professionals; do not hesitate to seek their help. Your Cooperative Extension advisor, qualified horticultural consultant, certified arborist, or certified nurseryperson may be able to make an identification or direct you to professional diagnostic services.

PROBLEM-SOLVING GUIDE
Common symptoms on many woody plant species, by plant part on which they frequently appear

Entire Plant May Exhibit Symptoms

WHAT THE PROBLEM LOOKS LIKE	PROBABLE CAUSE	COMMENTS
Foliage fades, discolors, then wilts, often in scattered portions of the canopy. Foliage drops prematurely. Branches, treetop, or entire plant may die.	Collar, foot, root, and crown rots.	May have bark cankers or ooze. See page 209.
	Verticillium wilt.	Discoloring often scattered throughout canopy. Vascular tissue may turn brown. See page 190.
	Armillaria root rot.	Possible mushrooms near trunk in fall and white mycelia fan beneath bark. See page 206.
	Dematophora root rot.	May be minute white growths beneath bark or white strands on soil. See page 208.
	Annosus root disease.	Affects mostly conifers in locations where conifers grow naturally. See page 211.
	Fusarium wilt.	See page 191.
	Too much or too little water.	See pages 32, 215.
	Nematodes.	See page 255.
	Scale insects.	See page 117.
	Moth larvae that bore in tissues.	See page 162.
	Gall makers.	See page 142.
	Wood-boring beetles.	See page 151.
	Twig blight fungi.	See page 185.
	Freeze damage.	See page 224.
Older needles or foliage drops. Lower branches may die back.	Normal maturation, not a disease, may be aggravated by poor pruning or improper irrigation.	Evergreen plants periodically drop old foliage. Lower, shaded branches naturally die and drop.
Yellow, dead, or prematurely dropping leaves or needles. Foliage discolored, flecked, sparse, stunted, or distorted. Plant grows slowly.	Air pollution.	See page 224.
	Mineral deficiency.	See page 215.
	Salt damage.	See page 220
	Herbicide toxicity.	See page 221
	Viruses.	Often irregular yellow patterns. See page 212.
Leaves, blossoms, or fruit have black or brown lesions or spots. Leaf veins may darken. Terminals may die back. Bleeding cankers or lesions may occur on stems.	Bacterial blight or bacterial canker.	See page 197.
Grayish, yellowish, or brownish encrustations form on plant. Leaves may yellow, branches may die back.	Scale insects.	See page 117.
Leafless, orangish stems entangle host plant. Clusters of small, white flowers in summer yield seeds that germinate from soil next season.	Dodder, *Cuscuta* spp., parasitic, annual plants sprouting from seeds and requiring sunny locations.	Repeatedly irrigate beneath host plant and till dodder seedlings or apply mulch. Control before seeds are produced. Flamers or herbicides kill dodder, but killing host plant may be unavoidable to kill dodder.

Foliage and Terminal Symptoms, Primarily

WHAT THE PROBLEM LOOKS LIKE	PROBABLE CAUSE	COMMENTS
Sudden wilting, blackening or browning of shoots, blossoms, or fruit. Plant appears scorched.	Fireblight, a bacterial disease.	Affects only rose family plants. See page 190.
Conspicuous spots or irregular dead areas form on leaves. Foliage or flowers curl, turn brown or black, may drop prematurely.	Sunburn. Frost damage. Wind or hot weather damage. Rust fungi. Leaf spots. Anthracnose, many different species of fungi.	Damage often starts between veins. See page 222. See page 224. See page 195. See Table 5-1, page 185. Affects many deciduous plants, especially ash, oak, sycamore, and Chinese elm in California. Lower branch foliage often more affected than upper foliage. Cankers on twigs or branches. See page 185.
Small, well defined, tan, reddish or black blotches form on leaves, often with yellowish border. Leaves may drop.	Entomosporium leaf spot fungus. Septoria leaf spot fungus.	See page 188. See page 187.
Foliage is flecked, yellowed, bleached, or bronzed by pests that suck plant juices.	Mites Thrips. Leafhoppers. True bugs. Sycamore scale.	See page 170. See page 139. See page 133. See page 135. See page 130.
Dark, varnishlike specks form on leaves.	True bugs. Greenhouse thrips. House flies.	See page 135. See page 141.
Light-colored powdery growth on plant. Leaves distort, discolor, or drop.	Powdery mildew, a fungal disease.	See page 193.
Dry, orangish or yellowish pustules occur, usually on leaf undersides.	Rust fungi.	See page 195.
Dark sooty growth on leaves and stems, washes from plant.	Sooty mold, a fungus growing on honeydew excreted by insects.	See page 194.
Clear, sticky substance appears on plant. May be white to clear cast skins on foliage or twigs.	Honeydew, excreted by plant-sucking insects: aphids, scales, leafhoppers, mealybugs, psyllids, and whiteflies.	Identify insect, then see that section.
Whitish, frothy material on foliage.	Spittlebugs.	See page 134.
Whitish, cottony, waxy material occurs on plant.	Adelgids. Mealybugs. Wooly aphids. Whiteflies. Cottony cushion scales, some others.	See page 102. See page 114. See page 96. See page 108. See page 130.
Winding or blotched tunnels or mines in foliage.	Leafminers or shield bearers.	See page 146.
Chewed, tattered, or scraped foliage, shoots, or blossoms.	Moth or butterfly larvae. Sawfly larvae. Leaf beetles or flea beetles. Weevils. Snails or slugs. Grasshoppers or katydids.	See page 63. See page 77. See page 80. Beetles feed at night. See page 86. Slimy or clear trails present. See page 176.
Silken tents, mats, or webbing occur on chewed foliage or terminals.	Tent caterpillars, webworms, or leafrollers.	See pages 74–77.

Foliage and Terminal Symptoms, Primarily (continued)

WHAT THE PROBLEM LOOKS LIKE	PROBABLE CAUSE	COMMENTS
Discolored foliage. Excessive or spindly growth.	Excess or deficient light.	See page 222.
Distorted, curled, swollen, or galled leaves, flowers, stems, or branches.	Gall mites. Thrips. Moth larvae. Psyllids. Gall makers. Aphids. *Taphrina* spp., fungi.	See page 173. See page 139. See page 63. See page 103. See page 142. See page 93. See Table 5-1, page 185.

Bark, Limb, And Trunk Symptoms, Primarily

WHAT THE PROBLEM LOOKS LIKE	PROBABLE CAUSE	COMMENTS
Fleshy or woody growths occur on bark, often mushroom- or seashell-shaped.	Trunk and limb rots, fungi decaying internal supportive wood tissue.	Decay often undetected except where bark cut or injured. Limbs or tree may fall. See page 198.
Bulging bark outgrowths or galls form.	Crown gall, a bacterial infection. Woolly apple aphid. Western gall rust, a fungal disease. Mistletoe, a parasitic plant.	Damage often around root crown. See page 203. See page 96. Affects only pines. See page 196. See page 252.
Bark splits or cracks.	Inappropriate water. Sunscald. Lightning damage. Freeze damage. Wind damage. Rapid growth.	See pages 32, 215. See page 222. See page 224. See page 224. Provide proper cultural care; see Chapter 3.
Areas of dead bark (canker) may be surrounded by callus tissue layers. Material may ooze from bark. Limbs or entire plant may die back.	Inappropriate water. Pruning wound. Sunburn. Injuries.	See pages 32, 200. See page 37. See page 222. See page 40.
Stained bark exudes dark liquid, often around crotches, or whitish frothy material, often from holes or cracks.	Wetwood or slime flux. Foamy canker or alcoholic flux.	Liquid odor, typically rancid. See page 204. Liquid has pleasant alcoholic or fermentative odor. See page 205.
Pitchy masses form on bark.	Moth larvae, insects bore under bark. Canker diseases, fungal infections.	See page 162. See page 200.
Holes, pitch tubes, boring dust, or stains occur on bark. Foliage may discolor and branches or entire plant may die.	Twig-, branch-, and trunk-boring insects. Pinewood nematode.	See page 151. See page 260.
Green plants with smooth stems and thick roundish leaves infest branches.	Large leaf mistletoe, parasitic, evergreen plant on host.	See page 252.
Small, leafless, orangish, upright plants grow on host stems. Distorted and slow plant growth. Branches die back.	Dwarf mistletoe, *Arceuthobium* spp., host specific parasitic plants that extract nutrients from host plant.	Prune out infected branches. Replace heavily infected plants with species from other genera; dwarf mistletoes won't spread to unrelated species.
Grayish, greenish, or orangish tissue grows on or hangs from bark.	Lichens, mosses, and algae.	Often grow on older trees. Generally harmless to host plant.

SEE PAGES 264–266 FOR ADDITIONAL COMMON CAUSES OF SYMPTOMS

TREE AND SHRUB PEST TABLES
Common Problems and their Causes, by Plant Species

WHAT THE PROBLEM LOOKS LIKE	PROBABLE CAUSE	COMMENTS
ABUTILON (*Abutilon* spp.), Chinese lantern, Flowering maple		
Leaves with yellowish blotches.	**Abutilon mosaic virus.**	Considered attractive. See pages 6, 213.
Chewed leaves or blossoms.	**Fuller rose beetle.** Pale brown adult snout weevils, about ³/₈ inch long.	Adults hide during day and feed at night. Larvae feed on roots. See page 88.
Foliage blackened by sooty mold. Twig or branch decline or dieback.	**Brown soft scale.** Small, brown or yellowish, flattened insects.	See page 126.
Twig or branch dieback. Grayish to brownish encrustations on twigs.	**Oleander scale.** Tiny, flattened, circular insects, up to ¹/₁₆ inch long.	See page 124.
ACACIA (*Acacia* spp.)		
Brown or dead terminals. White honey-dew pellets or blackish sooty mold.	**Acacia psyllid.** Tiny orange, green, or brown flattened or winged insects on new growth.	See page 105.
Foliage blackened by sooty mold. popcornlike bodies (egg sacks) on bark.	**Cottony cushion scale.** Orangish, flat immatures or cottony females on bark.	Normally controlled by natural enemies. See page 130.
Wet, white, frothy masses on foliage.	**Spittlebug,** *Clastoptera arizonica*. Greenish bugs in spittle. Suck sap.	Tolerate, does not damage plants. Hose plants with water. See page 134.
Stippled, flecked, or bleached foliage.	**Leafhopper,** *Kunzeana kunzii*. Green, up to ¹/₁₆ inch long insects. Suck sap.	Damage commonly minor, tolerate. Apply soap, oil, or botanical insecticide.
Chewed leaves. Foliage may be rolled and tied together with silk.	**Omnivorous looper.** Yellow, green, or pink larvae, up to 1¹/₂ inches long, with green, yellow or black stripes.	Larvae crawl in "looping" manner. See page 73.
Chewed leaves webbed with silk.	**Orange tortrix,** *Argyrotaenia citrana*. Larvae whitish with brown head and "shield" on back. Adults orangish to gray moths. Both up to ³/₄ inch long.	Larvae wriggle vigorously when touched. Vigorous plants tolerate moderate defoliation. Prune out webbing. Apply *Bacillus thuringiensis* or another insecticide. See Foliage-Feeding Caterpillars, page 63.
Chewed leaves or blossoms.	**Fuller rose beetle.** Pale brown adult snout weevils, about ³/₈ inch long.	Adults hide during day and feed at night. Larvae feed on roots. See page 88.
Leaves discolored, wilted, stunted, may drop prematurely. Discolored bark may ooze sap. Branches or plant may die.	**Collar, Foot, and Crown rots.** Decay fungi infect through wounds or roots in moist soil.	See page 209.
Declining or dead twigs or terminals. Gray to brownish, immobile encrustations (insects) on bark.	**California red scale, Greedy scale, Oleander scale, San Jose scale.** Tiny, circular to oval, flattened insects.	See pages 121–124.
Dieback of occasional twigs. Tunnels in twigs or branches, often at crotch.	**Lead cable borer,** *Scobicia declivis*. Black or brown beetles, ¹/₄ inch long.	Prune out affected parts. Eliminate nearby dead wood in which beetles breed.
ALBIZIA (*Albizia* spp.), Mimosa, Silk Tree		
Brown or dead terminals. White honey-dew pellets or blackish sooty mold.	**Acacia psyllid.** Tiny orange, green, or brown flattened or winged insects on new growth.	See page 105.
Chewed leaves. Silk tents in trees.	**Mimosa webworm.** Gray to brown larvae, up to ¹/₂ inch long, white stripes.	See page 77.

ALBIZIA (*Albizia* spp.), Mimosa, Silk Tree, continued

WHAT THE PROBLEM LOOKS LIKE	PROBABLE CAUSE	COMMENTS
Holes in wood. Boring dust. Branches may break and fall. Tree may decline.	**Carpenterworm.** Dark whitish larvae, up to 2½ inches long, boring in wood.	See page 168.
Yellowing and death of foliage, older foliage affected first. Browning of vascular tissue.	**Mimosa wilt,** *Fusarium* spp. Fungi infect plants through spores in soil.	Avoid injuring living tissue. Provide good drainage and appropriate irrigation. See page 191.

ALDER (*Alnus* spp.)

WHAT THE PROBLEM LOOKS LIKE	PROBABLE CAUSE	COMMENTS
Sticky honeydew, blackish sooty mold on leaves. Whitish cast skins on undersides of leaves.	**Aphids:** *Euceraphis gillettei, Pterocallis alni.* Yellowish green, tiny insects on leaves. Suck sap.	Natural enemies help control. Hose force-fully with water. Tolerate or apply insecti-cidal soap or oil. See Aphids, page 93.
Sticky honeydew, blackish sooty mold on leaves. Plant decline or dieback may occur.	**Cottony maple scale,** *Pulvinaria innumerabilis.* Females cottony. **European fruit lecanium scale.** Flat to bulbous, brown, up to ¼ inch long.	Plants tolerate moderate populations. Conserve natural enemies that help con-trol. If needed, monitor crawlers in spring and apply oil. See pages 117, 128.
Cottony white, waxy tufts on leaves.	**Cottony alder psyllid,** *Psylla alni.* Yellow to green, ¹⁄₁₆ inch long insects beneath wax. Suck sap.	Vigorous plants tolerate moderate populations. Tolerate or apply narrow-range oil or another insecticide. See Psyllids, page 103.
Stippled or bleached leaves. Dark, varnishlike specks and cast skins on undersides of leaves.	**Lace bugs,** *Corythucha* spp. Adults ⅛ inch long, wings lacy. Nymphs spiny.	See page 135.
Leaves skeletonized.	**Alder flea beetle,** *Altica ambiens.* Metallic blue adults, ¼ inch long. Larvae are brown to black.	Vigorous trees tolerate moderate defolia-tion. Provide plants proper cultural care. Apply oil or other insecticide to larvae on foliage if needed. See page 80.
Leaves cupped and thickened (galled) along midvein.	**Gall midge,** *Dasineura* sp. Tiny whitish to pink larvae in distorted tissue.	Apparently harmless to plant. Tolerate or prune out affected tissue. See page 144.
Stunting or dieback of woody parts. Gray to brown encrustations on bark.	**Oystershell scale.** Immobile, tiny oysterlike insects, often in colonies.	See page 124.
Dieback of branches. Gnarled, ridged bark with wet spots and D-shaped, ⅛ inch diameter emergence holes.	**Flatheaded alder borer.** Whitish larvae up to ½ inch long beneath bark.	See page 158.
Branches wilted or dying. Boring dust, swellings, holes on trunk or branches.	**Redbelted clearwing.** White larvae up to 1 inch long, head brown. Adult moths wasplike.	See page 167.
Galls or swellings on roots.	**Root knot nematode,** *Meloidogyne* sp.	See page 257.

ARAUCARIA (*Araucaria* spp.), Monkey puzzle tree, Norfolk island pine

WHAT THE PROBLEM LOOKS LIKE	PROBABLE CAUSE	COMMENTS
Whitish to yellow encrustations on or needles (scale insect bodies). Plant may decline and die back.	**Dictyosperum scale,** *Chrysomphalus dictyospermi.* Tiny, immobile, flattened insects suck plant juices. Have several generations per year.	Problem in California mostly in south. Vigorous plants tolerate moderate popula-tions. If needed apply oil when crawlers are active. See Scales and their monitoring, page 117.
Gray or brown encrustations on shoots or needles. Needles may yellow. More a problem in California in South.	**Black araucaria scale,** *Lindingaspis rossi.* Tiny circular to oval insects.	Conserve natural enemies that provide control. Monitor and apply narrow-range oil or another insecticide when crawlers numerous in spring.
Needles discolored. Plant growth slow. Sticky honeydew, blackish sooty mold, and grayish, flocculent material on plant.	**Golden mealybug,** *Nipaecoccus aurilanatus.* Females globular, ¹⁄₁₀ inch long, purplish with felty, golden band marginally and on back.	Several generations occur each year. Natural enemies or soap or oil sprays can help to control. See Mealybugs, page 114.

ARAUCARIA (*Araucaria* spp.), Monkey puzzle tree, Norfolk island pine, continued

Elongate, whitish material (mature female egg sacs) at leaf axils.	**Araucaria scale**, *Eriococcus araucariae*. A cottony cushion scale with orangish eggs in elongate, whitish females.	Vigorous plants tolerate moderate populations. See *Icerya purchasi*, for biology and picture of similar species, page 130. Monitor and if needed apply oil when crawlers are active.

ARBORVITAE (*Platycladus orientalis, Thuja* spp.)

Chewed needles.	**Sawflies**, *Neodiprion* spp. Up to 1 inch long, green larvae on needles.	See page 77.
Stickiness and blackening of foliage from honeydew and sooty mold.	**Arborvitae aphid**, *Dilachnus tujafilinus*. Brown to gray, ⅛ inch long insects on leaves and twigs.	Vigorous plants tolerate moderate populations. Hose forcefully with water. Tolerate or apply insecticidal soap or oil. See Aphids, page 93.
Discolored or dying foliage. Tiny, oval to circular bodies on foliage.	**Juniper scale**, *Carulaspis juniperi*; **Minute cypress scale**. Tiny insects.	Populations in California seldom warrant control. See page 125.
Browning of tips beginning in fall, browning worst late winter to spring.	**Cypress tip miner.** Greenish larvae, up to ⅛ inch long, tunnel in foliage.	See page 147.
Terminals distorted, wilting, or dead.	**Leaffooted bugs.** Mostly brown bug with yellow or bright colors, enlarged, flattened hind legs. Suck plant juices.	Control not investigated. Plants probably tolerate. See True Bugs, page 135.
Dead twigs on tree. Lateral twigs killed about 6 inches from tip.	**Cedar** or **cypress bark beetles.** Adults small, dark beetles that feed on twigs. Larvae and adults bore under bark.	See page 154.
Branches killed, sometimes to trunk. Coarse boring dust at trunk wounds and branch crotches.	**Cypress bark moth**, *Laspeyresia cupressana*. Larvae, up to ½ inch long under bark. Trunk and limbs of landscape trees attacked.	Provide plants with proper cultural care. Avoid excess water and fertilizer that promote rapid growth and thin bark. Avoid wounding bark, insects colonize wounds.

ARTEMISIA (*Artemisia* spp.), Mugwort, Sagebrush, Tarragon, Wormwood

Blackish sooty mold on leaves or twigs. Plants may decline.	**Black scale.** Brown to black, bulbous to flattened insects, up to ³⁄₁₆ inch long. Raised H-shape often on back.	See page 126.
Blackish sooty mold, sticky honeydew, whitish cast skins on plant.	**Aphids.** Small green, orange, black, often in groups on leaves or stems.	See Aphids, page 93.
Chewed foliage. Plant may be defoliated. Metallic, blue to green beetles, head yellowish.	**Leaf beetles**, *Trirhabda flavolimbata, T. pilosa*. Larvae brown to black, up to ½ inch long. Overwinter as eggs in soil, larvae crawl up trunk in spring and begin feeding.	One generation each year. Adults drop when disturbed. Vigorous plants tolerate damage. Sticky material around trunk may exclude larvae if foliage is trimmed back from ground. Foliar insecticide can be applied in spring.
Leaves or stems thickened, distorted, galled, or having felty patches.	**Eriophyid mites**, *Aceria* spp. Microscopic mites living in groups.	See Gall Mites, page 173.

ASH (*Fraxinus* spp.)

Sticky honeydew and blackish sooty mold on leaves and twigs. Tiny, white, mothlike adult insects.	**Ash whitefly.** Tiny oval nymphs are flattened and clear. Older nymphs have a band of white wax on the back.	See page 110.
Coarse, yellow stippling (flecking) of leaves. Dark, varnishlike excrement on undersides of leaves. Leaves may drop.	**Ash plant bugs.** Yellow to brown bugs about ³⁄₁₆ inch long.	See page 137.
Stippled, bleached leaves with dark specks of excrement on undersides.	**Lace bug**, *Leptoypha minor*. Pale brown, up to ⅛ inch long, wings lacelike.	See page 135.

ASH (*Fraxinus spp.*), continued

WHAT THE PROBLEM LOOKS LIKE	PROBABLE CAUSE	COMMENTS
Irregular tan, brown, or white areas on leaves. Premature leaf drop.	**Ash anthracnose,** *Discula fraxinea.* Fungus infects leaves and twigs. Splashing rain spreads spores.	Prune out/dispose of infected twigs before spring. Fungicide sprays offer some protection if properly applied. See page 185.
Leaves brown around edges and sometimes between veins.	**Scorch** or **Pierce's bacterium.** Disease caused by environmental conditions.	Caused by lack of water and bacteria plugging xylem. Irrigate deeply, thoroughly.
Leaves scraped, skeletonized, may be slime covered.	**Pear sawfly** or **pearslug.** Green, slimy, sluglike insects, up to ½ inch long.	See page 79.
Leaves chewed in spring, usually only on inner canopy near bark where the night-feeding larvae hide during day.	**Ash moth,** *Oncocnemis punctilinea.* Dark gray to brown larvae, up to 1½ inches long, with lighter longitudinal stripe. Head dark with light patterns.	Pest in San Joaquin Valley and southern deserts of California. One generation per year. Ash generally tolerates damage; no control recommended.
Leaves curled, twisted or galled at tips. Flocculent wax. Sticky honeydew on foliage.	**Ash leaf curl aphid,** *Prociphilus californicus.* Gray to green insects in distorted leaves.	Aphids alternate between conifer roots and ash. Vigorous plants tolerate many aphids. Tolerate or apply soap, oil, or other insecticide beginning in spring before damage occurs.
Foliage fades, yellows, browns, wilts, often scattered throughout canopy. Branches die. Entire plant may die.	**Verticillium wilt.** A soil dwelling fungus, infects through roots.	See page 190.
Dead or declining twigs and branches. Tan or gray encrustations on bark.	**Walnut scale.** Individuals up to ³⁄₁₆ inch diameter, often in colonies.	See San Jose Scale, page 122.
Branches wilted or dying. Boring dust, ooze, holes on trunk or branches.	**Ash borer, Redbelted clearwing.** White larvae up to 1 inch long, head brown.	Adult moths wasplike. See page 166.
Roughened twig bark. Possible twig dieback.	**Buffalo treehopper.** Bright yellow to green insects, horny or spiny.	See page 133.
Holes, up to ½ inch in diameter, in wood. Boring dust. Tree may decline.	**Carpenterworm.** Dark whitish larvae, up to 2½ inches long, bore in wood.	See page 168.
Foliage chewed, scraped, and webbed together.	**Moth,** *Platynota stultana.* Greenish larvae, head brown. Brown, blackish, and tan adult, up to ½ inch long.	Vigorous plants tolerate moderate defoliation. See Foliage-Feeding Caterpillars, page 63.
Green, plants with smooth stems, thick roundish leaves infesting branches.	**Large leaf mistletoe,** *Phoradendron* sp. Parasitic, evergreen plant on host.	See page 252.

AUCUBA (*Aucuba japonica*), Gold-dust plant, Gold spot aucuba, Japanese aucuba

WHAT THE PROBLEM LOOKS LIKE	PROBABLE CAUSE	COMMENTS
Whitish, yellowish, or grayish encrustations (insect bodies) on twigs or leaves. Plant may decline, die back.	**Yellow scale,** *Aonidiella citrina;* **Dictyosperum scale,** *Chrysomphalus dictyospermi;* **False oleander scale,** *Pseudaulacaspis cockerelli;* **Greedy scale; Oleander scale.**	Narrow-range oil or another insecticide can provide control when crawlers are active. Monitor crawlers to effectively time sprays. See Scales and their monitoring, page 117.
Plant blackened by sooty mold. Waxy, cottony material on leaves or twigs.	**Obscure mealybug.** Powdery, whitish insects up to ⅛ inch long with filaments, longest at tail. Suck sap.	See page 115.
Leaves blackened. Black cannot be scraped off as with above sooty mold.	**Excess light.** Abiotic disorder. Plant is adapted to grow well only in shade.	Provide some shade. Plant tall species and darken light-colored surfaces nearby.
Sticky honeydew and blackish sooty mold on plant. Leaves distorted, may drop prematurely. Plant growth slow.	**Foxglove aphid,** *Aulacorthum solani.* Small dull greenish or brownish to shiny yellowish, usually in groups.	See Aphids, page 93.
Yellowish or brownish spots on leaves, leaves may drop prematurely if severe.	**Phyllosticta leaf spot,** *Phyllosticta aucubae.* A fungal disease.	Spread and development promoted by rain. Avoid overhead watering.

WHAT THE PROBLEM LOOKS LIKE	PROBABLE CAUSE	COMMENTS

AUSTRALIAN WILLOW (*Geijera parviflora*)

Possible dieback. Bulbous, irregular, white and brown bodies (mature scale) on twigs.	**Chinese wax scale,** *Ceroplastes sinensis.* Whitish starlike nymphs on leaves.	Vigorous plants tolerate moderate populations. Monitor and if needed apply oil when crawlers are abundant. See Scale monitoring, page 117.

AZALEA (*Rhododendron* spp.)

Brownish spots and yellowing on leaves.	**Septoria leaf spot.** A fungal disease.	See page 187.
Wilted or dead plants. Roots missing, debarked, girdled near soil surface. Notched or ragged leaves, including on nearby hosts: rhododendron, photinia.	**Woods weevil,** *Nemocestes incomptus;* **Black vine weevil.** Adults dark brown to black snout weevils, up to ½ inch long. Larvae white grubs in soil.	Trap adults or apply insecticide to foliage in the spring. Apply nematodes to soil beneath infested plants to kill weevil larvae and pupae. See Weevils, page 86.
Browning of leaves or leaves tied together with silk.	**Azalea leafminer,** *Caloptilia azaleella.* Greenish larvae, up to ½ inch long, secretive. Young larvae mine, feed externally as mature.	Vigorous plants tolerate extensive leaf damage. Control difficult. Clip and dispose of infested leaves. If needed, apply oil to mature larvae or systemic insecticide for all larval stages.
Leaf partly or all thickened, distorted, and crisp. White or pinkish spores cover infected tissue.	**Leaf gall,** *Exobasidium vaccinii.* Fungus spreads by air only during wet weather.	Avoid overhead watering. Prune only when dry. Vigorous plants tolerate extensive leaf galling. Handpick or prune out galls.
Small round to larger spots on flowers. Flowers collapse, become soft and cling to leaves or stems.	**Flower blight,** *Ovulinia azaleae.* Fungus favored by cool, wet weather. Spores spread by splashing water.	Remove and dispose of diseased blossoms. Don't overhead water. Fungicide may prevent if applied before rainy season.
New foliage yellow, veins green.	**Iron deficiency.** Abiotic disorder.	See page 215.
Foliage yellows and wilts. Branches or entire plant dies.	**Root and crown rot,** *Phytophthora* sp. Fungal disease.	Disease usually caused by too much water or poor drainage. See page 206.
Foliage yellows, wilts, may prematurely drop. Plant stunted, may die back.	**Stunt nematode,** *Tylenchorhynchus* sp.	See page 260.

BACCHARIS (*Baccharis pilularis*), Coyote brush

Chewed foliage. Plant may be defoliated. Metallic, blue to green beetles, head yellowish.	**Baccharis leaf beetle,** *Trirhabda flavolimbata.* Larvae brown to black, up to ½ inch long.	Insect has one generation each year. Adults drop when disturbed. Vigorous plants tolerate moderate damage. Insecticide can be applied in the spring.
Chewed foliage. Plant may be defoliated.	**Looper,** *Prochoerodes truxaliata.* Brown to purplish caterpillars, up to ½ inch long, hide on ground during day.	Vigorous plants tolerate moderate damage. If needed, apply *Bacillus thuringiensis* or other insecticide when young larvae are abundant.
Chewed leaves. Foliage may be webbed. Plant may be defoliated.	**Omnivorous looper.** Yellow, green, or pink larvae, up to 1½ inches long, with green, yellow, or black stripes.	Larvae crawl in "looping" manner. See page 73.
Fleshy, knoblike swellings (galls) on shoot tips. Galled shoots stop growing.	**Gall fly,** *Rhopalomyia californica.* Orange maggots, up to ¹⁄₁₆ inch long, in galls. Adults tiny, delicate flies, lay tiny reddish eggs on terminals.	Plants are not killed. Tolerate galling. No known artificial controls. Many species of beneficial parasites attack gall fly larvae, conserve natural enemies.
Bead galls on leaves, open on leaf underside. Leaves may be deformed.	**Baccharis gall mite,** *Aceria baccharices.* A tiny eriophyid mite.	Plants apparently tolerate extensive galling. Control difficult. See Gall Mites, page 173.
Blackish sooty mold on leaves or twigs. Plants may decline.	**Black scale.** Brown to black, bulbous to flattened insects, up to ³⁄₁₆ inch long. Raised H-shape often on back.	See page 126.

SEE PAGES 264–266 FOR ADDITIONAL COMMON CAUSES OF SYMPTOMS

BACCHARIS (*Baccharis pilularis*), Coyote brush, continued

WHAT THE PROBLEM LOOKS LIKE	PROBABLE CAUSE	COMMENTS
Leaves stippled or bleached, with cast skins and varnishlike specks.	**Lace bug,** *Corythucha* sp. Brown adults, up to ⅛ inch long, wings lacelike.	See page 135.
Dead or declining branches or plant. Tunneling in wood.	**Flatheaded borer,** *Chrysobothris* sp. Whitish larvae up to 1¼ inches long with enlarged head, tunnel in wood.	See page 157.
Dead or declining branches, grayish encrustations on bark.	**Greedy scale.** Individuals circular, less than 1/16 inch long. Suck sap.	See page 123.

BAMBOO (*Bambusa* spp.)

WHAT THE PROBLEM LOOKS LIKE	PROBABLE CAUSE	COMMENTS
Yellowing leaves. Sticky honeydew, blackish sooty mold, and tiny, whitish cast skins on leaves.	**Bamboo aphids,** *Takecallis* spp. Pale yellow insects about 1/16 inch long with black marks.	Vigorous plants tolerate many aphids. Hose forcefully with water. Tolerate or apply soap or narrow-range oil. See Aphids, page 93.
Dead foliage, blackish sooty mold. Cottony material in leaf axils.	**Mealybugs.** Purplish, segmented, up to 3/16 inch long, under grayish wax.	Plants tolerate moderate populations. Apply soap or oil if needed. See Mealybugs, page 114.
Dieback of plant parts.	**Bamboo scale,** *Asterolecanium bambusae.* Yellow to black, circular, 1/16 inch long on leaves, stems, under sheaths.	Usually unimportant in landscapes. If severe, apply oil during dormant season or monitor and spray once or more in spring when crawlers are active. See Scales and their monitoring, page 117.

BEECH (*Fagus* spp.)

WHAT THE PROBLEM LOOKS LIKE	PROBABLE CAUSE	COMMENTS
Sticky honeydew, blackish sooty mold, and whitish cast skins on foliage.	**Woolly beech leaf aphid,** *Phyllaphis fagi.* Small, greenish insects in groups on underside of leaves.	Plants tolerate abundant aphids. Tolerate or apply insecticidal soap or oil if populations bothersome. See Aphids, page 93.

BIRCH (*Betula* spp.)

WHAT THE PROBLEM LOOKS LIKE	PROBABLE CAUSE	COMMENTS
Sticky honeydew, blackish sooty mold and tiny whitish cast skins on leaves.	**Aphids.** Yellow to green insects, about 1/16 inch long on leaf undersides.	See page 93.
Blackening of foliage by sooty mold.	**Frosted scale.** Hemispherical, brown or whitish, waxy insects, up to ¼ inch long. Suck sap.	See page 128.
Reddish yellow pustules on lower leaf surface (spores that reinfect birch). Leaves spotted, may drop.	**Rust,** *Melampsoridium betulinum.* Fungal spores overwinter around bud scales.	Rake and dispose of all birch leaves in the fall. See Rusts, page 195.
Stippled, flecked, or bleached leaves with whitish cast skins on undersides.	**Leafhoppers,** including: *Empoasca* sp.; *Alebra albostriella.* Green, wedgelike insects up to ⅛ inch long.	Quick insects, often on leaf underside. Plants generally tolerate, control rarely warranted. See Leafhoppers, page 133.
Leaves stippled or bleached, with cast skins and varnishlike specks.	**Lace bug,** *Corythucha* sp. Brown adults, up to ⅛ inch long, wings lacelike.	See page 135.
Chewed leaves. Foliage may be webbed or contain silken tents.	**Fall webworm, Tent caterpillars, Redhumped caterpillar.** Larvae up to 1½ inch long, may be hairy.	See pages 72–76
Foliage turns red, brown, then fades. May be small, pimplelike growths or brownish cankers on bark.	**Cytospora canker.** Fungal disease.	See page 201.
Branches wilted or dying. Boring dust, ooze, holes on trunk or branches.	**Carpenterworm, Redbelted clearwing, Western poplar clearwing.** Whitish larvae up to 2½ inches long, head brown, bore under bark.	See pages 162–69.

WHAT THE PROBLEM LOOKS LIKE	PROBABLE CAUSE	COMMENTS

BOTTLEBRUSH (*Callistemon* spp.)

Whitish to yellow encrustations on leaves and stems (scale insect bodies). Plant may die back and decline.	**Dictyosperum scale**, *Chrysomphalus dictyospermi*; *Parlatoria pittospori*. Tiny, flattened, oval, immobile insects, suck plant juices.	Oil or another insecticide may control if applied when crawlers are active. Monitor crawlers to effectively time any applications. See Scales, page 117.
Foliage or flowers curl, turn brown or black, and die. Terminals die back.	**Freeze or cold damage.**	See page 224.

BOX ELDER (*Acer negundo*)

Chewed leaves. Foliage may be rolled and tied together with silk.	**Omnivorous looper.** Yellow, green, or pink larvae, up to 1½ inches long, with green, yellow or black stripes. **Fruittree leafroller.** Larvae green, head black.	See pages 73–74.
Chewed leaves or blossoms.	**Fuller rose beetle.** Pale brown adult snout weevils, about ⅜ inch long.	Adults hide during day and feed at night. Larvae feed on roots. See page 88.
Spotted or yellow foliage, usually severe only on female trees.	**Boxelder bugs.** Gray and red adults, about ½ inch long. Nymphs red.	Trees tolerate damage. Adults invading houses may be a problem. See page 136.
Powdery white growth on leaves, tiny, black overwintering bodies later.	**Powdery mildew**, *Phyllactinia corylea*. Fungal disease.	Generally not severe enough to warrant control. See Powdery Mildew, page 193.
Foliage blackened by sooty mold. White popcornlike material on twigs (female scale egg sacs).	**Cottony maple scale.** *Pulvinaria innumerabilis*. Immatures flattened, yellow to tan, up to ¹⁄₁₆ inch long, on leaves. Suck sap.	Vigorous plants tolerate moderate populations. Monitor and if needed apply narrow-range oil or another insecticide when crawlers are active. See Scales and their monitoring, page 117.
Blackening of foliage from sooty mold.	**Calico scale.** Adults globular, black with white or yellow spots.	See page 128.
Twigs or limbs die back. Gray to brown encrustations on bark.	**Oystershell scale.** Individuals about ¹⁄₁₆ inch long, oysterlike. Suck sap.	See page 124.
Woody parts die back. Wet spots or sawdustlike frass on bark.	**Flatheaded appletree borer.** Whitish larvae up to ¾ inch long.	See page 157.
Bark stained brownish, exudes rancid fluid, often around crotches, wounds.	**Wetwood** or **Slime flux.** Bacterial infection.	Usually does not cause serious harm to trees. See page 204.

BOXWOOD (*Buxus* spp.), Box

Foliage black from sooty mold. popcornlike bodies (egg sacs) on bark.	**Cottony cushion scale.** Orangish, flat immatures or cottony females on bark.	Normally controlled by natural enemies. See page 130.
Cupping of leaves. American boxwood more susceptible than English boxwood.	**Boxwood psyllid.** Greenish adults, ⅛ inch long, nymphs flattened.	Tolerate, psyllids apparently do not harm shrubs. See Psyllids, page 103.
Foliage discolors, wilts, stunts, may drop. Discolored bark or cankers may ooze sap. Branches or plant may die.	**Collar, Foot, and Crown rots.** Decay fungi common in moist soils.	See page 209.
Twigs or branches die back, stunted growth. Grayish to brownish encrustations on bark.	**California red scale, Greedy scale, Oleander scale, Oystershell scale.** Tiny circular to elongate individuals.	See pages 121–124.

SEE PAGES 264–266 FOR ADDITIONAL COMMON CAUSES OF SYMPTOMS

BROOM (*Cytisus* spp.)

WHAT THE PROBLEM LOOKS LIKE	PROBABLE CAUSE	COMMENTS
Sticky honeydew and blackish sooty mold on foliage. Distorted terminals.	**Bean aphid,** *Aphis fabae.* Dull black insects, less than ⅛ inch long.	Plants tolerate moderate populations. Hose forcefully with water. Tolerate or apply soap or oil. See Aphids, page 93.
Plant parts die back. Grayish to brownish encrustations on bark.	**Greedy scale, Oleander scale, Oystershell scale.** Tiny circular to elongate individuals. Suck sap.	See pages 123–24.
Chewed leaves. Plants may be defoliated.	**Genista caterpillar,** *Uresiphita reversalis.* Caterpillars up to 1¼ inches long, green to orange with black and white hairs.	Released to control brooms, which are often considered weeds. In California more common in South than North. Apply *Bacillus thuringiensis* or another insecticide.

BUCKWHEAT (*Eriogonum* spp.)

Chewed flowers. Leaves chewed or surfaces scraped.	**Common hairstreak butterfly,** *Strymon melinus.* Larvae greenish with short brown hairs. Adult 1 inch long, gray above with marginal red wing spot.	Plants tolerate extensive feeding by larvae, which mature into attractive butterflies. See Foliage-Feeding Caterpillars, page 63.
Flowers chewed.	**Tumbling flower beetle,** *Mordella* sp. Dark, ⅙ inch long, narrow adults with tapered abdomen.	Feed mostly on pollen, damage usually minor. Adults often become very active when disturbed. No known controls.
Flowers drop prematurely or distort. Sticky honeydew or whitish cast skins.	**Aphids,** *Braggia* spp. Small grayish green to black insects in groups.	Plants tolerate many aphids. Flowers and seeds can be reduced. See Aphids, page 93.

BUDDLEIA (*Buddleia* spp.)

Leaves webbed, skeletonized. Leaves and terminal buds chewed.	**Buddleia budworm,** *Pyramidobela angelarum.* Yellow to green larvae, up to ⅓ inch long.	Adult tiny, grayish moth. Prune out infested foliage. Vigorous plants tolerate moderate defoliation. Spray only if severe.

BUSH ANEMONE (*Carpenteria californica*)

Leaves and shoots curled, distorted. sticky honeydew, blackish sooty mold, whitish cast skins on plant.	**Aphids.** Small green, brown, black, or yellowish insects, often in groups.	Inspect new growth regularly and hose aphids forcefully with water. Apply insecticidal soap or oil before damage occurs. See Aphids, page 93.
Thickening of sections of twigs. Shoots may be killed or distorted.	**Pit-making pittosporum scale,** *Asterolecanium arabidis.* Brown to white, up to ⅛ inch long, on twigs.	Occasional problem only. No known management.

CACTUS (*Opuntia* spp.)

Dieback of plant parts. Whitish to brownish encrustations on plant.	**Cactus scale,** *Diaspis echinocacti;* **Greedy scale; Oleander scale.** Tiny oval to circular, flattened insects.	Apply narrow-range oil or another insecticide when crawlers are abundant in spring or summer. See pages 123–24.
Plant blackened by sooty mold. Waxy, cottony material on plant.	**Longtailed mealybug.** Powdery, whitish insects up to ⅛ inch long with filaments longest at tail. Suck sap.	See page 116.
Stunting of plant. Pinhead-size white, yellow, or brown projections on roots.	**Cyst nematode,** *Heterodera cacti.*	See Chapter 8, Nematodes.
Galls or swellings on roots.	**Root knot nematode,** *Meloidogyne* sp.	See page 257.

CALIFORNIA BAY (*Umbellularia californica*), California bay laurel, Grecian laurel

WHAT THE PROBLEM LOOKS LIKE	PROBABLE CAUSE	COMMENTS
Small, black, angular spots and large, irregular, brown spots on leaves.	**Leaf blights:** *Pseudomonas* sp., *Kabatiella* sp., *Gloeosporium* sp.	Prolonged rainy springs promote disease. Usually not serious. No controls known.
Stickiness or blackening of foliage from honeydew and sooty mold.	**California laurel aphid,** *Euthoracaphis umbellulariae.* Grayish insects, ¹⁄₁₆ inch long, on undersides of leaves.	Ignore, even heavy populations apparently do not harm tree. Hose forcefully with water. Tolerate or apply soap or oil. See page 97.
Blackish sooty mold on leaves or twigs. Plants may decline.	**Black scale.** Brown to black, bulbous to flattened insects, up to ³⁄₁₆ inch long. Raised H-shape often on back.	See page 126.
Twig or branch dieback. Grayish to brownish encrustations on twigs.	**Greedy scale, Oleander scale.** Oval to circular insects, up to ¹⁄₁₆ inch long.	See pages 123–24.
Dieback of occasional twigs.	**Branch and twig borers:** *Scobicia declivis, Polycaon confertus.* Adults ¹⁄₄ to ¹⁄₂ inch long, tunnel in twigs.	Keep plants vigorous, provide proper cultural care. Prune out affected parts. Eliminate nearby dead hardwood where beetles breed.

CALIFORNIA BUCKEYE (*Aesculus californica*), Horse chestnut

WHAT THE PROBLEM LOOKS LIKE	PROBABLE CAUSE	COMMENTS
Yellowing and browning of leaves. Dead leaves may hang on tree.	**"Blight."** Normal dormancy, leaves drop sooner under drought conditions.	Early leaf drop is normal drought adaption. No control.
Chewed leaves. Foliage may be rolled and tied together with silk.	**Omnivorous looper.** Yellow, green, or pink larvae, up to 1¹⁄₂ inches long, with green, yellow or black stripes.	Larvae crawl in "looping" manner. See page 73.

CAMELLIA (*Camellia* spp.)

WHAT THE PROBLEM LOOKS LIKE	PROBABLE CAUSE	COMMENTS
Foliage blackened by sooty mold. Leaves cupped, curled, or twisted.	**Melon aphid; Black citrus aphid,** *Toxoptera aurantii.* Brown, black, or green insects on growing points.	Conserve natural enemies that provide control. Hose forcefully with water. Tolerate or apply soap or oil if severe. See Aphids, page 93.
Foliage blackened by sooty mold. Twig or branch decline or dieback.	**Black scale, Brown soft scale.** Small brown, yellowish or blackish insects, flattened or bulbous.	See page 126.
Foliage discolors, wilts, stunts, may drop. Discolored bark or cankers may ooze sap. Branches or plant may die.	**Collar, Foot, and Crown rots.** Decay fungi common in moist soils.	See page 209.
Dieback of twigs or branches. Plants grow slowly or are stunted. Grayish to brownish encrustations on bark.	**Greedy scale, Oleander scale, Oystershell scale.** Individuals oval to elongate, less than ¹⁄₁₆ inch long.	See pages 123–24.
Chewed leaves and blossoms.	**Fuller rose beetle.** Adults pale brown, ³⁄₈ inch long beetles with a snout.	See page 88.
Leaves with irregular, yellow mottling. Blossoms mottled whitish.	**Camellia yellow mottle virus.**	See page 212.
Buds drop prematurely.	**Premature bud drop.** Abiotic disorder caused by poor cultural practices.	Provide appropriate irrigation and good drainage. This spring's bud drop is caused by inadequate cultural care the previous summer and fall when buds were developing.
Blossoms rot. Brown lesions develop, centers discolor first. Blossoms drop prematurely.	**Camellia petal blight,** *Cibornia camelliae.* Fungal disease promoted by rainy weather.	Apply 4 inches of organic mulch beneath plants to reduce spore survival. Pick and dispose of all blighted blossoms. Avoid overhead irrigation.

SEE PAGES 264–266 FOR ADDITIONAL COMMON CAUSES OF SYMPTOMS

WHAT THE PROBLEM LOOKS LIKE	PROBABLE CAUSE	COMMENTS
CAMPHOR TREE (*Cinnamomum camphora*)		
Foliage fades, yellows, browns, wilts, often scattered throughout canopy. Branches die. Entire plant may die.	**Verticillium wilt.** A soil dwelling fungus, infects through roots.	See page 190.
Stickiness or blackening of foliage from honeydew and sooty mold.	**California laurel aphid,** *Euthoracaphis umbellulariae.* Grayish insects, $^1/_{16}$ inch long, on undersides of leaves.	Ignore; even heavy populations do not harm tree. Hose forcefully with water. Tolerate or apply soap or oil. See page 97.
CAPE HONEYSUCKLE (*Tecomaria capensis*)		
Foliage or flowers curl, turn brown or black, may die.	**Freeze or cold damage.**	See page 224.
CAROB (*Ceratonia siliqua*)		
Twig or branch dieback. Encrustations (scale insects) on twigs or foliage.	**Oleander scale.** Tiny, oval, immobile, tan to yellow insects.	See page 124.
CASSIA (*Cassia* spp.), Senna, Gold medallion tree		
Stippled or bleached leaves, varnish-like excrement specks on undersides.	**Thrips.** Tiny, slender blackish or orangish insects.	See Thrips, page 139.
CATALPA (*Catalpa* spp.)		
Sticky honeydew, blackish sooty mold, and whitish cast skins on foliage.	**Melon aphid.** Small greenish, blackish, or yellowish insects in groups.	See page 94.
Blackening of foliage from sooty mold. Cottony or waxy material on plant.	**Grape mealybug,** *Pseudococcus maritimus.* Powdery grayish, up to $^1/_4$ inch long with waxy filaments.	Vigorous plants tolerate moderate populations. Conserve natural enemies that help in control. See Mealybugs, page 114.
Foliage fades, yellows, browns, wilts, often scattered throughout canopy. Branches die. Entire plant may die.	**Verticillium wilt.** A soil dwelling fungus, infects through roots.	See page 190.
Galls or swellings on roots.	**Root knot nematode,** *Meloidogyne* sp.	See page 257.
CEANOTHUS (*Ceanothus* spp.)		
Spindle-shaped swellings (galls) on green stems. Reduced flowering.	**Ceanothus stem gall moth.** Gray larvae up to $^1/_4$ inch long inside gall.	See page 145.
Stippled or bleached leaves with dark specks of excrement on undersides.	**Ceanothus tingid,** *Corythucha obliqua.* Adults brown, $^3/_{16}$ inch long, wings lacelike. Nymphs smaller, flattened.	See Lace Bugs, page 135.
Foliage yellows, wilts, and drops. Branches die back or entire plant dies.	**Botryosphaeria canker and dieback, Oak root fungus,** *Phytophthora* spp.	Fungal diseases. See pages 203–09.
Dieback of twigs or branches. Grayish to brownish encrustations on bark.	**Greedy scale, Oystershell scale.** Tiny, flattened, round or elongate insects.	See pages 123–24.
Blackened foliage from sooty mold. Reduced shoot growth.	**Ceanothus aphid,** *Aphis ceanothi.* Small black to reddish brown insects.	Vigorous plants tolerate. Conserve beneficials. Tolerate or apply soap or oil. See Aphids, page 93.
Plant blackened by sooty mold. Waxy, cottony material on plant.	**Mealybugs.** Powdery covered, elongate to oval insects, up to $^1/_8$ inch long.	See page 114.
Cottony spots up to $^1/_4$ inch long on underside of leaves.	**Psyllid,** *Euphalerus vermiculosus.* Small greenish nymphs beneath cottony material. Suck sap.	Apparently do not damage plants. No controls known. See Psyllids, page 103.
Trunk or limbs with roughened, wet or oozing area. Cracked bark and dieback.	**Flatheaded borers.** Larvae under bark, whitish with enlarged head.	Adults bullet-shaped, metallic, coppery, gray, greenish, or bluish. See page 157.

SEE PAGES 264–266 FOR ADDITIONAL COMMON CAUSES OF SYMPTOMS

CEANOTHUS (*Ceanothus* spp.), continued

WHAT THE PROBLEM LOOKS LIKE	PROBABLE CAUSE	COMMENTS
Foliage turns red, brown, then fades. May be small, pimplelike growths or brownish cankers on bark.	**Cytospora canker.** Fungal disease.	See page 201.
Leaves wilted, discolored, may drop. Branches or entire plant may die.	**Dematophora root rot.** Minute white fungus growths may be visible in wood.	Less common than *Armillaria* or *Phytophthora.* See pages 206–09.
Leaves chewed, drop. May be silken webbing on plants.	**Tent caterpillars.** Hairy, colorful larvae up to 2 inches long.	See page 75.

CEDAR (*Cedrus* spp.), INCENSE CEDAR (*Calocedrus decurrens*)

WHAT THE PROBLEM LOOKS LIKE	PROBABLE CAUSE	COMMENTS
Stickiness and blackening of foliage from honeydew and sooty mold.	**Giant conifer aphids,** *Cinara* spp. Small, black, long-legged insects.	Often infest only a single branch. More common in California in South than in North. See page 95.
White waxy threads on bark. Yellowing, decline of young trees.	**Monterey cypress scale,** *Xylococculus macrocarpae.* Tiny, immobile insects on bark beneath wax.	On Monterey cypress and incense cedar. Only heavily infested young trees may be harmed. Apply oil to bark if needed.
Stunted, bushy branches. Orangish, gelatinous masses or galls on bark. Stem dieback.	**Gymnosporangium rusts.** Disease fungi.	See Rusts, page 196.
Foliage discolors, wilts, stunts, may drop. Discolored bark or cankers may ooze sap. Branches or plant may die.	**Collar, Foot, and Crown rots.** Decay fungi common in moist soils.	See page 209.
Branches, treetop dying. Some branches reddish, pitchy or grayish, bare.	**Botryosphaeria canker and dieback.** Fungus spread by splashing water.	Affects primarily drought stressed trees. Provide proper irrigation. See page 203.

CHESTNUT (*Castanea* spp.)

WHAT THE PROBLEM LOOKS LIKE	PROBABLE CAUSE	COMMENTS
Chewed leaves. Foliage may be rolled and tied together with silk.	**Omnivorous looper.** Yellow, green, or pink larvae, up to 1½ inches long, with green, yellow or black stripes.	Larvae crawl in "looping" manner. See page 73.
Sticky honeydew and black sooty mold on foliage. Tiny, mothlike adults.	**Crown whitefly.** Black, oval nymphs with spreading, whitish, waxy plates.	See page 111.
Leaves discolored, wilted, stunted, may drop prematurely. Discolored bark may ooze sap. Branches or plant may die.	**Collar, Foot, and Crown rots.** Decay fungi common in moist soils.	See page 209.

CHINESE PISTACHE (*Pistacia chinensis*)

WHAT THE PROBLEM LOOKS LIKE	PROBABLE CAUSE	COMMENTS
Foliage fades, yellows, browns, wilts, often scattered throughout canopy. Branches die. Entire plant may die.	**Verticillium wilt.** A soil dwelling fungus, infects through roots.	Foliage often wilts first on only one side. See page 190.

CHINESE TALLOW TREE, JAPANESE TALLOW TREE (*Sapium* spp.)

WHAT THE PROBLEM LOOKS LIKE	PROBABLE CAUSE	COMMENTS
Twig terminals die back in fall.	**Abiotic disorder.** Possibly result of freeze damage.	Provide proper cultural care. Avoid excess fertilization, irrigation, and pruning that stimulate excess growth, especially in fall.

CHOISYA (*Choisya ternata*), Mexican orange, Mock orange

WHAT THE PROBLEM LOOKS LIKE	PROBABLE CAUSE	COMMENTS
Stickiness and blackening of foliage from honeydew and sooty mold. Plant growth may slow.	**Black scale.** Brownish or orangish, flattened (immature) or blackish, bulbous (adult) insects.	Insects on twigs or leaves. Prominent H-shape on back of more mature stages. See page 126.
Stippled, flecked, or bleached leaves. Leaves may drop.	**Mites,** including Citrus red mite. Tiny, sand-size specks on leaves, often reddish. Suck sap.	See page 170.

WHAT THE PROBLEM LOOKS LIKE	PROBABLE CAUSE	COMMENTS
CISTUS (*Cistus* spp.), Rock rose		
Blackish sooty mold, sticky honeydew and whitish cast skins on foliage.	**Aphids.** Small insects, usually in in groups, often black.	See Aphids, page 93.
CITRUS (*Citrus* spp.), Lemon, Lime, Orange		
Sticky honeydew and blackish sooty mold on leaves and twigs. Whitish cast skins on undersides of leaves.	**Spirea aphid,** *Aphis citricola;* **Black citrus aphid,** *Toxoptera aurantii.* Tiny green to brownish insects in clusters.	In California mostly in coastal areas. Conserve natural enemies that help control. Tolerate or apply soap or oil if needed. See Aphids, page 93.
Stickiness and blackening of foliage from honeydew and sooty mold. Plant growth may slow.	**Black scale, Citricola scale, Brown soft scale, Cottony cushion scale.** Orange, brown, black, or cottony, bulbous or flattened insects.	Insects on twigs or leaves. See pages 126–130.
Blackening of foliage from sooty mold. Cottony or waxy material on plant.	**Mealybugs:** *Pseudococcus* and *Planococcus* spp. Powdery gray insects, up to ¼ inch long with waxy filaments.	Conserve natural enemies that provide control. See Mealybugs, page 114.
Blackening of foliage from sooty mold. Tiny, whitish, mothlike insects (adult whiteflies).	**Whiteflies,** including: Greenhouse whitefly, Woolly whitefly, Citrus whitefly, Ash whitefly. Nymphs oval, flattened, yellowish to greenish.	See page 108.
Stunted, declining, or dead branches. Grayish, orange, or brownish encrustations on bark.	**California red scale, Purple scale, Yellow scale.** Tiny circular to elongate insects.	See pages 121, 124.
Stippled, flecked, or bleached leaves. Leaves may drop.	**Citrus red mite, Pacific spider mite, Twospotted spider mite.** Tiny, sand-size specks on leaves.	See page 170.
Stippled, bleached leaves or fruit.	**Citrus thrips.** Tiny, slender, yellow.	See page 139.
Leaves chewed. Leaves may be tied together with silk.	**Orange tortrix,** *Argyrotaenia citrana;* **Fruittree leafroller; Western tussock moth; Omnivorous looper.** Naked to hairy larvae, up to 1½ inch long.	Vigorous plants tolerate moderate leaf damage. Prune out infested foliage. Apply *Bacillus thuringiensis* or another insecticide when young larvae are feeding. See pages 70–74.
Leaves chewed.	**Anise swallowtail,** *Papilio zelicaon.* Larvae up to 1½ inches long, green with black and yellow bands. Adults 2 inches, yellow with black.	Caterpillars mature into attractive butterflies. Control not recommended. Young larvae are killed by *Bacillus thuringiensis.* See Foliage-Feeding Caterpillars, page 63.
Chewed leaves or blossoms.	**Fuller rose beetle.** Pale brown adult snout weevils, about ⅜ inch long.	Adults hide during day and feed at night. Larvae feed on roots. See page 88.
Growth slow. Fruit may be few in number and undersized. Soil clings to roots and is difficult to wash off.	**Citrus nematode,** *Tylenchulus semipenetrans.*	See page 260.
COAST REDWOOD (*Sequoia sempervirens*)		
Gray or brown encrustations on shoots or needles. Needles may yellow. More a problem in California in South.	**Black araucaria scale,** *Lindingaspis rossi;* **Redwood scale,** *Aonidia shastae.* Tiny circular to oval insects.	Vigorous trees tolerate moderate populations. Conserve natural enemies. Tolerate or monitor and apply oil if needed. See Scales, page 117.
Browning of tips, beginning in fall, worst in late winter and spring.	**Cypress tip miner.** Silvery tan moths, green larvae, about ¼ inch long.	See page 147.

COAST REDWOOD (*Sequoia sempervirens*), continued

Terminals brown, dead several inches back from tip.	**Redwood bark beetle,** *Phloeosinus sequoiae.* Adults tiny, dark reddish.	Terminal feeding doesn't seriously harm trees. Provide trees proper cultural care, especially adequate water. Prune out and dispose of nearby dead cypress, *Chamaecyparis,* and redwood where beetles breed. See Bark Beetles, page 152.
Older foliage dark in color, stippled.	**Spruce spider mite.** Sand-sized specks on needles.	Mites feed during cool weather. See page 173.
Dead or dying branches. Cankers on trunk or limbs. Dying branches with resinous lesions.	**Botryosphaeria dieback and canker, Cytospora canker.** Fungal diseases.	Often on drought-stressed trees. Provide adequate irrigation. See page 200.
Resinous lesions or cankers on bark, branches or treetop die back.	**Redwood canker,** *Coryneum* sp. Fungal disease, usually at warm, dry sites.	Prune out and dispose of diseased branches. Irrigate adequately. See Cypress Canker, page 202.
Needles turn brown. Dead, dying, and falling branchlets.	**Drought stress.** Some needles and branchlets are shed naturally.	Provide adequate irrigation, drought stress increases normal shedding of needles.
Foliage discolors, wilts, stunts, may drop prematurely. Discolored bark may ooze sap. Branches or plant may die.	**Collar, Foot, and Crown rots.** Decay fungi common in moist soils.	See page 209.
Globular galls, up to several inches in diameter on branches.	**Genetic disorder.** Tree vigor not seriously affected.	No control except to eliminate tree. Tolerate, does not spread to other trees.

COTONEASTER (*Cotoneaster* spp.)

Sudden wilting then shriveling and blackening of shoots, blossoms and fruit. Plant appears scorched.	**Fireblight.** Bacterium enters plants through blossoms.	See page 190.
Stippled, bleached leaves with dark varnishlike specks on undersides.	**Lace bug,** *Corythucha* sp. Pale brown adults, up to ⅛ inch long, wings lacelike. Nymphs flattened.	See page 135.
Tiny reddish to brown leaf spots, may have yellow halos. Larger, dark areas on leaves. Leaves may drop.	**Entomosporium leaf spot.** A fungal disease.	See page 188.
Declining and dead twigs. Brownish to grayish encrustations on bark.	**Greedy scale, Oystershell scale, San Jose scale.** Tiny circular to elongate individuals, often in colonies.	See pages 123–24.
Sticky honeydew, blackish sooty mold, and whitish cast skins on plant.	**Apple aphid,** *Aphis pomi.* Tiny bright green insects clustered on new growth.	Plants tolerate moderate aphid populations. See Aphids, page 93.
Leaves wilted, discolored, may drop. Trunk or limbs with roughened, wet or oozing area. Cracked bark and die back.	**Flatheaded borers.** Whitish larvae with enlarged head, under bark.	Adults bullet-shaped, metallic, coppery, gray, greenish, or bluish beetles. See page 157.
Leaves wilted, discolored, may drop. Branches or entire plant may die.	**Dematophora root rot.** Minute white fungus growths may be visible in wood.	Less common than *Armillaria.* See page 206.
Foliage covered with silken webs. Leaves skeletonized.	**Cotoneaster webworm,** *Athrips rancidella.* Larvae brownish black. Tiny, grayish moths active at night.	Vigorous plants tolerate moderate defoliation. Prune out infested foliage. Tolerate or spray if larvae abundant. See Foliage-Feeding Caterpillars, page 63.

SEE PAGES 264–266 FOR ADDITIONAL COMMON CAUSES OF SYMPTOMS

CRAPE MYRTLE (*Lagerstroemia hirsuta*)

WHAT THE PROBLEM LOOKS LIKE	PROBABLE CAUSE	COMMENTS
Foliage covered with whitish growth. Shoots stunted, distorted.	**Powdery mildew.** A fungal disease.	See page 193.
Sticky honeydew, blackish sooty mold, and whitish cast skins on plant.	**Crapemyrtle aphid.** Yellowish green with black wing markings.	See page 93.

CYPRESS (Cupressus spp.), FALSE CYPRESS (*Chamaecyparis* spp.)

WHAT THE PROBLEM LOOKS LIKE	PROBABLE CAUSE	COMMENTS
Brown dying foliage on branches. Cankers on limbs or trunk.	**Cypress canker, Cytospora canker.** Fungi that infect cypress bark.	Infects Italian, Leyland, or Monterey cypress. See pages 201–02.
Stunted, bushy branches. Orange masses or gall on bark. Stems die back.	**Gymnosporangium rusts.** Disease fungi.	Occurs on cypress. See Rusts, page 196.
Dark scabby or velvety spots on leaves or fruit.	**Scab,** *Venturia* sp. Fungal disease spread by splashing water.	See Scabs, page 188.
Browning of tips beginning in fall, worst late winter to spring.	**Cypress tip miner.** Adults are small, silvery tan moths. Green larvae, up to $1/8$ inch long, tunnel in foliage.	See page 147.
Yellow or brown foliage. Whitish to brownish encrustations on foliage.	**Juniper scale,** *Carulaspis juniperi;* **Minute cypress scale.** Circular to elongate insects, $1/16$ inch long.	Populations in California rarely warrant control. Minute cypress scale not on *Chamaecyparis*. See page 125.
Stippled, flecked, or yellow foliage. Not on cypress.	**Spruce spider mite,** *Oligonychus ununguis.* Tiny green specks, may be fine webbing on foliage.	See page 172.
Stickiness and blackening of foliage from honeydew and sooty mold.	**Arborvitae aphid,** *Dilachnus tujafilinus.* Brown to gray insects, about $1/8$ inch long. Suck sap.	Plants tolerate moderate aphid populations. Hose with forceful water. Tolerate or apply soap or oil if severe. See Aphids, page 93.
Chewed needles.	**Sawflies,** *Neodiprion* and *Susana* spp. Green larvae, up to 1 inch long, on needles.	See Sawflies, page 77.
Dead and living foliage tied together with silk. Foliage may turn brown.	**Cypress leaf tier,** *Epinotia subviridis;* **Cypress webber,** *Herculia phoezalis.* Pink to dark larvae up to $3/4$ inch long, feed singly (*Epinotia*) or grouped (*Herculia*) in "nests."	More common in California in South than North. Vigorous plants tolerate moderate defoliation. Prune out infested foliage or tolerate. Apply broad-spectrum insecticide at high pressure in March or April if problem severe.
Twigs killed back about 6 inches from tips. Dead foliage hanging on tree.	**Cedar or Cypress bark beetles.** Adults small, dark beetles. Whitish larvae and adults bore beneath bark.	See page 154.
Branches killed, sometimes to trunk. Coarse boring dust at trunk wounds and branch crotches.	**Cypress bark moths,** *Laspeyresia cupressana; Epinotia hopkinsana.* Larvae up to $1/2$ inch long, feed under bark, in cones, or on foliage.	Provide plants proper cultural care. Avoid excess water and fertilizer, which promote rapid growth and susceptible thin bark. Avoid wounding bark. Control is generally not warranted. Often colonize cypress cankers (page 202). Insects are secondary, not cause of dieback.
White waxy threads on bark. Yellowing, decline of young trees.	**Monterey cypress scale,** *Xylococculus macrocarpae.* Tiny, immobile insects on bark beneath wax.	On Monterey cypress and incense cedar. Only heavily infested young trees may be damaged. Tolerate or monitor/apply oil to bark. See Scale monitoring, page 118.
Tufts of cottony material protruding from bark. Not on Chamaecyparis.	**Cypress bark mealybug.** Reddish insects about $1/16$ inch long under cottony wax.	See page 115.

CYPRESS (*Cupressus* spp.), FALSE CYPRESS (*Chamaecyparis* spp.), continued

Foliage discolors, wilts, stunts, may drop. Discolored bark or cankers may ooze sap. Branches or plant may die.	**Collar, Foot, and Crown rots.** Decay fungi common in moist soils.	See page 209.

DAPHNE (*Daphne* spp.)

Leaves discolored, wilted, stunted, may drop prematurely. Discolored bark may ooze sap. Branches or plant may die.	**Collar, Foot, and Crown rots.** Decay fungi common in moist soils.	See page 209.
Yellowing of foliage. Decline and death of branches or entire plant.	**Euonymus scale.** Tiny, elongate white male and purplish, oysterlike female insects encrusting leaves and stems.	See page 125.

DODONAEA (*Dodonaea viscosa*), Hopbush, Hopseed tree

Foliage fades, yellows, browns, wilts, often scattered throughout canopy. Branches die. Entire plant may die.	**Verticillium wilt.** A soil-dwelling fungal disease, infects through roots.	See page 190.
Blackish sooty mold on leaves or twigs. Twigs and branches die back.	**Black scale.** Brown to black, bulbous to flattened insects, up to ³⁄₁₆ inch long. Raised H-shape often on back.	See page 126.

DOGWOOD (*Cornus* spp.)

Small, circular, dirty yellow spots with purple margins on flowers, young shoots, and leaves.	**Spot anthracnose,** *Elsinoe corni.* A fungal disease.	Vigorous plants tolerate moderate leaf damage. Generally not serious enough in California to warrant control by preventive fungicide sprays.
Reddish, brown, or grayish circular to angular leaf spots.	**Septoria leaf spot.** A fungal disease.	Apparently does not harm plant. See page 186.
Foliage blackened by sooty mold. Tiny powdery white, mothlike adult insects.	**Greenhouse whitefly.** Immatures are green to yellow, flattened and oval.	See page 112.
Blackish sooty mold, sticky honeydew and whitish cast skins on foliage.	**Aphids.** Small green, yellowish, brown or blackish insects, often in groups.	See Aphids, page 93.
Leaves discolored, wilted, stunted, may drop prematurely. Discolored bark may ooze sap. Branches or plant may die.	**Collar, Foot, and Crown rots.** Decay fungi common in moist soils.	See page 209.

DOUGLAS FIR (*Pseudotsuga menziesii*)

Cottony white tufts on needles with yellow spots.	**Cooley spruce gall adelgid.** Tiny, purplish insects beneath cottony tufts.	See page 102.
Swollen, galled needles. Possible needle drop and twig dieback.	**Needle and twig midges,** *Contarinia* spp. White larvae in swollen needles. Adults emerge from pupae in soil.	Apparently do not harm trees. Prune out damaged shoots. New shoots on especially valuable (nursery) trees may be sprayed.
Brown to purplish insects clustered on foliage. May be sooty mold/honeydew.	**Giant conifer aphids.** Dark, long-legged, up to ⅕ inch long.	Apparently harmless to trees. See page 95.
Pitchy masses 1 to 4 inches in diameter protruding from trunks and limbs. Limbs occasionally break.	**Douglas-fir pitch moth.** Dirty whitish larvae, up to 1 inch long, in pitch.	See Sequoia Pitch Moth, page 168.
Needles chewed. Foliage browns.	**Douglas-fir tussock moth,** *Orgyia pseudotsugata.* Caterpillars hairy, brownish with orange and red.	Vigorous trees tolerate moderate damage. Apply *Bacillus thuringiensis* to control young larvae, if needed. See Tussock Moths, page 70.

WHAT THE PROBLEM LOOKS LIKE	PROBABLE CAUSE	COMMENTS

DOUGLAS FIR (*Pseudotsuga menziesii*), continued

WHAT THE PROBLEM LOOKS LIKE	PROBABLE CAUSE	COMMENTS
Branch terminals turn brown and die. Tree deformed. Growth retarded.	**Douglas-fir twig weevil,** *Cylindrocopturus furnissi.*	Beetle attacks primarily small, stressed trees. Provide appropriate irrigation and other care.
Needles yellow-spotted in fall. Needles red or brown spotted, drop in spring. Plant growth slow.	**Douglas-fir needle cast,** *Rhabdocline pseudotsugae* and **Swiss needle cast,** *Phaeocryptopus gaeumannii.* Fungi.	Fungi favored by moist conditions. Remove nearby plants and weeds, thin canopy, and prune off lower branches to reduce humidity.
Branches die back. Entire tree may die.	**Oak root fungus.**	See page 206.
Branches die back. Treetop or entire plant may die. Cankers on bark.	**Phomopsis canker,** *Phomopsis lokoyae.* A fungal disease.	Primarily affects young, stressed trees. Provide appropriate water and cultural care.

ELDERBERRY (*Sambucus* spp.)

WHAT THE PROBLEM LOOKS LIKE	PROBABLE CAUSE	COMMENTS
Leaves with blackish sooty mold, sticky honeydew, and whitish cast skins.	**Aphids,** including Bean aphid. Small green or black insects in groups.	See page 93.
Bark with wet spots, sawdustlike boring material. Limbs may decline and die.	**Elder borers,** *Desmocerus* spp. Adult longhorned beetles bluish, greenish, or blackish with gold or orange. Stressed or dying trees most affected. See Roundheaded Borers, page 160.	Larvae bore in living trees, which usually are not killed. Attractive adults feed on elderberry flowers. Valley elderberry longhorn beetle, *D. californicus,* is uncommon, its habitat may be protected by law.

ELM (*Ulmus* spp.), ZELKOVA (*Zelkova serrata*)

WHAT THE PROBLEM LOOKS LIKE	PROBABLE CAUSE	COMMENTS
Irregular, black, tarlike spots on leaves. Premature leaf drop. Perennial cankers on limbs and trunk. Dieback.	**Chinese elm anthracnose.** A fungal disease of Chinese (evergreen) elm.	See pages 185, 202.
Sticky honeydew, blackish sooty mold, and whitish cast skins on leaves.	**Elm leaf aphid,** *Tinocalis ulmifolii.* Tiny, green, clustered on leaves.	Trees not damaged. Tolerate or apply soap or oil. See Aphids, page 93.
Sticky honeydew and blackish sooty mold on plant. Possible dieback.	**European elm scale.** Dark, reddish, oval insects with white, waxy fringe.	Commonly at twig crotches or on undersides of limbs. See page 131.
Sticky honeydew and blackish sooty mold on leaves and twigs, dieback.	**European fruit lecanium scale.** Brown, flattened to bulbous insects on twigs.	See page 128.
Stippled, bleached leaves with sticky honeydew, blackish sooty mold, and (on undersides) whitish cast skins.	**Rose leafhopper,** *Edwardsiana rosae; Empoasca* sp. Pale green to white, 1/8 inch long, wedge-shaped insects.	Tolerate, apparently do not harm elms. Apply insecticidal soap or oil if not tolerable. See Leafhoppers, page 133.
Leaves discolored with irregular, yellowish pattern. Abnormal leaf size.	**Elm mosaic virus.**	Provide proper cultural care, especially proper water. No other treatment. See page 212.
Leaves skeletonized, some small holes. Leaves turn yellow, brown, and fall. Yellowish pupae around tree base.	**Elm leaf beetle.** Adults greenish with black, longitudinal stripes. Larvae black to green, up to 1/4 inch long.	See page 81.
Leaves chewed. Often only a single branch is defoliated.	**Spiny elm caterpillar.** Dark, hairy caterpillars, up to 1 1/2 inch long.	Ignore, they do not harm tree, or prune out infested branches. See page 75.
Leaves chewed, webbed together in groups of several containing larva.	**Western tiger swallowtail,** *Papilio rutulus.* Caterpillar bright green with eyespots, black and yellow markings. Adult 2 inches, yellow with black.	Caterpillars mature into highly attractive butterflies. Control not recommended. *Bacillus thuringiensis* kills young larvae. See Foliage-Feeding Caterpillars, page 63.
Chewed leaves. Foliage may be webbed or contain silken tents.	**Fall webworm, Fruittree leafroller, Omnivorous looper.** Larvae up to 1 inch long. May be in webbed foliage.	See pages 73, 74, 76.

ELM (*Ulmus* spp.), ZELKOVA (*Zelkova serrata*), continued

WHAT THE PROBLEM LOOKS LIKE	PROBABLE CAUSE	COMMENTS
Foliage yellows then wilts, usually first in one part of canopy. Curled, dead brown leaves remain on tree.	**Dutch elm disease.** Fungus spread by bark beetles and root grafts.	Do not confuse with elm leaf beetle feeding that causes skeletonized leaves. See page 192.
Woody swellings (galls), cottony, waxy material on branches and roots.	**Woolly apple aphid,** *Eriosoma lanigerum.* Tiny, reddish, cottony or waxy covered insects.	Conserve natural enemies that help control. Apply insecticidal soap or another insecticide. See Aphids, page 93.
Decline of branches or entire tree. Canopy yellowing but leaves not chewed. Tiny "shot holes" in bark.	**European elm bark beetle.** Small, dark, stout adults. Whitish larvae tunnel beneath bark.	Beetles can transmit Dutch elm disease. See pages 156, 192.
Bark exudes white, frothy material, often around wounds, has pleasant odor.	**Foamy canker.** Bacterial infection.	Foamy material appears for only short time during warm weather. See page 205.
Bark stained brownish, exudes rancid fluid, often around crotches, wounds.	**Wetwood** or **Slime flux.** Bacterial infection.	Usually does not cause serious harm to trees. See page 204.

ENGLISH LAUREL (*Prunus laurocerasus*)

Woody parts decline or die back. Gray to brown encrustations on bark.	**Greedy scale.** Insects are circular to flattened, less than $\frac{1}{16}$ inch long.	See page 123.
Dead twigs or branches. Plant declines, may die. Tiny "shot holes" in bark.	**Shothole borer.** Small brown adults, whitish larvae, tunnel beneath bark.	See page 156.
Stippled or bleached leaves, varnish-like excrement specks on undersides.	**Greenhouse thrips.** Tiny, slender blackish adults or yellowish nymphs.	See page 141.

EUCALYPTUS (*Eucalyptus* spp.), Gum

Dead tree or dying limbs. Broad galleries beneath bark.	**Eucalyptus longhorned borer.** Adults reddish brown with yellow on the back. Larvae whitish. Both about 1 inch long.	See page 161.
New shoots distorted, covered with whitish, waxy strands.	**Blue gum psyllid,** *Ctenarytaina eucalypti.* Tiny gray, green, or orange nymphs. Adults like tiny cicadas.	Established trees tolerate abundant psyllids. Insecticidal soap or oil may reduce populations if not tolerable. See page 106.
Galls or swellings around trunk base.	**Ligno-tubers.** Latent buds from which shoots sprout in response to stress.	Inspect plants for damage or stress. Provide proper cultural care. Ligno-tubers are not harmful, but may indicate tree stress or injury.
Leaves discolor, wilt, stunt, or drop prematurely. Discolored bark or cankers may ooze sap. Branches or plant dies.	**Armillaria root rot; Collar, Foot, and Crown rots.** Fungal diseases, often promoted by moist soil.	See pages 206–09.
Chewed leaves. Foliage may be rolled and tied together with silk.	**Omnivorous looper.** Yellow, green, or pink larvae, up to 1½ inches long, with green, yellow or black stripes.	Larvae crawl in "looping" manner. See page 73.

EUGENIA (*Syzygium paniculatum*), Australian bush cherry

Sticky honeydew and blackish sooty mold on foliage. Leaves and terminals pitted, distorted, and discolored.	**Eugenia psyllid.** Adults are tiny, leafhopperlike insects. Nymphs feed in pits on lower leaf surface.	See page 106.
Blackening of foliage from sooty mold. Tiny, whitish, mothlike adult insects.	**Woolly whitefly.** Nymphs are oval, waxy or cottony covered.	See page 114.

SEE PAGES 264–266 FOR ADDITIONAL COMMON CAUSES OF SYMPTOMS

WHAT THE PROBLEM LOOKS LIKE	PROBABLE CAUSE	COMMENTS
EUONYMUS (*Euonymus* spp.)		
Yellowing of foliage. Decline and death of branches or entire plant.	**Euonymus scale.** Tiny, elongate white male and purplish, oysterlike female insects encrusting leaves and stems.	See page 125.
Stunted, declining, or dead branches. Grayish, orange, or brownish encrustations on bark or foliage.	**California red scale.** Tiny, circular, flattened insects on stems or leaves.	See page 121.
Whitish patches of growth on foliage. Leaves may distort, drop prematurely.	**Powdery mildew.** A fungal disease.	See page 193.
Wilting or dead plants. Some roots striped of bark or girdled near soil. Foliage may be chewed, ragged.	**Black vine weevil.** Adults are black snout beetles, ½ inch long. Larvae are white grubs with brown head.	See page 87.
Sticky honeydew, blackish sooty mold, or whitish cast skins on plant.	**Melon aphid, Bean aphid.** Groups of small green, black, or yellow insects.	See pages 94–95.
Galls or swellings on trunk and roots, usually near soil, may be on branches.	**Crown gall.** Bacteria that infect plant via wounds.	See page 203.
Galls or swellings on roots.	**Root knot nematode,** *Meloidogyne* sp.	See page 257.
FICUS (*Ficus* spp.), Fig, Indian laurel, Laurel fig		
Blackening of foliage from sooty mold. Tiny, whitish, mothlike adults.	**Greenhouse whitefly,** Citrus whitefly. Nymphs oval, flat, green to yellow.	See page 111.
Curling and purple pitting of terminal leaves. In California, problem mostly in South.	**Cuban laurel thrips.** Slender, black adults, or yellow nymphs about ⅛ inch long, in curled leaves.	*Ficus microcarpa,* also sometimes called *F. nitida* or *F. retusa,* is preferred host. See page 140.
Whitish to yellow encrustations on leaves (scale insect bodies). Plant may decline and die back.	**Dictyosperum scale,** *Chrysomphalus dictyospermi.* Tiny, immobile, flattened insects suck plant juices. Several generations per year.	Problem in California mostly in south. Oil or another insecticide provide control if applied when crawlers are active. See Scales and their monitoring, page 117.
FIR (*Abies* spp.)		
Brown to purplish insects clustered on foliage. May be sooty mold/honeydew.	**Giant conifer aphids.** Dark, long-legged, up to ⅕ inch long.	Apparently harmless to trees. See page 95.
Chewed foliage. Tree may be defoliated.	**Rusty tussock moth,** *Orgyia antiqua;* **Douglas-fir tussock moth.** Hairy caterpillars, up to 1 inch long.	See page 70.
Chewed needles.	**Sawflies,** *Neodiprion* spp. Up to 1 inch long, green larvae on needles.	See page 77.
Pitchy masses 1 to 4 inches in diameter on trunks and limbs.	**Douglas-fir pitch moth.** Dirty whitish larvae, up to 1 inch long, in pitch.	See page 168.
Treetop or entire tree killed.	**Fir engraver.** Adults are small, brown beetles. White larvae bore under bark.	See page 154.
Distorted, stunted twigs or needles. Needles may drop.	**Balsam twig aphid,** *Mindarus abietinus.* Tiny greenish yellow, powdery insects.	Vigorous plants tolerate. Control generally not warranted except on high value (nursery) trees. See Aphids, page 93.
Foliage discolors, wilts, stunts, may drop. Discolored bark or cankers may ooze sap. Branches or plant may die.	**Collar, Foot, and Crown rots.** Decay fungi common in moist soils.	See page 209.

FIR (*Abies* spp.), continued

Branches turn red, brown, then fade. May be small, pimplelike growths or brownish cankers on bark.	**Cytospora canker.** Fungal disease.	See page 201.
Bark stained brownish, exudes rancid fluid, often around crotches, wounds.	**Wetwood** or **Slime flux.** Bacterial infection.	Usually does not cause serious harm to trees. See page 204.
Small, leafless, orangish, upright, plants on host stems. Distorted and slow plant growth. Branches die back.	**Dwarf mistletoe,** *Arceuthobium* spp. Host specific parasitic plants that extract nutrients from host plant.	Prune out infected branches. Replace heavily infected plants with broadleaf species or conifers from other genera; dwarf mistletoes don't spread to unrelated host species.
Needles turn brown, drop prematurely. Slow plant growth.	**Needle casts,** *Virgella robusta* and *Lirula abietis-concoloris.* Fungal diseases.	Fungi favored by moist conditions. Remove nearby plants/weeds, thin canopy, prune off lower branches to reduce humidity.

FLANNEL BUSH (*Fremontia, Fremontodendron* spp.)

Decline or dieback of branches, twigs. Grayish to brownish bark encrustations.	**Greedy scale.** Tiny circular to elongate individuals on twigs, branches.	See page 123.
Foliage yellows and wilts. Branches or entire plant dies.	**Root and crown rot,** *Phytophthora* spp. Fungus disease.	Disease caused by too much water and/or poor drainage. See page 209.

FRUIT TREES: Apple, crab apple (*Malus* spp.); Apricot, cherry, nectarine, peach, plum (*Prunus* spp.); Natal plum (*Carissa macrocarpa*); Pear (*Pyrus* spp.); Pomegranate (*Punica granatum*)

Sticky honeydew and blackish sooty mold on foliage. Twigs and branches may decline and die.	**Aphids,** several species. Small gray to green insects on leaves and terminals.	See page 93.
Sticky honeydew and blackish sooty mold on leaves and twigs. Tiny, white, mothlike insects (adults) present.	**Ash whitefly, Citrus whitefly.** Tiny, flattened, oval, whitish, green, yellow, or waxy nymphs.	See pages 110–11.
Sticky honeydew and blackish sooty mold on leaves and twigs. Dieback of twigs or branches possible.	**Black scale, Brown soft scale.** Yellow, brown, or black, flattened or bulbous, up to ⅕ inch long.	See page 126.
Sticky honeydew, blackish sooty mold on leaves and twigs. Possible dieback.	**Kuno scale,** *Eulecanium kunoense.* Adult scales beadlike and mahogany colored.	Plants tolerate moderate populations. Monitor and apply oil if needed. See Scales, page 117.
Sticky honeydew, blackish sooty mold on foliage. Slow growth and possible premature leaf drop.	**Pear psylla,** *Cacopsylla pyricola.* Tiny orangish nymphs in honeydew droplets. Brown adults look like tiny cicadas.	On pear. Conserve natural enemies that help in control. Apply narrow-range oil in dormant season, thoroughly covering terminals where eggs occur. See Psyllids, page 103.
Blackening of foliage from sooty mold. Cottony or waxy material on plant.	**Grape mealybug,** *Pseudococcus maritimus;* Obscure mealybug. Powdery, grayish, up to ¼ inch long with waxy filaments.	Vigorous plants tolerate moderate populations. Conserve natural enemies that help in control. See Mealybugs, page 114.
Small brownish leaf spots, center tan. Holes in leaf from dropped, infected tissue. Concentric lesions on branch.	**Shot hole.** A fungal disease.	Affects stone fruit and ornamental *Prunus* spp. See page 187.
Tiny reddish to brown leaf spots, may have yellow haloes. Larger, dark areas on leaves. Leaves may drop.	**Entomosporium leaf spot.** A fungus.	Affects apple, evergreen pear, pear. See page 188.

SEE PAGES 264–266 FOR ADDITIONAL COMMON CAUSES OF SYMPTOMS

FRUIT TREES: Apple, crab apple (*Malus* spp.); Apricot, cherry, nectarine, peach, plum (*Prunus* spp.); Natal plum (*Carissa macrocarpa*); Pear (*Pyrus* spp.); Pomegranate (*Punica granatum*), continued

WHAT THE PROBLEM LOOKS LIKE	PROBABLE CAUSE	COMMENTS
Reddened, distorted foliage in spring. Shoots thickened, distorted, may die. Leaves may drop prematurely.	**Leaf curl,** *Taphrinia deformans.* Fungal disease promoted by moist spring weather or splashing irrigation water.	Affects peach, nectarine. Apply fungicide with at least 50% copper or synthetic fungicide in fall after leaf drop, repeat when buds swell.
Dark scabby or velvety spots on leaves or fruit.	**Scab,** *Venturia* spp. Fungi spread by splashing water in spring.	Affects apple and pear. See Scabs, page 188.
Stippled, flecked, or bleached leaves. Leaves may drop.	**Citrus red mite, Pacific spider mite, Twospotted spider mite.** Tiny, sand-size specks on leaves.	See page 170.
Darkening or bronzing of leaves. Plant growth may slow.	**Pear rust mite,** *Epitrimerus pyri.* An eriophyid mite.	Affects *Pyrus calleryana.* See Gall Mites, page 173.
Spotted or yellow foliage, dimpled pears.	**Boxelder bugs.** Gray and red adults, about $\frac{1}{2}$ inch long. Nymphs red.	Trees tolerate damage. Primarily affects box elder, maple, but also pear. See page 136.
Leaves scraped, skeletonized, may be slime covered.	**Pear sawfly** or **pearslug.** Green, slimy, sluglike insects, up to $\frac{1}{2}$ inch long.	See page 79.
Leaves chewed. Single branches or entire plant may be defoliated.	**Redhumped caterpillar, Western tent caterpillar, Tussock moths.** Up to $1\frac{1}{2}$ inches long, caterpillars.	See pages 70–75.
Chewed leaves. Foliage may be rolled and tied together with silk.	**Fruittree leafroller, Omnivorous looper.** Moth larvae.	See pages 73–74.
Leaves chewed, webbed together in groups of several containing larva.	**Western tiger swallowtail,** *Papilio rutulus.* Caterpillar bright green with eyespots, black and yellow markings. Adult 2 inches, yellow with black.	Caterpillars mature into attractive butterflies. Control not recommended. *Bacillus thuringiensis* kills young larvae. See Foliage-Feeding Caterpillars, page 63.
Chewed leaves or blossoms. Larvae feed on roots.	**Fuller rose beetle.** Pale brown adult snout weevils, about $\frac{3}{8}$ inch long.	Adults hide during day and feed at night. Attacks *Pyrus* and *Prunus* spp. See page 88.
Some leaves or fruit wilted, distorted.	**Chinch bugs.** Small, slender, mostly brownish or blackish bugs.	See page 138.
Stems, flowers, or fruit with dark lesions. Cankers possible on branches.	**Bacterial blight.**	See page 197.
Sudden wilting then shriveling and blackening of shoots, blossoms and fruit. Plant appears scorched.	**Fireblight.** Bacterium enters plants through blossoms.	Affects apple, crab apple, evergreen pear, pear. See page 190.
Leaves discolored, wilted, stunted, may drop prematurely. Discolored bark may ooze sap. Branches or plant may die.	**Collar, Foot, and Crown rots.** Decay fungi common in moist soils.	See page 209.
Leaves wilted, discolored, may drop. Branches or entire plant may die.	**Dematophora root rot.** Minute white fungus growths may be visible in wood.	Less common than *Armillaria* or *Phytophthora.* See page 208.
Galls or swellings on roots.	**Root knot nematode,** *Meloidogyne* sp.	See page 257.
Foliage fades, yellows, browns, wilts, often scattered throughout canopy. Branches die. Entire plant may die.	**Verticillium wilt.** A soil dwelling fungal disease, infects through roots.	See page 190.
Roughened twig bark. Possible twig dieback.	**Buffalo treehopper.** Bright yellow to green insects, horny or spiny.	See page 133.

WHAT THE PROBLEM LOOKS LIKE	PROBABLE CAUSE	COMMENTS

FRUIT TREES: Apple, crab apple (*Malus* spp.); Apricot, cherry, nectarine, peach, plum (*Prunus* spp.); Natal plum (*Carissa macrocarpa*); Pear (*Pyrus* spp.); Pomegranate (*Punica granatum*), continued

Foliage turns red, brown, then fades. May be small, pimplelike growths or brownish cankers on bark.	**Cytospora canker.** Fungal disease.	See page 201.
Decline or dieback of twigs and branches. Grayish to brownish encrustations on bark.	**Greedy scale, Oystershell scale, San Jose scale.** Tiny circular to elongate individuals on twigs and branches.	See pages 122–24.
Dead twigs or branches. Plant declines, may die. Tiny "shot holes" in bark.	**Shothole borer.** Small brown adults, whitish larvae, tunnel beneath bark.	See page 156.
Roughened bark, reddish brown granular material (frass) at base of trunk and main limbs. May be dark ooze from bark.	**Peachtree borer,** *Synanthedon exitiosa*. Brown to pink larvae bore under bark. Adults wasplike, blue and orange.	Attacks stone fruit and ornamental *Prunus* spp. Prevent injuries to bark. Provide proper cultural care. Applying nematodes may kill moth larvae. See Clearwing Moths, page 162.
Woody swellings on bark. Cottony, waxy material on branches.	**Woolly apple aphid.** Tiny reddish insects covered with cottony wax.	See page 96.
Galls or swellings on trunk and roots, usually near soil, may be on branches.	**Crown gall.** Bacteria infect plant via wounds.	*Prunus* spp. (cherry, plum, peach) common hosts. See page 203.

FUCHSIA (*Fuchsia* spp.)

Foliage fades, yellows, browns, wilts, often scattered throughout canopy. Branches die. Entire plant may die.	**Verticillium wilt.** A soil-dwelling fungal disease, infects through roots.	See page 190.
Leaf undersides with orangish pustules. Leaves may be spotted, drop.	**Rust,** *Pucciniastrum pustulatum*. Fungus requires moisture to develop.	Avoid overhead watering. Plants tolerate moderate populations. See Rusts, page 195.
Shoots and leaves thickened, distorted or galled.	**Fuchsia gall mite.** Microscopic, wormlike eriophyid mites.	See page 173.
Foliage blackened from sooty mold. Tiny, whitish, mothlike adult insects.	**Greenhouse whitefly.** Nymphs oval, flattened, yellow to greenish.	See page 112.
Plant blackened by sooty mold. Waxy, cottony material on plant.	**Mealybugs.** Oblong, waxy, slow-moving insects, up to 1/8 inch long.	See page 114.

GARDENIA (*Gardenia augusta*), Cape jasmine

Sticky honeydew and blackish sooty mold on plant. Elongated, whitish material (egg sacs) on bark.	**Cottony cushion scale.** Females brown, orange, red, or yellow with elongated, white, fluted egg sacs when mature.	Insects on twigs or leaves. Natural enemies usually provide good control. See page 130.
Leaves with blackish sooty mold, sticky honeydew, and whitish cast skins.	**Aphids.** Groups of small, pearshaped insects on succulent foliage.	See Aphids, page 93.

GIANT SEQUOIA (*Sequoiadendron giganteum*), Big tree, Sierra redwood

Stippled foliage. Foliage color abnormally light green or yellowish.	**Spruce spider mite.** Greenish specks, often in fine webbing at foliage base.	Highest populations occur during spring and fall. See page 172.
Grayish or brownish encrustations on foliage. Foliage may yellow.	**Redwood scale,** *Aonidia shastae*. Oval to circular insects, each about 1/16 inch long, often in colonies.	Conserve natural enemies that provide control. Vigorous plants tolerate moderate populations. Monitor, apply oil if severe. See Scales, page 117.
Treetop, branches dying. Some branches reddish, pitchy or grayish, bare.	**Botryosphaeria canker and dieback.** Fungus spread by splashing water.	Avoid planting sequoia in hot areas outside of native range. Affects drought-stressed trees. Provide proper irrigation. See page 203.

WHAT THE PROBLEM LOOKS LIKE	PROBABLE CAUSE	COMMENTS
GRECIAN LAUREL (*Laurus nobilis*)		
Stippled or bleached leaves with varnishlike specks on undersides.	**Greenhouse thrips.** Tiny, slender black adults or yellow nymphs.	See page 141.
Leaf margins rolled inward, forming galls, which turn red then brown.	**Laurel psyllid,** *Trioza alacris*. Nymphs about ¹/₁₆ inch long, powdery covered, within galls.	Conserve natural enemies that help control. Vigorous plants tolerate. If not tolerable, inspect terminals regularly and apply oil or soap when nymphs abundant. See Psyllids, page 103.
Dead or declining twigs or branches. Grayish encrustations on plant.	**Oleander scale.** Tiny, circular to oval insects on twigs, branches and leaves.	See page 124.
GREVILLEA (*Grevillea* spp.)		
Sticky honeydew and blackish sooty mold on plant. Elongated, whitish material (egg sacs) on bark.	**Cottony cushion scale.** Females brown, orange, red, or yellow with elongated, white, fluted egg sacs when mature.	Insects on twigs or leaves. Natural enemies usually provide good control. See page 130.
HACKBERRY (*Celtis* spp.)		
Stickiness and blackening of foliage from honeydew and sooty mold. Plant growth may slow, foliage may yellow.	**Citricola scale, European fruit lecanium.** Brownish or grayish flattened or bulbous insects.	See pages 127–28
HAWTHORN (*Crataegus* spp.)		
Sudden wilting then shriveling and blackening of shoots, blossoms and fruit. Plant appears scorched.	**Fireblight.** Bacterium enters plants through blossoms.	See page 190.
Tiny reddish to brown leaf spots, may have yellow haloes. Larger, dark areas on leaves. Leaves may drop.	**Entomosporium leaf spot.** A fungus.	See page 188.
Leaves with orangish pustules. Leaves yellow, spotted, may drop. Swellings possible on leaves, twigs.	**Rusts,** *Gymnosporangium* species. Fungus alternates hosts on juniper, cedar.	Avoid overhead watering. Vigorous plants tolerate moderate populations. See page 196.
Leaves chewed, may be tied with silk. Plant may be defoliated.	**Fruittree leafroller, Tussock moths.** Larvae green or hairy, up to 1½ inch long.	See page 70.
Leaves scraped, skeletonized, may be slime covered.	**Pear sawfly** or **pearslug.** Green, slimy, sluglike insects, up to ½ inch long.	See page 79.
Roughened twig bark. Possible twig dieback.	**Buffalo treehopper.** Bright yellow to green insects, horny or spiny.	See page 133.
Leaves with blackish sooty mold, sticky honeydew, and whitish cast skins.	**Aphids.** Groups of small, pearshaped insects on succulent foliage.	See Aphids, page 93.
HEATHER (*Calluna vulgaris*)		
Leaves discolored, wilted, stunted, may drop prematurely. Discolored bark may ooze sap. Branches or plant may die.	**Collar, Foot, and Crown rots.** Decay fungi common in moist soils.	See page 209.
HEBE (*Hebe, Veronica* spp.)		
Leaves with reddish, brownish, or yellowish spots or blotches.	**Septoria leaf spot.** A fungal disease.	Avoid overhead irrigation. See page 187.
Foliage fades, yellows, browns, wilts, often scattered throughout canopy. Branches die. Entire plant may die.	**Verticillium wilt.** A soil-dwelling fungal disease, infects through roots.	See page 190.

WHAT THE PROBLEM LOOKS LIKE	PROBABLE CAUSE	COMMENTS

HEBE (*Hebe, Veronica* spp.), continued

Yellowing and death of foliage, older foliage affected first. Browning of vascular tissue.	**Fusarium wilt**, *Fusarium oxysporum.* Fungus infects plant through roots.	Avoid injuring live tissue. Provide proper drainage, irrigation, and fertilization. Avoid planting hebe. See page 191.
Twigs distorted, swollen, and pitted. Leaves dwarfed. Shoots may die back.	**Pit-making pittosporum scale**, *Asterolecanium arabidis.* Brown to white, up to ⅛ inch long, on twigs, often in pits.	Occasional problem in northern California. Management not investigated. See Scales, page 117.

HEMLOCK (*Tsuga* spp.)

Foliage discolors, wilts, stunts, may drop. Discolored bark or cankers may ooze sap. Branches or plant may die.	**Collar, Foot, and Crown rots.** Decay fungi common in moist soils.	See page 209.
Bark stained brownish, exudes rancid fluid, often around crotches, wounds.	**Wetwood** or **Slime flux.** Bacterial infection.	Rarely causes serious harm to trees. See page 204.

HIBISCUS (*Hibiscus* spp.)

Leaves with yellow to brownish spots or blotches.	**Hibiscus chlorotic ringspot virus.**	Keep plants vigorous by providing proper cultural care. No other treatment. See page 212.
Chewed leaves or blossoms.	**Fuller rose beetle.** Pale brown adult snout weevils, about ⅜ inch long.	Adults hide during day and feed at night. Larvae feed on roots. See page 88.
Blackish sooty mold, sticky honeydew. Tiny, whitish, mothlike adult insects.	**Greenhouse whitefly.** Nymphs oval, flattened, yellowish to translucent.	See page 112.
Plant blackened by sooty mold. Waxy, cottony material on plant.	**Mealybugs** including Longtailed mealybug. Up to ⅛ inch long with waxy filaments, longest around tail.	See page 114.
Sticky honeydew, blackish sooty mold, and whitish cast skins on foliage.	**Melon aphid.** Small greenish, blackish or yellowish insects in groups.	See page 94.
Galls or swellings on roots.	**Root knot nematode**, *Meloidogyne* sp.	See page 257.

HOLLY (*Ilex* spp.)

Blackening of foliage from sooty mold. Possible decline or dieback of twigs and branches.	**Black scale, Brown soft scale.** Yellow, orange, brown, or black, flattened to bulbous insects, often in groups.	See page 126.
Dead or declining twigs or branches. Grayish to brownish encrustations on twigs, branches, or leaves.	**Greedy scale, Oleander scale, Oystershell scale.** Tiny circular to oval insects, often in colonies.	See pages 123–24.
Slender, winding or blotched mines. Pinpricklike scars in leaves. Mines occur in American holly, puncture scars on American and Japanese hollies.	**Native holly leafminer**, *Phytomyza ilicicola.* Adults are tiny, black flies. Flattened, pale larvae are in mines in leaves.	Ignore or prune out damage. Plants tolerate abundant mines. An organophosphate insecticide may be applied once about April to June if not tolerable.
Leaves discolored, wilted, stunted, may drop prematurely. Discolored bark may ooze sap. Branches or plant may die.	**Collar, Foot, and Crown rots.** Decay fungi common in moist soils.	See page 209.
Leaves wilted, discolored, may drop. Branches or entire plant may die.	**Dematophora root rot.** Minute white fungus growths may be visible in wood.	Less common than *Phytophthora.* See page 208.

WHAT THE PROBLEM LOOKS LIKE	PROBABLE CAUSE	COMMENTS
HONEY LOCUST (*Gleditsia triacanthos*)		
Leaflets terminating in podlike galls. Foliage browns and drops prematurely.	**Honeylocust pod gall midge.** Adult is tiny fly. White larvae occur in pods.	See page 114.
Chewed leaves. Silken tents in tree.	**Mimosa webworm.** Larvae gray to brown with white stripes, up to ½ inch long.	See page 77.
Blackening of foliage from sooty mold. Tiny, whitish mothlike adult insects.	**Greenhouse whitefly.** Nymphs are oval, flattened, yellow to greenish.	See page 112.
HYPERICUM (*Hypericum* spp.), Gold flower, St. Johnswort		
Chewed leaves. Entire plant may be defoliated.	**Klamathweed beetle.** Adults metallic, oval, bluish, about ¼ inch long.	See page 86.
Leaves stippled, bleached, with varnishlike specks on undersides.	**Greenhouse thrips.** Tiny, slender, black adults or yellowish nymphs.	See page 141.
Leaves with orangish pustules. Leaves spotted, discolored, drop.	**Hypericum rust,** *Melampsora hypericorum.* A fungal disease.	Avoid overhead watering. Vigorous plants tolerate moderate rust infections. See Rusts, page 195.
JACARANDA (*Jacaranda* spp.)		
Leaves with blackish sooty mold, sticky honeydew, and whitish cast skins.	**Aphids,** including Bean aphid. Small green or black insects in groups.	See page 93.
JASMINE (*Jasminum* spp.), Star jasmine		
Plant blackened by sooty mold. Waxy, cottony material on plant.	**Mealybugs,** including Longtailed mealybug. Up to ⅛ inch long with waxy filaments, longest around tail.	See page 114.
Blackish sooty mold on leaves or twigs. Plants may decline.	**Scales,** including Black scale. Bulbous to flattened insects, yellowish to black. May be H-shape on back.	See page 117.
JUNIPER (*Juniperus* spp.)		
Brown to purplish insects clustered on foliage. May be sooty mold/honeydew.	**Giant conifer aphids.** Dark, long-legged, up to ⅕ inch long.	Apparently harmless to trees. See page 95.
Chewed needles.	**Sawflies,** *Neodiprion* spp. Up to 1 inch long, green larvae on needles.	See page 77.
Browning of tips beginning in fall, worst late winter to spring.	**Cypress tip miner.** Adults are small, silvery tan moths. Green larvae, up to ⅛ inch long, tunnel in foliage.	See page 147.
Browning of plant tips. Plant appears brown most of the year. In California, problem along south coast.	**Juniper needle miner,** *Stenolechia bathrodyas.* Green larvae, up to ⅛ inch long, mine leaflets. Adults are silvery moths, about ¼ inch long.	See similar cypress tip miner, page 147. Plants tolerate extensive needle mining. If not tolerable, may be sprayed during three annual flights of moths. Shake foliage regularly March–October, spray only if moths abundant.
Tufts of cottony material protruding from bark.	**Cypress bark mealybug.** Reddish insects about 1/16 inch long under cottony wax.	See page 115.
Yellow or brown foliage. Whitish to brownish encrustations on foliage.	**Juniper scale,** *Carulaspis juniperi;* **Minute cypress scale.** Circular to elongate insects, 1/16 inch long.	Populations in California rarely warrant control. See page 125.
Foliage yellows and wilts. Branches or entire plant dies.	**Root and crown rot,** *Phytophthora* spp. Fungus disease.	Disease caused by too much water and/or poor drainage. See page 209.

SEE PAGES 264–266 FOR ADDITIONAL COMMON CAUSES OF SYMPTOMS

WHAT THE PROBLEM LOOKS LIKE	PROBABLE CAUSE	COMMENTS
JUNIPER (*Juniperus* spp.), continued		
Scattered dying or dead branches. Entire plant never dead.	**Juniper twig girdler.** Off-white larva with brown head, up to ⅜ inch long, occurs in tunnel beneath twig bark.	See page 169.
Stunted, bushy branches. Orangish, gelatinous masses or galls on bark. Stem dieback.	**Gymnosporangium rusts.** Fungi alternate on deciduous hosts.	See page 196.
Dieback of branches.	**Flatheaded borer,** *Chrysobothris* sp. Whitish larva up to 1¼ inch long with enlarged head, tunnels in wood.	In California affects mostly Hollywood (Twisted Chinese) juniper in San Joaquin Valley. Keep plants vigorous. See Flatheaded Borers, page 157.
Galls or swellings on roots.	**Root knot nematode,** *Meloidogyne* sp.	See page 257.
KOELREUTERIA (*Koelreuteria* spp.), Chinese flame tree, Golden rain tree		
Trunk or limbs with roughened, wet or oozing area. Cracked bark and dieback.	**Flatheaded borers.** Whitish larvae enlarged behind head, under bark.	Adults bullet-shaped, metallic, coppery, gray, greenish or bluish beetles. See page 157.
LANTANA (*Lantana montevidensis*), Sage		
Blackish sooty mold, sticky honeydew. Tiny, whitish, mothlike adult insects.	**Greenhouse whitefly.** Nymphs oval, flattened, yellowish to translucent.	See page 112.
Flowers, leaves, and shoots discolor, wilt, decay, and drop.	**Botrytis blight,** *Botrytis cinerea.* A fungal disease.	Avoid overhead watering. Thin canopy to improve air circulation. Provide proper care. Prune out dying tissue, make cuts in healthy wood.
LARCH (*Larix* spp.)		
Foliage discolored, wilted, stunted, drops. Discolored bark or cankers may ooze sap. Branches or plant may die.	**Collar, Foot, and Crown rots.** Decay fungi common in moist soils.	See page 209.
LINDEN (*Tilia* spp.)		
Sticky honeydew, blackish sooty mold, and whitish cast skins on leaves.	**Linden aphid,** *Eucallipterus tiliae.* Small yellowish insects, with black.	See Aphids, page 93.
LIQUIDAMBAR (*Liquidambar* spp.), Sweet gum		
Blackening of foliage from sooty mold.	**Calico scale.** Adults globular, black with white or yellow spots.	See page 128.
Webbing or tents on branch terminals. Chewed foliage.	**Fall webworm.** Larvae white to yellow, hairy, up to 1 inch long.	See page 76.
Leaves chewed, may be tied with silk. Plant may be defoliated.	**Fruittree leafroller, Tussock moths.** Larvae green or hairy, up to 1½ inches long.	See pages 70–74.
Chewed foliage. Typically only single branches are defoliated.	**Redhumped caterpillar.** Larvae with red head, body yellowish with reddish and black stripes, up to 1 inch long.	See page 72.
Bark exudes white, frothy material, often around wounds, has pleasant odor.	**Foamy canker.** Bacterial infection.	Foamy material appears for only short time during warm weather. See page 205.

LOCUST, BLACK LOCUST (*Robinia* spp.)

WHAT THE PROBLEM LOOKS LIKE	PROBABLE CAUSE	COMMENTS
Large holes, up to ½ inch diameter, in trunks and limbs. Slow tree growth.	**Carpenterworm.** Whitish larvae, up to 2½ inches long, with brown head, tunnel in wood.	See page 168.
Dying or dead limbs. Many tiny, round holes in bark from beetle emergence.	**Bark beetles,** *Chramesus* spp. Adults ¹⁄₁₀ inch long, dark, cylindrical. Whitish maggotlike larvae under bark.	Attack only severely stressed trees and dying limbs. Prune out infested wood. Provide trees proper care. See Bark Beetles, page 152.
Bark discolored, oozing, or swollen. Boring dust in crevices, at tree base. Dying limbs. Tree may decline.	**Black locust borer,** *Megacyllene robiniae.* Whitish larvae bore under bark. Adult is yellow and black longhorned beetle.	Attacks primarily stressed trees, provide trees proper cultural care. See Round-headed Borers, page 160.

LOQUAT (*Eriobotrya japonica*)

Sudden wilting then shriveling and blackening of shoots, blossoms and fruit. Plant appears scorched.	**Fireblight.** Bacterium enters plants through blossoms.	See page 190.
Black to dark olive spots on fruit and sometimes on leaves. Leaves yellow and may drop prematurely.	**Scab,** *Spilocaea pyracanthae.* A fungal disease spread by water from infected leaves and twigs.	Avoid overhead watering. Prune out infected twigs in fall, make the cuts in healthy wood. Collect/dispose of infected leaves.

MADRONE (*Arbutus menziesii*), STRAWBERRY TREE (*Arbutus unedo*)

Dark, immobile bodies (pupae) about ¹⁄₁₆ inch long on underside of leaves. Blackish sooty mold.	**Madrone whitefly,** *Trialeurodes madroni.* Fringe of white filaments on sides of dark pupal cases.	Apparently does not damage plants. No known management. See Whiteflies, page 108.
Blackening of foliage from sooty mold. Scalelike bodies on twigs.	**Madrone psyllid,** *Euphyllura arbuti.* Tiny reddish winged adults or flattened, grayish waxy nymphs.	Plants tolerate psyllid. No management known. See Psyllids, page 103.
Foliage blackened by sooty mold. Twigs or branches may decline or die back.	**Black scale, Brown soft scale.** Yellow, brown, or black, flattened or bulbous.	See page 126.
Blackish sooty mold, sticky honeydew, and whitish cast skins on plant.	**Aphids.** Small green, brown, black or yellowish insects, often in groups.	See Aphids, page 93.
Small discrete spots to irregular, large spots or holes over most of leaf surface. Tree may defoliate if severe.	**Leaf spots,** *Cryptostictis arbuti, Mycosphaerella arbuticola, Phyllosticta fimbriata, Sphaceloma* sp.	Diseases apparently promoted by wet winters. Plants tolerate extensive leaf spotting. No control measures known.
Mined blotches or dead patches on leaves. Lower leaf surface scraped.	**Blotch leaf miner,** *Gelechia panella.* Moth larva up to ⅔ inch long.	Does not harm plant. Tolerate or clip and dispose of infested leaves. See Foliage Miners, page 146.
Leaves with elliptical holes, ⅛ to ¼ inch long, and winding tunnels.	**Madrone shield bearer,** *Coptodisca arbutiella.* Larvae, up to ¼ inch long, mine leaves. Adult is tiny moth.	Vigorous plants tolerate moderate leaf damage. No management known. See page 149.
Winding, silvery or whitish tunnels on leaf upper surface.	**Leafminer,** *Marmara arbutiella.* Moth larva.	Does not harm plant. Tolerate or clip and dispose of infested leaves. See Foliage Miners, page 146.
Chewed leaves. Tents or mats of silk on leaves.	**Western tent caterpillar.** Hairy larva, mostly brown, up to 2 inches long.	See page 75.
Dying and dead branches. Cankers on large branches and trunk. Dead branches turn black.	**Fungi:** *Botryosphaeria dothidea, Phomopsis* spp., *Fusicoccum aesculi.* Attack weakened trees.	Prune out dead and diseased branches in summer. Provide appropriate water and other cultural care to improve tree vigor. See page 203.

WHAT THE PROBLEM LOOKS LIKE	PROBABLE CAUSE	COMMENTS

MADRONE (*Arbutus menziesii*), STRAWBERRY TREE (*Arbutus unedo*), continued

WHAT THE PROBLEM LOOKS LIKE	PROBABLE CAUSE	COMMENTS
Trunk or limbs with roughened, wet or oozing area. Cracked bark and dieback.	**Flatheaded borers.** Larvae whitish, with enlarged head, under bark.	Adults bullet-shaped, metallic, coppery, gray, greenish, or bluish. See page 157.
Leaves yellow, wilt and drop. Branches die back and entire plant may die.	**Annosus root disease.** Fungal disease and decay spread through roots and airborne spores.	See page 211.
Declining or dead twigs or branches. Grayish encrustations on twigs/bark.	**Greedy scale.** Circular, flattened, up to ¹/₁₆ inch long, often in colonies.	See page 123.

MAGNOLIA (*Magnolia* spp.)

WHAT THE PROBLEM LOOKS LIKE	PROBABLE CAUSE	COMMENTS
Blackening of foliage from sooty mold. White popcornlike bodies on bark.	**Cottony cushion scale.** Orangish, flat immatures or cottony females on bark.	Usually under good biological control. See page 130.
Blackening of foliage from sooty mold.	**Obscure mealybug.** Powdery gray insects with waxy filaments.	Conserve natural enemies that help in control. See page 115.
Stippled or bleached leaves with varnishlike specks on undersides.	**Greenhouse thrips.** Tiny, slender black adults or yellow immature insects.	See page 141.
Chewed leaves. Foliage may be rolled and tied together with silk.	**Omnivorous looper.** Yellow, green, or pink larvae, up to 1½ inches long, with green, yellow or black stripes.	Larvae crawl in "looping" manner. See page 73.
Dead or dying twigs or branches. Grayish to brown bark encrustations.	**California red scale, Greedy scale, Oleander scale.** Tiny circular to oval individuals, often in colonies.	See pages 121–24.
Bark stained brownish, exudes rancid fluid, often around crotches, wounds.	**Wetwood** or **Slime flux.** Bacterial infection.	Usually does not cause serious harm to trees. See page 204.

MAHONIA (*Mahonia, Berberis* spp.), Barberry, Oregon grape

WHAT THE PROBLEM LOOKS LIKE	PROBABLE CAUSE	COMMENTS
Poor plant growth. Oval, yellow, or tan nymphs, black pupae on undersides of leaves.	**Deer brush whitefly,** *Aleurothrixus interrogationis.* Tiny, mothlike adults.	Plants tolerate moderate densities. If severe, insecticidal soap may be applied. See Whiteflies, page 108.
Leaves stippled, bleached. Varnishlike specks on underside.	**Greenhouse thrips.** Tiny, slender, black adults or yellowish nymphs.	See page 141.
Leaves chewed. Plants may be defoliated.	**Barberry looper,** *Coryphista meadii.* Green caterpillars, up to 1 inch long.	Vigorous plants tolerate moderate defoliation. Tolerate or apply *Bacillus thuringiensis* or another insecticide. See Foliage-Feeding Caterpillars, page 63.
Foliage discolored, reddening with irregular brown to black dead spots. Orangish pustules or coating on leaves.	**Mahonia rusts,** *Cumminsiella mirabilissima, Puccinia* spp. Fungal diseases.	Avoid overhead watering. Vigorous plants tolerate moderate infection. See Rusts, page 195.
Blackish sooty mold, whitish flocculent material on leaves, stems.	**Mealybug,** *Pseudococcus fragilis.* Oval, whitish insects with rows of bare points, waxy filaments.	See Mealybugs, page 114.
Dead or declining twigs or branches. Grayish encrustations on bark.	**Greedy scale.** Nearly circular insects, less than ¹/₁₆ inch long.	See page 123.

MAIDENHAIR TREE (*Ginkgo biloba*), Ginkgo

WHAT THE PROBLEM LOOKS LIKE	PROBABLE CAUSE	COMMENTS
Chewed leaves.	**Omnivorous looper.** Yellow, green, or pink larvae, up to 1½ inches long, with green, yellow or black stripes.	Larvae crawl in "looping" manner. See page 73.
Galls or swellings on roots.	**Root knot nematode,** *Meloidogyne* sp.	See page 257.

SEE PAGES 264–266 FOR ADDITIONAL COMMON CAUSES OF SYMPTOMS

MANZANITA (*Arctostaphylos* spp.)

WHAT THE PROBLEM LOOKS LIKE	PROBABLE CAUSE	COMMENTS
Leaves with ⅛ to ¼ inch long elliptical holes and winding tunnels.	**Madrone shield bearer,** *Coptodisca arbutiella.* Larvae, up to ¼ inch long, mine leaves. Adult is tiny moth.	Vigorous plants tolerate extensive leaf mining. No management known. See page 149.
Leaves chewed, drop. May be silken webbing on plant.	**Tent caterpillar, Western tussock moth.** Hairy brown or colorful caterpillars up to 2 inches long.	See pages 70, 75.
Fleshy red galls on leaves. Plants may grow slowly.	**Manzanita leaf gall aphid.** Tiny, gray or greenish insects in leaf galls.	See page 96.
Sticky honeydew, blackish sooty mold, whitish cast skins on leaves. Shoots may die back.	**Aphid,** *Wahlgreniella nervata.* Pink to green insects in colonies on leaves and terminals.	Plants tolerate moderate populations. Hose forcefully with water. Apply soap or oil if not tolerable. See Aphids, page 93.
Blackening of foliage from sooty mold. Possible twig and branch dieback.	**Brown soft scale.** Yellow to brown, flattened insects in groups.	See page 126.
Blackening of foliage from sooty mold. Immobile, dark, oval bodies (pupae) 1/16 inch long on leaf undersides.	**Whiteflies,** including Iridescent whitefly, *Aleuroparadoxus iridescens;* Crown whitefly. Tiny mothlike adults.	Conserve natural enemies that help control. Insecticidal soap may be applied if severe. See Whiteflies, page 108.
Blackening of foliage from sooty mold. Cottony waxy material on plant.	**Mealybugs:** *Puto arctostaphyli, Puto albicans.* Powdery white insects, up to ¼ inch long, with waxy fringe.	Apply soap or oil if intolerable. See Mealybugs, page 114.
Dying and dead branches. Cankers on large branches and trunk. Dead branches turn black.	**Fungi:** *Botryosphaeria dothidea, Fusicoccum* spp. attack weakened trees.	Prune out dead and diseased branches in summer. Provide appropriate water and other cultural care to improve tree vigor. See page 203.
Dead or dying twigs or branches. Grayish to brownish encrustations on twigs and branches.	**Manzanita scale,** *Diaspis manzanitae;* **Greedy scale; Oleander scale.** Tiny oval to circular insects.	Vigorous plants tolerate moderate populations. If needed, apply oil during the dormant season or monitor and apply oil in the spring or early summer when crawlers are abundant. See pages 123–24.
Trunk or limbs with roughened, wet or oozing area. Cracked bark and dieback.	**Flatheaded borers.** Larvae whitish with enlarged head, under bark.	Adults bullet-shaped, metallic, coppery, gray, greenish or bluish. See page 157.

MAPLE (*Acer* spp.)

WHAT THE PROBLEM LOOKS LIKE	PROBABLE CAUSE	COMMENTS
Sticky honeydew, blackish sooty and whitish cast skins on leaves.	**Aphids,** including *Periphyllus* spp.; Painted maple aphid, *Drepanaphis acerifolii.* Tiny green insects clustered on leaves.	Plants tolerate moderate populations. Hose forcefully with water. Insecticidal soap or oil (these may injure Japanese maple) or another insecticide may be applied if severe.
Sticky honeydew and blackish sooty mold on foliage. Dead or dying twigs and branches. Cottony white material (*Pulvinaria* egg sacs) on plant.	**Cottony maple scale,** *Pulvinaria innumerabilis;* **Black scale; Calico scale.** Yellow, brown, black, or white with spots, flattened to bulbous.	Vigorous plants tolerate moderate populations. Conserve natural enemies. If severe, consider a dormant oil spray or treat when crawlers are abundant; oil may damage maple foliage.
Dead or dying twigs or branches. Grayish to brownish encrustations on twigs and branches.	**Oleander scale, Oystershell scale, San Jose scale.** Tiny circular to elongate individuals, often in groups.	See pages 122–24.
Spotted or yellow foliage, usually severe only on female trees.	**Boxelder bugs.** Gray and red adults, ½ inch long. Nymphs red.	Trees tolerate damage. Adults invading houses may be a problem. See page 136.
Oval or irregular, glossy black, thick tarlike raised spots on upper leaf surface.	**Tar spot,** *Rhytisma punctatum.* Fungus most prevalent in moist environments.	Rake and dispose of leaves in the fall. See Leaf Spots, page 185.

WHAT THE PROBLEM LOOKS LIKE	PROBABLE CAUSE	COMMENTS

MAPLE (*Acer* spp.), continued

WHAT THE PROBLEM LOOKS LIKE	PROBABLE CAUSE	COMMENTS
Foliage fades, yellows, browns, wilts, often scattered throughout canopy. Branches die. Entire plant may die.	**Verticillium wilt.** A soil-dwelling fungus, infects through roots.	See page 190.
Foliage turns red, brown, then fades. May be small, pimplelike growths or brownish cankers on bark.	**Cytospora canker.** Fungal disease.	See page 201.
Dieback of woody plant parts. Tunnels and larvae in wood.	**Flatheaded appletree borer, Pacific flatheaded borer.** Whitish, larvae up to 1 inch long with enlarged head.	See page 157.
Leaves chewed. Foliage may be webbed, defoliated, or contain silk tents.	**Fall webworm, Fruittree leafroller, Omnivorous looper.** Caterpillars.	See pages 73–76.
Bark stained brownish, exudes rancid fluid, often around crotches, wounds.	**Wetwood** or **Slime flux.** Bacterial infection.	Usually does not cause serious harm to trees. See page 204.

MAYTEN (*Maytenus boaria*)

Blackening of foliage from sooty mold.	**Black scale, Nigra scale.** Yellowish to brown, flattened oval insects or black and elongate or bulbous.	See page 126.
Leaves discolored, wilted, stunted, may drop prematurely. Discolored bark may ooze sap. Branches or plant may die.	**Collar, Foot,** and **Crown rots; Verticillium wilt.** Soil-dwelling fungi, infect primarily through roots.	See pages 190, 209.

METROSIDEROS (*Metrosideros* spp.), Iron tree, New Zealand Christmas tree

Sticky honeydew and blackish sooty mold on foliage. Leaves and terminals pitted, distorted, and discolored.	**Eugenia psyllid.** Adults are tiny, leafhopperlike insects. Nymphs feed in pits on lower leaf surface.	Young foliage of *Metrosideros excelsus* may be infested during winter in southern California. See page 106.
Dead tree or dying limbs. Broad galleries beneath bark.	**Eucalyptus longhorned borer.** Adults reddish brown with yellow on the back. Larvae whitish. Both about 1 inch long.	See page 161.

MONKEY FLOWER (*Diplacus, Mimulus* spp.)

Leaves stippled or bleached. Leaves and shoots may die back.	**Seed bugs,** *Kleidocerys* spp. Small, brown, oval insects, suck plant juices.	No known controls. See Bugs, page 135.
Stippled or bleached leaves, varnish-like excrement specks on undersides.	**Thrips.** Tiny, slender blackish or orangish insects.	See Thrips, page 139.
Flower buds mined or distorted. Flowering reduced. Insect pupal skins (exuviae) attached to flower buds.	**Gall midge,** *Asphondylia* spp. Larvae maggotlike, often several per bud. Adults tiny flies.	No known controls. Larvae reduce seeds, but established plants not threatened. Several generations per year. See Gall Midges, page 144.
Foliage discolored. Plant growth slow. Sticky honeydew, blackish sooty mold, and grayish, flocculent material on plant.	**Golden mealybug,** *Nipaecoccus aurilanatus*. Females globular, 1/10 inch long, purplish with felty, golden band marginally and on back.	Several generations occur each year. Natural enemies or soap or oil sprays can help to control. See Mealybugs, page 114.

MOUNTAIN MAHOGANY (*Cercocarpus* spp.)

Blackish sooty mold, sticky honeydew, and whitish cast skins on plant.	**Aphids.** Small, greenish to black, often in groups on leaves and stems.	See Aphids, page 93.

WHAT THE PROBLEM LOOKS LIKE	PROBABLE CAUSE	COMMENTS
MULBERRY (*Morus* spp.)		
Webbing or silk tents on ends of branches. Chewed leaves.	**Fall webworm.** Hairy, white to yellow larvae, up to 1 inch long, in colonies.	See page 76.
Angular blackened areas on leaves. Young leaves and shoots distorted. Elongated lesions may occur on twigs.	**Bacterial blight.** Bacteria ooze from infected twigs in wet weather.	See page 197.
Sticky honeydew, blackish sooty mold on leaves. Blackish, oval bodies with white waxy fringe (nymphs) on leaves.	**Mulberry whitefly,** *Tetraleurodes mori.* Tiny adults, white or yellowish and mothlike.	Conserve natural enemies that help to control. Difficult to control with sprays. Soap or oil can reduce populations. See Whiteflies, page 108.
Declining or dead twigs and branches. Grayish to brownish encrustations on twigs and branches.	**California red scale, Oleander scale, San Jose scale.** Circular to oval insects, less than $1/16$ inch long.	See pages 121–24.
Bark stained brownish, exudes rancid fluid, often around crotches, wounds.	**Wetwood** or **Slime flux.** Bacterial infection.	Usually does not cause serious harm to trees. See page 204.
Galls or swellings on roots.	**Root knot nematode,** *Meloidogyne* sp.	See page 257.
NANDINA (*Nandina domestica*), Heavenly bamboo, Sacred bamboo		
Whitish, cottony material on bark or underside of leaves.	**Comstock mealybug,** *Pseudococcus comstocki.* Oblong, soft, powdery, waxy covered insects with filaments.	Control ants, reduce dust, avoid persistent pesticides that disrupt effective natural enemies. See Mealybugs, page 114.
Foliage blackened by sooty mold. Popcornlike bodies (egg sacs) on bark.	**Cottony cushion scale.** Orangish, flat immatures or cottony females on bark.	Normally controlled by natural enemies. See page 130.
Foliage mottled, reddish.	**Nandina virus.** Disease spread by aphids.	Plants usually tolerate. No control. See page 212.
NYSSA (*Nyssa* spp.), Sour gum, Tupelo gum		
Chewed foliage. Typically only single branches are defoliated.	**Redhumped caterpillar.** Larvae with red head, body yellowish with reddish and black stripes, up to 1 inch long.	See page 72.
Blackening of foliage from sooty mold. Possible plant decline or dieback.	**European fruit lecanium.** Brown, flat or bulbous, immobile scale insects.	See page 128.
OAK (*Quercus* spp.), TANBARK OAK (*Lithocarpus densiflorus*)		
Blackening of foliage from sooty mold. Dark oval bodies (nymphs), about $1/16$ inch long on underside of leaves, often with white, waxy fringe.	**Stanford whitefly,** *Tetraleurodes stanfordi;* **Gelatinous whitefly,** *Aleuroplatus gelatinosus;* **Crown whitefly.** Adults tiny, mothlike.	Ignore insects, they apparently do not damage trees. See Whiteflies, page 114.
Blackening of foliage from sooty mold.	**Aphids,** *Myzocallis* spp. Tiny, green to yellow insects, clustered on leaves.	Plants tolerate moderate aphid populations. Conserve natural enemies. Hose forcefully with water. Apply soap or oil if not tolerable. See Aphids, page 93.
Blackened foliage from sooty mold.	**Oak lecanium scale,** *Parthenolecanium quercifex.* Flattened orangish (nymphs) to bulbous brown (adults) on twigs.	Scale has one generation/year. Control usually not warranted. If severe, monitor in spring, apply oil when crawlers are abundant. See page 128.
Blackening of foliage from sooty mold.	**Obscure mealybug.** Powdery gray insects with waxy filaments.	Conserve natural enemies that help in control. See page 115.

OAK (*Quercus* spp.), TANBARK OAK (*Lithocarpus densiflorus*), continued

WHAT THE PROBLEM LOOKS LIKE	PROBABLE CAUSE	COMMENTS
Blackened foliage from sooty mold. Twig bark roughened. Some bark may be dead.	**Oak treehopper.** Adults green to brown with red dots and horn on head, often on twigs with group of nymphs.	See page 133.
Leaves with many tiny, irregular brown and yellow spots. Young plants most susceptible.	**Oak leaf phylloxera,** Phylloxeridae. Tiny, yellowish insects on underside of leaves. Suck sap.	Plants apparently not damaged. Tolerate or thoroughly apply soap to leaf underside when nymphs present, before severe spotting.
Chewed leaves. Tree may be defoliated.	**California oakworm.** Dark larvae, up to 1¼ inches long, with yellow stripes.	See page 68.
Leaves chewed, tied together with silk. Tree may be defoliated.	**Fruittree leafroller.** Green larvae, with black head and "shield" behind head. Larvae up to ¾ inch long.	Larvae wriggle vigorously when touched. See page 74.
Chewed leaves. Silken mats or "tents" sometimes seen in trees. Tree may be defoliated.	**Pacific tent caterpillar, Western tent caterpillar, Tussock moths.** Hairy, brownish to colorful caterpillars.	See pages 70–75.
Chewed leaves or blossoms.	**Fuller rose beetle.** Pale brown adult snout weevils, about ⅜ inch long.	Adults hide during day and feed at night. Larvae feed on roots. See page 88.
Leaf surface etched. These "windows" may turn brown.	**Oak ribbed casemaker.** Larvae are up to ¼ inch long.	White, ribbed cigar-shaped cocoons on leaves or bark. See page 148.
Leaves mined with elliptical holes.	**Shield bearers.** Tiny larvae cut mined foliage from leaf.	See page 149.
Gouged and etched leaves. Leaves may turn brown.	**Live oak weevil,** *Deporaus glastinus*. Adults are dark, metallic-blue snout beetles, about ¼ inch long.	Most common on live oak, which tolerates much damage. Most damage occurs from April to June. Tolerate. A foliar insecticide may be applied when weevils are present if not tolerable.
Leaves with rolled margins.	**Woolly oak aphid,** *Stegophylla quercicola*. Small, greenish to bluish, cottony wax covered, in rolled leaves.	Plants tolerate moderate aphid densities. Commonly on coast live oak. No known control. See Aphids, page 93.
Leaves yellowish, except along veins. Leaves small, drop. Branches die back.	**Iron deficiency.** Abiotic disorder.	Especially common in pin oak, *Quercus palustris*. See page 218.
Patches of dead leaves at end of branches of live oaks.	**Oak twig girdler.** Adult cylindrical, metallic beetle, larvae whitish.	See page 159.
Leaves discolor, wilt, stunt, may drop prematurely. Discolored bark may ooze sap. Branches or plant may die. Trees may fall over.	**Collar, Foot, and Crown rots,** including Oak root fungus. *Ganoderma applanatum*, a sapwood and heartwood decay fungus of roots and trunks.	See page 209. *Ganoderma* produces large, fan-shaped basidiocarps on lower trunks. These are reddish brown above; their whitish undersides turn dark where touched (thus are called artist's conks).
Wilting and browning leaves. Wood is stained brown. Cambium, sapwood, and bark are killed. Branches die.	**Branch dieback,** *Diplodia quercina*. A fungal disease.	See page 189.
Death of current season's twigs. Dead white leaves remain on twigs, scattered throughout canopy.	**Twig blights:** *Cryptocline cinerescens, Discula quercina*. Fungal diseases more severe if oak pit scale present.	Infects primarily *Quercus agrifolia*. See page 189.
Brown, dead areas along leaf veins. Lower branch leaves most affected.	**Anthracnose,** *Apiognomonia quercina*. Fungal disease active in the spring.	Commonly infects *Quercus kelloggii*. Usually not serious enough to warrant control. See page 185.

SEE PAGES 264–266 FOR ADDITIONAL COMMON CAUSES OF SYMPTOMS

OAK (*Quercus* spp.), TANBARK OAK (*Lithocarpus densiflorus*), continued

WHAT THE PROBLEM LOOKS LIKE	PROBABLE CAUSE	COMMENTS
Shoots short, bushy. Leaves stunted, covered with white, powdery growth. Terminals brown, shriveled ("brooms").	**Witches' broom** or **powdery mildew**, *Sphaerotheca lanestris*. Fungus attacks new growth.	Avoid cultural practices that stimulate excess growth, such as summer irrigation and heavy pruning. Prune out infected growth in winter. Rake and dispose of infected leaves.
Green, plants with smooth stems, thick roundish leaves infesting branches.	**Large leaf mistletoe**, *Phoradendron* sp. Parasitic, evergreen plant on host.	See page 252.
Rough bark, ring-shaped swellings. Dead twigs and branches. Dead leaves persist over winter on deciduous oak.	**Oak pit scales.** Pinhead-size, brown to green, on bark in roundish swellings.	See page 132.
Swellings (galls) sometimes colorful on leaves, flowers, twigs, or branches.	**Cynipid gall wasps.** Adults tiny wasps. Larvae whitish maggots in galls.	Most galls apparently do not harm trees. No control known, except pruning. See page 143.
Raised blisters on leaves with orange felty depressions on undersides.	**Coast live oak erineum mite.** Minute (microscopic-size) wormlike mites.	No management known. See Gall Mites, page 173.
Bulges on upper leaf surface. Leaves galled, curled, may drop.	**Oak leaf blister**, *Taphrina caerulescens*. Fungal disease promoted by wet foliage during leaf flush.	Provide oaks proper cultural care. No control generally recommended.
Greatly roughened bark on lower trunk or major limb crotches. Slow growth.	**Sycamore borer.** Pink larvae up to ¾ inch long, bore in bark or wood.	See page 167.
Large holes, up to ½ inch diameter, in trunks and limbs. Slow tree growth.	**Carpenterworm.** Whitish larvae, up to 2½ inches long, with brown head, tunnel in wood.	See page 168.
Bleeding or frothy material bubbling from tiny holes in trunk or limbs. Fine boring dust may surround holes.	**Oak bark beetles.** Adults brown, ⅛ inch long. White larvae tunnel beneath bark.	See page 155.
Trunk or limbs with roughened, wet or oozing area. Cracked bark and dieback.	**Flatheaded borers.** Larvae whitish with enlarged head, under bark.	Adults bullet-shaped, metallic, coppery, gray, greenish, or bluish. See page 157.
Bark stained brownish, exudes rancid fluid, often around crotches, wounds.	**Wetwood** or **Slime flux.** Bacterial infection.	Usually does not cause serious harm to trees. See page 204.
Holes in acorns. Tunnels inside acorns may contain whitish larvae.	**Filbert weevil**, *Curculio occidentis*; **Filbertworm**, *Melissopus latiferreanus*. Adults tiny beetle (*Curculio*) or moth.	Acorns on shady tree side more likely attacked. May reduce natural oak regeneration, but established trees are not damaged.
Brownish sticky material dripping from acorns.	*Erwinia quercina*. A bacterial disease of acorns.	Apparently associated with filbertworm and filbert weevil. No control recommended in landscapes.

OLEANDER (*Nerium oleander*)

WHAT THE PROBLEM LOOKS LIKE	PROBABLE CAUSE	COMMENTS
Blackened foliage from sooty mold.	**Black scale.** Orangish flat immatures or brown to black bulbous adults with raised H-shape on back.	See page 126.
Blackened foliage from sooty mold. May be cottony waxy material on plant.	**Longtailed mealybug, Obscure mealybug.** Grayish, powdery waxy, with filaments.	See page 116.
Sticky honeydew, blackish sooty mold, and whitish cast skins on leaves and terminals. New growth may be deformed.	**Oleander aphid**, *Aphis nerii*. Yellow and black insects clustering on leaves, shoots, and flowers.	Water and prune less to reduce new growth that promotes aphids. Conserve natural enemies that help control. Hose forcefully with water. Tolerate or apply soap. See Aphids, page 93.

WHAT THE PROBLEM LOOKS LIKE	PROBABLE CAUSE	COMMENTS
OLEANDER (*Nerium oleander*), continued		
Black to brown lesions, spots, streaks on blossoms, leaves and stems. Cankers and brown streaks on wood. Dieback.	**Bacterial blight.**	See page 197.
Galls or knots on stems, bark, and occasionally on leaves. Twig dieback.	**Bacterial gall.**	See page 198.
OLIVE (*Olea europaea*)		
Blackened foliage from sooty mold.	**Black scale.** Orangish flat immatures or brown to black bulbous adults with raised H-shape on back.	See page 126.
Blackening of foliage from sooty mold. Tiny, whitish, mothlike adults.	**Citrus whitefly.** Nymphs oval, flattened, green to yellow.	See page 111.
Declining or dead twigs and branches. Gray to brown encrustations on bark.	**Olive scale,** *Parlatoria oleae;* **Oleander scale.** Circular to oval, less than $\frac{1}{16}$ inch long, on twigs and branches.	Plants tolerate moderate populations. Conserve natural enemies. Monitor in spring and apply oil when crawlers are abundant if populations are damaging. See Scales, pages 124.
Foliage fades, yellows, browns, wilts, often scattered throughout canopy. Branches die. Entire plant may die.	**Verticillium wilt.** A soil-dwelling fungus, infects through roots.	See page 190.
Branches wilted or dying. Boring dust, holes in trunk or branches.	**Ash borer.** Larvae white, up to 1 inch long, head brown. Adult moth wasplike.	See page 166.
Dieback of some twigs. Tunnels under bark. Adults, family Bostrichidae, similar to bark beetles.	**Branch/twig borer,** *Polycaon confertus.* Adults black to brown beetles, up to $\frac{1}{2}$ inch long. Larvae whitish.	Prune out affected parts. Eliminate nearby hardwood in which beetles breed. Provide trees with proper cultural care.
Galls or knots on stems, bark, and occasionally on leaves. Twig dieback.	**Bacterial gall.**	See page 198.
Galls or swellings on roots.	**Root knot nematode,** *Meloidogyne* sp.	See page 257.
PALM (*Arecastrum, Chamaedorea, Phoenix, Washingtonia* spp.)		
Yellowing and death of fronds, often older fronds or leaflets on one side die first. Vascular tissue brown.	**Fusarium wilt,** *Fusarium oxysporum.* Fungus infects through roots.	Attacks primarily Canary Island palm. Avoid injuring living tissue. See page 191.
Premature yellowing of lower fronds.	**Abiotic disease.** Causes include excess or deficient water; magnesium, nitrogen, or potassium deficiency; and pesticide or other chemical injury.	Provide proper cultural care.
Yellowing of main shoots. Odorous rot.	**Bud rot,** *Phytophthora cactorum.* Fungus most severe during warm, moist, or humid weather.	Provide good soil drainage and proper cultural care. Bordeaux mixture helps to prevent further infection if applied at first signs of damage. See Root Rots, page 209.
Yellowing fronds and plant death. Boring insects, family Bostrichidae, similar to bark beetles (page 152), except much larger.	**Giant palm borer,** *Dinapate wrighti.* Larva stout, yellowish. Adult brown to black. Both up to $1\frac{1}{2}$ inches long, tunnel in wood.	Primarily a secondary pest, attacks dead and dying palms. Provide proper cultural care. Dispose of dead palms in which beetles breed.
Yellowing or dieback of fronds. Gray, brownish, yellowish, or black encrustations on fronds. Fronds may blacken from sooty mold.	**Boisduval scale,** *Diaspis boisduvalii;* **California red scale; Greedy scale.** Tiny circular to oval insects. **Black scale; Brown soft scale; Hemispherical scale,** *Saissetia coffeae.* Flattened oval to bulbous, yellow to black.	Vigorous plants tolerate moderate populations. If damaging, monitor and apply oil (which may injure some palms) or other insecticide when crawlers are abundant in spring or summer. See Scales, page 117.

SEE PAGES 264–266 FOR ADDITIONAL COMMON CAUSES OF SYMPTOMS

SEE PAGES 264–266 FOR ADDITIONAL COMMON CAUSES OF SYMPTOMS

WHAT THE PROBLEM LOOKS LIKE	PROBABLE CAUSE	COMMENTS
PALM (*Arecastrum, Chamaedorea, Phoenix, Washingtonia* spp.), continued		
Blackened foliage from sooty mold. Cottony waxy material on plants.	**Longtailed mealybug, Obscure mealybug.** Powdery gray insects with waxy fringe filaments.	See pages 115–16.
Stippled or bleached foliage with varnishlike specks on undersides.	**Greenhouse thrips.** Tiny, slender black adults or yellow nymphs.	See page 141.
Leaf stalk bases rot and die. Terminal bud dies. Trunk cankers on Queen palm.	**Pink rot.** A fungal disease of palms.	Most serious near the coast and on plants of low vigor. See page 205.
Galls or swellings on roots.	**Root knot nematode,** *Meloidogyne* sp.	See page 257.
PECAN (*Carya illinoensis*)		
Yellowish to brown angular patches, sticky honeydew, and blackish sooty mold on leaves. Premature leaf drop.	**Aphids,** including Black pecan aphid, *Melanocallis caryaefoliae.* Black, green, or yellowish insects.	Feeding may cause portions of leaves to die. See Aphids, page 93.
PEPPER TREE (*Schinus molle*), California pepper tree		
Chewed leaves. Foliage may be rolled and tied together with silk.	**Omnivorous looper.** Yellow, green, or pink larvae, up to 1½ inches long, with green, yellow or black stripes.	Larvae crawl in "looping" manner. See page 73.
Roundish pits in leaflets, petioles, and twigs. Trees grayish green with sparse foliage.	**Peppertree psyllid.** Tiny green adults, ¹⁄₁₆ inch long. Nymphs flattened and in pits. Suck sap.	See page 108.
Stippled, bleached foliage.	**Citrus thrips.** Tiny, slender, yellow.	See page 142.
Blackened foliage from sooty mold. Declining or dead twigs or branches.	**Barnacle scale,** *Ceroplastes cirripediformis;* **Hemispherical scale,** *Saissetia coffeae;* **Black scale.** Flat, brown to yellow or bulbous gray, black, or brown insects.	Vigorous plants tolerate moderate populations. If damaging, monitor and apply oil or another insecticide in spring when crawlers are are abundant. See page 126.
Declining or dead twigs or branches. Gray to brown encrustations on bark.	**Greedy scale, Oleander scale.** Tiny oval to circular insects on bark.	See pages 123–24.
Foliage fades, yellows, browns, wilts, often scattered throughout canopy. Branches die. Entire plant may die.	**Verticillium wilt, Armillaria root rot.** Fungi infect through roots.	See pages 190, 206.
PHOTINIA (*Photinia* spp.)		
Stippled, bleached or reddened leaves with varnishlike specks on undersides.	**Greenhouse thrips.** Slender black adults or yellow nymphs.	Look for insects to distinguish from similar damage caused by lace bugs. See page 141.
Stippled or bleached leaves with varnishlike specks on undersides.	**Lace bug,** *Corythucha incurvata.* Adults with lacelike wings, somewhat robust.	Look for insects to distinguish from similar damage caused by thrips. See page 135.
Tiny reddish to brown leaf spots, may have yellow haloes. Larger, dark areas on leaves. Leaves may drop.	**Entomosporium leaf spot.** A fungal disease.	See page 188.
Blackish sooty mold, sticky honeydew, and whitish cast skins on plant.	**Aphids.** Small green, brown, black or yellowish insects, often in groups.	See Aphids, page 93.
Leaf margins chewed, notched. Young plants may decline.	**Weevils,** *Otiorhynchus* or *Brachyrhinus* sp. Adults chew foliage. Larvae chew roots.	See Weevils, page 86.

PINE (*Pinus* spp.)

WHAT THE PROBLEM LOOKS LIKE	PROBABLE CAUSE	COMMENTS
Stickiness, varnishing, or blackening of foliage from honeydew and sooty mold. Possible yellowing of needles.	**Aphids:** *Essigella californica*; *Schizolachnus piniradiatae.* Tiny, slender, green to gray insects.	More common in California in South than in North. Plants tolerate moderate populations. Hose forcefully with water. Tolerate or apply soap or oil if damaging. See Aphids, page 93.
Brown to purplish insects clustered on foliage. May be sooty mold/honeydew.	**Giant conifer aphids.** Dark, long-legged, up to $1/3$ inch long.	Apparently harmless to trees. See page 95.
Blackened foliage from sooty mold. Possible yellowing of older needles. Male scales resemble rice grains on needles.	**Monterey pine scale,** *Physokermes insignicola.* **Irregular pine scale.** Females $1/4$ inch long, resemble chips of marble or dark, shiny, beads on twigs.	Vigorous trees tolerate moderate populations. See page 129.
Yellow mottling or dieback of needles.	**Pine needle scale,** *Chionaspis pinifoliae*; **Black pine leaf scale,** *Nuculaspis californica.* White, gray, or black, $1/16$ inch long, on needles.	Scales have several generations a year in warm areas, only one at cool sites. Plants tolerate moderate populations. Conserve natural enemies. If damaging, monitor and apply oil. See Scales, page 117.
Stippled or bleached needles, more common on young pines.	**Spider mites,** *Oligonychus* spp. Green to pink specks on needles. Suck sap.	See page 170.
Cottony white or grayish material on bark or needles. Slow pine growth.	**Pink bark adelgids,** *Pineus* spp. Tiny purplish insects under cottony wax.	See page 103.
Waxy, whitish material and blackish sooty mold on needles, twigs.	**McKenzie pine mealybug,** *Dysmicoccus pinicolus*; **Obscure mealybug.** Oval, waxy fringed, up to $1/8$ inch long.	Conserve natural enemies. Plants tolerate moderate populations. Insecticidal soap can be applied. See Mealybugs, page 114.
Needles chewed, notched along length. Needles turn brown in late winter or spring.	**Pine needle weevils,** *Scythropus* spp. Adults $1/4$ inch long, brownish snout beetles.	Adult damage to needles and larvae feeding on roots appear not to harm trees. Damaged needles soon drop. No control known. See Weevils, page 86.
Chewed needles.	**Sawflies,** *Neodiprion* spp. Up to 1 inch long, green larvae on needles.	See page 77.
Chewed needles webbed with silk.	**Silverspotted tiger moth,** *Lophocampa* or *Halysidota argentata.* Dark larvae, up to $1 1/4$ inches long, dense brown, blue and yellow hairs. Adults brownish to tan moths with silvery spots.	Vigorous pines tolerate moderate damage. Prune out and dispose of colonies. Tolerate or apply *Bacillus thuringiensis* or other insecticide if young larvae abundant. See Foliage-Feeding Caterpillars, page 63.
Mined buds and shoot tips. Killed tips give tree red or brown appearance. Foliage becomes bunchy looking.	**Monterey pine tip moth,** *Rhyacionia pasadenana*; **Ponderosa pine tip moth,** *R. zozana*; **Nantucket pine tip moth.** Adults $1/3$ inch long yellow, gray, to brown moths. Orangish larvae in mines.	Pines tolerate extensive tip mining. *R. pasadenana* occurs along coast, *R. zozana* in inland California, have one generation a year. Foliage can be sprayed in spring to kill adults if damage not tolerable. See page 150.
Terminals distorted, chewed, dead. Foliage may become bushy, crooked.	**Pine weevils,** *Pissodes* spp. Adults black to brown, rough-surfaced, snout beetles with lighter blotches on back. See page 88.	Grublike larvae of damaging species mine shoots. Tolerate or prune out damage. On high aesthetic value (nursery) trees, a foliar insecticide spray in the spring may be applied when adults feed and lay eggs.
Sections of shoot with greatly shortened needles with swollen bases.	**Monterey pine midge,** *Thecodiplosis piniradiatae.* White or orangish larvae in swollen needles.	Control generally not warranted. No management known.
Wet, white, frothy masses of spittle on twigs or cones.	**Spittlebugs,** *Aphrophora* spp. Green to black insects in spittle.	Tolerate; spittlebugs cause no apparent harm to pines. See Spittlebugs, page 134.

SEE PAGES 264–266 FOR ADDITIONAL COMMON CAUSES OF SYMPTOMS

PINE (*Pinus* spp.), continued

WHAT THE PROBLEM LOOKS LIKE	PROBABLE CAUSE	COMMENTS
Tips of Monterey pine mined, but only for 1 or 2 inches. Tips die, often in crooked position.	**Monterey pine bud moth,** *Exoteleia burkei*. Larvae brownish yellow, up to $^3/_{16}$ inch long, in mines.	Damage very localized and unlikely to harm tree. Prune out and dispose of affected tips, no other control known.
Pitchy masses 1 to 4 inches in diameter protruding from trunks and limbs. Limbs occasionally break.	**Sequoia pitch moth, Douglas-fir pitch moth.** Dirty, whitish larvae, up to 1 inch long, in pitch. Adults wasplike.	Avoid injuring pines, wounds attract moths. Plants tolerate these insects that feed shallowly beneath bark. See page 168.
Dead branches with clinging needles, mostly in upper canopy. Trunk cankers and branches exuding copious pitch.	**Pine pitch canker.** A fungal disease.	See page 201.
Stunted, bushy foliage, possible dieback. Round swellings on branches, orangish (spore covered) in spring.	**Western gall rust.** Fungus infects 2- and 3-needle pines.	See page 196.
Yellow or brown dead spots on needles. Yellow to white blisters on bark. Galls, cankers, dieback may occur.	**Pine rusts.** Fungal diseases.	See page 196.
Black to brown lesions, spots, streaks on needles, stems. Cankers and brown streaks on wood. Branches may die back.	**Needle cast fungi.**	Moist conditions favor fungi. Remove nearby plants/weeds, thin canopy, prune off lower limbs to reduce humidity.
Needles discolor, wilt, stunted, may drop prematurely. Discolored bark may ooze sap. Branches or plant may die.	**Collar, Foot, and Crown rot and decay,** including *Armillaria, Heterobasidion*.	See page 209.
Small, leafless, orangish, upright, plants on host stems. Distorted and slow plant growth. Branches die back.	**Dwarf mistletoe,** *Arceuthobium* spp. Host-specific parasitic plants that extract nutrients from host plant.	Prune out infected branches. Replace heavily infected plants with broadleaf species or conifers from other genera; dwarf mistletoes won't spread to unrelated host species.
Tree declining or dead. Boring dust or coarse granular material around tree base or on bark plates or branch crotches. Pitch tubes on bark.	**Bark beetles.** Brown to black, stout beetles up to $^1/_4$ inch long. Larvae white grubs under bark.	See page 152.
Tree dead, sometimes dying quickly.	**Pinewood nematode,** *Bursaphelenchus xylophilus*.	See page 260.
Declining or dead tree.	**Flatheaded and Roundheaded borers.** Whitish larvae, up to 1 inch long tunneling beneath bark.	See pages 157–60.

PITTOSPORUM (*Pittosporum* spp.), Mock orange, Tobira, Victorian box

WHAT THE PROBLEM LOOKS LIKE	PROBABLE CAUSE	COMMENTS
Twigs distorted, swollen, and pitted. Leaves dwarfed. Shoots may die back.	**Pit-making pittosporum scale,** *Asterolecanium arabidis*. Brown to white, up to $^1/_8$ inch long, on twigs, often in pits.	Occasional problem in northern California. Management not investigated. See Scales, page 117.
Sticky honeydew, blackish sooty mold, and whitish cast skins on plant.	**Apple aphid,** *Aphis pomi*. Bright green insects on terminals or leaves.	Conserve natural enemies that provide control. Tolerate or apply soap or oil. See Aphids, page 63.
Blacked foliage from sooty mold. popcornlike bodies (egg sacs) on bark.	**Cottony cushion scale.** Orangish, flat immatures or cottony females on bark.	Normally controlled by natural enemies. See page 130.
Declining or dead twigs or branches. Grayish encrustations on bark.	**Greedy scale.** Nearly circular insects, $^1/_{16}$ inch long, on bark.	See page 123.

WHAT THE PROBLEM LOOKS LIKE	PROBABLE CAUSE	COMMENTS

PITTOSPORUM (*Pittosporum* spp.), Mock orange, Tobira, Victorian box, continued

WHAT THE PROBLEM LOOKS LIKE	PROBABLE CAUSE	COMMENTS
Leaves discolored, wilted, stunted, may drop prematurely. Discolored bark may ooze sap. Branches or plant may die. Trees may fall over.	**Heart rot or decay fungi,** including *Ganoderma applanatum.*	See page 198. *Ganoderma* produces large, fan-shaped basidiocarps on lower trunks. These are reddish brown above; their whitish undersides turn dark where touched (thus are called artist's conks).
Galls or swellings on roots.	**Root knot nematode,** *Meloidogyne* sp.	See page 257.

PODOCARPUS (*Podocarpus* spp.), African fern pine, Yew pine

Declining or dead twigs or branches. Brownish encrustations on bark.	**California red scale.** Circular to oval insects, less than $1/16$ inch long.	See page 121.
Bluish white bloom covering foliage. Whitish cast skins on leaves.	**Podocarpus aphid,** *Neophyllaphis podocarpi.* Grayish insects, about $1/16$ inch long, grouped on stems or leaves.	Plants tolerate extensive aphid feeding. Hose with forceful water. Tolerate or apply soap or oil if damaging. See Aphids, page 93.

POPLAR, COTTONWOOD, ASPEN (*Populus* spp.)

Leaves with circular to irregular tan or darker spots on leaves. Branch cankers on some hosts.	**Leaf spots,** *Mycosphaerella populorum* (on cottonwood), *Marssonina* spp. (on aspen and poplar). Fungal diseases. Spores spread by water.	Vigorous plants tolerate leaf spotting. Branches with infected leaves may be pruned, dispose of them away from host trees. See Septoria, page 187.
Leaves with orangish pustules, light to dark spots. Leaves may drop.	**Rusts,** *Melampsora* species. Fungi require moist conditions.	Avoid overhead watering. Vigorous plants tolerate moderate infection. See page 195.
Leaves stippled or bleached, with cast skins and varnishlike specks.	**Lace bug,** *Corythucha* sp. Brown adults, up to $1/8$ inch long, wings lacelike.	See page 135.
Black to brown lesions, spots, streaks on blossoms, leaves and stems. Cankers and brown streaks on wood. Dieback.	**Bacterial blight.**	See page 197.
Leaves chewed. Tree may be defoliated. Leaves may be tied together with silk. May be silken tents in tree.	**Silver spotted tussock moth,** *Lophocampa* or *Halysidota maculata*; **Fall webworm; Fruittree leafroller; Redhumped caterpillar, Tent caterpillars.**	*L. maculata* larvae are up to 1 inch long, and black with yellow, white and/or reddish hairs. Other larvae are naked to hairy. Vigorous plants tolerate much defoliation. See page 63.
Leaves chewed, webbed together in groups of several containing larva.	**Western tiger swallowtail,** *Papilio rutulus.* Caterpillar bright green with eyespots, black and yellow markings. Adult 2 inches, yellow with black.	Caterpillars mature into highly attractive butterflies. Control not recommended. *Bacillus thuringiensis* kills young larvae. See Foliage-Feeding Caterpillars, page 63.
Leaves mined with elliptical holes.	**Poplar shield bearer,** *Coptodisca* sp. Moth larvae mine foliage.	See page 149.
Skeletonized leaf surfaces. No silk.	**Leaf and flea beetles,** *Chrysomela* spp. *Altica* spp. Adults dark or metallic, oval, up to $3/8$ inch long.	Larvae are dark, up to about $1/2$ inch long. See Leaf Beetles, page 80.
Sticky honeydew, blackish sooty mold, and whitish cast skins on leaves.	**Aphids,** including Cloudywinged cottonwood aphid, *Periphyllus populicola*; *Chaitophorus* spp.	Tiny green to grayish insects, clustered on leaves. Plants tolerate abundant aphids. Hose forcefully with water. If severe, soap or oil may be applied. See Aphids, page 93.
Blackened foliage from sooty mold. Possible decline or dieback of twigs or branches.	**Cottony maple scale,** *Pulvinaria innumerabilis*; **Brown soft scale; Black scale; European fruit lecanium.** Oval yellow to brown and flattened or black, brown, or cottony and bulbous.	Conserve natural enemies that help in control. Vigorous plants tolerate moderate populations. Monitor and if damaging apply oil when crawlers are abundant in spring or summer. See pages 126–28.
Swellings (galls), often purselike, on leaves and leaf petioles.	**Poplar gall aphid.** Tiny, grayish, waxy insects in galls.	See page 96.

POPLAR, COTTONWOOD, ASPEN (*Populus* spp.), continued

WHAT THE PROBLEM LOOKS LIKE	PROBABLE CAUSE	COMMENTS
Brownish, sunken lesions on trunk and large limbs. Small branches and twigs killed without any apparent canker.	**Canker**, *Cytospora chrysosperma*. Fungal disease most serious on low vigor trees. Often infects through wounds.	Provide moderate fertilizer, adequate water, and proper cultural care. Prune out dead and diseased branches. See page 201.
Declining or dead twigs or branches. Gray to brown encrustations on bark.	**Oystershell scale, San Jose scale.** Tiny oval to circular insects on bark.	See pages 123–24.
Dieback of branches or sometimes entire tree. Wet or dark spots on bark. Bark gnarled.	**Carpenterworm, Clearwing moths, Flat-headed borers, Roundheaded borers.** Whitish larvae up to 2½ inches long, mine beneath bark or in wood.	See pages 157–68.
Leaves wilted, discolored, may drop. Branches or entire plant may die.	**Dematophora root rot.** Minute white fungus growths may be visible in wood.	Less common than *Armillaria*. See page 208.
Roughened twig bark. Possible twig dieback.	**Buffalo treehopper.** Bright yellow to green insects, horny or spiny.	See page 133.
Warty, woody swellings (galls) on twigs.	**Cottonwood gall mite.** Wormlike and and microscopic, in galls.	Plants tolerate extensive galling. No known management. See Gall Mites, page 173.
Bark stained brownish, exudes rancid fluid, often around crotches, wounds.	**Wetwood** or **Slime flux.** Bacterial infection.	Usually does not cause serious harm to trees. See page 204.

PRIVET (*Ligustrum* spp.)

WHAT THE PROBLEM LOOKS LIKE	PROBABLE CAUSE	COMMENTS
Blackened foliage from sooty mold.	**Black scale.** Orangish, flattened, oval or bulbous, black, H-shape on back.	See page 126.
Declining or dead twigs or branches. Gray to brown encrustations on bark.	**California red scale, San Jose scale.** Tiny circular to oval insects on bark.	See pages 121–22.
Twigs distorted, swollen, and pitted. Leaves dwarfed. Shoots may die back.	**Pit-making pittosporum scale,** *Asterolecanium arabidis*. Brown to white, up to ⅛ inch long, on twigs, often in pits.	Occasional problem in northern California. Management not investigated. See Scales, page 117.
Leaves wilted, discolored, may drop. Branches or entire plant may die.	**Dematophora root rot.** Minute white fungus growths may be visible in wood.	Less common than *Armillaria* or *Phytophthora*. See page 208.
Foliage stunted, brown. Buds distorted, galled, dead.	**Privet rust mite,** *Aceria ligustri*; **Privet bud mite,** *Vasates ligustri*. Microscopic pests, suck plant juice.	Vigorous plants tolerate mite feeding. Eriophyid mites are difficult to control. See Gall Mites, page 173.

PYRACANTHA (*Pyracantha* spp.)

WHAT THE PROBLEM LOOKS LIKE	PROBABLE CAUSE	COMMENTS
Sudden wilting, shriveling, blackening of shoots, blossoms, fruits.	**Fireblight.** Bacteria enter plant through blossoms.	Plant appears scorched. See page 190.
Black to dark olive spots on fruit and sometimes on leaves. Leaves yellow and may drop prematurely.	**Scab**, *Spilocaea pyracanthae*. A fungal disease spread by water from infected leaves and twigs.	Avoid overhead watering. Prune out infected twigs and leaves in fall. See Scabs, page 188.
Reddening or bronzing of foliage.	**Spider mite,** *Oligonychus platani*. Greenish or brownish specks on leaves.	See Sycamore Spider Mite, page 170.
Sticky honeydew, blackish sooty mold, and whitish cast skins on plant.	**Apple aphid,** *Aphis pomi*; Bean aphid. Small green or black insects grouped on leaves or terminals.	Conserve natural enemies that provide control. Hose with forceful water. Tolerate or apply soap or oil if severe. See Aphids, page 93.
Sticky honeydew and blackish sooty mold on plant. Slow plant growth.	**Kuno scale,** *Eulecanium kunoense*. Bead-like, mahogany colored, on bark.	Tolerate or monitor and apply oil or another insecticide when crawlers abundant. See page 117.
Blacked foliage from sooty mold. popcornlike bodies (egg sacs) on bark.	**Cottony cushion scale.** Orangish, flat immatures or cottony females on bark.	Normally controlled by natural enemies. See page 130.

WHAT THE PROBLEM LOOKS LIKE	PROBABLE CAUSE	COMMENTS
PYRACANTHA (*Pyracantha* spp.), continued		
Declining or dead twigs or branches. Gray to brown encrustations on bark.	**Greedy scale, San Jose scale.** Tiny circular to oval, often in colonies.	See pages 121–23.
Chewed leaves. Plant may be defoliated.	**Tussock moths.** Hairy larvae, up to 1 inch long, may have colorful spots.	See page 70.
Woody swellings (galls), cottony, waxy material on branches and roots.	**Woolly apple aphid,** *Eriosoma lanigerum.* Tiny, reddish, cottony or waxy covered insects.	Conserve natural enemies that help control. Tolerate or apply soap or another insecticide if severe. See Aphids, page 93.
REDBUD (*Cercis* spp.)		
Foliage turns red, brown, then fades. May be small, pimple-like growths or brownish cankers on bark.	**Cytospora canker.** Fungal disease.	See page 201.
Declining or dead twigs and branches. Gray to brown encrustations on bark.	**Greedy scale, Oleander scale.** Tiny oval insects, often in colonies.	See pages 123–24.
Blackening of foliage from sooty mold. Tiny, powdery white mothlike insects.	**Greenhouse whitefly.** Flat, oval, tiny, yellow to green, on leaf undersides.	See page 112.
Chewed leaves. May be silken tents or mats on plant.	**Tussock moths, Tent caterpillars, Redhumped caterpillar.** Larvae up to 2 inches long, may be hairy or colorful.	See pages 70–75.
Leaves chewed, tied together with silk. Tree may be defoliated.	**Fruittree leafroller.** Green larvae, with black head and "shield" behind head. Larvae up to ¾ inch long.	Larvae wriggle vigorously when touched. See page 74.
RHAMNUS (*Rhamnus* spp.), Buckthorn, Coffeeberry, Redberry		
Sticky honeydew, blackish sooty mold, whitish cast skins on plant.	**Aphids,** *Aphis* and *Sitobion* species. Colonies of tiny, often green insects.	Vigorous plants tolerate moderate aphid populations. Hose plants forcefully with water. Tolerate or apply soap or oil if severe. See Aphids, page 93.
Sticky honeydew, blackish sooty mold on plant. Tiny, white mothlike adults.	**Grape whitefly,** *Trialeurodes vittata.* Tiny yellowish to translucent, oval nymphs. Mature nymphs (pupae) dark brown or mottled dark and yellowish.	Usually most severe on *Rhamnus californica* near grapes, especially in fall when insects move from senescent grape leaves. See Whiteflies, page 108.
Dark scabby or velvety spots on leaves or fruit.	**Scab,** *Venturia rhamni.* Fungal disease promoted by moist spring weather.	See Scabs, page 188.
RHAPHIOLEPIS (*Rhaphiolepis* spp.), Indian hawthorn		
Tiny reddish to brown leaf spots, may have yellow haloes. Larger, dark areas on leaves. Leaves may drop.	**Entomosporium leaf spot.** A fungus.	See page 188.
Leaf margins chewed, notched. Young plants may decline.	**Weevils,** *Otiorhynchus* or *Brachyrhinus* sp. Adults chew foliage. Larvae chew roots.	See Weevils, page 86.
Trunk or limbs with roughened, wet or oozing area. Cracked bark and dieback.	**Flatheaded borers.** Larvae whitish, with enlarged head, under bark.	Adults bullet-shaped, metallic, coppery, gray, greenish, or bluish. See page 157.
RHODODENDRON (*Rhododendron* spp.)		
Stippled or bleached leaves with varnishlike specks on undersides.	**Greenhouse thrips.** Tiny, slender black adults or yellow nymphs.	See page 141.
Blackening of foliage from sooty mold. Tiny powdery white mothlike insects.	**Greenhouse whitefly.** Flat, oval, tiny yellow to green, on leaf undersides.	See page 112.

SEE PAGES 264–266 FOR ADDITIONAL COMMON CAUSES OF SYMPTOMS

RHODODENDRON (*Rhododendron* spp.), continued

WHAT THE PROBLEM LOOKS LIKE	PROBABLE CAUSE	COMMENTS
New foliage yellow, veins green.	**Iron deficiency.** Abiotic disorder.	See page 218.
Leaves with orangish pustules, spots, or discoloring. Leaves may drop.	**Rusts,** *Chrysomyxa* species. Fungi require moisture to reproduce.	Avoid overhead watering. Vigorous plants tolerate moderate populations. See page 195.
Wilting or dead plants. Some roots stripped of bark or girdled near soil. Foliage may be notched around margins.	**Black vine weevil.** Adults are black snout beetles, $\frac{1}{2}$ inch long. Larvae are white grubs with brown head.	Larvae feed on roots. Adults hide during day and feed at night. See page 87.
Leaves discolored, wilted, stunted, may drop prematurely. Discolored bark may ooze sap. Branches or plant may die.	**Collar, Foot, Crown, and Root rots.** Decay fungi common in moist soils.	See page 209.
Leaves with dead margins.	**Abiotic disorder.** Caused by improper irrigation, poor soil, low humidity.	Provide proper cultural care, especially appropriate irrigation. Plant other species.

RHUS (*Rhus* spp.), Sugarbush, Sumac, Wax tree

WHAT THE PROBLEM LOOKS LIKE	PROBABLE CAUSE	COMMENTS
Whitish, waxy material on leaves and shoots. May be blackish sooty mold.	**Sumac psyllids,** *Calophya* spp. Nymphs flattened, brown, orangish, or greenish. Tiny eggs black.	Plants tolerate abundant psyllids. Conserve natural enemies, no other management recommended. See Psyllids, page 103.
Blackish sooty mold, sticky honeydew and whitish cast skins on plant.	**Aphids.** Small green, brownish or yellowish insects, often in groups.	See Aphids, page 93.

RIBES (*Ribes* spp.), Currant, Gooseberry

WHAT THE PROBLEM LOOKS LIKE	PROBABLE CAUSE	COMMENTS
Blackish sooty mold, sticky honeydew and whitish cast skins on plant.	**Aphids.** Small green, brown, black or yellowish insects, often in groups.	See Aphids, page 93.
Slightly raised, yellowish spots on undersides of leaves and young stems. Leaves may drop prematurely.	**White pine blister rust.** Alternate host stage of fungal disease that also damages pines.	See page 196.

ROSE (*Rosa* spp.)

WHAT THE PROBLEM LOOKS LIKE	PROBABLE CAUSE	COMMENTS
Stippled or bleached leaves. Leaves may dry up and drop.	**Spider mites,** *Tetranychus* spp. greenish specks. Suck sap.	Conserve natural enemies that help control. See page 170.
Leaves bleached or stippled with spots larger than mite stippling. Cast skins on underside of leaves.	**Rose leafhopper,** *Edwardsiana rosae.* Greenish to whitish, wedge-shaped insects, up to $\frac{1}{8}$ inch long.	Plants tolerate moderate stippling. Apply insecticidal soap or another insecticide if severe. See Leafhoppers, page 133.
Sticky honeydew, blackish sooty mold, and whitish cast skins on plant. Blossoms may be distorted.	**Aphids,** including Cotton aphid, *Aphis gossypii*; Rose aphid. Tiny greenish to pink insects on terminals and buds.	See Aphids, page 93.
Blackening of foliage from sooty mold. Possible decline of canes.	**Black scale, Brown soft scale, European fruit lecanium.** Flattened or bulbous and yellow, brownish or black.	See pages 126–28.
Blackening of foliage from sooty mold. Tiny powdery white mothlike insects.	**Greenhouse whitefly.** Flat, oval, tiny yellow to greenish nymphs on leaves.	See page 112.
White to gray growth, often powdery, on leaves, shoots, and buds. Leaves become distorted and may drop.	**Powdery mildew.** A fungal disease.	See page 193.
Small orange pustules, primarily on leaf undersides. Upper leaf surface may discolor. Leaves may drop.	**Rust,** *Phragmidium disciflorum.* Fungus favored by cool, moist weather. Spores airborne.	Avoid overhead watering and condensation. Fungicides help prevent damage. See page 195.
Black spots with fringed margins on upper surface of leaves and succulent stems. Yellow areas develop around spots. Leaves may drop.	**Black spot,** *Diplocarpon rosae.* Fungal spores spread by splashing water.	Avoid wetting foliage. Prune out and dispose of infected tissue. Remove fallen leaves. Fungicides help control.

ROSE (*Rosa* spp.), continued

WHAT THE PROBLEM LOOKS LIKE	PROBABLE CAUSE	COMMENTS
Purplish, red, or dark brown spots on leaves. Leaf undersides covered with downy fungal growth. Leaves may yellow and drop.	**Downy mildew,** *Peronospora sparsa*. Spores produced only on living plants. Resistant spores carry fungus over unfavorable periods. Favored by moist, humid conditions.	Prune plants to improve air circulation. Reduce humidity around plants, such as through drip or low-volume irrigation. Avoid overhead watering. Fungicide applications help prevent damage.
Leaves yellow or with yellow blotches, lines, or intricate patterns. Leaves may distort. Plants may be stunted.	**Mosaic virus.** Includes prunus necrotic ringspot and other viruses.	Severity of symptoms varies greatly with rose variety. Many infected varieties tolerate and exhibit few symptoms. See page 212.
Leaves curl downward and canes die. Leaves readily drop from new shoots, which are typically pointed with a broad base.	**Rose leaf curl.** Probably a virus.	Obtain virus-free stock. No known treatment. Tolerate or destroy infected plants.
Leaves emerging in spring are balled or curved on very short shoots with conspicuous vein clearing. Symptoms tend to disappear later in season.	**Rose spring dwarf.** Probably a virus.	Obtain virus-free plants. No known treatment. Tolerate or destroy infected plants.
Foliage fades, yellows, browns, wilts, often scattered throughout canopy. Branches die. Entire plant may die.	**Verticillium wilt.** A soil-dwelling fungus, infects through roots.	See page 190.
Leaves yellow. Growth stunted. Roots smaller, darker than on healthy plants.	**Root lesion nematode,** *Pratylenchus* sp.	See page 258.
Blossom petals streaked with brown.	**Western flower thrips; Madrone thrips,** *Thrips madroni*. Tiny, slender, yellow or black insects in blossoms.	See page 141.
Chewed leaves or blossoms. Leaf margins notched, ragged.	**Fuller rose beetle.** Pale brown adult snout weevils, about ³⁄₈ inch long.	Adults hide during day and feed at night. Larvae feed on roots. See page 88.
Chewed blossoms, especially white and yellow flowers.	**Hoplia beetle,** *Hoplia callipyge*. Adult beetles about ¼ inch long, mostly reddish brown with silver, black or white. Larvae feed on roots.	Larvae not known to damage woody plant roots, also feed in turf, alfalfa, other hosts. Hand pick adults chewing on blossoms. Spray blossoms with a synthetic insecticide in spring if damage cannot be tolerated.
Leaf undersides scraped, skeletonized. Large holes may be eaten in leaves.	**Bristly roseslug.** Shiny black to pale green, bristly larvae, up to ⁵⁄₈ inch.	See page 79.
Holes punched in flowers and canes. Blossoms ragged.	**Rose curculio,** *Rhynchites bicolor*. Red to black snout weevil, ¼ inch long. Small, whitish larvae in buds.	Avoid yellow and white roses apparently preferred by beetle. A broad-spectrum synthetic pesticide can be applied if severe.
Chewed leaves. Leaves may be tied together with silk.	**Caterpillars,** including: Orange tortrix, *Argyrotaenia citrana*; Tussock moths; Fruittree leafroller; Tent caterpillars; Omnivorous looper.	Hairy to naked larvae up to 1½ inches long. See page 63.
Semicircular holes cut in margins of leaves or blossoms.	**Leafcutting bees,** *Megachile* spp. About ½ inch long, robust bees.	Bees line their nests with cut plant parts. Bees are important pollinators and should not be killed. No effective nonchemical controls known.
Flower petals spotted. Buds rot. Twig dieback and cane canker. Woolly, gray fungal spores on decaying tissue.	**Botrytis blight,** *Botrytis cinerea*. Favored by high humidity. Spores are airborne.	Remove and dispose of fallen leaves and debris around plants. Reduce humidity around plants by modifying irrigation, pruning, reducing ground cover. Some fungicides can prevent damage.
Grayish or whitish encrustations on canes. Canes may decline or die back.	**Rose scale,** *Aulacaspis rosae*; **Greedy scale; San Jose scale.** Tiny circular to oval insects, often in colonies.	Conserve natural enemies that help control. If damaging, apply oil during dormant season or monitor and apply soap, oil, or another insecticide when crawlers abundant. See pages 122–23.

SEE PAGES 264–266 FOR ADDITIONAL COMMON CAUSES OF SYMPTOMS

ROSE (*Rosa* spp.), continued

WHAT THE PROBLEM LOOKS LIKE	PROBABLE CAUSE	COMMENTS
Brown cankers, sometimes with gray centers. Small, black, spore-producing structures (pycnidia) on dead tissue.	**Stem cankers and dieback:** *Coniothyrium fuckelii, Botryosphaeria dothidea, Cryptosporella umbrina,* and others. Often infect through wounds, many are spread or promoted by water and rain.	Provide proper cultural care to keep plants vigorous. Prune off diseased or dead tissue, make cuts at an angle in healthy tissue and just above a node. Avoid otherwise wounding tissue. Avoid overhead water.
Decline or death of canes or entire plant. Larvae, up to 1 inch long, tunneling in canes.	**Flatheaded appletree borer, Pacific flatheaded borer.** Whitish larvae with enlarged head in tunnels.	Keep plants vigorous. Remove and dispose of cane stubs from earlier pruning. See page 157.
Tips of canes wilt in the spring and die back in summer. Spiral girdling (by larvae) in canes.	**Raspberry horntail,** *Hartigia cressoni.* Segmented white larvae up to 1 inch long. Adult sawflies black or black and yellow, ½ inch long, wasplike.	In California, mostly in interior valleys. Inspect canes regularly in spring, prune them off just below discolored egg-laying incision and pronounced swelling caused by larva.
Galls or enlarged, distorted tissue on stems and roots.	**Crown gall.** Bacteria in soil spread in water, infects through wounds.	See page 203.
Galls or swellings on roots.	**Root knot nematode,** *Meloidogyne* sp. **Dagger nematode,** *Xiphinema index.*	See page 257. See page 258.

ROSEMARY (*Rosmarinus officinalis*)

WHAT THE PROBLEM LOOKS LIKE	PROBABLE CAUSE	COMMENTS
Blackish sooty mold, sticky honeydew and whitish cast skins on plant.	**Aphids.** Small green, brown, black or yellowish insects, often in groups.	See Aphids, page 93.
Wet, white, frothy masses of spittle on twigs or cones.	**Spittlebugs.** Insects covered in spittle, suck plant juices.	Tolerate, does not harm plants. Wash with forceful water. See Spittlebugs, page 134.

RUBUS (*Rubus* spp.), Raspberry, Salmonberry, Thimbleberry

WHAT THE PROBLEM LOOKS LIKE	PROBABLE CAUSE	COMMENTS
Blackish sooty mold, sticky honeydew and whitish cast skins on plant.	**Aphids.** Small green, brown, black, or yellowish insects, often in groups.	See Aphids, page 93.
Tips of canes wilt in the spring and die back in summer. Spiral girdling (by larvae) in canes.	**Raspberry horntail,** *Hartigia cressoni.* Segmented white larvae up to 1 inch long. Adult sawflies black or black and yellow, ½ inch long, wasplike.	In California, mostly in interior valleys. Inspect canes regularly in spring, prune them off just below discolored egg-laying incision and pronounced swelling caused by larva.

SALVIA (*Salvia* spp.), Sage

WHAT THE PROBLEM LOOKS LIKE	PROBABLE CAUSE	COMMENTS
Blackish sooty mold, sticky honeydew and whitish cast skins on plant.	**Aphids.** Small green, brown, black or yellowish insects, often in groups.	See Aphids, page 93.
Stippled or bleached leaves, varnish-like excrement specks on undersides.	**Thrips.** Tiny, slender blackish or orangish insects.	See Thrips, page 139.

SERVICEBERRY (*Amelanchier* spp.), Shadbush

WHAT THE PROBLEM LOOKS LIKE	PROBABLE CAUSE	COMMENTS
Tiny reddish to brown leaf spots, may have yellow haloes. Larger, dark areas on leaves. Leaves may drop.	**Entomosporium leaf spot.** A fungus.	See page 188.
Leaves with orangish pustules, light to dark spots. Leaves may drop.	**Rusts,** *Gymnosporangium* spp. Fungi require moist conditions.	Avoid overhead watering. Vigorous plants tolerate moderate infection. See page 196.

SPIREA (*Spirea* spp.)

WHAT THE PROBLEM LOOKS LIKE	PROBABLE CAUSE	COMMENTS
Foliage blackened by sooty mold. Sticky honeydew and whitish cast skins on leaves. Leaves curled.	**Spirea aphid,** *Aphis citricola.* Green insects, less than ⅛ inch long, clustered on growing leaves and tips.	Vigorous plants tolerate moderate populations. Hose with forceful water. Tolerate or apply soap or oil. See Aphids, page 93.

WHAT THE PROBLEM LOOKS LIKE	PROBABLE CAUSE	COMMENTS

SPRUCE (*Picea* spp.)

WHAT THE PROBLEM LOOKS LIKE	PROBABLE CAUSE	COMMENTS
Brown to purplish insects clustered on foliage. May be sooty mold/honeydew.	**Giant conifer aphids.** Dark, long-legged, up to ⅕ inch long.	Apparently harmless to trees. See page 95.
Stippled foliage. Foliage color abnormally light green or yellowish.	**Spruce spider mite.** Greenish specks, often in fine webbing at foliage base.	Highest populations occur during spring and fall. See page 172.
Interior needles turn yellow and drop, leaving only young terminal needles.	**Spruce aphid,** *Elatobium abietinum.* Green insects about ⅟₁₆ inch long.	Most common late winter to early spring. Apply insecticidal soap if abundant. See Aphids, page 93.
Yellow mottling of needles.	**Pine needle scale,** *Chionaspis pinifoliae.* White, immobile bodies about ⅟₁₆ inch long. Suck sap.	Vigorous plants tolerate moderate populations. Conserve beneficials and tolerate. Monitor, if damaging, apply soap to crawlers. See Scales, page 117.
Chewed needles.	**Sawflies,** *Neodiprion* spp. Up to 1 inch long, green larvae on needles.	See page 77.
Pineconelike galls on branch tips. Galls turn brown and become obvious.	**Cooley spruce gall adelgid.** Tiny, rarely seen insects, may be in galls.	Galls common in California only in North. Plants usually tolerate damage. See page 102.

SYCAMORE (*Platanus* spp.), London plane tree

WHAT THE PROBLEM LOOKS LIKE	PROBABLE CAUSE	COMMENTS
Blackening of foliage from sooty mold. Tiny powdery white mothlike insects.	**Greenhouse whitefly.** Flat, oval, tiny yellow to green, on leaf undersides.	See page 112.
Yellow, then brown spots on leaves. Premature leaf drop. Cottony material in bark crevices overwinter.	**Sycamore scale.** Bulbous insects, less that ⅟₁₆ inch long, in center of yellow spot on lower leaf surface.	See page 130.
Leaves, buds and shoots distorted and discolored. Irregular brown dead areas along leaf veins. Twig dieback.	**Anthracnose,** *Discula veneta.* A fungal disease.	See page 185.
White powdery growth on leaves/shoots. Terminals dwarfed and fungus covered.	**Powdery mildew,** *Microsphaera alni.* A fungal disease.	Disease most damaging on severely pruned trees. Plant resistant 'Yarwood' cultivar. See page 193.
Stippled leaves, may become bleached.	**Sycamore spider mite.** Green specks, suck sap.	Problem in California mostly in interior valleys. See page 173.
Stippled, bleached leaves with cast skins and varnishlike specks.	**Western sycamore lace bug.** *Corythucha confraterna.* Adult wings lacelike.	See page 135.
Webbing or silk tents on ends of branches. Chewed leaves.	**Fall webworm.** Hairy, white to yellow larvae, up to 1 inch long, in colonies.	See page 76.
Young leaves skeletonized. Holes in leaves.	**Sycamore leaf skeletonizer,** *Gelechia desiliens.* Greenish larvae, up to ½ inch long, in tubular nest on leaves.	Plants tolerate extensive skeletonization. Tolerate or apply *Bacillus thuringiensis* if young moth larvae are abundant.
Sparse foliage. Undersized leaves. Rapid decline and death of entire tree.	**Canker stain,** *Ceratocystis fimbriata.* Fungus occurs in San Joaquin Valley and eastern U.S. Enters wounds, spread by contaminated tools.	Avoid wounding trees; don't nick shallow roots with mowers. Sterilize pruning tools and equipment when moving between trees and sites.
Stunted or dead twigs and branches. Gray to brown encrustations on bark.	**Oystershell scale.** Look like tiny oysters, in colonies on bark.	See page 124.
Decline or death of limbs or entire plant. Roughened, cracked, wet, or oozing areas on bark.	**Flatheaded appletree borer, Pacific flatheaded borer.** Whitish larvae with enlarged head, tunnel under bark.	Keep plants vigorous. See page 157.
Greatly roughened bark and boring dust on lower trunk and branch crotches. Slow tree growth.	**Sycamore borer.** Pink larvae, up to ¾ inch long, in tunnels in bark or cambium.	Trees are not seriously harmed. See page 167.

SEE PAGES 264–266 FOR ADDITIONAL COMMON CAUSES OF SYMPTOMS

SYRINGA (*Syringa* spp.), Japanese tree lilac, Lilac

WHAT THE PROBLEM LOOKS LIKE	PROBABLE CAUSE	COMMENTS
Stunted or dying woody parts. Brown to gray encrustations on twigs/branches.	**Oystershell scale.** Individuals like miniature oysters, $\frac{1}{16}$ inch long.	See page 124.
Black to brown spots and streaks on leaves, which may shrivel. Elongated, possibly oozing, lesions on twigs.	**Bacterial blight.**	See page 197.

TAMARISK (*Tamarix* spp.)

Stunted or dead twigs and branches. Gray to brown encrustations on bark.	**Oystershell scale.** Look like tiny oysters, in colonies on bark.	See page 124.
Wilting or dead plants. Some roots stripped of bark or girdled near soil. Foliage may be notched or clipped.	**Black vine weevil.** Adults are black snout beetles, $\frac{1}{2}$ inch long. Larvae are white grubs with brown head.	Larvae feed on roots. See page 87.
Galls or swellings on roots.	**Root knot nematode,** *Meloidogyne* sp.	See page 257.

TAXUS (*Taxus* spp.), Yew

Blackening of foliage from sooty mold. Cottony waxy material on plant.	**Obscure mealybug.** Powdery, grayish, heavily segmented insects with fringe filaments, longer at tail.	See page 115.
Declining or dead twigs or branches. Gray to brown encrustations on bark.	**Purple scale,** *Lepidosaphes beckii*; **Oleander scale.** Tiny circular to elongate insects, often in colonies.	Plants tolerate moderate populations. Conserve beneficials. Tolerate or monitor and applying oil if damaging. See page 124.
Needles notched or clipped. General decline of plant may occur.	**Black vine weevil.** Adults $\frac{1}{2}$ inch long, black snout beetles, active at night.	Larvae feed on roots. See page 87.
Foliage discolored, wilted, stunted, drops prematurely. Discolored bark may ooze sap. Branches or plant may die.	**Collar, Foot, and Crown rots.** Decay fungi common in moist soils.	See page 209.

TOYON (*Heteromeles arbutifolia*), Christmas berry

Terminal leaves severely curled and twisted. Damage occurs early in season.	**Toyon thrips,** *Rhyncothrips ilex.* Tiny, slender black (adult) and orangish (immature) insects in new terminals.	Insect has one annual generation. Tolerate damage. Keeping soil bare beneath plants or applying oil or soap to new growth may reduce damage.
Stippled, bleached leaves, with varnishlike specks on undersides.	**Greenhouse thrips.** Tiny, slender, black adults or yellowish nymphs.	See page 112.
Stippled, bleached leaves with varnishlike specks on undersides.	**Lace bugs,** *Corythucha* spp. Body, wings lacelike. Nymphs yellowish, spiny.	See page 135.
Sticky honeydew and blackish sooty mold on leaves and twigs. Tiny, white, mothlike insects (adults) present.	**Iridescent whitefly,** *Aleuroparadoxus iridescens*; **Ash whitefly; Crown whitefly.** Tiny, oval flattened nymphs, often white wax on fringe or back.	Conserve natural enemies, no other control generally recommended, plants tolerate. Soap spray provides some control. See page 108.
Blackening of foliage from sooty mold. Possible plant decline or dieback.	**European fruit lecanium.** Brown, flat or bulbous, immobile scale insects.	See page 128.
Tiny reddish to brown leaf spots, may have yellow haloes. Larger, dark areas on leaves. Leaves may drop.	**Entomosporium leaf spot.** A fungus.	See page 188.
Dark scabby or velvety spots on leaves or fruit.	**Scab,** *Spilocaea photinicola.* Fungal disease promoted by moist spring.	See Scabs, page 188.

WHAT THE PROBLEM LOOKS LIKE	PROBABLE CAUSE	COMMENTS

TOYON (*Heteromeles arbutifolia*), Christmas berry, continued

Sudden wilting then shriveling and blackening of shoots and blossoms. Plants appear scorched.	**Fireblight.** Bacteria enters plants through blossoms.	See page 190.
Dieback of branches or entire plant.	**Pacific flatheaded borer.** Whitish larvae with enlarged head in tunnels.	See page 157.
Foliage discolored, wilted, stunted, drops prematurely. Discolored bark may ooze sap. Branches or plant may die.	**Collar, Foot, and Crown rots.** Decay fungi common in moist soils.	See page 209.
Chewed leaves. May be silken tents or mats of silk in plant.	**Western tent caterpillar, Western tussock moth.** Hairy caterpillars, up to 2 inches long, dark or colorful.	See pages 70–75.

TULIP TREE (*Liriodendron tulipifera*), Yellow poplar

Sticky honeydew, blackish sooty, and whitish cast skins on leaves. Possible premature leaf yellowing.	**Tuliptree aphid,** *Illinoia liriodendri.* Tiny green insects in colonies on underside of leaves.	Plants tolerate extensive aphid populations. Apply insecticidal soap or another insecticide if not tolerable. See page 93.
Dark spots on leaves.	**Physiological leaf spotting.** Caused by heat, drought, poor cultural care.	Provide adequate summer irrigation. Improve drainage and increase organic content of soil.

VIBURNUM (*Viburnum* spp.)

Stippled, bleached leaves with varnishlike specks on undersides.	**Greenhouse thrips.** Tiny, slender, black adults or yellow immatures.	See page 141.
Sticky honeydew and blackish sooty mold on foliage. Distorted terminals.	**Bean aphid,** *Aphis fabae.* Dull black insects, less than ⅛ inch long.	Plants tolerate moderate populations. Hose forcefully with water. Insecticidal soap or oil can be applied. See Aphids, page 95.
Stunting or dieback of woody parts. Brown encrustations on bark.	**Oystershell scale.** Tiny, immobile, insects, look like miniature oysters.	See page 124.
Leaves wilted, discolored, may drop. Branches or entire plant may die.	**Dematophora root rot.** Minute white fungus growths may be visible in wood.	Less common than *Armillaria* or *Phytophthora.* See page 208.

WALNUT (*Juglans* spp.)

Sticky honeydew, blackish sooty mold, and whitish cast skins on foliage.	**Walnut aphid,** *Chromaphis juglandicola;* **Duskyveined aphid,** *Callaphis juglandis.* Tiny, yellowish to brown insects on either leaf surface.	Conserve natural enemies that provide control. Plants tolerate aphids, control is rarely needed. If severe, apply insecticidal soap or oil. See Aphids, page 93.
Foliage blackened by sooty mold. Woody parts may decline and die back.	**Calico scale, European fruit lecanium, Frosted scale, Citricola scale.** Oval, flat or bulbous. Brown, yellow, spotted, or whitish waxy covered.	See pages 127–28.
Stippled, bleached, or reddened foliage.	**European red mite, Pacific spider mite, Twospotted spider mite.** Yellowish to reddish specks.	See page 170.
Leaves stippled or bleached, with cast skins and varnishlike specks.	**Lace bug,** *Corythucha* sp. Brown adults, up to ⅛ inch long, wings lacelike.	See page 135.
Chewed leaves. Silken tents may occur on terminals. Single branch or entire tree may be defoliated.	**Fall webworm, Redhumped caterpillar, Tussock moths.** Smooth to hairy caterpillars, up to 1½ inches long.	See pages 70–76.

SEE PAGES 264–266 FOR ADDITIONAL COMMON CAUSES OF SYMPTOMS

SEE PAGES 264–266 FOR ADDITIONAL COMMON CAUSES OF SYMPTOMS

WALNUT (*Juglans* spp.), continued

WHAT THE PROBLEM LOOKS LIKE	PROBABLE CAUSE	COMMENTS
Declining or dead twigs or branches. Gray to brown encrustations on bark.	**Italian pear scale,** *Epidiaspis leperii*; **Walnut scale,** *Quadraspidiotus juglansregiae*; **Oystershell scale; San Jose scale.** Tiny circular to elongate insects.	Plants tolerate moderate populations. Conserve natural enemies. Apply oil during delayed dormant season or monitor and spray when crawlers abundant in spring. See pages 122–24.
Leaves discolored, wilted, stunted, may drop prematurely. Discolored bark may ooze sap. Branches or plant may die.	**Collar, Foot, and Crown rots.** Decay fungi common in moist soils.	See page 209.
Leaves discolored. Growth stunted. Lack of fine roots on feeder roots.	**Root lesion nematode,** *Pratylenchus* sp.	See page 258.

WILLOW (*Salix* spp.)

WHAT THE PROBLEM LOOKS LIKE	PROBABLE CAUSE	COMMENTS
Stickiness and blackening of foliage from honeydew and sooty mold.	**Melon aphid; Giant willow aphid,** *Lachnus salignus*; *Chaitophorus* spp. Green to brown insects, up to ⅛ inch long, clustered on leaves or twigs.	Plants tolerate moderate aphid populations. Conserve natural enemies. Hose forcefully with water. Tolerate or apply soap or oil in spring. See Aphids, page 93.
Sticky honeydew and blackish sooty mold. Possible decline and dieback of woody parts. May be cottony material on plant.	**Brown soft scale; Cottony maple scale;** *Pulvinaria innumerabilis*. Yellow to brown, oval, flattened insects or cottony white, popcornlike bodies.	Cottony maple scale has one generation a year. Conserve natural enemies and tolerate moderate populations or monitor and apply oil in spring when crawlers are abundant. See page 126.
Leaves stippled or bleached, with cast skins and varnishlike specks.	**Lace bug,** *Corythucha* sp. Brown adults, up to ⅛ inch long, wings lacelike.	See page 135.
Blackening of foliage from sooty mold. Cottony or waxy material on plant.	**Obscure mealybug.** Powdery, grayish, up to ¼ inch long with waxy filaments.	Conserve natural enemies that help in control. See page 115.
Decline or dieback of twigs or branches. Grayish to brownish encrustations on bark.	**Greedy scale, Oystershell scale, San Jose scale.** Tiny circular to elongate insects on twigs and branches.	See page 121–24.
Decline or dieback of some branches or entire tree. Roughened bark may have dark or wet spots.	**Flatheaded borers, Roundheaded borers, Clearwing moths, Carpenterworm.** Whitish larvae up to 2½ inches long, tunnel beneath bark or in wood.	See pages 157–68.
Brownish, sunken lesions on trunk and large limbs. Small branches/twigs die without any definite canker evident.	**Canker,** *Cytospora chrysosperma*. Fungal disease most serious on low vigor trees.	Provide moderate fertilizer, adequate water, and proper cultural care. Prune out dead and diseased branches. See page 201.
Leaves skeletonized.	**Leaf beetles,** including *Chrysomela aeneicollis*; *Chrysomela scripta*; *Altica bimarginata*; *Syneta albida*; California willow beetle, *Melasomida californica*. Brown to metallic black adults, larvae are dark, elongate.	Vigorous plants tolerate moderate leaf damage. Provide proper cultural care, including adequate water for willows, which are adapted to moist soils. Tolerate or apply oil or another insecticide to kill eggs and larvae. See Leaf Beetles, page 80.
Leaves chewed. May be silken tents in tree.	**Fall webworm, Redhumped caterpillar, Spiny elm caterpillar, Tussock moths, Tent caterpillars, Omnivorous looper, Fruittree leafroller.** Naked, spiny or hairy larvae, up to 2 inches long.	Vigorous plants tolerate moderate defoliation. Prune out colonies of caterpillars confined to a few branches. Apply *Bacillus thuringiensis* or other insecticide when caterpillars are young if damage not tolerable. See pages 70–76.
Leaves chewed, webbed together in groups of several containing larva.	**Western tiger swallowtail,** *Papilio rutulus*. Caterpillar bright green with eyespots, black and yellow markings. Adult 2 inches, yellow with black.	Caterpillars mature into highly attractive butterflies. Control not recommended. *Bacillus thuringiensis* kills young larvae. See Foliage-Feeding Caterpillars, page 63.

WHAT THE PROBLEM LOOKS LIKE	PROBABLE CAUSE	COMMENTS
WILLOW (*Salix* spp.), continued		
Prominent red globular or elongate swellings (galls) on leaves.	**Willow leaf gall sawfly.** Tiny, whitish larvae sometimes found in galls.	Adults are small, stout wasps. Galls apparently do not harm plant. See page 78.
Yellow to orangish powdery pustules on lower surface of leaves.	**Rust,** *Melampsora* spp. Fungal diseases.	Damage usually not severe enough to warrant control action. See page 195.
Black to dark olive spots on leaves in early spring. Leaves yellow and may drop prematurely.	**Scab,** *Venturia saliciperda.* A fungal disease spread by water from infected leaves and twigs.	Avoid overhead watering. Prune out infected twigs and leaves in fall. See Scabs, page 188.
Galls or swellings on trunk and roots, usually near soil, may be on branches.	**Crown gall.** Bacteria infect plant via wounds.	See page 203.
WISTERIA (*Wisteria* spp.)		
White encrustations on woody parts and leaves.	**Wisteria scale,** *Chionaspis wistariae.* Elongate, less than 1/16 inch long.	Effect of scale on plant unknown. See Scales, page 117.
Decline of plant. Dying branches.	**Spotted tree borer,** *Synaphaeta guexi.* Larvae are whitish grubs up to 3/4 inch long, tunnel in woody parts.	Borer attacks injured and dying wisteria. Provide proper cultural care to keep plants vigorous. Prune out and dispose of damaged plant parts, no other management known. See Roundheaded Borers, page 160.
XYLOSMA (*Xylosma congestum*)		
Dark, brown circular spots on leaf upper surface, up to about 3/4 inch in diameter. Orangish pustules on leaf underside. Leaves may drop prematurely.	**Xylosma rust,** *Xylosma congestum.* Fungal disease requiring moist conditions.	Avoid overhead watering. Vigorous plants can tolerate a moderate infection. See Rusts, page 195.
YUCCA (*Yucca* spp.)		
Blackening of plant from sooty mold. Cottony waxy material on plant.	**Large yucca mealybug,** *Puto yuccae.* Powdery, white oval insects, up to 1/8 inch long.	Conserve natural enemies that provide control. Apply soap, oil, or another insecticide if not tolerable. See Mealybugs, page 114.
Declining or dead plant parts. Grayish to brownish encrustations on bark.	**Oleander scale, Oystershell scale.** Tiny, circular to elongate insects.	See page 124.
Blackened foliage from sooty mold. Possible yellowing and dieback of foliage.	**Hemispherical scale,** *Saissetia coffeae.* Yellowish or brown, oval, flattened or bulbous insects.	Conserve natural enemies. Tolerate moderate populations or monitor and apply oil or other insecticide if crawlers numerous. See Scales page 117.
Decline of plant. Holes punctured in leaves.	**Yucca weevil,** *Scyphophorus yuccae.* Adult is black snout weevil about 1/2 inch long. Larva is white grub.	Larvae tunnel in base of green flower stalks and heart of plant. Provide plants with proper cultural care. No other management known.

SEE PAGES 264–266 FOR ADDITIONAL COMMON CAUSES OF SYMPTOMS

References

Choosing the Correct Plant

Compatible Plants Under and Around Oaks. 1991. California Oak Foundation, Sacramento, CA.

An Annotated Checklist of Woody Ornamental Plants of California, Oregon, & Washington. 1979. UC Publication 4091.[a]

A Guide to Shrubs for Coastal California. 1980. UC Leaflet 2584.[a]

Generalized Plant Climate Map of California. 1988. UC Publication 3328.[a]

Landscape Trees for the Great Central Valley of California. 1979. UC Leaflet 2580.[a]

Native California Plants for Ornamental Use. 1981. UC Leaflet 2831.[a]

Ornamentals for California's Middle Elevation Desert. 1968. UC Publication 1839.[a]

Ornamental Shrubs for Use in the Western Landscape. 1980. E. L. Labadie. Sierra City Press, Sierra City, CA.

Ornamental Trees: An Illustrated Guide to Their Selection and Care. 1955. E. Maino and F. Howard. University of California Press, Berkeley, CA.

Trees for Saving Energy. 1991. UC Leaflet 21485.[a]

Trees Under Power Lines: A Homeowner's Guide. 1989. UC Leaflet 21470.[a]

Cultural Care

Arboriculture: Integrated Management of Landscape Trees, Shrubs, and Vines. 1992. R. W. Harris. Prentice-Hall, Englewood Cliffs, NJ.

Fertilizing Woody Plants. 1977. UC Leaflet 2958.[a]

A New Tree Biology. 1986. A. L. Shigo. Shigo and Trees Associates, Durham, NH.

Protecting Trees When Building on Forested Land. 1988. UC Leaflet 21348.[a]

Questions and Answers About Tensiometers. 1981. UC Leaflet 2264.[a]

Staking Landscape Trees. 1972. UC Leaflet 2576.[a]

Western Fertilizer Handbook: Horticultural Edition. 1990. Interstate Publishers, Danville, IL.

Diseases

California Plant Disease Handbook and Study Guide for Agricultural Pest Control Advisors. 1990. UC Publication 4046.[a]

Compendium of Rose Diseases. 1989. R. K. Horst. American Phytopathological Society, St. Paul, MN.

Diagnosing Ornamental Plant Diseases, An Illustrated Guide. 1988. UC Publication 21446.[a]

Diseases of Forest and Shade Trees of the United States. 1971. U.S. Dept. Agriculture Handbook 386. Washington, D.C.

Diseases of Pacific Coast Conifers. 1979. R. V. Bega. U.S. Dept. Agriculture Handbook 521. Washington, D.C.

Diseases of Shade Trees. 1989. T. A. Tattar. Academic Press, San Diego, CA.

Diseases of Trees and Shrubs. 1987. W. A. Sinclair, H. H. Lyon and W. T. Johnson. Cornell University Press, Ithaca, NY.

Foliage and Branch Diseases of Landscape Trees. 1988. UC Leaflet 2616.[a]

Fungi on Plants and Plant Products in the United States. 1989. D. F. Farr, G. F. Bills, G. P. Chamuris, and A. Y. Rossman. American Phytopathological Society, St. Paul, MN.

Plants in California Susceptible to Phytophthora cinnamomi. 1980. UC Leaflet 21178.[a]

Plant Pathology. 1988. G. N. Agrios. Academic Press, San Diego, CA.

Plants Resistant or Susceptible to Verticillium Wilt. 1981. UC Leaflet 2703.[a]

Reducing Root Rots in Plants. 1975. UC Publication 4004.[b]

Resistance or Susceptibility of Certain Plants to Armillaria Root Rot. 1979. UC Leaflet 2591.[a]

Soil Solarization: A Nonchemical Method for Controlling Diseases and Pests. 1984. UC Leaflet 21377.[a]

Insects and Mites

Biological Control and Insect Pest Management. 1979. UC Publication 1911.[a]

Biological Control of Insect Pests and Weeds. 1964. P. DeBach and E. I. Schlinger, eds. Reinhold Publishing Corp., New York, NY.[b]

Biological Control of Pests by Mites. 1983. UC Publication 3304.[a]

California Insects. 1979. J. A. Powell and C. L. Hogue. University of California Press, Berkeley, CA.

Color-Photo and Host Keys to the Armored Scales of California. 1982. R. J. Gill. Scale and Whitefly Key #5. Calif. Dept. Food Agri., Sacramento, CA.

Color-Photo and Host Keys to California Whiteflies. 1982. R. J. Gill. Scale and Whitefly Key #2. Calif. Dept. Food Agri., Sacramento, CA.

Color-Photo and Host Keys to the Mealybugs of California. 1982. R. J. Gill. Scale and Whitefly Key #3. Calif. Dept. Food. Agri., Sacramento, CA.

Color-Photo and Host Keys to the Soft Scales of California. 1982. R. J. Gill. Scale and Whitefly Key #4. Calif. Dept. Food Agri., Sacramento, CA.

Common Names of Insects & Related Organisms. 1989. Entomological Society of America, Lanham, MD.

Destructive and Useful Insects: Their Habits and Control. 1993. R. L. Metcalf and R. A. Metcalf. McGraw-Hill, New York, NY.

DDU: Degree-Day Utility. 1991. A program for computers using MS-DOS. UC Statewide IPM Project. Univ. Calif., Davis, CA.

Insects Affecting Ornamental Conifers in Southern California. 1967. L. R. Brown and C. O. Eads. California Agricultural Experiment Station Bulletin 834.[b]

Insects That Feed on Trees and Shrubs. 1988. W. J. Johnson, H. H. Howard, C. S. Koehler and J. A. Weidhaas. Cornell University Press, Ithaca, NY.

Insects of Western North America. 1926. E. O. Essig. MacMillan, New York, NY.[b]

Insect Pest Management Guidelines for California Landscape Ornamentals. 1988. UC Publication 3317.[a]

A Key to Ants of California. 1987. UC Leaflet 21433.[a]

A Manual of Acarology. 1975. G. W. Krantz. Oregon State Univ. Book Stores, Corvallis, OR.

Natural Enemies Are Your Allies. 1991. Color poster. UC Publication 21496.[a]

A Technical Study of Insects Affecting the Elm Tree in Southern California. 1966. L. R. Brown and C. O. Eads. California Agricultural Experiment Station Bulletin 821.[b]

A Technical Study of Insects Affecting the Oak Tree in Southern California. 1965. L. R. Brown and C. O. Eads. California Agricultural Experiment Station Bulletin 810.[b]

A Technical Study of Insects Affecting the Sycamore Tree in Southern California. 1965. L. R. Brown and E. O. Eads. California Agricultural Experiment Station Bulletin 818.[b]

Urban Entomology. 1978. W. Ebeling. UC Publication 4057.[b]

Western Forest Insects. 1977. R. L. Furniss and V. M. Carolin. U.S. Dept. Agriculture Miscellaneous Pub. 1339. Washington, D.C.

General Pest Management

Advances in Implementing Integrated Pest Management for Woody Landscape Plants. 1992. M.J. Raupp, C.S. Koehler and J.A. Davidson. Annual Review of Entomology 37: 561-585.

Common-Sense Pest Control. 1991. W. Olkowski, S., Daar, and H. Olkowski. The Tauton Press, Newton, CT.

Common Sense Pest Control Quarterly. Bio-Integral Resource Center, Berkeley, CA.

Integrated Pest Management for Almonds. 1985. UC Publication 3308.[a]

Integrated Pest Management for Apples and Pears. 1991. UC Publication 3340.[a]

Integrated Pest Management for Citrus. 1991. UC Publication 3303.[a]

Integrated Pest Management for Walnuts. 1987. UC Publication 3270.[a]

An Introduction to Biological Control. 1982. R. van den Bosch, P. S. Messenger, and A. P. Gutierrez. Plenum Press, New York, NY.

Introduction to Integrated Pest Management. 1981. M. L. Flint and R. van den Bosch. Plenum Press, New York, NY.

The IPM Practitioner. Bio-Integral Resource Center, Berkeley, CA.

Peaches, Plums, and Nectarines: Growing and Handling for Fresh Market. 1989. UC Publication 3331.[a]

Pests of the Garden and Small Farm: A Grower's Guide to Using Less Pesticide. 1990. UC Publication 3332.[a]

Prune Orchard Management. 1981. UC Publication 3269.[a]

Wood Preservation. 1992. UC Publication 3335.[a]

Pesticides

Managing Insects & Mites With Spray Oils. 1991. UC Publication 3347.[a]

Pesticides: Theory and Application. 1983. G.W. Ware. W.H. Freeman Co., San Francisco, CA.

Residential, Industrial, and Institutional Pest Control. 1990. UC Publication 3334.[a]

Safe and Effective Use of Pesticides. 1988. UC Publication 3324.[a]

Safety

Evaluation of Hazard Trees in Urban Areas. 1991. N. P. Matheny and J. R. Clark. International Society of Arboriculture, Urbana, IL.

Landscape for Fire Protection. 1976. UC Leaflet 2401.[a]

Vertebrates

Wildlife Pest Control Around Gardens and Homes. 1984. UC Leaflet 21385.[a]

Weeds

Growers Weed Identification Handbook. 1992. UC Publication 4030.[a]

Guide to Turfgrass Pest Control. 1988. UC Leaflet 2209.[b]

Mistletoe Control in Shade Trees. 1980. UC Leaflet 2571.[a]

Nursery and Landscape Weed Control. 1986. R. P. Rice, Jr. Thompson Publications, Fresno, CA.

Principles of Weed Control in California. 1989. California Weed Conference. Thompson Publications, Fresno, CA.

Soil Solarization: A Nonchemical Method for Controlling Diseases and Pests. 1984. UC Leaflet 21377.[a]

Turfgrass Pests. 1989. UC Publication 4053.[a]

Weed Control in Ground Covers. 1987. UC Leaflet 2782.[a]

Weeds of California. 1970. W. Robbins, M. Bellue, and W. Ball. State of California Documents and Publications, North Highlands, CA.[b]

Weeds of the West. 1991. Wyoming Agricultural Extension. Available as UC Publication 3350.[a]

a. UC Leaflets and Publications are available from Agriculture and Natural Resources Publications, University of California, 6701 San Pablo Avenue, Oakland, CA 94608-1239. A free catalog lists titles on related topics. For ordering information, telephone (510) 642-2431.

b. Publications out of print. Copies may be available for reference at libraries.

Suppliers

Beneficial Organisms

Directory of Least-Toxic Pest Control Products. The IPM Practitioner. Bio-Integral Resource Center, Berkeley, CA.

Gardens Alive! Lawrenceberg, IN.

Some Biological Control Agents Commercially Available in California. UC Publication 7115.

Suppliers of Beneficial Organisms in North America. C. D. Hunter. 1992. Calif. EPA, Dept. Pesticide Regulation, Sacramento, CA.

A Worldwide Guide to Beneficial Animals (Insects/Mites/Nematodes) Used for Pest Control Purposes. 1992. W. T. Thompson. Thompson Publications, Fresno, CA.

Monitoring and Diagnostic Equipment

AgriSense, Fresno, CA.

BioQuip Products, Gardena, CA.

Disease diagnostic test kits. Agri-Diagnostics Associates, Cinnaminson, NJ.

Pest Management Supply, Inc., Hadley, MA.

Sentry Monitoring Products. Sentry Inc., Buckeye, AZ.

Trece, Inc., Salinas, CA.

Water-sensitive paper for monitoring honeydew. Spraying Systems Co., Wheaton, IL.

Glossary

allelopathy. the ability of a plant species to produce substances that are toxic to certain other plants.

annual. a plant that normally completes its life cycle of seed germination, vegetative growth, reproduction, and death in a single year.

bacterium. a single-celled, microscopic, plantlike organism that does not produce chlorophyll. Most bacteria obtain their nitrogen and energy from organic matter; some bacteria cause plant or animal diseases (plural: bacteria).

biological control. the action of parasites, predators, or pathogens in maintaining another organism's population density at a lower average level than would occur in their absence. Biological control may occur naturally in the field or result from manipulation or introduction of biological control agents by people.

botanical. derived from plants or plant parts.

broad-spectrum pesticide. a pesticide that is toxic to many different species.

canker. a dead and discolored, often sunken area (lesion) on the stem, branch, or twig of a plant.

canopy. the leafy parts of trees or shrubs.

caterpillars. immature stages of butterflies and moths.

cotyledons. leaves formed within the seed and present on seedlings immediately after germination. These "seed leaves" typically appear different from the leaves on more mature plants.

crown. the point at or just below the soil surface where the main stem (trunk) and roots join. Also used to refer to the topmost limbs on a tree or shrub.

degree-day. a unit combining temperature and time used in monitoring growth and development of organisms.

dormant. to become inactive during winter or periods of cold.

dormant spray. a pesticide applied during the time when trees are inactive.

frass. solid fecal material produced by insects.

fungicide. a pesticide used to control fungi.

fungus. a multicellular lower plant lacking chlorophyll, such as mold, mildew, smut, or rust. The fungus body normally consists of filamentous strands called mycelium and reproduces through dispersal of spores (plural: fungi).

gall. a localized swelling or outgrowth of plant tissue, often formed in response to the action of a pathogen or other pest.

girdled. having a ring of dead or damaged tissue around the stem or root; girdling usually kills the plant.

herbicide. a pesticide used to control weeds.

honeydew. an excretion from insects, such as aphids, mealybugs, and soft scales, consisting of modified plant sap.

host. a plant or animal that provides sustenance for another organism.

inorganic. containing no carbon; generally used to indicate materials (for example, fertilizers) that are of mineral origin.

instar. the period between molts in larvae of insects. Most larvae pass through several instars; these are usually given numbers, such as first or second instar.

integrated pest management (IPM). a pest management strategy that focuses on long-term prevention or suppression of pest problems through a combination of techniques such as encouraging biological control, use of resistant varieties, and adoption of alternate cultural practices such as modification of irrigation or pruning to make the habitat less conducive to pest development. Pesticides are used only when careful monitoring indicates they are needed according to preestablished guidelines, treatment thresholds, or to prevent pests from significantly interfering with the purposes for which plants are being grown.

larva. the immature form of insects that develop through the process of complete metamorphosis including egg, several larval stages, pupa, and adult. In mites, the first-stage immature is also called a larva (plural: larvae).

lesion. a localized area of diseased or discolored tissue.

ligule. in many grasses, a short membranous projection on the inner side of the leaf blade at the junction where the leaf blade and leaf sheath meet.

metamorphosis. the process of change from an immature insect into an adult.

microbial pesticides. pesticides that consist of bacteria, fungi, viruses, or other microorganisms used for control of weeds, invertebrates, or plant pathogens.

molt or moult. the periodic formation of a new cuticle or outer skin in insects and other arthropods, followed by the shedding of old skin before entering another stage of growth.

monitoring. carefully watching and recording information on the activities, growth, development, and abundance of organisms or other factors on a regular basis over a period of time, often utilizing very specific procedures.

mulch. a layer of material placed on the soil surface to prevent weed growth, modify environmental factors such as moisture and heat, and, in the case of certain organic materials that decay, to gradually improve soil quality. Plant-derived (organic) or synthetic materials may be used.

mycelium. the vegetative body of a fungus, consisting of a mass of slender filaments called hyphae (plural: mycelia).

mycorrhizae. beneficial associations between plant roots and fungi.

narrow-range oil. a highly refined petroleum or seed-derived oil that is manufactured specifically to control pests on plants, also called horticultural oil.

natural enemies. predators, parasites, or pathogens that are considered beneficial because they attack and kill organisms that we normally consider to be pests.

nymphs. immature forms of insects that go through gradual metamorphosis with no pupal stage; also the immature forms of mites after the first larval stage.

organic. a material (for example, pesticide) whose molecules contain primarily carbon and hydrogen atoms. Also may refer to plants or animals which are grown without the use of synthetic fertilizers or pesticides.

parasite. an organism that derives its food from the body of another organism, the host, without killing the host directly; also an insect that spends its immature stages in the body of a host that usually dies just before the parasite emerges (this type is also called a parasitoid).

pathogen. a microorganism that causes disease.

perennial. a plant that lives longer than two years—some may live indefinitely. Some perennial plants lose their leaves and become dormant during the winter; others may die back and resprout from underground root structures each year.

pesticide. any substance or mixture intended for preventing, destroying, repelling, killing, or mitigating problems caused by any insects, rodents, weeds, nematodes, fungi, or other pests; and any other substance or mixture intended for use as a plant growth regulator, defoliant, or desiccant.

pheromone. a chemical produced by an animal to attract other animals of the same species.

photosynthesis. the process by which plants convert sunlight into energy.

predator. an animal that kills other animals and feeds on them.

pupa. the nonfeeding, usually immobile, stage between larva and adult stages in insects that undergo complete metamorphosis (plural: pupae).

resistant. able to tolerate conditions (such as pesticide sprays or pest damage) harmful to other strains of the same species.

resistant varieties. strains of a plant species able to resist or tolerate damage by a pest normally damaging to that plant species.

rhizome. a horizontal underground stem, especially one that forms roots at the nodes to produce new plants.

roguing. removal of individual diseased or undesirable plants.

sclerotium. a firm, compact mass of mycelium that serves as a dormant stage for some fungi (plural: sclerotia).

seed leaves. the first leaf (grasses) or two leaves (broadleaf plants) on a seedling; synonymous with cotyledons.

selective pesticide. pesticides that are toxic primarily to the target pest (and perhaps a few related species), leaving most other organisms, including natural enemies, unharmed.

solarization. the practice of heating soil to levels lethal to pests through application of clear plastic to the soil surface for 4 to 6 weeks during sunny, warm weather.

spore. a reproductive structure produced by some plants and microorganisms that is resistant to environmental influences.

stolon. an aboveground runner or rooting structure found in some plants.

synthetic organic pesticides. manufactured pesticides produced from petroleum and containing largely carbon and hydrogen atoms in their basic structure.

tuber. a much enlarged, fleshy underground stem.

virus. a submicroscopic particle that can reproduce only within the living cells of other organisms; some are capable of producing disease symptoms.

Index

UNIVERSITY OF CALIFORNIA

ANR Publications

6701 San Pablo Avenue • Oakland, California 94608-1239

TO ORDER, TELEPHONE **510-642-2431** OR FAX **510-643-5470**

Our indispensible publications include:
- *Pests of the Garden and Small Farm* #3332
- *Natural Enemies Are Your Allies* (poster) #21496
- *Managing Insects & Mites with Spray Oils* #3347
- *Insect Pest Management Guidelines for California Landscape Ornamentals* #3317
- *Wildlife Pest Control Around Gardens and Homes* #21385
- *Turfgrass Pests* #4053
- *The Safe and Effective Use of Pesticides* #3324
- *Residential, Industrial, and Institutional Pest Control* #3334

Order by phone or fax. We accept checks, money order, VISA or MasterCard

For a free catalog of publications, send in the form below.

NAME _____

ADDRESS _____

_____

CITY, STATE, ZIP_____